MINUTES
FOREVER

www.mascotbooks.com

**48 Minutes Forever: The History of High School Football
in New Jersey's Shore Conference**

For more information, please contact:
Mascot Books, an imprint of Amplify Publishing Group
620 Herndon Parkway, Suite 220
Herndon, VA 20170
info@amplifypublishing.com

Library of Congress Control Number: 2023903649
CPSIA Code: PRV0423A
ISBN-13: 978-1-63755-622-1
Printed in the United States

To Nana and Pop-Pop

To Kevin Carter, a great teammate and friend

48
MINUTES
FOREVER

The History of High School Football
in New Jersey's Shore Conference

NICK SCERBO

MASCOT
BOOKS
an imprint of Amplify Publishing Group

CONTENTS

FOREWORD AND ACKNOWLEDGMENTS   1

PROLOGUE   21

PART 1: THE BIRTH OF THE SHORE
CONFERENCE, 1936-1941   27

CHAPTER 1
THE CREATION OF THE SHORE
CONFERENCE   29

CHAPTER 2
THE EARLY YEARS, 1936-1938   43

CHAPTER 3
STORM CLOUDS GATHERING, 1939-1941   59

PART 2: THE WAR YEARS, 1942-1945   81

CHAPTER 4
LIFE IN WARTIME   83

CHAPTER 5
ASBURY PARK AND LONG BRANCH   89

CHAPTER 6
THE SHORE CONFERENCE   93

CHAPTER 7
THE T FORMATION ARRIVES   103

CHAPTER 8
THE BAYSHORE BOYS   111

PART 3: THE AGE OF THE TITANS:
SHORE CONFERENCE FOOTBALL
FROM 1946-1961   **115**

CHAPTER 9
THE RIVALRY: ASBURY PARK VS. LONG
BRANCH, 1932-1948   117

CHAPTER 10
THE POSTWAR SHORE CONFERENCE,
1946-49   129

CHAPTER 11
THE SHORE IN THE EARLY 1950s   137

CHAPTER 12
THE SHORE IN THE MIDDLE 1950s   153

CHAPTER 13
GOLDEN HOUR   189

CHAPTER 14
SHORE CONFERENCE FOOTBALL,
1957-1961   201

PART 4: THE RISE OF THE SHORE CONFERENCE, 1960-1974   **223**

CHAPTER 15
THE BIRTH OF BRICK   225

CHAPTER 16
THE RISING TIDE:
CLASS A IN THE 1960s   241

CHAPTER 17
THE GREATEST SEASON EVER PLAYED
IN THE SHORE CONFERENCE   263

CHAPTER 18
CLASS B FOOTBALL IN THE 1960s   279

CHAPTER 19
CLASS C FOOTBALL:
FROM 1966 TO 1969   305

CHAPTER 20
THE INDEPENDENTS: RBC, RUMSON,
AND ASBURY PARK   313

CHAPTER 21
BRICK AT THE TOP   319

CHAPTER 22
CLASS B FOOTBALL IN THE
EARLY 1970s   341

CHAPTER 23
STREAKS AND SHOWDOWNS   351

CHAPTER 24
THE AUTUMN WIND BLOWS
THROUGH RED BANK   363

PART 5: THE CATHOLIC GOLDEN AGE   381

CHAPTER 25
THE MONSIGNOR'S DREAM: MATER DEI   383

CHAPTER 26
SOARING WITH THE GRIFFINS
(ST. JOSEPH'S)   389

CHAPTER 27
THE LUCK OF THE IRISH
(RED BANK CATHOLIC)   397

CHAPTER 28
THE NEW POWER (ST. JOHN VIANNEY)   401

CHAPTER 29
IN COME THE CATHOLICS (1980)   407

EPILOGUE   415

ENDNOTES   429

ABOUT THE AUTHOR   465

FOREWORD AND ACKNOWLEDGMENTS

A note for the reader: this book forms the first of two planned volumes about the history of the Shore Conference. This first volume will take us from the founding of the league in 1936, ending with the emergence of the state playoffs in 1974 (as well as a section on the Catholic schools, which joined the Shore Conference for the first time in 1980). The completed-but-not-yet-published volume two will cover the story of the Shore Conference after 1974.

It is not possible to write a truly complete history of every game that has been played in Monmouth and Ocean County over the past century of high school football. However, my guiding principle has been that every school's tale should be told. There are doubtless worthy players, coaches, games, and stories that have not appeared in my book. For that, I apologize. At the very least, though, I hope that the stories I have managed to include prompt the remembrance and the telling of the ones that I haven't.

More importantly, any book requires a great deal of thanks. To everyone in my family—Mom, Dad, Tommy, Chris, and Hunter—thank you for putting up with my repeated telling of some new story or character that I had discovered, and thank you for supporting me as I put all of these notes together into a book. I also owe similar thanks to all my friends who were also subjected to these stories. Additionally, I owe thanks to everyone who donated to the Kickstarter that allowed this dream of a book to become a reality. Among those many people, I'd like to express special gratitude to my great-uncle, George Degnon, whose life and actions have been an inspiration for all blessed to know him.

I also owe more gratitude than I can ever express to my teammates, coaches, and role models who introduced me to and cultivated my love for the game of football. It has enriched my life in so many different and unexpected ways. So let this be a thank you to every one of the Monsignor Donovan Griffins with whom I was lucky enough to share a uniform, and to all of our coaches who pushed us to be better people at every stage of our lives. My senior class had the good fortune to play for two fine role models in Coach Tobin and Coach Duddy, who built a program that truly used the football field as a classroom for life. We also had the good fortune of playing for more quality assistant coaches than space permits me to name. I will mention two as representatives—Coach Haupt, who guided us for all three years of our varsity careers, and Coach Sciarappa, who would again be a role model for me when I worked for him at Mater Dei in my first teaching and coaching job. I owe all of them, named specifically or not, more than I can ever repay.

I also have to thank everyone that I was blessed to share a football season with—from Gettysburg College to Mater Dei to Lacey to Monsignor Donovan and now to Pascack Hills. Together we created memories that have enriched every day of my life, and I'm forever grateful for the times we had together. These are the bonds that have inspired me to write this book.

I also have to thank the people who were willing to be interviewed for this project. They took time out of their busy days to sit down with me and answer the questions of a stranger. Without their stories, this would have been a lifeless recitation of scores and records. Instead, they were willing to share with me their descriptions of what it meant to be involved with football in New Jersey's Shore Conference. I know how important those stories are to anyone who is involved with the game, and I hope that this book fulfills the trust that they placed in me. Each person I interviewed is given a brief capsule biography on the following pages. However, there are a few who must be thanked individually for specific contributions.

When Dan Duddy was our head coach at Monsignor Donovan, he made a point to make all of us aware of the rich history of the Shore Conference. His passion for the league, and for his alma mater, Brick Township, was how I first became aware that there was enough history in Monmouth and Ocean County to write a book like this. Pat Toland was kind enough to give me access to his vast archive of Shore Conference football film and highlights, something which made the writing of this book much easier. And Lou Vircillo was not only willing to sit with me in his office at Lacey Township High School for a lengthy and extensive interview, but also helped put me in contact with other coaches that I would never have otherwise met.

Finally, I want to thank my Mom and Dad again for supporting everything that I have ever done, for encouraging my growing love for the game of football, and for putting up with all the craziness that comes with raising a football player and fan.

CONTRIBUTORS: THE ORAL HISTORIES

The following people were interviewed as part of the process of writing this book. Their words and stories are woven throughout both the first and second volumes of this history.

STEVE ANTONUCCI grew up in Keyport and followed the Red Raider football team from an early age. A member of Keyport's class of 1988, he played football under Head Coach Mike Ciccotelli and was a senior starter on the 1987 championship team. He worked as an assistant under Coach Ciccotelli at Keyport, Coach Skip Edwards at Holmdel, and Coach Keith Comeforo at Middletown South. He became head coach himself in 1998. His tenure with the Eagles has been the longest and most successful in the history of a very proud program; his South teams have won eleven division and six state championships. In both 2005 and 2015, they were ranked No. 1 in the state of New Jersey. He remains the head coach at Middletown South today.

BOB BADDERS is a graduate of Brick Memorial High School (class of 2000) and has been covering Shore-area sports since 2004. Currently the managing editor for the Shore Sports Network, he has been witness to nearly two decades of the Shore's best games, best players, and best rivalries.

CHRIS BARNES grew up in Middletown and was a fan of Middletown North's football team from an early age. He played for the Lions under Head Coach Vic Kubu, earning All-Shore honors for them in 1982. After playing at Syracuse, he returned to the Shore as an assistant at Middletown North under Head Coach Mike Galos. From 1994 to 1999, he was the head coach at Jackson, laying the groundwork for a Jaguar program that would transform into a dynasty under Head Coach Reggie Lawrence. From 2000 to 2011, he was the head coach at Wall, coaching teams that won five division titles and the 2002 state championship. Those teams also helped create one of the Shore's most treasured Thanksgiving traditions— the annual game between Wall and Manasquan.

RICHARD BONELLI became involved in Shore Conference football as a player at Manasquan High School under Head Coach Hal Manson. A member of Manasquan's class of 1960, he was a member of two highly successful Warrior teams—the 1958 team went undefeated and won the Class A championship, and the 7-2 1959 team. He retains many fond memories of playing for the Warriors.

The late **BILL BRUNO** grew up watching his father, legendary Asbury Park Coach William "Butch" Bruno, coach the Bishops to great success. Later, he entered coaching himself, working as an assistant at Asbury Park under Head Coach LeRoy Hayes. He was later the head coach at Pinelands from 1989 to 1992 and 1998 to 1999, and coached track at CBA,

Asbury Park, and Pinelands. He won accolades throughout the state as both as a coach and athletic director.

STEVE BUSH has coached football at the high school, college, and professional levels. He first became involved with Shore Conference football in 1993 as the head coach at Manalapan. He worked there until 1999, during which time the Braves won three division championships and made three playoff appearances. In 2013, he returned to the Shore Conference as the head coach at Middletown North, where he remains today. His 2015 North team won back-to-back playoff games and reached the state finals for the first time in almost two decades. He remains a teacher and head coach at the high school.

PETE CAHILL became involved with Shore Conference football in Middletown, playing for Middletown North and Head Coach Vic Kubu. He was an assistant throughout Coach Kubu's legendary tenure at Manasquan, eventually becoming defensive coordinator for the Big Blue. When Coach Kubu passed away in 2007, he succeeded him as his head coach. His own tenure as head coach lasted from 2007 to 2010 and saw the Warriors win three division titles and a Central Jersey Group II championship. He is currently Manasquan's athletic director.

WENDY KUBU CALLAHAN has many reasons to follow Manasquan football—she is a graduate of the high school, her children played in the program, and she is the daughter of Manasquan's legendary Head Coach Vic Kubu. She grew up watching her father's teams compete at Middletown North. In 1985, her freshman year at Manasquan, her father became the head coach at his alma mater. She has followed Warrior football ever since.

GARY CARMODY has been involved with Shore Conference football since the early 1960s, when he began his playing career at Red Bank Catholic. After college, he was an assistant at Keansburg and then at Central Regional under Head Coach John Gardi. He later became the head coach at Central from 1981 to 1991, leading the Eagles to three consecutive Thanksgiving wins over Lacey and the 1988 B South title. He later was an assistant coach at Mater Dei, the head coach of the Seraphs from 2002-2003, and Mater Dei's athletic director.

HARRY CHEBOOKJIAN first became involved with Shore Conference football as a player at Red Bank Catholic under Head Coach Lou Montanaro. He then became an assistant at Red Bank Regional under Head Coach Barry Sullivans. He was the head coach of the Bucs in his own right from 1999 to 2005. The 2003 team won ten games and reached the CJ III finals. He is currently the athletic director at Shore Regional in West Long Branch.

LJ CLARK grew up in Lakewood and followed Piner athletics from an early age. He played football at Lakewood under Head Coaches Len Rivers and Chip LaBarca Jr. After college, he returned to Lakewood as a teacher and coach. He was on staff with Head Coach Warren Wolf in 2010 when the Piners ended a lengthy thirty-three-game losing streak. He has been the head coach since 2011. His Lakewood teams have made six playoff appearances, won two playoff games, and claimed a division title in 2015 (the school's first since 2000). He remains the head coach at his alma mater today.

MARK COSTANTINO is both the longest-tenured and winningest coach in the history of Shore Regional High School. He first arrived at the high school as an assistant to Head Coach Bob Rolak in 1987. He became head coach himself in 1992. In his tenure, the Blue Devils have won eight division and four state titles. He remains the head coach of the Blue Devils today.

DAN CURCIONE is a graduate of Brick Memorial High School, where he played for the Mustangs under Head Coach Jim Calabro. He was an assistant at Lakewood, Toms River North, and Wall before becoming the head coach at Wall Township in 2014. He remained the head coach there until 2016, when his Crimson Knights went 10-2 and won the SJ III championship. He is currently the head football coach at Donovan Catholic.

WALT CURRIE grew up in Toms River and is a member of the Toms River East Class of 1987. While there, he played football for the Raiders under Head Coaches George Jeck and Ken Snyder. He first began coaching at his alma mater under Coach Snyder and then later at Toms River South under Head Coach Ron Signorino Sr. From 2001 to 2006, he was an assistant coach at Point Boro under Head Coaches Shaun Boylan and Calvin Thompson. In his final year with the Panthers, he was the offensive coordinator for a team that went 12-0 and won the 2006 South Jersey Group II title. In 2007, he became the head coach at Brick Memorial, where he remains today. His teams have won three division titles and in 2008 won a Central Jersey Group IV championship. He is the longest-tenured and winningest coach in the history of the high school.

CORY DAVIES first arrived in the Shore Conference as the head coach at Howell High School. He was with the Rebels from 1991 to 2011, the longest tenure of any head coach in Howell history. His Rebel teams won ninety-five games, two division titles, and the first state championship in program history in 2009. He has been the head coach at Freehold Township since 2015, and in his tenure has led the Patriots to three playoff appearances and their first-ever playoff victory.

ROB DAVIS became involved in Shore Conference football as a high schooler, playing at Southern Regional under Head Coach Ron Emmert. After college, he became a teacher and coach, working first at his alma mater and then at Lacey Township under Head Coach Lou Vircillo. He then became the first head football coach at Barnegat High School, coaching the Bengals in varsity action from 2006 until he stepped down as head coach at the end of the 2020 season. In that time, his teams won two division champions, made six playoff appearances, and reached South Jersey Group III finals in 2013.

BILL DICKINSON is a legend and mentor to generations of Mater Dei students. His children attended Mater Dei in the late 1970s and early 1980s. He worked as an assistant coach at Mater Dei to both his daughter Jeanne (a 400-game-winning softball coach) and his son Bill (head football coach at Mater Dei from 1985 to 1988). In later years, he worked as an assistant to various head coaches at both Monmouth Regional and Mater Dei, using his wisdom and experience to help develop countless younger coaches.

CHARLIE DISKIN first arrived in the Shore Conference as an assistant coach at Point Beach. He was an assistant there for seven years, and the head coach for the 2000 season. After that, he was an assistant at Toms River East under Head Coach Joe Arminio, and the head coach himself from 2006 to 2015. His Raider teams won three division titles and made three playoff appearances. The 2006 and 2009 teams were both undefeated in the Shore Conference and reached the SJ IV semifinals. Still an active Shore Conference coach, he is currently an assistant at Manchester.

DAN DUDDY has been a Shore Conference fixture for decades. He grew up in Brick Township, where he was a fan of the Green Dragons from an early age. A member of Brick's class of 1974, he played for the legendary Warren Wolf. During his time as a starter, the Dragons were 17-1, won back-to-back A South championships, and finished the 1972 season as the No. 1 team in New Jersey. He later returned to Brick as an assistant, working under Coach Wolf for many years. He was later the head coach at Central Regional from 1992 to 2003 and Monsignor Donovan from 2006 to 2015. He won division championships at both schools, and in 1994 coached the Golden Eagles to an appearance in the SJ III finals.

JOE DUNNE grew up in Point Pleasant Beach and was a fan of the high school team from a young age. A member of the high school's class of 1967, he played at Point Beach under Coaches John Kelly and Al Michigan and captained the team his senior year. He still lives at the Jersey Shore and retains many fond memories of playing Shore Conference football.

SKIP EDWARDS grew up in Long Branch and has followed Shore Conference football since his childhood. He played for the Green Wave under Head Coach Ken Schroeck, and as a senior in 1969 kicked a game-winning field goal on Thanksgiving against Red Bank. After college, he became a teacher and football coach, and has worked at a number of schools around the state of New Jersey. In the Shore Conference, he has been an assistant coach at St. John Vianney, Keansburg, and Holmdel, and has been the head coach at Holmdel (1987 to 1998), Lakewood (2005 to 2007), and St. John Vianney (2009 to 2010). His twelve-year tenure at Holmdel was the longest in school history, and in 1992 saw the Hornets make their first-ever appearance in a state title game. He is still the head coach for West Windsor Plainsboro.

SHANE FALLON was introduced to Shore Conference athletics at an early age by his father, George Fallon, a longtime athletic director at Red Bank Regional. A member of Rumson-Fair Haven's class of 1990, he played for the Bulldogs under Head Coach Jim "Biff" Wilbur, starting at quarterback on teams that won a division title in 1988 and reached the Central Jersey Group II finals in 1989. In 1996, he returned to his alma mater as a teacher and assistant coach. He was Rumson's head coach from 1998 to 2012, a time during which the Bulldogs won five division championships and the 2010 Central Jersey Group II title, the school's first-ever playoff championship. He stepped down as the winningest coach in Rumson history. He is currently the head coach at Red Bank.

PAUL FARLEY grew up as a fan of Brick football, spending many Saturday afternoons at Keller Memorial Field. In high school, he played for the Green Dragons under Head Coach Warren Wolf. As a senior in 1987, he earned second-team All-Shore honors on a 7-2 Brick team. After college, he returned to the Shore as a teacher and assistant coach. From 1992 until 1999, he was an assistant under Head Coach Dan Duddy at Central Regional, working with some highly successful Golden Eagle teams. He is currently a middle school principal.

TOM FARRELL played football at St. Joseph's/Monsignor Donovan high school under Head Coaches Bob Tormollan and Mike Schuld. He is a member of the school's class of 1985. Farrell was later an assistant with the Griffins under Head Coaches Denny Toddings and Bob Mussari. During that tenure, he was part of the first Donovan team to play for a state championship (1992) and the first Donovan team to win a division title (1993). He was the head coach at his alma mater from 1997 to 2001. His teams made back-to-back playoff appearances in 1999 and 2000.

DENNIS FILIPPONE grew up in Brick Township and played football in Brick's youth system from an early age. He played on some of legendary Head Coach Warren Wolf's most successful teams, including the 1972 state champions, who finished the year ranked No. 1 in all of New Jersey. He later returned to Brick as an assistant coach under Warren Wolf, working with Green Dragon football for nearly two decades. He worked in Brick Township schools for forty-one years, retiring in 2019 after fourteen years as the principal at the high school from which he graduated.

GARY FOULKS grew up in Middletown, learning the lore of Middletown football from his grandfather, a lifelong Middletown resident, graduate of Leonardo High School, and mayor of Middletown. He began attending Middletown North football games from an early age and played for the Lions under Head Coach Mike Galos. He still teaches physics at his alma mater.

LEROY HAYES began his relationship with Asbury Park High School as a student. A 1969 graduate, he played football for Head Coaches Tony Frey and Ed Hudson. After college, he returned to his alma mater as a teacher and coach. He was a football assistant under Head Coaches Ed Hudson and George Conti Jr., and then became head coach from 1982 to

1990. His Blue Bishop teams won four division titles and a Central Jersey Group I title in 1984. After stepping down as head coach, he continued to work as an assistant with Asbury Park's football team for many years. In addition to football, he also coached track and girls' basketball at the high school, directing championship teams in both sports. He is an Asbury legend and in 2016 was deservingly inducted into the Asbury Park High School Hall of Fame.

SEAN HENRY grew up in Point Boro and attended Panther football games from a young age. He played at Point Boro under Head Coach Shaun Boylan, and then returned to his alma mater in 2003 as a teacher and assistant coach under Head Coach Calvin Thompson. He was head coach from 2010 to 2015, a time during which the Panthers made four playoff appearances and won the 2015 B South title. He remains a teacher at the high school.

BILL HILL is one of the greatest athletes to ever come through Howell High School. A star in football, basketball, and baseball at Howell, after graduation Hill played major college football, minor league baseball, and in both the USFL and NFL. He later worked as an assistant at Neptune, Lakewood, and Asbury Park (where he was part of the famed 1998 team). He has also been a head coach at Toms River South from 2008 to 2010 and at Asbury Park in 2014.

TOM O'KEEFE grew up in Keansburg and remembers watching the Titans play from when he was a young child. He is a graduate of Keansburg High School, where he played for the Titans under Head Coach Frank Kuhl. A longtime assistant coach at Keansburg, he was on the staffs of Head Coaches Jon Schultheis, Craig Palmer, and Brian Kmak. He is considered an authority on the history of Keansburg football.

WALT KRYSTOPIK grew up in Jackson Township. A member of the high school's class of 1993, he played football for the Jaguars under Head Coach Bill Ruddy. After college, he returned to his alma mater as a teacher and assistant coach. He was on staff there from 1998 until 2010, working under Head Coaches Chris Barnes, Reggie Lawrence, and Mike Smith. He was a part of teams that won four division titles and three state championships. He was the head coach from 2011 until 2016, coaching Jaguar teams that won a division title in 2013 and consecutive Central Jersey Group IV titles in 2014 and 2015. He remains a teacher at the high school today.

BRIAN KMAK grew up in Keansburg and remembers watching the Titans play from when he was a young child. A graduate of Keansburg High School, he played for the Titans under Head Coach Skip Cox. He later worked for many years as an assistant at Keansburg High School under Head Coaches Frank Kuhl, Jon Schultheis, and Craig Palmer. Head coach from 2003 to 2012, his teams won a division title and reached the 2007 CJ I championship game.

CHIP LABARCA JR. is a graduate of Toms River High School South. At the time, South's head coach was his father, Shore Conference Hall of Famer Chip LaBarca Sr. LaBarca Jr. was a three-time All-Shore receiver (1985-87) on teams that won three consecutive A South titles. After continuing his football career at Penn State, he returned to the Shore to begin a lengthy coaching career. He was the head coach at Lakewood from 1997 to 1998 and at Toms River North from 2006 to 2012. His Mariner teams won two division championships and a state title at the end of an undefeated season in 2007. He has also been an assistant at a number of Shore schools, working as the offensive coordinator on state championship teams at Brick and Wall. He is currently an assistant coach at Donovan Catholic.

GREG LACAVA first became involved in Shore Conference football as a player at Middletown South, under Head Coaches Rich Mosca and Keith Comeforo. After college, he became an assistant at a number of Shore Conference schools as well as the head coach at Allentown High School. From 2009 to 2013, he was the head coach at Colts Neck. His

Cougar teams won the first playoff game in school history (2012) and made the program's first state title appearance (2013). He has also been the head coach at Holmdel and worked as an assistant at St. John Vianney. He still teaches at Colts Neck High School today.

TYLER LAVINE is a member of Mater Dei Prep's class of 2014. During his time as a student at Mater Dei, he was a loyal supporter of Seraph athletics, organizing cheering sections at football and basketball games and playing on the school's baseball team. He was also active in fundraising efforts to keep the school open during its near-closure in 2015.

BRIAN LEE has been involved in some of the greatest seasons in the legendary history of Manasquan football. As a player, he played under Manasquan's legendary Head Coach Vic Kubu, and was part of Warrior teams that won four division and three state titles. After college, he returned to his alma mater, and worked as an assistant under Coach Kubu, as well as Head Coaches Pete Cahill and Jay Price. He is currently an assistant football and assistant baseball coach at the high school.

MIKE MCARTHUR first arrived in the Shore Conference as an assistant under Head Coach Steve Bush at Manalapan High School. In 1998, he became the first head coach at newly opened Colts Neck High School. He was the head coach of the Cougar program until 2008 and remains today the winningest and longest-tenured coach in school history. His teams made five playoff appearances and won a Constitution Division title in 2008. He remains an active teacher in the Freehold Regional School District.

CHRIS MELVIN grew up in Red Bank and played high school football at Red Bank Regional under Head Coach Ty Lewis. He later returned to the Shore as an assistant coach at Red Bank under Head Coach Barry Sullivan. He is currently a respected recruiting analyst, and for the past two decades has covered Shore Conference football for a variety of publications. In his time, he has seen many of the best athletes in the history of the Shore Conference in action.

BOB NANI is a member of the Shore Conference Football Hall of Fame. A graduate of Admiral Farragut High School in Pine Beach, New Jersey, he was a long-time football coach at Toms River North, first as an assistant and later as a head coach from 1989 to 2004. During that time, he won 103 games, four division titles, and three state titles.

JOHN OXLEY first became introduced to Shore Conference football while watching his father (Joe Oxley) coach Raritan's teams in the early 1960s. A member of Middletown North's class of 1983, he played on very strong teams coached by the legendary Vic Kubu. After graduating college, he returned to his alma mater as a coach. He spent over a decade as an assistant to Head Coach Mike Galos, and then served as head coach from 2000 to 2005. He still teaches math at Middletown North today.

CRAIG PALMER grew up in Keansburg and watched Titan football from an early age. He played for Keansburg under Head Coach Chip La-Barca and graduated as a member of the class of 1980. He became a Shore Conference coach, first as an assistant under Skip Edwards at Holmdel and later at his alma mater under fellow Keansburg graduate Jon Schultheis. He was the offensive coordinator on Titan teams that three division championships and claimed state titles in both 1994 and 1996. He was head coach from 1999 until 2002.

FRANK PAPALIA is a member of Central Regional's class of 1998. He first became involved in high school football as a player for the Golden Eagles under Head Coach Dan Duddy. He later became involved in coaching, first as an assistant to Coach Duddy at Central and then to Andy Carlstrom at Holmdel. He has been the head coach at Holmdel (2009 to 2013) and Point Beach (2018), as well as an assistant coach on two state championship teams at Rumson.

GARY PENTA first became involved with Shore Conference football as a young child, watching games officiated by his father (a Shore Conference referee). He attended Long Branch High School and played there under Head Coach Ken Schroeck. After college, he returned to Long Branch as an assistant under Head Coaches Frank Glazier and Jack Levy. He later became the head coach at St. John Vianney from 1986 to 1997. His tenure remains the longest (twelve years) and winningest (fifty-six victories) in school history.

ALEX PISKO played high school football at Toms River East under Head Coach Charlie Diskin and at Monsignor Donovan under Head Coach Dan Duddy (where the author was very proud to call him a teammate). He is a member of Donovan's class of 2009 and has fond memories of being involved in Shore Conference football.

JAY PRICE has been involved with Manasquan football since his time in high school. A member of the class of 1988, Price played his freshman year under Head Coach Gary Chapman and then the rest of his career under Head Coach Vic Kubu. In 1995, he returned to his alma mater as a teacher and coach. He remained on staff for the rest of Coach Kubu's tenure, and then assisted Head Coach Pete Cahill after Coach Kubu's passing. He has been Manasquan's head football coach since 2011, and in that time his Big Blue teams have both a state championship and a division title. He still teaches and coaches at the high school today.

DON REID has been involved with some of the winningest programs in the history of the Shore Conference. He both played at Brick Township under the legendary Warren Wolf in the late 1950s and early 1960s. After college, he returned to his alma mater and worked as an assistant with the Green Dragons for many years. When Brick Memorial opened, he was its first head coach, running the program from 1980 to 1984. After that, he became a defensive coordinator at Manasquan High School under the legendary Vic Kubu, winning a number of division and state championships with the Big Blue.

AL SANER is a member of the Shore Conference Hall of Fame and one of the Shore's most revered head coaches. He founded the Point Boro football program, serving as the school's head coach from 1964 to 1983 and again from 1986 to 1992. During that time, he won 150 games, eleven division championships, and back-to-back state titles in 1977 and 1978. His tenure saw the Panthers win thirty-four straight games between 1966 and 1970 (at the time, a Shore Conference record).

STEVE SCIARAPPA became involved in Shore Conference football at Monsignor Donovan, where he is a member of the class of 1993. He played for the Griffins under Head Coaches Pat Shea and Denny Toddings, and in 1992 he was a starting linebacker on a Donovan team that won the first playoff game in school history and reached the Parochial A South finals. He became a teacher and a coach, working as an assistant at his alma mater. He entered administration and became the principal at Mater Dei Prep; from 2010 to 2014, he was also the school's head football coach. Under his direction, the Seraphs became a winning football program, with playoff victories coming in both 2013 and 2014. His efforts were also instrumental in ensuring the school's survival. He is currently the offensive coordinator at Montclair State University.

JIM SHARPLES first came to the Shore Conference as an assistant coach at Jackson Liberty under Head Coach Tim Osborn. When Coach Osborn tragically passed away, he became the second head coach in the history of Jackson Liberty. He still coaches the Lions today.

DWIGHT SHEEHAN has been a supporter of Mater Dei football since childhood, when he remembers attending games to cheer for the 1999 Seraph team, which reached the Parochial I finals. In later years, he was a key part of Mater Dei's football revival. As a member of Mater Dei's class of 2011, he played on a team that snapped one of the longest losing streaks in Shore Conference history. He returned in later years as an assistant under Head Coaches Steve Sciarappa, Shannon Hoadley, and Dino Mangiero.

RON SIGNORINO SR. began his association with the Shore Conference in 1964, when he became the head coach at what was then Toms River High School and what is now Toms River South. He was the head coach there from 1964 until 1978, winning three division championships and a 1978 South Jersey Group IV title. He returned to coaching in 1981 as Brick's defensive coordinator under legendary Head Coach Warren Wolf. While with the Green Dragons, he was a part of teams that won ten division and three state championships. He then returned to head coaching at Toms River South, running the program from 1997 to 2000, winning another division championship with the Indians. He is the winningest coach in the school's history. He also worked as an assistant at Toms River East, Monsignor Donovan, and to his son Ron Signorino Jr. at Toms River South.

SAL SPAMPANATO became a fan of Shore Conference football at an early age, watching Asbury Park games on Saturday afternoons. A member of Ocean Township's class of 1987, he played football for the Spartans under legendary Head Coach George Conti Jr. After college, he returned to his alma mater, working as a teacher and assistant coach there from 1993 to 2002. He was the head coach from 2003 to 2006; his teams won a Central Jersey Group III title in 2005 and a Federal Division championship in 2006. He was then the head coach at Monmouth Regional from 2007 to 2010. He is currently an assistant principal at that high school.

FRED SPRENGEL first became involved in Shore Conference football as a player at Wall Township under the legendary John Amabile. He was an All-Shore lineman on Wall's 1982 team, which went 11-0 and won the school's first state football championship. He later returned to the Shore Conference and became an assistant coach at Wall, Raritan, and Long Branch. He was the head coach at Long Branch from 1995 to 1998, and then at Brick Memorial from 2000 to 2006. His 1996 Long Branch team reached the CJ II finals, while his Brick Memorial teams won two division championships and in 2003 won the first state championship in

Mustang football history (they also reached a second title game in 2005). He is currently a teacher in the Brick Township school district.

SCOTT STUMP has followed Shore Conference athletics since he was a student-athlete at Red Bank Catholic in the early 1990s. After college, he became a sports reporter for the *Asbury Park Press*, and over the years he has covered the Shore Conference football in many forms, including his tenure as the managing editor of the Shore Sports Network.

BARRY SULLIVAN is a longtime Shore Conference assistant and head coach. He was an assistant to the renowned Ty Lewis at both Howell and Red Bank, and after Coach Lewis's untimely passing, he became the head coach at Red Bank Regional in 1990. He coached the Bucs from 1990-98, guiding them to six winning seasons in nine years. After leaving Red Bank, he became an assistant under Head Coaches Vic Kubu and Pete Cahill at Manasquan High School.

PAT TOLAND first became involved in Shore Conference football while playing at Middletown North under Head Coach Vic Kubu. A two-year starter at running back for the Lions, he earned All-Shore honors in 1983 while helping North complete a perfect 11-0 season. The team won both division and state championships, while Toland earned a scholarship to the University of Virginia. Among other projects, he is currently creating a digital archive of Shore Conference football film.

CALVIN THOMPSON is a graduate of Manasquan High School, where he played under Head Coaches Jack Hawkins and Gary Chapman. As a senior, he earned All-Shore honors at end. He was later an assistant coach at Red Bank and Point Beach and after that the head coach at Point Boro from 2002 to 2010. His Panther teams won sixty-four games, three division titles, and a South Jersey Group II title in 2005.

JOHN TIERNEY is a member of Mater Dei's class of 1997. While a student there, he played football under Head Coach Craig Cicardo. After college, he entered teaching and coaching. In addition to coaching basketball (he was a longtime head basketball coach at Pinelands), he has worked as an assistant coach under Gary Carmody at Mater Dei, Craig Cicardo and Sean DeRosa at Pinelands, and Lou Vircillo at Lacey. He is currently the head football coach at Pinelands.

DENNY TODDINGS has been involved in Shore Conference football since the 1950s. He played high school football at Brick Township, on some of the first teams coached by the legendary Warren Wolf. After playing college football at Delaware, he returned to the Shore as an assistant at Long Branch under Head Coach Ken Schroeck (in later years, he would also work as an assistant to Al Saner at Point Boro). The Shore school with which he is most associated, however, is St. Joseph's/Monsignor Donovan in Toms River. He was the head coach of the Griffins from 1976 to 1980 and again 1991 to 1993. His teams won the 1976 Parochial C South championship and made additional playoff appearances in 1980, 1992, and 1993. His 1993 team won the first division title in the school's football history. He is still the longest-tenured and winningest head coach in school history. After retiring as football coach, he served as Monsignor Donovan's athletic director for many years.

BILL VANORE is a graduate of St. Joseph's/Monsignor Donovan High School. He played for Head Coach Denny Toddings and was a member of the 1976 Parochial C South championship team. He later worked for many years as a guidance counselor at Monsignor Donovan.

JOE VALENTI grew up in Long Branch and followed Green Wave football from an early age. He played at Long Branch under legendary Head Coach Army Ippolito. He has followed Long Branch football specifically and Shore football in general ever since.

LOU VIRCILLO is a Shore Conference Hall of Famer and the Shore's winningest active coach. He arrived in the Shore Conference as an assistant to Head Coach Tom Lally at Red Bank Catholic. In 1975, he moved across town to Red Bank Regional to work as offensive coordinator under Head Coach Bob Strangia. Red Bank went undefeated that season, winning its first and to date only state championship. He became the head coach when Strangia retired at the end of the season and stayed with the Bucs from 1976 until 1980. His teams won two division titles and made three playoff appearances (twice reaching the state finals). In 1981, he moved to Lacey to found the football program at Lacey Township High School. In his tenure, Lacey has become a Shore Conference power, winning thirteen division and four state championships. He is still active as a head coach today.

KEVIN WILLIAMS became involved in Shore Conference football while playing at Central Regional High School. A member of Central's class of 1973, he played under legendary Head Coach Joe Boyd, the founder of the Golden Eagle program. He has covered high school sports in Monmouth and Ocean County for over forty years, including live radio broadcasts of Shore Conference football games. During that time, he has covered some of the greatest teams, coaches, and athletes in the history of Shore athletics. He is currently the director of the Shore Sports Network.

PROLOGUE

NOVEMBER 17, 2005

It was a cold, crisp November night, and high school gridirons across the Jersey Shore were alive with activity. The glow of those magical Friday night lights illuminated young athletes warming up, walking through their assignments, and dreaming of their moments of glory. Fans, bundled up in layers of coats and blankets, were wedging their way into bleachers all throughout Monmouth and Ocean County. At the biggest games, sports reporters were preparing to write stories that would be read across the state the next morning. New Jersey's high school football season was rapidly approaching its climax.

This was the eleventh week of a season that had started in the heat of September. The stakes were high—the state playoffs had reached their semifinal round, and any teams that won would earn the right to play for a championship. Every game had deep meaning. Some teams were trying to become the number-one team in all of New Jersey. Some had unfinished business with a rival. And some were trying to live up to rich traditions established by teams gone before.

The game that I will never forget had no such stakes. Neither my school, Monsignor Donovan, nor our fierce rivals, Manchester, had made the playoffs. And yet to every player on the field that night, this game was as important as any state championship. We cared as much about the proceedings that night as any playoff team did. Although few outside the community of our schools were aware of it, this was a very big rivalry.

The two teams had been playing in the season finale since before any of us had been born. The winner got to keep the traveling trophy for a year. A golden football sat on top of a pedestal, on which the scores of every game in the series were listed. If Monsignor Donovan had it, it sat proudly in the school's front lobby. It was obvious when it was there, and it was obvious when it wasn't. For the first three months of my sophomore year, it wasn't in our school.

As we dressed for the game, piling on extra layers to ward off against the chill, I tried to envision the forty-eight minutes of action to follow. This would be by third MonDon-Manchester game. The first time I saw this game, I'd been in eighth grade and had seen a previously winless Griffin team upset Manchester in overtime. I could vividly remember the student section pouring onto the field to celebrate with their classmates. If there had been any doubt in my mind about where I wanted to go to high school, it disappeared then. The second time I saw this game, I was a freshman football player, watching the game from the stands at Manchester. The spectacular Kevin Malast scored in every possible way to beat us almost singlehandedly.

As much as I loved the sport, pregame was always torture to me. Time seemed to slow to a crawl as kickoff approached. This was especially the case tonight, on homecoming, because there was so much to play for. We were 5-4, and if we could beat Manchester, we would finish with a winning record. That would be irrefutable proof that we were, after all, pretty good. It would also be our first winning season since 1993. That team had won a division title, marked by a banner hanging in the gym. I often looked at it, wondering what their season had been like, who their stars had been, who their rivals were. Could we live up to their legacy?

Whether my friends and I knew it or not, we were swimming in a sea of football history. The teams we felt were rivals, the teams that we spoke of with awe, the teams that we spoke of with disdain, those feelings had been shaped by an epic drama of which we knew only a small corner.

There were times we could get a glimpse of the larger world—when we gazed at the towering façade of Asbury Park's stadium; when we went to a passing scrimmage with Brick Township and heard the reverence with which our coaches spoke of Coach Warren Wolf, Brick's lionized, long-time leader; when we heard the marching bands from Toms River South down the street. Still, we could not fully understand it.

What we did know was that the Shore Conference was special. We went to the All-Shore game on warm summer nights, cheering our recently graduated friends. We grabbed at the *Asbury Park Press* on Thursdays and flipped to Bill King's cartoon, hoping to see a Griffin among the crowd of mascots fighting for football glory. We devoured the preseason previews and held onto them as keepsakes, letting them yellow as the years went by and dreams became memories. When the playoffs came, we hoped that Shore teams would go out and prove what we all already knew—the Shore Conference was the best in the land.

Most athletes feel that way about their league, especially in New Jersey; all of the many high school sports in the state are intensely competitive and extremely well coached. However, it has been my experience that this feeling of collective pride is especially strong in the Shore Conference. There are several reasons why. Most obviously, the Shore has produced a litany of great teams, epic games, transcendent athletes, and legendary coaches. Few know all, but all know some, and all sense that there is more. However, this alone is not enough. The Shore Conference is special because of its long continuity and close community ties.

The league started in 1936, and although it has grown tremendously from that first season, the Shore sports world remains an interconnected family. Pretty much every school in the conference knows about every other school. The fact that most, but not all, schools have lights helps strengthen this part of its football culture. It isn't unusual for football players to go out on a Friday (or Saturday afternoon) and catch whatever big game happens to be nearby. Coaches regularly see each other at clinics and friendships develop between staffs. Players also develop relationships with friends and competitors from neighboring towns.

Sometimes these relationships are antagonistic (victories in one season are often used to taunt opponents in the next one), and sometimes they are supportive (Shore athletes often root for even fierce rivals if they're playing an out-of-area foe). But few are apathetic. Teams at the Shore care about other league teams, a sentiment captured best at the annual All-Shore game. Recently graduated seniors take the field representing either Monmouth or Ocean County. They wear the helmet of their high school alma mater, but by the end of practice, those helmets look starkly different. Players trade helmet decals with their new teammates, creating designs that represent a collage of new connections and new friendships.

In a way, those helmets are the perfect emblem of the Shore Conference. Some logos appear larger and more important than others. Yet take one away, no matter how small, and the entire picture is forever diminished. Every school, every player, every coach has made a contribution to the history of the Shore Conference. So have the fans, the cheerleaders, and the marching bands. As the years have gone by, all have come together to tell the unfolding story of football at the Jersey Shore. It is a story written in red and green and blue and purple, in black and silver and gold. It has been authored by a wide variety of birds, cats, and horses, by every imaginable type of warrior, by rockets and waves and bishops, even by seraphs and griffins.

Every piece matters. Every story counts. In writing this book, I have done my best to include as many of them as I could. Some (too many) have been left out, and for that I ask the reader's forgiveness. The story of the Shore Conference is so big that some omissions are inevitable. One thing I have made a point to do, however, is to mention every school, since it has taken the efforts of all forty-three football-playing members of the Shore Conference (as well as two who once played) to make this league what it is.

In writing this book, I have tried to capture a feeling I have often felt walking into school on a Friday in the fall. Perhaps if you played or coached at the high school level, you have felt it too. The air is crisp and clear, with just a bit of a chill. The leaves have turned. The school is abuzz—there's a game tonight. You walk down the hallway, and friends and teachers wish you good luck. Butterflies flit around your stomach. The last bell rings, and the hallways empty. Most people are rushing toward the parking lot, but you walk slowly—you're staying after school anyway, so what's the rush? There's a game tonight.

That's the way I felt on November 17, 2005, from the moment I walked through the front doors of Monsignor Donovan High School to the moment that the last bell rang at 2:20 p.m. Classes, the team dinner, the team movie, the pregame stretching—all seemed interminable. Kickoff couldn't come fast enough. And then, as it always did, things started to accelerate. Coach Tobin gave us his pregame speech. We said our pregame prayer as a team and packed into the tunnel that ran from the basement to the field. It was time for Donovan to take the field to do battle with Manchester. What our teams did over the next forty-eight minutes would last forever.

PART 1: THE BIRTH OF THE SHORE CONFERENCE, 1936-1941

CHAPTER 1
THE CREATION OF THE SHORE CONFERENCE

"We just don't recognize the most significant moments when they're happening."
Doc Graham, *Field of Dreams*

The winter of 1936 was quiet, as most winters were at the Jersey Shore in those days. Summers were busy, especially in the tourist centers of Asbury Park and Long Branch, but tourists didn't come to Monmouth and Ocean Counties in the dead of winter. The area was still primarily farmland, home to fewer than 200,000 year-round residents. February was the quietest month. It was a time for thinking. It was a time to stay home and stay indoors, especially since a bitter cold snap was helping to make the winter one of the worst on record.

One man who was not home on the evening of February 10, 1936, was Freehold High School Athletic Director Roy Maurer. Like many of his colleagues at the Jersey Shore, Maurer had a problem. Although his school drew students from most of Western Monmouth County, its enrollment was small. Under the system used by the NJSIAA, Freehold was a Group II (Group Is were the smallest, Group IVs were the largest). Finding enough games against schools of similar size was a constant struggle, and Freehold's teams often had to travel far and wide in order to find suitable opponents.

They couldn't easily stay local because Monmouth County athletics were dominated by a trio of large schools—Red Bank, Long Branch, and most of all Asbury Park—that dwarfed their smaller counterparts in both student population and athletic success. Scheduling them regularly, especially in contact sports such as football, was out of the question.

Equally frustrating was the lack of media attention. The *Asbury Park Press*, the region's main daily newspaper, provided extensive coverage for its hometown high school and its archrival, Long Branch. A game between the Colonials football team and an out-of-area foe was not likely to draw much attention. Even matchups with local foes such as Lakewood or Neptune were not well-covered unless some sort of title was at stake.

Freehold was not the only school with such a problem. The Jersey Shore was home to ten other schools of similar size, and all of them faced similar problems. Atlantic Highlands had been forced to transport its football team as far west as Bernards and as far north as Lodi, while Manasquan played an annual game against distant Rancocas Valley. Neptune still had three open dates for the 1936 football season, including Thanksgiving (then the biggest date on the football calendar).[1]

Maurer, however, believed that he had a solution. If the small schools of Monmouth and Ocean County would cooperate and form a league of their own, they could all gain full schedules and ensure that local games would always have some stakes. Local papers might not have been interested in one-off games, but they would certainly cover a league championship race.

On February 10, principals, athletic directors, and coaches from across Monmouth and Ocean County gathered in the gymnasium at Freehold High School. The men at the meeting weren't there just to chat. This was a working meeting. By the time it was over, nine schools had officially decided to create the first interscholastic sports league in Central Jersey (two more would join later that week). They had formed committees to develop schedules in the league's four original sports (football, basketball, baseball, and track). They had elected a president (Maurer) and they had chosen a name. The Shore Conference was born.[2]

Today, the Shore Conference is a sporting juggernaut, the oldest continuously operating athletic high school league in New Jersey. It offers championships in twenty different sports, with major events held at neutral sites throughout Monmouth and Ocean County. Its forty-three member schools compete for statewide honors at all group sizes. Decades of rapid growth have transformed the region it serves into a heavily populated, bustling region. It looks very different now than it did when the league was first created back in 1936.

At that time, the combined population of Monmouth and Ocean Counties was still just a third the size of Hudson County's and a quarter the size of Essex County's. Beyond Asbury Park, the Shore was mostly an afterthought. A quick tour of the region shows how true this was.

We'll start in Asbury Park, the region's main population hub. One of New Jersey's premier resorts, it was annually flooded with tourists who stepped off their railroad cars and right onto the boardwalk. Locals too made their way to Asbury, taking advantage of its huge business district and many entertainment options. Its downtown dominated local commerce, and its newspaper was the main source of information. In 1936, over 10 percent of Monmouth County's population lived in either the city itself or its near suburbs.

> **PHILLIP MAY (Monmouth County resident)**: *"As a child growing up, I went there to the amusements and the business district. We went shopping in the business district, maybe once a month . . . in the summertime, the boardwalk was unbelievable. My mother and father would bring us down there for fireworks, for the rides, or for whatever . . . I mean, they had the best of everything there in Asbury Park. Beautiful area, beautiful homes, well-kept, nice city, as far as stores and commercial areas."[3]*

That large population was also one of the county's most diverse. Essential to the city's tourist trade were the workers who kept its hotels running, serving as porters, maids, and bellhops. Many of them were African Americans drawn up from the South. Asbury Park was no utopia and working in a hotel was not an easy or comfortable job, but there were some appealing features to it. Asbury's hotels offered relatively good wages, uniforms, and a chance to be addressed with more respect than would be found working manual labor in the South.[4]

The city's growing Black population crowded into the West Side—a quarter-mile square neighborhood some distance off the beach. There was clear racial segregation in the town's theaters and beachfronts, and the conditions on the West Side lagged far behind those on the wealthier, all-white East Side. But there was also a community, with four churches, mutual aid societies, an active social life, and plenty of Black-owned businesses.[5]

Thomas Smith Jr. (Asbury Park resident and policeman):
"As a Black American in Asbury Park at that time, we all had to live on the West Side, close to the tracks and south of Asbury Avenue. There were no Blacks north of Asbury Avenue except three Black families that lived on Second Avenue . . . the beachfront was segregated, too. We were down at the lower end of the beach, just before you get to Ocean Grove, and there was a sewer pipe that ran through there, but that was the only beach that we could use. A lot of young people started to go to Belmar to swim."[6]

This brings up an important point—Shore Conference athletics never had a color line, and none of its high schools were segregated. From the league's first season, African American and white athletes competed side by side. Yet in 1936, the region was not entirely integrated, either. Patterns of residential segregation ensured that African American families were clustered into certain areas of Monmouth and Ocean County. Many towns had only a tiny population of African Americans. The more diverse ones often had several clear color barriers.

These were most clearly seen at the elementary school level. In Asbury, for example, students of all races shared the Bangs Avenue School *building* but did not actually share its facilities. Students walked through either a "colored" entrance or a "white" entrance, and once within found themselves in separate classrooms, with separate teachers and separate bathrooms. This system lasted until 1946.[7]

The prejudice that greeted immigrants from Southern and Eastern Europe was not as extreme, nor were the legal barriers erected against them as high. Nonetheless, there was still prejudice, and those groups also clustered into specific ethnic neighborhoods. The largest such community at the Shore were Italian-Americans, who packed themselves into Long Branch or into their own section of Asbury's West Side. However, the barriers in their way dropped much more quickly than they did for the Shore's African American community, and it wasn't long before Italian last names could be found in every high school at the Shore.[8]

Truly integrated or not, Asbury Park did tower over its neighbors—economically, culturally, and athletically. Its much larger high school was the only one in the area to enjoy statewide athletic renown. The Blue Bishops already had a total of eight state championships in football, including four consecutive from 1929-32. The 1929 team had allowed just six points all season and finished as the number-one team in all of New Jersey. Asbury had also produced a major star, quarterback Bill "Butch" Bruno, who in 1936 was playing for the University of Notre Dame.

Any town near Asbury was closely linked with the city, economically and culturally. The smaller suburbs sent their children into the city for school. Neptune was large enough to run its own school system but was nonetheless tightly tied to Asbury. Its wealthier areas were summer cottages, and its working-class areas were generally filled with those who worked in Asbury's hotels. Only the inland portions of the town, still dotted with farms, looked elsewhere.[9]

The close links between the two towns carried over into football. During the 1920s, Neptune's football teams (then known as the Sea Kings) had been highly competitive, strong enough to meet Asbury Park in an annual

Thanksgiving rivalry. By 1928, that feud had grown so intense that it led to a complete break in athletic relations between the two schools.

That was Bill Flynn's first season as head coach at Asbury Park. The team, which had been struggling for a few years, immediately revived thanks to Flynn's skilled coaching and the brilliant play of linemen Damon Tucker and William White. As Thanksgiving neared, Asbury was favored to complete an undefeated season with a victory over a middling Sea King team. That was when the Neptune Board of Education started a huge controversy.

The board filed a complaint with the NJSIAA claiming that Tucker and White were overage. Asbury Park produced birth certificates refuting the charge, but by then Neptune's accusations had shifted. Tucker and White were both African Americans and natives of Virginia; in a typical Asbury Park story, they had come up to New Jersey to work at one of the boardwalk hotels. Rather than return home at the end of the summer, they used their savings to rent rooms in the city, where they enrolled at the high school and joined the football team.

Neptune charged that the two athletes were actually ringers, secretly recruited off the hotel staff to play football. Asbury countered witheringly, accusing Neptune of having used ringers themselves in the past, and with having used extreme and inappropriate methods to investigate Tucker and White. One board member, they charged, had disguised himself as a city teacher and visited the two at their homes. Despite this burst of righteous anger, the NJSIAA sided with Neptune and suspended both players.

The Thanksgiving game itself provided the final blow to the already damaged relationship. Neptune won, 19-18, after which their jubilant fans stormed the field and tore down Asbury's goalposts. After that, the two schools decided that athletic relations should cease for a while. For Neptune, this was a blow—the Sea Kings had lost their greatest rival.

Since the break was still ongoing in 1936, their teams were doubtless excited about the opportunity to compete for a local title and create some new rivalries. Asbury football quickly rebounded, as Flynn coached the team to sectional titles in each of the next four seasons. They also quickly developed a new rival to fill the void left by Neptune. That was Long Branch.[10]

Long Branch, just six miles north of Asbury, was the only Shore town that at this point could bear comparison to Asbury. It was also a resort town, with a long history of attracting fashionable crowds (including a string of seven different presidents that stretched back to Ulysses S. Grant). It, too, was a diverse city, with a significant African American population and the area's largest Italian community.

Its high school also had a rich football tradition. The Green Wave had been playing football since before World War I. Their most recent period of success had seen them win CJ III titles in 1932 and 1935, and they had sent a star of their own to the college ranks—end Amadeo "Army" Ippolito, who would earn All-East honors at Temple, under the legendary Pop Warner. The presence of Ippolito at Temple, like the presence of Bruno at Notre Dame, was validation for the young-but-growing traditions of these two high schools.

The tourist Shore ran northward from Long Branch, through a string of resort towns and beaches that ran all the way up to Sandy Hook. These towns were smaller than Asbury or Long Branch, but similar in content—boardwalks, music halls, and hotels. Head inland, though, and the atmosphere changed. One distinct area was Red Bank. Like Long Branch and Asbury, it was a shopping hub and possessed an active nightlife, centered around the popular Carlton Theater (today known as the Count Basie Theater). It too had a substantial African American population, large enough to draw regular appearances from touring Negro League teams (featuring stars such as Josh Gibson and Satchel Paige). But Red Bank was not a tourist town.

Red Bank existed because of the Navesink River, a navigable body of water that allowed its ships access to New York City. That had long made it a center for farmers and other businessmen looking to easily ship goods elsewhere. Its economy was further strengthened by nearby Fort Monmouth, home to the U.S. Army's Signal Corps Training School. The fort provided valuable jobs to residents and valuable business for local merchants.[11]

Daniel Dorn (Red Bank resident) : *"Red Bank grew because they had access to New York City before there was any railroad . . . the farmers used to come to Red Bank and send their products to New York . . . so that's why this area grew . . . the whole county was here shopping."*[12]

A traveler who exited Red Bank eastward, driving along Ridge Road into Fair Haven and Rumson, would find a different atmosphere yet. The main roads here were dotted by large, luxurious estates; wealthy New Yorkers had long been spending their summers in this area. Elements of the aristocracy could still be found in 1930s Rumson, where it wasn't unusual for the large estates to employ multiple domestic servants. But the area wasn't quite as homogenous as all that—it was also home to the staff of those houses, to successful professionals, and to merchants and storekeepers selling goods and services to all of them.[13]

The symbol of the community was its imposing high school. Although it held less than 300 students (barely a quarter the size of Asbury Park), the high school was nonetheless striking. Much of the money for its construction had come from the WPA, a federal program designed to relieve unemployment stemming from the Great Depression. Funds for its bell tower, however, had come from a philanthropic school board member named Bertram Borden. That was the sort of community this was—it took pride in its high school, and it had the resources to show it.[14]

East of Rumson was the ocean, so now our traveler was at a literal crossroads. Southward lay the tourist Shore and Asbury Park. Northward, along State Route 36, lay the bluffs of Atlantic Highlands. Beneath their towering heights, one could pause and see Sandy Hook far below, marking the division between the Atlantic Ocean and New York Bay. In that direction, the road curved westward, along the Raritan Bayshore, itself a unique region.

At times, it seemed that each Bayshore town was its own little world. This was especially the case for Atlantic Highlands and Keyport. Both were home to a nautical working class, fishers and clammers who worked the waters, then sold their produce to New York City. Both also had their own small downtowns, complete with a full range of stores. The occasions when one would need to venture out of these close-knit communities were rare indeed.

That spirit was epitomized by the effort both communities put into establishing and maintaining their own high schools. Keyport had been educating its own high schoolers since the 1880s and had thrown up a gleaming new three-story building to do it in 1928. Atlantic Highlands, with an even smaller student population, also educated all their students, grades K-12, in a single building in their own downtown.[15]

One of several towns that separated Atlantic Highlands and Keyport was one of the Bayshore's more unique towns—Middletown. This was a sprawling township of fifty-eight square miles. Much of the town was "rolling, with many farms and country estates."[16] The town had no center but was instead a collection of seven different census-designated places, each with its own identity and community.

The town's sections were very different from one another, ranging from nautical Belford and Port Monmouth to rural Lincroft. Each had its own little downtown, and so a traveler who wasn't paying close attention could easily have thought that he had passed through seven towns. The high school reflected that reality—although its official name was Middletown High School, most residents called it Leonardo High School, after the section of town where it was located. By the late 1930s, that building held just over 700 students. That was larger than most area schools, but still quite a bit smaller than Asbury or Long Branch.[17]

Of all the Bayshore towns, Middletown was really the only one that had a football tradition. The Lions didn't have the enrollment to compete with the likes of Asbury or Long Branch, but against schools their own size they could be fierce, and they'd won Central Jersey titles in 1925 and 1926. More than that, they'd produced a bona fide star, maybe the first in the history of the Shore—Swede Hanson.

Hanson had been part of an all-star backfield on those 1925 and 1926 teams, a group so dangerous it was nicknamed the "Four Horsemen of Leonardo." He played both football and baseball at Temple, becoming a legend for his heroic performance in a 1930 gridiron upset of Bucknell. In that game, Hanson returned a kickoff 78 yards for a touchdown to secure a narrow 7-6 victory over the Bison (who started future NFL Hall of Famer Clark Hinkle). Hanson himself played in the NFL for eight years, twice earning All-Pro honors. In 1936, he was still playing for the Philadelphia Eagles, a point of pride for Middletown football fans of all ages.

West of Middletown, the Bayshore began to give way to New Jersey's fertile farm belt, a rich agricultural region that produced the fruits, dairy, and potatoes that fed cities across the Northeast. Matawan, the next major town, carried elements of both regions. Like the tight-knit fishing villages to its east, it was its own little world, where everyone knew everyone else. It also was not totally removed from the sea; the northwestern part of the township still touched the water. It had a modern downtown, which at times could look as bustling and modern as Red Bank's. It also had busy rail links to North Jersey, connecting commuters to ferries from which they could reach New York City. But stray too far out of the town center, and suddenly you'd find yourself in farm country, with the barns and open fields of the farm belt to its southwest.[18]

Drive far enough through that farm belt, and eventually you'd hit Freehold, the county seat and the anchor of western Monmouth County. In 1936, this was a quintessential American small town, fusing farmland, residential neighborhoods, a downtown shopping section, and even a small industrial area. If it wasn't for three distinguishing features, Freehold could have stood in for just about any small town in the Northeast.

The first was Freehold's unusually strong connection to the American Revolution. The Battle of Monmouth, a key coming-of-age moment for George Washington's Continental Army, had been fought nearby, and the battle site and memory were well-preserved in town. The second key feature was the Freehold Racetrack, the oldest in the United States and a reliable summer attraction. The third was the town's largest employer, the Karagheusian Carpet Factory. This massive building employed 1,500 people in its production of huge rugs, fulfilling orders to carpet places such as Radio City Music Hall and the US Supreme Court Building.[19]

Freehold's football tradition was practically nonexistent, and student support shallow.[20] The situation may not have been quite as dire at Monmouth County's other small schools, but outside of Leonardo there was nobody with a championship tradition. This wasn't a football wasteland, but it was still very much uncharted territory.

If our traveler headed south out of Freehold, he would see things start to change. The soil south of town was less productive and less attractive to farmers. Thus, the rolling fields of Northern Monmouth County started to give way to trees, bracketing either side of US 9. Those pine trees didn't break up until County Line Road, when our traveler crossed into Ocean County and entered the winter resort town of Lakewood.

Ocean County was very sparsely populated in 1936, and while Lakewood may have been home to just 7,000 people, it was nonetheless the county's largest town. It had first risen to prominence in the 1880s and 1890s, when its reputation for warm winters attracted celebrities such as President Grover Cleveland, author Mark Twain, and robber barons John D. Rockefeller and Jay Gould. That, in turn, attracted entrepreneurs who opened restaurants and hotels. Although the town was inland from the beach, the tourist trade soon became the backbone of its economy.

In some ways, Lakewood would be unrecognizable to a modern visitor— the modern version of the town is much more urbanized and more than ten times the size. However, there were some elements that would seem familiar. The town was easily the most diverse in Ocean County, home not only to a significant African American population but also a substantial Jewish population. Although not as popular as the Catskills, Lakewood did draw a fair number of Jewish vacationers from New York City. The guests stayed only for the season, but the proprietors and staff of the establishments stayed in town year-round. It wasn't unusual to see Jewish names among the Lakewood athletes listed in the *Asbury Park Press*.

Piner athletic teams frequently did appear in the paper, in large part due to their colorful coach, Russ Wright. Wright stood out in Lakewood—he had been a football star in West Virginia's coal country, earning All-State honors and a scholarship to the state university. After starring for the Mountaineers, he bounced around the fringes of semipro football and minor league baseball, then entered coaching. At Lakewood, he was *the* coach. During his tenure, Wright would coach football, basketball, base-ball, track, golf, and bowling.

And his teams won, in all sports but especially football. The year 1936 was Wright's seventh at the helm; in his first six years, the team had won two Central Jersey titles and established dominance over their archrivals from Toms River. The two high schools were Ocean County's largest, and therefore they were natural enemies. The Piners and Indians had started playing in 1919, and then moved their rivalry to Thanksgiving in 1928. It quickly became a hit, regularly drawing a huge crowd and becoming the focal point of the season. Toms River had won the first holiday meeting, but in six years under Wright, Lakewood was 4-1-1 and hadn't lost since 1930.

Although it was not Lakewood's equal in football, the town of Toms River would still have been worth a visit to our traveler, and so we'll send him farther down US 9, deeper into what was then the northern fringes of the Pine Barrens. The road then would have been surrounded by swamps, many of them used by local farmers as cranberry bogs. It would have been a relief, then, to reach little Toms River, then known as "an attractive fishing community" clustered around the banks of the river that named the town.

Toms River had a long history, and in the American Revolution had been home to a blockhouse from which Patriots raided the British mil-itary. An incident in which loyalist forces captured and hanged Patriot captain Joshua Huddy turned out to be one of the last major affairs of the Revolution. The town at the time was still a small one, home to fewer than 4,000 people. They were mostly clustered by the courthouse and riv-erbanks, the section that now goes to Toms River High School South.[21]

At that time, of course, it was just Toms River High School. This was a quintessential small town, and it had a small-town's love for sports. Prin-cipal Nathaniel Detwiler, a local legend for whom the football stadium would one day be named, had coached all of Toms River sports back in the 1920s, and he made sure that the locals were informed of the success their students found on fields of friendly strife. They didn't need to go to the games or even read the paper to know how Toms River did; they just needed to listen for the "Singer of Victories." This bell (which hung over the high school) rang out loud and clear after every football victory. And those victories were frequent; the 1935 Indians were 8-2.

South of Toms River, Ocean County changed. Houses got sparser, the land got sandier, and the pines got thicker. These were the Pine Barrens, a vast, empty region shrouded in legend, and highly unwelcoming to outsiders. Travel guides warned that outside of the main route, the roads were "wretched, unmarked, and not safe for automobile travel except in dry weather."

No tourist would have thought to turn west, into the forest. The few scattered residents of the pines were subject to all kinds of wild rumors— that they were descended from Tories and British deserters, that they brewed illegal moonshine and robbed unwary travelers, and they were so hostile that they would shoot at the US Navy blimps that drifted over the area. The pines were frightening and best avoided, most travelers would have thought.[22]

The land east of the road was considered more hospitable, but not more interesting. Few travelers would have had much desire to spend time among the small, scattered villages of this swampy, sandy region. Even Long Beach Island, today a major vacation area, attracted only a few visitors to its "resort hamlets." It was really thought of as a rugged place for fishermen and whalers to ply their trade.[23] No, in 1936 travelers didn't expect to find much south of Toms River unless they were heading all the way to Atlantic City, and our intrepid explorer was not.

There was, though, one more part of the Shore left to be seen. Perhaps no part of Monmouth and Ocean Counties was more representative of them than the banks of the Manasquan River. On the south side (in Ocean County) was Point Pleasant, on the northern side (in Monmouth County) was Manasquan. To outsiders, the two towns were very similar—beachfront communities whose populations swelled significantly in the summer. The nearby beach and inlet drew vacationers of all sorts—boaters, swimmers, sport fishermen, and tourists for the summer. And the locals took sports seriously all year round.[24]

That was especially true of the town's youngsters. But they would not have agreed that Manasquan and Point Pleasant were identical, since the two towns were rivals in just about everything. Town teams had been playing each other in organized games of football and baseball since the 1890s, and in 1935 the high school football teams had begun playing on Thanksgiving. The game became a fixture of local sports almost immediately. That Manasquan was already playing on Thanksgiving will be no surprise to the modern reader; that the greater championship tradition belonged to Point Pleasant probably will be.

The Garnet Gulls were, like everyone else in Ocean County, too small to ever challenge Asbury Park or Lakewood, but they had won consecutive Central Jersey titles at their size in 1927 and 1928, and they were never intimidated by the thought of competing with their northern siblings from across the river. Manasquan, meanwhile, had not yet become the title town it would one day be. Nonetheless, the raw materials were there. The town and students cared deeply about competitive sports, and within a few years they would be wildly celebrating titles.

Going north from Manasquan, our traveler would pass through a few more tourist towns like Sea Girt, Spring Lake, and Belmar, but it wouldn't be long before he was back in Asbury Park. And so, our circuit of Monmouth and Ocean Counties in the 1930s is now complete. It was in this landscape, still an open canvas, that the Shore Conference would be created. And these early teams, competing in a landscape very different from the teams that take the field today, would lay the groundwork for the glorious decades of Shore football to come.

CHAPTER 2
THE EARLY YEARS,
1936-1938

The Shore Conference started quickly. In the spring of 1936, only a few months after forming the league, its member schools managed to organize a track meet and crown a baseball champion. The track meet (which immediately became an annual fixture) was held at Long Branch and won by Toms River. The baseball season, meanwhile, ended in controversy.

Lakewood finished 6-1 in the Shore and acquitted themselves well against a tough nonconference schedule. However, they faced neither 5-1 Keyport nor 6-2 Manasquan. In order to settle the matter, the Shore Conference arranged a playoff between Lakewood and Keyport. Lakewood, however, felt that they'd already played too many games and had the better record; they refused to participate. Instead, Keyport played Manasquan at Memorial Park in Belmar. In front of a respectable crowd, the Red Raiders won 3-2 in fourteen innings, bringing an end to the first athletic season in Shore Conference history.[1]

That first season revealed two key facts about the early years of the Shore Conference. First, it was a great idea—students and adults alike followed it very closely. Second, its loose organization was going to be a problem. The league had not issued a schedule in baseball, which meant that some teams played each other twice, others once, and others not at all. The standings were a mess and would be in football as well—the first Shore Conference season would see teams play as few as four and as many as six league opponents. The plan was instead to award the title based on the Dickinson System, a mathematical rating formula.

The result was constant controversy. On seven occasions, there was either a tie for the title or it remained disputed by teams that hadn't played each other. Not until 1952, when the league split into two divisions, would it be possible to determine titles on the field. Nonetheless, interest in the league was intense, and the controversy only fueled the fire.

The Shore's first football season began in earnest on September 1, 1936. Under the rules of the time, that was the first date that coaches could assemble their teams, issue equipment, and begin workouts. After a long summer away from organized high school athletics, the young men of Monmouth and Ocean County were eager to get to work.

The football they played then was very different than the football played today. Coaching from the sideline was strictly forbidden, and substitution was limited. Unable to call individual plays or shuttle messengers in with direct instructions, coaches had to educate their players in tactics and strategy, then sit back and hope that they would make the right decisions. During timeouts and between possessions, there would be opportunities to share instructions, but the play-to-play conduct of the game was in the hands of the boys themselves.

There were other differences. The ball was fatter in the middle and rounder at the edges, making it harder to throw accurately. Long passes were very rare; Sammy Baugh (arguably the first modern passing quarterback) was still just a college football player at TCU. This meant offensive drives were harder to sustain, and the game was much lower scoring; a team that scored once a quarter was considered an offensive machine. Teams were therefore quick to punt (even on third down) if a possession went poorly. The punt was actually a crucial weapon; a good one could reverse field position and turn the tide of an entire game.

Although the game was run-based, it certainly wasn't stodgy. Teams used a wide array of offensive formations and systems, many that would seem strange to the modern eye. Just about every offensive formation seen in the modern game is in some way based on the principles of the T formation. Although the original formation is now rarely used, most of its innovations are now standard—a quarterback who is both a passer and ballhandler, a "hand to hand snap" in which the quarterback takes the ball from under center, and a balanced line (with one tackle and one guard on each side of the center). But that offense hadn't really been developed yet and wouldn't hit the national scene until the Chicago Bears put Sid Luckman under center in 1939.

The three most popular formations of the day were the single wing, the Notre Dame Box, and the short punt. The single wing (also known as "the Pop Warner system" after the coach who developed it) was easily the most common and was run by just about every team at the Shore. It featured an unbalanced line and an unbalanced backfield, with a clear strong side and a clear weakside. The center would snap the ball shotgun style to any of the three backs in the backfield (quarterback, fullback, or tailback), who could then either carry the ball himself or hand it to a teammate.

This offense offered plenty of opportunities for straight power plays, with three backs leading for the fourth. However, reverses and "spinner" plays, in which the action started one way and then went another, were common. The key man was the tailback, who needed to be able to run, pass, and punt if necessary. The quarterback called the plays, but his responsibilities were more often blocking and faking. Passing was rare.

One common variant of the single wing was the Notre Dame Box, so named because it had been made famous by Knute Rockne's Irish teams of the 1920s. This was an offense based on deception, with the four backs frequently motioning or shifting before the snap, then using fake handoffs to each other afterward. One of the tight ends would occasionally "flex" out to a split position, creating a genuine passing threat. This was the spread offense of its day, and it had powered the Green Bay Packers to

NFL titles in 1929, 1930, and 1931. In 1936, Matawan, Point Pleasant, Atlantic Highlands, and Leonardo were all using this formation at least occasionally.

The final, and least common offense was the short punt formation, which was most often used in desperate situations. It didn't offer much power, but the position of the backs gave the tailback plenty of time to throw the ball, and five different potential receivers who could head out for passes. It also forced the defense to back off a little, as it always carried the threat of a quick kick. In 1936, Manasquan intended to use this as its primary set.

Information about who was using which offense could be found (along with a wealth of other information) in the detailed previews published by the *Asbury Park Press*. The paper's football-hungry audience received daily previews of local teams all through September. Most teams could find at least some reason to be excited—Asbury Park and Long Branch had sectional crowns to defend, and any of the conference schools had a shot at the title. It was all building toward the last weekend in September, when the season would officially begin.

A quick look at the *Asbury Park Press* on that Friday afternoon gives a glimpse at the Shore world of 1936. It was a presidential election year, so most of the front page was dedicated to the ongoing race between Democratic incumbent Franklin Delano Roosevelt and his Republican challenger, Alf Landon. The Shore (always a Republican stronghold) narrowly preferred Landon, but not by nearly enough to offset the huge margins that Roosevelt would run up in other parts of the state. That was typical—New Jersey was one of the forty-six states Roosevelt would win in one of the most decisive landslides in American history.

Inside, a few articles covered the ongoing Spanish Civil War, and an editorial questioned why so many democracies were falling to dictatorships. These were hints that the United States could no longer focus solely on domestic concerns, but those whispers remained quiet and distant. More representative of these sleepy days at the Shore, though, were some of its regular sections. The "Local Happenings" column informed readers which of their neighbors were going away for the weekend and which ones were holding cocktail parties. Another feature, "News of Interest to Farmers," was authored by the Monmouth County agriculture agent. This half-page spread contained all sorts of advice, ranging from the most efficient way to light a henhouse to the best way to handle seed potatoes. The Shore was still a farming area, and there were doubtless many locals who found the advice practical, rather than quaint.

The sports pages were just as local. Although the *Press* did preview the upcoming World Series (an all-New York affair between the Yankees and the Giants), it spent far more space on the arrival of "king football." The weekend's big game, between New Brunswick and Asbury Park, was previewed in detail. Additional space was devoted to recounting a scrimmage between Red Bank and Rumson.[2] New York may have been the nearest major city, but its teams were not the home teams. The local high schools were.

The most popular team was usually Asbury Park, followed by Long Branch. Those two, plus Red Bank, were the area's independents, and they focused on three goals. The first was to win the sectional title—for Asbury's Blue Bishops that was Central Jersey Group IV, while for Long Branch's Green Wave and Red Bank's Bucs, that was CJ III. These titles were based off mathematical ranking systems, rather than playoffs, so no one team truly controlled its own destiny. However, Asbury played several of its key rivals in the title race, and so knew that seven wins usually gave them a shot at the crown.

The second goal was to beat local rivals, which in the case of the so-called "big three" meant beating each other. Especially heated was the rivalry between Long Branch and Asbury Park. The third and final goal was to win on Thanksgiving, the traditional climax of the season and usually played in front of the year's biggest crowd.

Asbury Park's 1936 season was representative. The Blue Bishops dominated their local rivals (shutting out Long Branch and Red Bank), acquitted themselves well against out-of-area foes (tying statewide power Garfield and routing Phillipsburg), and were tightly competitive with their CJ IV rivals (beating New Brunswick and tying Perth Amboy). They entered the Thanksgiving game at 6-1-2, knowing that a win over South

River would probably be enough to claim their second consecutive CJ IV crown.

In 1936 and for many decades afterward, Thanksgiving was the high point of the football season. Most teams ended their year against their archrivals, and all the state's big cities, from Jersey City (St. Peter's Prep vs. Dickinson) to Camden (Woodrow Wilson vs. Camden) had at least one game. Even with the traditional Neptune series suspended, the Blue Bishops could still attract 4,000 fans to the stadium to see them play South River.

Unfortunately, those 4,000 went home disappointed. The Bricktowners, as South River teams were called in those days, played Asbury tooth and nail and led 13-7 in the fourth. With time running down, Asbury's Tommy Smith blocked a punt, which Jerry Thixton fell on in the end zone for a tying touchdown. The extra point, however, sailed wide; the game ended in a tie and the CJ IV title would instead go to New Brunswick.[3]

The lack of a title was disappointing, but the 6-1-3 record was still nothing to complain about. A number of individual Bishop players received postseason honors, filling six of the eleven slots on the annual "Monmouth-Ocean All-Star Team" picked each December by the *Asbury Park Press*. Two of them, Tom Smith and Courtleigh Halikman, played major college football, Smith at Howard and Halikman at Villanova and George Washington.

There was no doubt that the Blue Bishops honored by the *Asbury Park Press* deserved the accolades they received that winter. However, their dominance was a reminder of why the smaller schools wanted the Shore Conference so badly. They had plenty of good athletes too, but received scant coverage compared to the detail that the *Press* focused on the Blue Bishops. Still, lack of media coverage didn't mean lack of excitement. Every town loved its team, as evidenced by the annual Long Branch-Red Bank Thanksgiving spectacular.

1936 had been mildly disappointing for Long Branch (which entered Thanksgiving at 3-4-1) and an unmitigated catastrophe for Red Bank (which came in at 0-7). Despite those records, their yearly game remained exciting. The two teams had been playing on the holiday since 1926, always drawing a large crowd (this year, it drew 4,500 fans). What happened on this day salvaged Red Bank's season and turned Long Branch's from mixed to miserable.

Two touchdown runs by Red Bank tailback Jack Henry tilted the game toward the Bucs early, and it never tilted back. By the time the clock ran out, the home fans were headed home with their heads held high after a thrilling 15-0 victory.[4] Thanksgiving could do that to you.

In total, there were six Thanksgiving games at the Shore in 1936. The Asbury-South River game had been a marriage of convenience and would end after just one year. A second game, between Freehold and Matawan, would within three years be superseded by the more natural Matawan-Keyport rivalry. The other four, though, were all naturals. Both Red Bank-Long Branch and Lakewood-Toms River already had rich traditions. The Manasquan and Point Pleasant Thanksgiving series was younger, but the two towns had been competing in everything for years anyway, and so the rivalry was hugely popular. Even the Leonardo-Rumson rivalry, which would one day turn into a mismatch, was at this time a good contest.

And while Thanksgiving may have been the biggest attraction of the year, it was far from the only one. The intensity of the very first Shore Conference title race helped get the league off to a fast start. From the first, the clear favorite had been Lakewood. By enrollment the league's largest school, the Piners also had their most established coach (Russ Wright) and the most recent track record of success, including two sectional crowns and an 8-2 season in 1935.

Most importantly, they had talent. End Purnell Mincey and center Paul Protin both earned All-Shore honors, but the real punch came from the backfield, which featured workhorse back Earl Childress. However, the team suffered some early blows—a key lineman left the team in order to work, while another dropped football to pick up professional boxing. That left the door open a crack for local challengers, most prominently Manasquan and Leonardo.

Leonardo, under new Head Coach Gil Augustine, had the conference's best backfield, featuring tailback Ed Mooney and fullback James O'Neill.

They also had a literal homefield advantage—their gridiron was known for its unusually steep incline, something that their teams often tried to take advantage of. Manasquan, meanwhile, was breaking in a new head coach (Red Griswold) but returned most starters, particularly quarterback Joe LaVance, fullback Phil Towne, and All-Shore tackle Jack Hyde.[5]

All three teams reached mid-November with undefeated league records. The key game remaining was between Lakewood and Manasquan, but since neither team played Leonardo, a disputed title was likely. That would have been a sour note on which to start the new league. Fortunately, an unlikely Atlantic Highlands team grabbed Shore's first big upset and launched the career of its first star coach.

Arnie Truex had been a triple-threat tailback on the 1934 Rutgers football team, earning an honorable mention on that year's All-American team. He then became the all-sports coach at tiny Highlands. He had at his disposal a talented, speedy backfield featuring the Keyes brothers, Jim and Thomas, plus hammering halfbacks Ed "Alabama" Pitts and Abe Pleasant. The Tigers overcame a 1-2 start to climb over .500 with wins over Matawan and Rumson.

That set the stage for the Bayshore's biggest game of the year, the annual clash between Leonardo and Atlantic Highlands. Leonardo usually dominated; they'd won seventeen years running. However, 1936 saw the streak come to an abrupt halt, as Abe Pleasant's touchdown and extra point secured Highlands a shocking 7-6 win and eliminated Leonardo from the title race.[6]

That same day, Lakewood drilled Manasquan 24-0. They went on to clinch the league title with a 14-0 Thanksgiving Day victory over Toms River (Earl Childers and Purnell Mincey both scored). So ended a season of glory—the CJ II crown, a 9-0 record, and the first-ever Shore Conference title. Not bad at all.[7]

In 1937, the Shore Conference's second title race received greatly expanded coverage from the *Asbury Park Press*; every league game was detailed in the Sunday paper. Readers could now follow the twists and turns of individual games. With both Asbury and Long Branch enduring difficult seasons, the league race provided a nice focus for local sports coverage.

The early spotlight shone on Neptune. Area sports were always more exciting when Neptune was good, because the flashy Scarlet Fliers usually had plenty of athletes and were well-supported by an enthusiastic student body. Head Coach Bob Woolley was a sharp, disciplined football mind, and in 1935 he had coached his team to their first title in almost ten years.

The young 1936 team had struggled to a 2-5-1 finish, but with so many key players returning for 1937, hopes were high. The biggest star was spectacular triple-threat back Joe Vetrano. A classic single-wing tailback, Vetrano could run, kick, and pass, and was capable of breaking a game open at any moment. To take advantage of the expected large crowds, the Neptune booster club arranged to hold four night games at Belmar's Memorial Field.

Over 1,500 fans packed the field on September 24 to see Neptune take on Rumson. They saw the first edition of the Joe Vetrano Show. His booming punt in the second quarter pinned the Bulldogs back on their own 2. When Rumson tried to kick out of their precarious situation, Vetrano returned it for the game's only score.

Neptune won, 6-0. Crowds swelled a week later, with 2,000 fans wedging into the bleachers to see Vetrano score the only touchdown of a 7-0 win over Toms River. The town had caught "Flier Fever."[8]

When that fever went too far, though, it threw the entire season into jeopardy. After the game, a group of Neptune fans and players took part in a "midnight motorcade" to Toms River to celebrate their victory. The exuberant youths paraded through the town, then started a bonfire before they were caught by unamused authorities. Vetrano played no part in the bonfire, but he was at the parade, and for that he was suspended by Head Coach Bob Woolley. With the title chase entering its final stages, locals angrily demanded that Woolley reinstate his star. He refused. And so, Neptune entered its biggest game yet, against Lakewood, shorthanded.[9]

The Piners were the surprise of the season. Russ Wright predicted their doom to the *Asbury Park Press*, and he was borne out by two early defeats—the first in a scrimmage against some local alumni and the second against Princeton High School. However, Wright's Piner teams could never be counted out, and with Neptune depleted, they had a puncher's chance.

Memorial Field was mobbed for a tense game. Even without Vetrano, Neptune mounted a second quarter drive to the Lakewood 1. However, the Piners held, and the game went into the half scoreless. In the third quarter, though, Lakewood's Oscar Wood and Joe Page took over with their line plunges. Wood eventually scored the winner from short range and Lakewood escaped, 6-0.[10]

After that, the title race seemed to tilt toward the Piners. Thanks to the running of Wood, Page, and Frank Aufiero, they won six straight games, four of them in the league. By Thanksgiving, Wright's team was 7-1, one win away from their second consecutive league crown. But they were not alone at the top. They weren't even the story of the season.

That honor belonged to tiny Atlantic Highlands. The Tigers had just twenty-four players on their roster (eight of them freshmen), but Arnie Truex's team was second to none in terms of talent. They had a big line, featuring All-Shore end Tom Minor, center Ed Cardner, and speedy Thomas "Boonie" Keyes. Keyes was as dangerous as Vetrano and a threat to score on any play.

The Tigers caved in opposition defenses, scoring blowout wins over Freehold (40-0) and Matawan (33-0). It fast became clear that the Tigers were serious contenders for a Shore Conference title. By November, the Tigers were one of only six unbeaten and untied teams left in the entire state. Their biggest remaining hurdle was the annual game with Leonardo. Here the usual roles were reversed; the Lions had lost three straight and were heavy underdogs.

Since schools were closed on Thursday, November 11, to celebrate Armistice Day, the game was moved up to that morning in order to serve as a holiday feature. The atmosphere resembled Thanksgiving, with 3,500 fans jamming the bleachers for the showdown. For nearly the entire game, the score was deadlocked with neither side able to move. Then, in the final five minutes, things started happening.

First, Leonardo back Herbie Haulbosky raced 70 yards for a go-ahead touchdown. He tried to run for the extra point but was stopped short. Highlands answered with a drive of their own. Boonie Keyes did most of the work on a 10-play, 72-yard drive, eventually scoring on a short run. But he too was stopped on the conversion, and the game finished 6-6. The Tigers were still unbeaten, but they were perfect no more, and even after a victory over Toms River they still sat second to Lakewood.[11] Highlands was 7-0-1 and could do nothing but wait.

The fate of the race now lay with Lakewood. Thanks to their more difficult schedule, the Piners needed only a win over Toms River to repeat as Shore Conference champions. This was the year's big game, and 4,000 fans came out to see it. Toms River was fired up, eager to grab their first win over Lakewood since 1930 and deny the Piners the league title. They forced three first-half fumbles, one leading to Bill Zeimer's short touchdown run. In the second half, the Piners marched up and down the field, but the Indians held them at the 5, 8, and 10. They took an intentional safety after that last stop and ran out 6-2 winners.[12]

Shore Conference seasons and championship races have come down to the final quarter of the final game on many occasions since, but this was the first, and it helped solidify the league as one in which anything could happen. Atlantic Highlands, the smallest team in the league, had outraced Lakewood, the largest, to claim the Shore Conference title. The press loved it, especially when Lakewood gave them something else to write about by challenging the undefeated Highlanders to a postseason game. Atlantic Highlands, however, quickly declined. They had won the title fair and square, and now it was time for basketball season.[13]

Two Tigers, Boonie Keyes and senior tackle Tom Minor, received All-Shore honors, a list on which they were joined by Lakewood end John Melton. They were among six conference players to make the team, up from only three the year before. The status of the league was rapidly improving in the eyes of the local media. Among those six was the young man who consensus held was the area's best player, even better than the spectacular Keyes.

That was Joe Vetrano. He and his teammates had rebounded from the Lakewood loss with four straight wins. Two performances in that stretch particularly stood out. One was at Memorial Field, in the season's final night game against Freehold. Vetrano ran for touchdowns of 70, 63, 49, and 40 yards, helping Neptune to a 51-0 romp.[14] A week later, though, he did something even better—he helped the Fliers validate the new league by upsetting Long Branch.

Long Branch was struggling in 1937, but Neptune's 27-13 upset still carried a great deal of weight. Vetrano was his usual solid self in that game, running for touchdowns of 43 and 50 yards, and throwing a long pass to set up another score. This was a huge step forward.[15] It didn't help Neptune in the league standings, where they finished third. It did, however, help them claim the CJ II title, their second in three years, and it helped Vetrano win the area's scoring championship. He accepted a scholarship to Southern Mississippi, starring for that school's 1941 undefeated team.

After serving in the US Army during World War II, Vetrano went on to kick for the San Francisco 49ers in the All-American Football Conference from 1946-49. During that stretch, he hit an AAFC-record 108 extra points. Vetrano remained popular at the Shore, and locals closely followed his exploits in the professional ranks. In later years, he would serve as a scout with the 49ers, and eventually return to the Shore as a coach at Neptune.

The Shore Conference may have taken center stage in 1937, but Asbury Park and Long Branch were major draws even when their records were just okay. On Thanksgiving, 6,500 fans packed Deal Lake Stadium to see Asbury's loss to New Brunswick, while another 6,000 turned out in Long Branch to see the Green Wave beat Red Bank for their first win of the season. That set the stage for a hotly anticipated postseason matchup with the Blue Bishops.

The game's original date had been washed out by rain, but the rivalry was important enough that it was rescheduled for a Saturday in early December. Nothing was at stake but all-important bragging rights. With that on the line, the two teams produced a classic. Asbury led after three quarters on a Maurice Klitzman touchdown run, but Long Branch rallied.

The hero was tailback Claude Paxton, who had missed most of the season with injury. First, he hit Jim Renzo on a perfect short pass to the flat, which Renzo lugged 37 yards for a touchdown. That cut the lead to 7-6. In the fourth, Paxton caught a pass at his own 45-yard line, reversed his field, and raced down the sideline for the game-winning touchdown. The final was 12-7. The jubilant Long Branch fans tore down Asbury's goalposts and marched off with them. Their final record was just 2-4-2, but the wins over Red Bank and Asbury Park had made the season a success. It was a measure of how important local rivalries were at the Shore.[16]

Those rivalries remained important as the 1938 season started. Neptune was the biggest attraction; last season's experiment with Belmar night games was such a success that they played almost all their home games under the lights in 1938 and continued to draw enthusiastic, cheering crowds. They may well have been the best team, even without Joe Vetrano. Their experienced line was good enough to shut out five of eight opponents, and the hard-charging runs of Arnie Moore were usually enough to keep the ball moving. The season's highlight, once again, came at Long Branch. Neptune was undefeated at the time and chasing a CJ II title. Unusually for 1938, the game turned on an aerial display. Don Van Note caught two touchdown passes, one in the fourth quarter to secure a 14-8 victory.[17]

Since Neptune didn't play on Thanksgiving, their season was scheduled to end with a Saturday night home game against Red Bank. Since a win would complete an undefeated season and secure the CJ II crown, it drew the season's largest crowd—5,000 fans. Every aspect of the Flier team contributed to the victory. Jack Whitworth ran for a touchdown, while Arnie Moore added a 40-yard field goal for a 10-0 lead. Red Bank scored late to cut the deficit to 10-7, but the Flier line foiled any remaining drives and completed the championship quest.[18]

Neptune's final record was 6-0-2. Their two season-ending wins over Group III foes Red Bank and Long Branch had been decisive for them in the sectional title race. But they could not help in the Shore Conference race, where two ties with Toms River and Lakewood proved fatal.

Much like in 1937, the front-runners were Lakewood and Atlantic Highlands. The Piners, who returned their entire backfield from 1937, had a good mix of talent. Frank Aufiero was the hammer, a big fullback known for his line plunges, while Joe Wood and Oscar Page were the speedsters, smaller, faster, and dangerous big-play threats. Lakewood started 5-1-1, and their lone loss (to Group IV Phillipsburg) was also to their credit. For the third year in a row, they were the league's most intimidating force.

However, the sentimental favorites remained the little school that could—Atlantic Highlands. The Shore's smallest school was also its most exciting; Boonie Keyes could run like the wind, while Bob Morse at quarterback orchestrated what for 1938 was an impressive aerial offensive. The season peaked on Armistice Day with a thrilling 7-0 win at Leonardo, in which Morse hit George Janus for the winning touchdown on the final Tiger possession.[19] A tie for the title between the Tigers and Piners looked very likely.

The season's final two weeks, though, saw the emergence of Toms River. Bob Reigle had predicted only a fair season for his team at the start, and their quiet 0-0 tie at Neptune in the season opener seemed to confirm that. But as the season went on, workhorse back Fred Gesser and the Indians started to gain ground. They ran their record to 5-0-1, which gave them control of their own destiny in the race. But they were still dark horses, especially after an unimpressive win over lowly Freehold.

Their underdog status disappeared just before Thanksgiving when Toms River upset Atlantic Highlands. The "Truex Machine" scored first on a short Fred Bedle touchdown run, but the Ocean County boys tied the game on a trick play, a triple reverse to left guard Henry Klee. After that came the saving storm. The rain turned the field to muck, nullifying the Highlands speedsters and creating the conditions for Toms River's second score. In the bad weather, a botched Tiger punt attempt left the ball loose in the end zone, allowing Fred Combi to fall on it for what proved to be the winning touchdown. Toms River prevailed, 13-6.[20]

And so, for the second year in a row, the Shore Conference title came down to Toms River and Lakewood. The winner would claim the loop title, while the loser would get nothing. The 8,000 fans who ignored a snowstorm to pack the bleachers that morning was further proof that the league idea was a success; the championship stakes had drawn the largest crowd in series history. Unfortunately for the Lakewood fans, they had little to cheer about.

The Toms River defense quickly put the shackles on Aufiero, Wood, and Page, while the Lakewood defense struggled to contain Gesser, who set up the first touchdown (a short run by Wee Willie Collins) with four consecutive line plunges. He scored the clincher himself in the fourth. The final was 12-0, and Toms River was alone at the top. Three years, three different champions. The Shore Conference was off and running.[21]

Further validation for the league came a few weeks later, when the *Asbury Park Press* and New Jersey Blind Men's Club came together to organize an all-star game between the best players in the Shore Conference and the best players in what they called "the Big Three" (Asbury Park, Long Branch, and Red Bank). The game was held on December 3 at Deal Lake Stadium and drew a huge crowd of 6,000 fans. This was really 1938 football—it was a scoreless tie, and the player of the game was the punter, Manasquan's Harry Brevoort.

It wasn't until the 1970s that this game was held again. Local principals didn't like extending the season, and neither did the local basketball coaches (who wanted to get their season started). Still, it was clear that the Shore Conference teams were playing football as well as anybody.[22] In three short years, the Shore Conference had become a fixture on the Monmouth and Ocean County sporting landscape. Its titles were hotly contested, its league games drew huge crowds, and even partisans of Long Branch and Asbury Park had to admit that they put out a quality product. A tradition had been born, and it wouldn't go away any time soon.

CHAPTER 3
STORM CLOUDS GATHERING, 1938-1941

For most of the 1930s, Americans only acknowledged international affairs grudgingly. Most residents of Monmouth and Ocean County preferred to ignore the increasingly worrying news coming out of Europe and Asia. As the decade wore on, though, and the pace of events began to quicken, that changed. Many were left with a sinking feeling that the United States couldn't help but be drawn into events occurring "over there." Even the most ardent isolationist had no choice but to admit that people needed to be aware of the rapidly rising fascist powers in Europe and the increasingly bitter war being fought in China.

The change could be seen on the front pages of the *Asbury Park Press*. In 1936, the paper had lightly covered the accelerating violence in Spain. By 1937 and 1938, there was no avoiding what had become the Spanish Civil War, or the Sino-Japanese War, or the ongoing crisis over the Sudetenland. By November of 1938, the *Press* began to devote front-page space to Nazi persecution of the Jews. Perceptive observers looked at the flood of news and sagely noted that the war clouds were gathering.

They finally burst on September 1, 1939. On the same day that the Asbury Park football team gathered for its first practice of the season, German planes began bombing cities across Poland. Extra-sized headlines on the front page of the *Evening Press* brought word of the invasion, and of the resulting preparations for war that were then being undertaken in Britain and France. World War II had started in earnest.

At first, most Americans were complacent, much to the frustration of President Roosevelt. At one point, he complained in frustration that "public opinion over here is patting itself on the back every morning and thanking God for the Atlantic Ocean (and Pacific Ocean)." That confidence was shaken in the summer of 1940, when Nazi Germany took just six weeks to overrun France and drive the Western Allies off the European continent entirely.

Suddenly things seemed much more serious. Americans listened intently to Winston Churchill urge the British Empire to fight on alone against Nazi tyranny and to Edward R. Murrow's nightly broadcasts from the beleaguered rooftops of London. The war became the central issue of the 1940 presidential campaign. Roosevelt would use it as his justification to run for, and win, an unprecedented third term in office. It also became the justification for some equally unprecedented acts of Congress.

The Selective Service Act of 1940 initiated the first peacetime draft in American history. The Lend-Lease Act, passed in March of 1941, started a massive flow of supplies and military equipment to Great Britain and the other allies. The third and final big step was the massive rearmament program, which turned the United States military from a small and undersupplied force to one of the world's largest fighting forces. It was a hurricane of spending.[1]

And yet as tense as the situation was, the last three years of peace were in some ways a miniature golden age for sports. The summer of 1941 saw one of the most romanticized seasons in the history of baseball. Ted Williams hit .406, Joe DiMaggio hit safely in 56 consecutive games, and the New York Yankees beat the Brooklyn Dodgers in a historic Subway Series. The glow spread to other sports—Long Island University's basketball team won two NIT titles in a packed Madison Square Garden, the

Chicago Bears crushed the Washington Redskins 73-0 in a nationally broadcast NFL title game, and Billy Conn very nearly upset Joe Louis in a legendary heavyweight boxing match.

The same was true for New Jersey sports. Bergen County-ites beamed with pride as Garfield stormed through the 1939 football season undefeated, earning a trip to the Orange Bowl to take on Miami High School. This Health Bowl game was billed as a high school national championship, and when Garfield beat the Stingarees, they could chant, "We're number one!" and mean it.

No teams from the Shore went to Miami in the years before World War II (although Asbury Park came close). But Shore football was nonetheless spectacular, and the area's loyal fans were rewarded with some superb seasons and exciting games. It all started in 1939, when a Shore Conference fixture took its first turn in the spotlight.

THE RISE OF THE BIG BLUE

Manasquan had always been home to an active community. Its inlet had attracted fishermen long before the arrival of the first English colonists, and its beaches had been drawing day visitors since the early 1800s. After the railroad arrived in 1878, and the area's population grew, locals began competing against nearby towns in games of football and baseball.

The town's high school (which dated back to the 1800s) had fielded its first football team in 1906. However, the school was still small in those days, and the team popped in and out of existence. It wasn't until 1926 that enrollment grew large enough to make the team a permanent fixture. Seven years later, in 1933, the high school moved to its own building on Broad Street in Manasquan. By then, Warrior football tradition was already starting to take root.

The man most responsible for that was Abe Smith. A graduate of Bound Brook High School, Smith was *the* coach at Manasquan from 1931 to 1935, coaching football, basketball, and track. By the time he left to take a new job at Mountain Lakes, athletic enthusiasm in the school was higher than ever. That was especially true for the football team, which enjoyed four winning seasons in five years. The groundwork was being laid for what was to come.

A key part of the foundation was laid down in Smith's final game as head football coach—the Thanksgiving rivalry with Point Pleasant High School. Proximity made the two teams natural rivals, and clashes between the Warriors and Gulls had always drawn large crowds. In 1935, the schools agreed to move their game to Thanksgiving Day. It was a brilliant idea; the holiday series would last thirty-seven years.

> **Jay Price (current Manasquan head coach):** *"I think from talking to the elders in town, it was the thirties that the first parade started happening. . . . It started in the thirties and moved through the war. It was something that the town used to look forward to. Even in the thirties they used to spray the street down (it was a dirt road) for the parade . . . so they caught on pretty early."*[2]

The first game looked a bit different than the ones that would follow. Perhaps unsure that football alone could sustain the rivalry, the schools scheduled some unusual halftime entertainment—a live turkey was released onto the field, with the bird awarded as a prize to whichever spectator could successfully wrangle it before the teams returned.[3] Manasquan won 46-0, routing Point Pleasant in what at the time was reported as a jinx breaker (the Warriors had in the past struggled to beat the Gulls). It was difficult to say who enjoyed the game more—the Manasquan players, or John Coryell, the fortunate spectator who tackled the turkey and went home with a free dinner.[4]

Smith left Manasquan that spring and was succeeded for one season by Red Griswold, who coached the team to a 5-2-1 record and another Thanksgiving win. The first golden era of Manasquan football, though, really began in 1937 with the arrival of Head Coach Granville Magee. Magee had been an All-State football player at South River and had played both football and baseball at Rutgers. Before arriving at Manasquan, he had served as an assistant at Metuchen and at his college alma mater.

Always clad in suit and hat on the sidelines, Magee was the perfect image of a 1930s football coach. His teams, too, were the perfect image of 1930s teams. Well-disciplined and primed for action, under Magee the Big Blue were a force to be reckoned with. He demanded excellence of his players at all times, something helped by his skill at picking assistants. One of his first assistants was Line Coach Butch Bruno, the former Asbury Park star and future Asbury Park head coach. In later years, his staff would be joined by luminaries such as Jack Schellenger and Hal Manson, later championship-winning head coaches in their own right.

He also had the ability to adjust. Magee's first season was chaotic; the Warriors were struggling even before their coach was felled by a midseason attack of appendicitis. By the end of November, the team was 0-5-1. Magee kept working, reshuffled his offense, and guided the team to a three-game winning streak to finish the season. The masterstroke came on Thanksgiving, in front of the season's biggest crowd. He moved Vernon King to fullback and let King's passing shred the Point Pleasant defense in a 28-0 holiday win.[5]

Manasquan took a step back in 1938, finishing 3-4-2 and going five games without scoring. However, there were signs of hope. The defense was stout, holding opponents to just three points per game, and the team was not intimidated by anyone. Even Lodi (which finished the season unbeaten, untied, and unscored upon) was held to a narrow 7-0 victory. Magee could sense that things were, in his words, "starting to click."[6] Some young faces were starting to make their way into the lineup, which meant that the Warriors returned six starters for 1939.

> **Granville Magee**: *"There has been a complete change in attitude on the part of the squad. The boys listen to what I have to say, and they are trying hard to do things the right way. We really haven't much in the way of material, but the change in attitude makes up for a lot of things. If willingness counts at all, they'll surprise a lot of people."*[7]

Magee was being quite honest about his team's attitude and willingness to surprise, but his claim to lack material was more than a little misleading. End Hal "Buck" Thompson was a star receiver, 200-pound fullback Harry "Roll out the Barrel" Brevoort might have been the Shore's best runner, and center Earl Heyniger may have been its best blocker. All three earned All-Monmouth/Ocean honors that December.

The 1939 Warriors opened the season against Atlantic Highlands, a team that had in recent years made a habit of bedeviling larger schools. The Warriors blitzed them, with Harry Brevoort running for one touchdown and throwing for three more in a 31-3 romp. That turned some heads.[8] A thrilling win at Toms River a week later turned some more.

The Indians, one of the early contenders for the Shore Conference title, had taken a 7-0 halftime lead on an end around to Dick Carriker. Their line was stopping Brevoort's plunges and seemingly had control of the game. The tide turned after the half. Manasquan's defense held Toms River without a single first-half first down, while Brevoort's effective passing led a Warrior rally. In the final moments, with 'Squan still down 7-6, the Warriors perfectly executed a hook and lateral. Brevoort hit Thompson, who flipped to Lafayette "Lace" Campbell. That put the ball on the 4, from where Brevoort scored the winner with 1:35 to play.[9]

More drama followed the next Friday night. In front of a packed house at Belmar's Memorial Field, Manasquan beat Neptune 7-0 on Brevoort's 52-yard fourth-quarter touchdown pass to sophomore John Campbell. The week after that, the Big Blue beat Lakewood 12-6 to take a commanding lead in the title race.[10] Manasquan finished the year with wins over Freehold and Point Pleasant, securing both the Shore Conference and CJ II titles. It was the first time that the Warriors had won either title, and the first time in the history of the young league that a team had won both in a single season.[11]

The winter season continued Buck Thompson's year of athletic glory, as he earned all-state honors on a 17-2 basketball team. He lettered in track that spring, spent a postgraduate year at a military academy in Pennsylvania, and then went to Delaware, where he played on undefeated Blue Hen teams in 1941 and 1942. His future, though, lay on other fields.

Thompson joined the U.S. Army after the 1942 season, serving in the 222nd Infantry Regiment of the 42nd Division. This regiment landed in France just one day after D-Day, then fought their way across Europe, from Normandy to the Ardennes. They also helped to liberate the

Dachau concentration camps. Thompson came home from the war un-
wounded, and in 1946 starred on another undefeated Delaware team (this
one claimed a small college national title). He went on to play two years
in AAFC before becoming a teacher and coach. In 2008, Thompson was
posthumously inducted into the Manasquan High School Hall of Fame.[12]

Thompson is rightfully a Manasquan legend, but he was not the only
player on the 1939 team to do special things. Harry Brevoort earned All-
State honors in football, basketball, and baseball. He spent one year as
a pitcher in the minor league system of the Brooklyn Dodgers before
World War II interrupted his rise.[13] His baseball career ended with his
induction into the army. Like so many others, he never found out how far
he could have gone.

The graduation of players like that would have left many programs
grasping at straws, but between Magee's determined coaching and a few
key returning veterans, the Big Blue were back in form again for the 1940
season. This time the keys were the Campbell brothers, John and Lafayette (also known as Lace). Even with the Campbells, though, Manasquan
looked shaky. They had to rally from 7-0 down to beat Atlantic Highlands 12-7, and they could only manage a scoreless tie with Toms River.
The team was struggling and the hardest part of the season, back-to-back
games against Neptune and Lakewood, was looming.

The Big Blue rose to the challenge. Bill Moore threw three touchdowns to Lace Campbell in a 24-0 rout of Neptune, then hit Tom Deter
for another in a 14-0 win over Lakewood.[14] Manasquan won their remaining games with ease and looked impressive in season-ending routs
of Freehold and Point Pleasant. Lace Campbell closed his football career
in sensational fashion by scoring seven touchdowns in those two games.
Manasquan finished 7-0-1, undefeated for the second consecutive year.
The only thing they couldn't celebrate was a Shore Conference title. The
scoreless tie with Toms River turned out to be a costly one.[15]

THE LIONS' ROAR: ARNIE TRUEX AND LEONARDO

Manasquan didn't win a Shore Conference championship in 1940 because that was the year that Leonardo came as close to true perfection as any team in the Shore Conference ever had or ever would. It was a long time coming. When the league was formed in 1936, Lion fans expected success and plenty of it. After all, they had an old football tradition dating back to Swede Hanson and the 1920s. Yet things didn't quite work out.

The Lions started 3-0 in 1936, but a late-season loss to Atlantic Highlands ended up costing them the Shore Conference title. Disappointing seasons followed in 1937 and 1938, made worse by a tie and then a loss to Highlands. A coaching change followed, accompanied by suggestions that the school administration had not provided enough support for its staff.[16]

With the football job now opened, Leonardo adopted a time-honored strategy—they hired the man they couldn't beat. In this case, that meant Arnie Truex from Atlantic Highlands. Truex, who had coached the Tigers to titles in football, basketball, and baseball, was one of the most highly regarded coaches in the Shore. Since the school's total male enrollment never topped 100, this was quite a feat. It wasn't long before Truex became a Middletown legend.[17]

The Chip Hilton series of books, written by former Long Island Versity Basketball Coach Claire Bee, immortalized a certain image of high school athletics. Hilton was a three-sport star, leading his team to championships in everything. There at every step of the way was Coach Hank Rockwell. Rockwell wasn't the coach of a specific sport, he was just "Coach," and he shepherded Hilton and company through "football, basketball, baseball, and life's lessons." That was the role that Truex would play at Leonardo for the next twenty years.[18]

Truex's first season saw the Lions improve from 2-5 to 4-3-1; among their wins was a 6-0 victory over Atlantic Highlands. The key to the operation was talented junior halfback Joe Bolger, the focal point of Truex's

Notre Dame Box attack. With him returning in 1940, great things were expected. Still, few could have predicted exactly how good Leonardo would be.

Bolger carried the ball behind a line that by 1940 standards was enormous. It averaged 177 pounds a man, anchored by 220-pound tackle John Koleda. Several other players (guard Harry Adubato and fullback Harry Huber) neared the 200-pound barrier.[19] They were tough, strong, and motivated—all through the preseason Truex reminded his team that Red Bank had embarrassed them 38-0 in the 1939 opener.

That didn't happen this season. Bolger ran for a first-quarter touchdown, while Joe Adubato secured the 6-0 victory by recovering a fumble to end Red Bank's final drive. Leonardo had not just won; they had shut out their opponents. That would become a season-long trend.[20] Four straight shutouts followed. The Lions were fast closing in on a double triumph—the Shore Conference and CJ II titles.

They surrendered points to Keyport (Rudy Buntenbach returned a kickoff for a touchdown), which marred their unscored-upon record. However, they still rolled to a 42-12 victory. Nothing could slow their march to the title. In mid-November, 1,800 fans attended the annual rivalry game with Atlantic Highlands and saw Bolger (the Shore's leading scorer) cross the goal line twice in a 21-0 win.[21] That set up the dramatic finale against Rumson.

Rumson, one of the league's smallest schools, presented a serious challenge. Even at this early date, there was a clear hierarchy in the standings, based mostly on size. The Group II schools (Leonardo, Neptune, Manasquan, Lakewood, and Toms River) were the title contenders, while the Group Is (Keyport, Matawan, Rumson, and Point Pleasant) squabbled with each other for the scraps. There were a few notable exceptions—Group II Freehold struggled, while tiny Atlantic Highlands punched above its weight—but the pattern generally held. Even strong Group I teams could rarely get a high enough Dickinson Rating to be title contenders.

Rumson, though, had a rich athletic tradition. They'd gone 4-2-1 in 1937 and hoped to better that record in 1940. Bulldog teams were typically light, but fast and dangerous, much like Mickey Walker, the boxer every boy in Rumson had idolized for years. Walker, an Elizabeth native, had become a pro boxer at the young age of seventeen. During a career that lasted from 1919 to 1935, Walker had held both the world welterweight and world middleweight championship belts. Despite his diminutive stature (just five-foot-seven), Walker was a legendarily aggressive fighter, even holding his own in exhibition matches against many heavyweights.

Walker had relatives in Rumson, and he made his training runs through the town. In reference to that, and to both his small size and aggressive style, sportswriters dubbed him the Rumson Bulldog. In honor of their hero, the young athletes at Rumson decided to take his nickname as their own. And this season, they'd live up to it.[22]

Lou Jacoubs had been the head coach at Rumson since 1932, and this was easily his greatest team. There was lanky speedster Howell Harris, accurate passer Henry Hitzwabel, and workhorse tailback Tony Mellaci. Together, they would terrorize the Shore Conference's bigger schools. It started on a Friday night at Neptune when Harris ran for a 34-yard touchdown and caught a long pass to set up a Mellaci score. That let the Bulldogs escape with a 15-6 win.[23] The win started a seven-game winning streak, which featured four victories by a touchdown or less.

The most dramatic was the regular season finale against Toms River. That game epitomized the Bulldog spirit—in the first half, Rumson held Toms River at the 16-, 6-, and 2-yard lines, keeping the game scoreless until the fourth. That's when Harris's interception set up Mellaci for the game-winning touchdown.[24] So the Rumson-Leonardo Thanksgiving game would also determine the Shore Conference champion. The winner would hoist the crown (a tie would result in a split title). The biggest crowd of the season, 6,000 fans, packed the bleachers at Leonardo High School. They saw a struggle worthy of the stakes.

The difference was ultimately Leonardo's size, which even Rumson's fighting spirit could not overcome. The Bulldogs spent the game pinned in their half of the field, and eventually even their gallant defense faded against the running of Joe Bolger, who scored twice. Leonardo won, 13-0, claiming both the Shore and CJ II titles.[25]

That evening, fans celebrated the title with a bonfire on the field. Coach Truex spoke to the crowd, Joe Bolger lit the flame, and then players, fans, teachers, and even school board members paraded through town. It was the first of many titles that Truex would win with the Lions.[26] Bolger, guard Joe Adubato, and center Ray Goclon were all named to the All-Shore Conference team by the *Long Branch Daily Record*. Bolger also earned All-State honors and a scholarship to the University of Pennsylvania. World War II ultimately kept him from becoming a college star, but after the war Bolger enhanced his reputation as one of the area's greatest backs by starring for the Leonardo Field Club, a local semipro team. He would later return to the area as a coach at Red Bank Catholic and the superintendent of Keansburg schools.

Rumson star Tony Mellaci also earned All-Shore honors. He spent a postgraduate year playing football at Admiral Farragut Academy in Ocean County, then entered the service during the war. His coach, Lou Jacoubs, spent one more successful season at Rumson; the Bulldogs went 6-3, beating Leonardo 14-0 on Thanksgiving. He then took a job at Red Bank before joining the service himself. The groundwork he laid at Rumson would eventually form the basis for the long and successful tenure of his assistant, Joe Rosati, who became head coach in 1946.

THE OCEAN COUNTY POWERS

The 1941 season saw the balance of power shift southward. The Monmouth County powers were young, and Toms River was experienced. It was never a surprise to see Bob Reigle field a strong team. His Indians had enjoyed three winning seasons in the previous five seasons. Even their youthful 1940 team had turned out a respectable (if odd) record of 3-3-3.

The 1941 club returned eight starters from that team, including All-Shore tackle Norm Galinkin. He was strong enough that the Indians could run behind him and fast enough that he could run down plays from behind. The other star was All-Shore tailback Al Sica. He could kick, he could pass, and he could run like a deer for long, game-breaking scores.

Toms River won their first eight games, two of them dramatic streak-breaking victories. The first came against Manasquan in mid-October and ended a twenty-one-game unbeaten streak for the Warriors. The hero, as expected, was Al Sica. His fourth-quarter touchdown pass to Ed Gibson snapped a scoreless tie and handed the Indians a 6-0 victory.[27] The second came later in the season, against the defending champions from Leonardo, unbeaten in fifteen games.

The Lions were unbeaten, unscored upon, and one win away from essentially sealing the league title. When Ernie Bonnette's touchdown run put them up 6-0, it looked like the streak would go on. In the third quarter, though, Sica, Dick Clement, and Jay DeGraw alternated line plunges as the Indians steadily drove to the 2-yard line. Joe Barulic's touchdown run tied the game, and Sica's conversion pass to DeGraw won it, 7-6.[28] Wins over Rumson and Keyport followed, setting up a Thanksgiving showdown with Lakewood. This was the big one.

It had been an odd season for the Piners. Although they were one of the Shore's premier football teams, they had a difficult time finding games. Including their Thanksgiving rivalry with Toms River, Lakewood had only four league games. It seemed as though no one wanted to play them. The sources are unclear as to exactly why, but the *Asbury Park Press* did hint at a few possibilities. One was size—Lakewood's enrollment (almost 300 boys) made them one of the largest schools in the league. Few opponents wanted to play a large, traditionally strong foe.

But it also appears that some bitterness existed between Lakewood and the conference's other schools. Reasons varied—sometimes it was said that the Piners liked to run up the score, other times that Lakewood's crowd was too hostile to outsiders and provoked brawls. A brawl *had* erupted midway through the Manasquan game, a free-for-all involving players and spectators of both teams, and that certainly didn't help their image.[29] Whatever the reason, scheduling was a problem, would remain a problem for years to come. In the long term, it meant rumors that the Piners were getting ready to secede from the Shore Conference. In the short term, it meant that they played an extremely difficult statewide schedule.

The 1941 Piners took on all comers. They hosted Bernardsville, and took long bus rides to Phillipsburg, Springfield, and Memorial High School of West New York. They beat everyone but Phillipsburg and gave the few Shore schools they did schedule (Neptune, Manasquan, and Freehold) identical treatment. Come Thanksgiving, Lakewood was 6-1, one win from the title.

The main man in that surge was All-Shore back Al Childers. Running behind All-Shore guard Bob Weiss, Childers menaced every defense in the state with his blend of power and speed. In his finest performance of the season, he scored four touchdowns in a 26-0 rout of Manasquan.[30] The Thanksgiving game promised a duel between Sica and Childers, the two best backs in the Shore Conference, and it drew a crowd of 5,000 to Lakewood's field.

What they saw was one of the year's tensest games. Lakewood's stronger line was able to push around the Indians, allowing the Piners to drive to the 17 in the first quarter and the 7 in the second quarter. The Toms River defense, however, held each time, and Sica's booming punts kept flipping the field and erasing Lakewood's gains. The game went into halftime scoreless.

A similar pattern prevailed in the second half. Lakewood reached the 10 in the third quarter and the 22 in the fourth quarter but went scoreless on both drives. Toms River was experiencing similar struggles. They had driven to the 15, only for their own field goal try to be blocked. They had the ball at midfield with time for one play. A scoreless tie looked likely, especially when the Piner line trapped Sica in his own backfield. But the star still had one bullet left in his chamber.

Sica slipped two tacklers and then burst into the clear. A Lakewood safety got a shot at Sica at the 25, and though he didn't tackle him, he did slow him up enough that Childers and Bill Malayter were able to run him down at the 20. He was tackled there, and as soon as he hit the dirt, the final gun sounded. The two exhausted backs simply lay on the field, too tired to move as the crowd applauded the thriller they had just seen. Lakewood 0, Toms River 0.[31]

It had been an instant classic. However, what happened next put a sour twist on the whole affair. In order to ensure that the Piners had enough games to make the rating system work, the Shore Conference had agreed to count Lakewood's win over Bernardsville in the standings. Two days after the epic scoreless tie, Pompton Lakes upset the Mountaineers. That changed Lakewood's season rating, untying the league rankings and dropping Lakewood into second place. Toms River claimed the outright Shore Conference championship for 1941.[32]

Toms River's Norm Galinkin enjoyed a fine spring season, setting a school record in the javelin and starring at first base for the school's baseball team. He spent three years in the Marines (1943-46), then played football and baseball at North Carolina. He also bounced around some of the lower-level minor leagues before giving up the sport in 1950.

Galinkin's teammate Al Sica was also a track star, setting a record in the high hurdles and helping the school's 4x100 relay team win at the Penn Relays. He went on to play football at UPenn, where he was All-American in 1944. A twenty-ninth round pick in the 1948 NFL Draft, Sica's football career was ultimately ended by a knee injury. It didn't end his role in Shore athletics, though; Sica would eventually return as one of the first coaches at St. Joseph's in Toms River.

Toms River's joy was matched by Lakewood's bitterness. The absurdity of a game in North Jersey breaking a tie between two Shore teams that had tied on the field was frustrating enough. What happened next was worse—the Piners had expected to win the CJ II title, only to learn after the season that their enrollment actually placed them in the large CJ III group. Toms River won the CJ II title, while Lakewood was a distant second to undefeated Carteret in the CJ III standings. A season that had ended so dramatically on the field had been completely undercut by mathematical rankings. It looked like these debates would fuel the hot stove league all through the offseason. As it turned out, events in the Pacific meant that there wouldn't be much time and energy left in December of 1941 to debate high school football.

THE ASBURY MACHINE

When people in Asbury Park talked about the glory days, they meant 1929-32, when Bill Flynn's Blue Bishop teams had won four consecutive CJ IV titles and totaled a record of 36-2. Those accomplishments set the bar impossibly high, and although Flynn's successor Bob Heisel led the team to a CJ IV title in 1935, that only bought tolerance, not love. Middling seasons each of the next two years were accompanied by losses to Long Branch, and Heisel stepped down under pressure after the 1938 season. His successor, Red Young, lasted through only one 3-6 season and a third straight loss to the Green Wave. And so, the job was open again in 1940.

Despite the pressure, Asbury Park was considered an attractive job. Flynn's dominant teams of the 1930s were well-remembered, and coaches from all over the state applied. The Bishop athletic administration settled on Bill Smith, a former Notre Dame star and the head coach at Clifford Scott High School in East Orange. Smith's first move was a wise one—he added former Asbury Park star Butch Bruno as his assistant and line coach. His second move, installing the Notre Dame box formation, proved to be a perfect choice for the talent on hand.

Asbury's 1939 team had been young, starting more than its share of sophomores. That meant that the 1940 team was unusually experienced, returning guards Bill Supthen and Bill Brown, center Ernie Siciliano, tackles Ralph Martorella and George Reiss, and end Eddie Etoll. They also had a good stable of backs—Ed Ehring, Les Dugan, Fred Reichey, Frank Savoth, and Tony Falco. But the key back was a junior, the spectacular Jack Netcher.

A native of Niagara Falls, Canada, Netcher had moved with his family to Asbury Park at the age of six. He became a star in Asbury's youth sports' leagues, and by the time he entered high school his talent was known around the city. By his junior year, he was regarded as its best athlete.[33] Smith spotted Netcher's potential early and built the offense around him. The results would be so spectacular that the *Asbury Park Press* would use every page of the thesaurus describing him—sensational, brilliant, a shining star, a sparkplug, a workhorse, a one-man team. Eventually, they just gave up and said that "anything written here would be superfluous."[34] He could run for power and run for speed, he could kick, he could throw, he could tackle.

Netcher broke out in the 1940 season opener, running for two touchdowns and threw for another in a 20-0 win over South River. A week later, against Thomas Jefferson (Elizabeth), he returned an interception and a blocked punt for touchdowns in a 19-0 Bishop romp.[35] His fourth quarter touchdown run against Perth Amboy secured a 14-7 victory, Asbury's first in the series since 1936. Now 3-0, the Bishops were on the inside track to the CJ IV crown.[36]

After avoiding a near-upset at Irvington, the Bishops started mauling people. Netcher scored four touchdowns in a 32-0 rout of Red Bank, then helped the team blister Weequahic 21-0. It wasn't just the CJ IV title in reach now; observers were starting to suggest that Asbury Park might have the best team in all New Jersey.[37]

Only there was a catch. Netcher and fellow back Vic Musto were both playing with sore knees, and neither would be available for the annual rivalry clash with Long Branch. Fortunately, the Bishops had lineman George Reiss. He blocked one punt that Tom Layton returned for a touchdown, and he blocked another through the end zone for a safety. In the fourth, Joe Petillo stepped in to fill Netcher's shoes and threw two touchdown passes, one to Les Dugan and another to Tom Scott, as Asbury secured a 21-0 victory.[38]

That game had drawn about 7,000 fans. The final game, against New Brunswick, drew a similar crowd. The tension in the air was thick; fans remembered three years of losses to New Brunswick, and they remembered how a Thanksgiving tie with South River had cost them the 1936 title. The whole city wanted to see if the Bishops could clear the hurdle this time. What they saw was dominance.

George Reiss and Ralph Martorella threw Zebra linemen around in the trenches, clearing huge holes for a newly healthy Netcher. He gave his usual balanced performance, kicking two field goals and running for a short touchdown, while Joe Petillo added a touchdown pass to Les

Dugan in the fourth to clinch the game. The Zebra offense, meanwhile, was totally stymied. The final was 19-0, and after the game jubilant players threw both Bill Smith and Butch Bruno into the showers in celebration.[39]

The honors poured in. Asbury Park won the CJ IV title, and Netcher was rightfully honored as an All-Shore and All-State tailback. The *Newark Sunday Call* dubbed the Bishops the number-one team in all of New Jersey. It had been a season of glory. The crazy thing was that 1941 promised to be even better. Netcher was one of *eight* returning starters, including linemen Reiss, Martorella, and Siciliano, quarterback Tom Scott, and end Eddie Etoll. The *Asbury Park Press* noted in awe that the 1941 team would likely be a bigger, more experienced version of the 1940 champions.[40]

First, though, there was the little matter of the winter and spring seasons, both of which saw Netcher and the Bishops attain sporting glory. A starter on the basketball team, Netcher helped the Bishops roll to the statewide Group IV title. He was key in the biggest games, scoring sixteen points in the CJ IV finals against New Brunswick and another seventeen in the statewide finals against Memorial (West New York).[41] He might have been even better at baseball, playing outfield and catcher for the high school team and several local sandlot outfits. He was a sensation, and his return for 1941 set the bar almost impossibly high.

The *Asbury Park Press* was rabid to see what the Bishop football team would do that fall, printing daily practice reports from their preseason camp in Brielle. And they were as good as advertised—Netcher was better than ever, while his backfield mates Scott, Pete Vetrano, and Hal Manson carried their own share of the load. Their quest to repeat as the state's number-one team made it as far as November, when a scoreless tie with Phillipsburg ended their chances of receiving that ranking from the *Newark News* (that trophy ultimately went to Montclair). It did not, however, end their quest for the CJ IV crown.[42]

The road toward that crown was difficult, but the Bishops nonetheless made it to Thanksgiving at 7-0-1. Still, that last hurdle was a tough one. New Brunswick could take the title with a win, and the Bishops were not at full strength. The Long Branch win had been a very physical one, and a number of stars were banged up.[43]

With New Brunswick so strong, an unusual number of visiting fans made the trek down to Monmouth County on Thanksgiving morning, so the stadium was jammed with 8,500 fans, the largest crowd to see a game at the Shore in over a decade. They saw a tense defensive struggle. The injury-depleted Bishops had to hang on by their fingernails against repeated Zebra drives. Only the effective punting of Joe Petillo and the desperate defensive efforts of Netcher at safety kept New Brunswick from scoring. The game wasn't decided until the final moments, when Asbury blocked a late field goal try to preserve the scoreless tie.

As soon as the 0-0 game ended, an exhausted Jack Netcher collapsed on the field and had to be helped into the locker room. In the moment, the Asbury football team was bitterly disappointed at their inability to win. That the tie had preserved a second straight undefeated season and ensured the team a share of the CJ IV crown took some time to sink in. It was almost as if the unrelenting pressure of trying to repeat had sucked some of the joy out of the season. The season had been so draining, in fact, that Netcher decided to take a break from sports entirely, skipping the first month of basketball season.[44]

He spent December recovering and accepting accolades for earning All-State honors a second straight season. In January, Netcher returned to action and helped Asbury win another CJ IV title and reach the state finals (where they lost a rematch to Memorial of West New York). In the spring, he starred again on the baseball team, leading the Bishops in hitting with a .419 average.[45] Netcher graduated with All-State honors in all three sports, and was designated by the Newark Athletic Club as New Jersey's best athlete. Recruited by all the major eastern colleges, Netcher ultimately settled on the University of Pennsylvania, where he intended to play football, basketball, and baseball. However, that plan was interrupted by World War II. After his freshman football season, he enlisted in the Army Air Corps.[46]

Not long after enlisting, Netcher was transferred to military intelligence. He served in North Africa and Italy, continuing all the while to play baseball on various service teams. Since some of those service teams included major league-level talent, Netcher was highly recruited again after the war ended. He chose William & Mary, where he intended to play baseball and football. He made it through one baseball season, hitting .350 in the spring of 1946 before signing a minor league contract with the Washington Senators.[47] He spent two years in the minor leagues, then gave up baseball after an arm injury.

Netcher returned to college, playing a year of football at Carson-Newman in Tennessee, and then began an itinerant career as a teacher, coach, and administrator. He earned a doctorate from Indiana, coached at Humboldt State in California, then served as the athletic director and baseball coach at High Point in North Carolina and Central Florida Junior College. His fame as a high school athlete gradually faded, and Netcher slowly transitioned into a steady career as a college administrator. When he passed away in 2013, his obituary noted only that he had been the dean of the Department of Health at the University of North Florida. There was no acknowledgement that he had at one time been the best high school athlete in all New Jersey.[48]

Netcher was not Asbury's only star. George Reiss went on to Fordham, which in 1942 was still a football power. With freshmen eligible due to the war, Reiss won a starting position on the line and helped the Rams to a 5-3-1 record, beating Purdue, West Virginia, and Missouri. After that season, Reiss joined the Army and saw combat with the 82nd Airborne. He returned to Fordham after the war, and although the Rams were no longer the power that they'd been, he personally was still good enough to make the training camp of the New York Football Giants.

Asbury Park football teams have hoisted championship banners many times. On numerous occasions, they have been renowned around New Jersey, even finishing number one in the state again in 1953. But there's something special about the 1940-41 teams, the only Asbury squads to ever go undefeated in back-to-back seasons. Perhaps it was the brilliance of Netcher and his teammates, or the huge crowd that saw their final Thanksgiving game against New Brunswick. Or perhaps it was the timing. After all, within two weeks of the final gun against the Zebras, high school athletics would be knocked off the front pages. The storm clouds that had gathered across the world burst on American soil, and the world would never be the same.

IN THE BACKGROUND: RED BANK

In the 1930s, Red Bank was not a sports power. Strong during the 1920s, the team had since fallen on hard times. They were caught in between; too large for the fledgling Shore Conference, they were also too small to reliably compete with Asbury Park and Long Branch. By the time Dick Guest took over the football team in 1936, few feared the Bucs.

Facing a brutal schedule, Guest's team struggled to a combined record of 4-20-2 over his first three years in charge. They entered the 1939 season on a thirteen-game losing streak. Things looked grim. But Guest was not easily dissuaded. He had eight returning lettermen, four on the line (All-Shore tackle Dom Scala stood out) and four in the backfield (led by halfback Bill Geroni and fullback Angelo DeGeorge). More than that, the Bucs were hungry.

> **Dick Guest**: *"We've got spirit to burn. The boys have plenty of fight, and it is going to go a long way toward giving us a good team. These eight lettermen have had their share of disappointments, and they are out to make up for last season."*[49]

Red Bank started the year with a 38-0 rout of local rivals Leonardo, then went up to Linden and beat the hosts 19-0. They nearly upset South River, did upset Morristown, and pushed Asbury Park to the limit in a heartbreaking 13-7 loss. So, they were 3-2 at the midway point of the season with a great chance for a winning record. Then came two fine performances, with Geroni scoring two times apiece in wins over Princeton and Neptune.[50]

Word then arrived that a greater prize was possible. South River had slipped up, losing in a stunning upset to Bound Brook. If the Bucs could beat Long Branch on Thanksgiving, they would be CJ III champions. However, the Green Wave would be tough. They were 5-1-1, and they had impressive wins over Dickinson (Jersey City) and Asbury Park to their name. They too could be champions with a holiday victory. Rain postponed the game from Thanksgiving, but 4,500 fans packed the bleachers anyway. This was basically a title game.

Long Branch struck first, with Tony Bevacqui recovering a blocked punt for a touchdown and a 6-0 lead. However, the extra point failed due a muffed snap, leaving the door open for the Bucs. They charged through it in the third, when Bill Geroni returned a punt 44 yards to the 6-yard line, setting up John Summonte for the tying score. Angelo DeGeorge followed with the extra point, winning the game and the sectional title for the Bucs.[51]

It wasn't the CJ IV crown, and it didn't get the attention that Asbury Park would get in the next two seasons. However, it did bring Red Bank its first championship in nine years, helping to reestablish the winning Buck tradition. More would come during the war years.

PART 2: THE WAR YEARS, 1942-1945

CHAPTER 4
LIFE IN WARTIME

On December 7, 1941, the Imperial Japanese Navy launched a surprise aerial assault on the United States naval base at Pearl Harbor, in Hawaii. No declaration of war was given until after the attack, which lasted from 7:53 a.m. until about 10 a.m. (local time). The attack achieved complete surprise, sinking eighteen ships, destroying 180 aircraft, and killing 2,403 American soldiers and sailors. Later that day, Nazi Germany declared war on the United States. The United States was now fully immersed in World War II.

Now a member of the Allied Powers, the United States was fighting alongside the United Kingdom and its empire, the Soviet Union, the Republic of China, and over a dozen smaller countries. Opposing them were three major dictatorships—Nazi Germany, Fascist Italy, and the Empire of Japan—as well as a collection of satellite states and puppet governments, many operated at the point of a Nazi bayonet. The US had joined the worldwide struggle between democracy and dictatorship, freedom and tyranny.

US entry into World War II prompted the most rapid transformation of American life in the twentieth century. Although the United States had been serving as the "arsenal of democracy" for over a year, its full weight of manpower and materiel had not yet been thrown into the fray. Three million men were still unemployed, and the average factory was used only forty hours a week. Some industries were still operating at half capacity. That was about to change.[1]

The most obvious transformation involved the military. The Selective Service Act of 1940 had instituted a draft, but deferments were available for essential professions and married men. Fathers were almost untouchable. After Pearl Harbor, these were sharply scaled back. By the end of the war, more than sixteen million men and women were in uniform. Nearly one out of every five families contributed at least one member to the armed forces by war's end.[2]

The expansion of the military was matched by a similarly massive expansion in war production. In January 1942, President Roosevelt asked Congress for a "crushing superiority of equipment in any theater of the world war" and set unbelievably ambitious targets for producing new tanks, new guns, new airplanes, and new shipping. Men and women from all over the country were now enlisted in putting the nation's production on a war footing. Production figures were truly staggering—1,556 naval vessels, 299,293 aircraft, 634,569 jeeps, 88,410 tanks, 2.3 million trucks, 6.5 million rifles, and 40 billion bullets. These dwarfed friends and enemies in every conceivable category.[3]

Achieving those upgrades meant rationing, and rationing brought changes of its own. Diets changed in response to strict rationing of meat, butter, and coffee; fashion had to adjust to equally strict rationing of fabrics. Everywhere, Americans were making do with less. At the same time, though, American standards of living were rising. Rearmament finally ended the lingering impacts of the Great Depression, sending consumer spending to record highs.[4]

Another area transformed by the war was travel. Recreational trips ended almost entirely. The production of automobiles for private use was prohibited, and both gasoline and tires were rationed. Trains were reserved for soldiers heading to military training camps or workers on their way to essential jobs. Further restrictions were put on the size of crowds.[5]

It was this type of rationing that would most severely affect the world of American sports.

There were initially concerns that the war effort would bring an end to professional sports entirely; both England and Scotland had suspended their national soccer leagues for the duration. In January of 1942, however, President Roosevelt expressed his hope that baseball would continue through the war as a morale booster. This was taken by sports at all levels as a go-ahead to continue. Still, each league and each sport had to make adjustments.

Baseball, America's most popular sport at this time, came through the war in the best shape. In all four wartime seasons, the major leagues managed to play a full slate of 154 games, plus the World Series. No teams folded and fan interest remained high. The same was true of Black baseball; the Negro National League and Negro American League may have enjoyed their highest attendances ever and successfully revived their own World Series. Still, some things did change. Teams were not permitted to go south as they usually did for spring training, a change that brought the Yankees to Asbury Park in 1943. In all, a total of 500 major league players left for the war effort, including big stars such as Joe DiMaggio, Buck O'Neil, Bob Feller, Jackie Robinson, Hank Greenberg, Larry Doby, and Ted Williams.

Football had it harder. In the 1940s, that sport was most popular at the college level, and many small colleges suspended their teams until the war was over. Many that continued to play were only able to do so because the Navy put training programs on their campus. Those schools still often saw their stars depart to join the war effort. Notre Dame, for example, lost Heisman Trophy-winning quarterback Angelo Bertelli to the Marines midway through the 1943 season. His replacement, Johnny Lujack, led the Irish to a national championship before then joining the Navy himself. So did Head Coach Frank Leahy. Neither would return until 1946.

The National Football League, far from the entertainment juggernaut it is today, was hit even harder. The Cleveland Rams sat out the 1943 season, while the Pittsburgh Steelers twice merged with other teams just to survive—they joined the Philadelphia Eagles to become the Steagles in

1943 and joined the Chicago Cardinals to become Card-Pitt in 1944. The league as a whole barely made it.

Still, the sport remained popular. Fans packed stadiums and tuned their radios to listen to games, sometimes featuring "super teams" assembled at training stations across the country. The most powerful of those teams came from Great Lakes Naval Air Station. Coached by the legendary Paul Brown, the Bluejackets terrorized some of the nation's best college teams. During the war years, they beat Notre Dame twice and Ohio State once. They weren't alone; Iowa Pre-Flight was the nation's No. 2 team in 1943, while Randolph Field was No. 3 in 1944.

No team, however, did quite so well in the war years as Army. With applications to West Point at an all-time high, Red Blaik had his pick of the nation's best athletes, and he assembled them into some of the greatest college football teams ever seen. The Cadets finished undefeated three years in a row (1944-46), winning two national championships and producing two Heisman trophy winners (Doc Blanchard and Glenn Davis). The sold-out stadiums to see Army play every Saturday proved beyond a doubt that war or not, fans wanted to see football.

Wartime high school football faced the same challenges and attracted the same passion that wartime college and professional football did. Six Shore area coaches left their peacetime jobs for wartime service. The Army claimed Jack Daly of Atlantic Highlands after the 1940 season and Joe Barlie of Keyport midway through 1941. Two more, Manasquan's Granville Magee and Matawan's Paul Bednard, signed up immediately after Pearl Harbor. Magee oversaw prisoner of war camps in upstate New York, eventually reaching the rank of captain, while Bednard was promoted to major for his service in North Africa and Europe. Two more, Freehold's Les Goodwin (Army) and Lakewood's Russ Wright (Navy), left after the 1943 season. There were also numerous assistants, such as Asbury's Butch Bruno, who departed for the service.

School teams were also affected by gasoline rationing, which drove athletic departments to reduce travel. This wasn't much of a problem for the Shore Conference teams, who by now were staying local anyway. Independent teams had it harder; the challenges led Red Bank to join the league in 1943. It also led Asbury Park and Long Branch, who remained independents, to play twice a year in both 1943 and 1944. That helped fill out their schedule while keeping travel light. It also helped keep Shore football a major attraction.

CHAPTER 5
ASBURY PARK
AND LONG BRANCH

The prewar years had seen Asbury Park gain ascendancy over their archrivals from Long Branch; war or no war, Bill Smith's goal was to keep the Bishops on top in 1942. Considering the wealth of talent that had graduated and the number of teams that wanted revenge on the Bishops, this would be a difficult task. Smith, though, was undaunted.

He took his lone backfield veteran, Pete Vetrano, and put him at fullback. Vetrano would handle the inside runs, while sophomore halfback John Lee would hit the outside. Up front, senior center Nick Seganos and junior tackle Milt Aronis stood out on an inexperienced but fiery line. It was almost enough to carry the Bishops to another title.

Asbury finished the year 7-2, beating Group IV rivals such as Perth Amboy, Irvington, and Thomas Jefferson (Elizabeth) and handling local foes Red Bank and Asbury Park. They even represented the area well in a 10-0 loss to powerful Phillipsburg. Their only blemish in Central Jersey, and the game that denied them the CJ IV crown, was a Week 2 loss to New Brunswick. It was a heartbreaker. Lee's 59-yard touchdown run had put the Bishops ahead 6-0, but a last-minute New Brunswick touchdown pass and a dropkicked extra point undid it. Asbury lost 7-6, missing their chance at a third straight CJ IV crown.[1]

Still, it had been a good season, with big crowds filling the stadium each Saturday. Thanksgiving provided an appropriate cap, with 3,000 fans turning out to see the Bishops down the Iron Dukes of Newark East Side, 20-7. The hero, as usual, was Vetrano, who scored three touchdowns to win the area scoring crown.[2] Their celebrations continued into the basketball season, as Vetrano earned All-State honors for captaining the Bishops to their second state championship in three years. Then he completed an incredible triple play, earning all-state honors on the baseball diamond as well. It was the first time in school history that anyone had done all three in one year (Jack Netcher had won all three, but over two separate years). Every major college football program wanted him, as did baseball's Brooklyn Dodgers.

But this was the summer of 1943, and graduation brought with it induction to the United States Army. Vetrano was sent to France as part of an anti-tank division and was seriously wounded at St. Nazaire on August 29, 1944. He received sixty-eight stitches and spent thirty days in a hospital bed. At times, it looked as though he wouldn't survive, and later it appeared he would never walk again. Vetrano did recover, but he also carried shrapnel in his leg for the rest of his life. There would be no college football or pro baseball for him.[3]

In terms of athletic ability, there were few who were like Pete Vetrano. In terms of the cost of the Second World War, there were many like him, and many who sacrificed even more, in order to preserve freedom and democracy across the globe. That the cause was just and the war necessary does not change the fact that the cost was high. In that sense, Vetrano's story stands as a memorial for all those young Americans who paid that cost.

Asbury's 1943 season was not nearly as successful as the three preceding years. The Bishops struggled to a disappointing 3-6-1 record, their worst in many years. This mostly dismal season, however, was enlivened on November 2 when word was released to the *Asbury Park Press* that

Neptune and Asbury would resume their rivalry on the Saturday before Thanksgiving. It was the first time the two teams had played since 1928, and its return drew intense interest and plenty of pageantry.

Uniformed members of the Army, the Navy, the Marine Corps, the Coast Guard, the Royal Navy, and the Royal Canadian Air Force turned out for the game, as did 3,500 cheering local fans. The disappointments of the season were quickly forgotten as the Blue Bishops played their best game of the year. Their size made the difference, springing Wheaton Pearce and Steve Pappaylion for touchdowns in a hard-fought 13-7 victory. After the game, Asbury's band celebrated by parading down Sunset Avenue.[4] The Bishops finished the season with a rout of Newark South Side, ending an otherwise disappointing year on a high note.

Bill Smith resigned after the season, moving back to Northwest Jersey to raise his family's herd of cattle. At this point, the natural choice was for the Asbury Board of Education to hire a coach that they'd been considering for some time—the city's greatest-ever football star, Butch Bruno. Since he was in the Navy, they couldn't have him just yet. Instead, they appointed a caretaker, Lachman Rinehart, on the understanding that Bruno would inherit the job as soon as the war ended. Rinehart shepherded the Bishops through the 1944 and 1945 seasons, then stayed on as an assistant under Bruno.

Long Branch, meanwhile, was also looking to their own legendary graduate—Army Ippolito. The Branchers had been middling in the 1940s, neither particularly strong nor particularly weak. The high points of their season remained their annual battles with Asbury and Red Bank. The board of education hoped that Ippolito would get them out of that rut and bring them the titles they so craved. He would do that quickly, coaching the Green Wave to a championship in 1945. The groundwork was being laid for the golden years of both programs.

CHAPTER 6
THE SHORE CONFERENCE

Meanwhile, the Shore Conference was building up its own traditions. In 1942, both Arnie Truex's Leonardo Lions and Russ Wright's Lakewood Piners took the lead, engaging in a heated race that once again came down to the final day of the season. Both coaches started the year by claiming that their rosters were depleted by graduation and that the teams would at best be in the middle of the pack. By now, though, the *Asbury Park Press* was wise to the ways of Truex and Wright, and sarcastically dismissed their gloomy predictions. Everyone knew that these were the two favorites.[1]

Leonardo relied on two main weapons—end Doug Foulks (a great receiver and a stout defender) and Swede Reinertson, who could seemingly do everything. He started the season on the line, moved to the offensive backfield due to injury, and continued to dominate the trenches on defense. He even threw the ball when necessary. With players like that, it was no surprise that Leonardo started the season 4-0. Then they slipped, stumbling to a 6-6 tie with Toms River.

Leonardo responded to the tie with its three best games of the season, overwhelming Keyport and Atlantic Highlands before blasting Rumson

53-0 on Thanksgiving morning. Eight different players scored in that win. Now all the Lions could do was wait for word from the Lakewood game and wonder how the conference's point system would play out.[2]

Much like in 1941, Lakewood was playing perhaps the toughest schedule in the Shore Conference. Unable to fill a full slate of league foes, they lined up games with Bernardsville, Somerville, Cranford, and parochial power St. Peter's of New Brunswick. The Piners went 3-1 against that group, losing only to St. Peter's. In the area, they bordered on dominant, thrashing the few local teams willing to play them.

The key was their powerful offensive line, which cleared big holes for sophomore back Jim Royle. Against Neptune, the Piners racked up 406 yards of total offense and romped to a 32-13 win. Against Manasquan, they sloshed through the mud to a 13-0 victory, and against Freehold they scored four third-quarter touchdowns in a 32-0 romp. [3] Thanksgiving, though, would prove far less certain.

Jim Royle had injured his stomach against Somerville and sat out the regular season finale against Cranford to be full strength for the holiday classic. The stakes were high, for the team and for Royle personally. Not only would a win avenge last year's Thanksgiving disappointment, but it would also give the Piners a share of the Shore Conference title and probably sole possession of the CJ II crown. Royle, meanwhile, held a slim lead over Asbury Park's Pete Vetrano in the Shore scoring race. It would be a big morning in Toms River.

The game was scoreless through the first quarter, which had Lakewood fans shuddering as they remembered last year's tie. Then All-Shore guard Bill Malayter turned the tide of the game with an interception that he returned to the 27. That set up Royle for a short touchdown, which was all the Piners needed to grab a hard-fought 6-2 win. Vetrano's three scores let him pass Royle in the scoring chase, but the Piners still secured their fourth sectional title under Wright.

The conference race was more complex. Although Leonardo had won more games, they also had a tie and Lakewood had played a tougher schedule. Ultimately, the Dickinson System rated the two teams as equals and the league declared them co-champions. The *Asbury Park Press* called for a playoff, but the conference had no interest, especially not in a war year.[4]

The war continued into 1943, and it dominated the headlines. People voraciously consumed every scrap of news they could get, whether about the ongoing U-Boat war in the North Atlantic, the grinding Allied advance up the Italian peninsula, or the steady Soviet push through Eastern Europe. The news also affected its readers practically; they needed to know the specifics on changes to the gas ration, as well as the welfare of friends and family.

Signs of the war even made the sports pages—in addition to its annual previews of high school teams, the *Asbury Park Press* reported on a service team assembled at Lakehurst Naval Air Station. The Aviators had no home games and no major college stars, but their schedule (which included games against Penn, Villanova, and Bucknell) drew some local interest.[5] Still, the high schools were the main draw. There was plenty of drama to hold fans' attention.

Entering the season, Lakewood felt like the league's unwanted child. Once again, they could only get four league games (one less than the required five) and needed special permission just to stay eligible in the title race.[6] This was just one of many headaches that Russ Wright was dealing with in the offseason. He was taken ill late in the school year and spent much of the summer recovering in West Virginia. When he returned, he found that a number of his players had been drafted. As usual, he predicted a middling season.[7]

Adding to Wright's stress was the schedule. In addition to a Shore Conference schedule that included a championship-caliber Manasquan team, Wright's Piners had to face St. Peter's and a long trip to face a team from the National Farm School, a residential school in Pennsylvania that no one knew anything about. Still, Lakewood did return Jimmy Royle and Rudy Kurinsky, two devastatingly effective backs. They hoped that would be enough.

It wasn't enough to beat the Farmers, who humbled Lakewood 12-6 in the season opener. However, the motivated Piners put forth a much better effort in Week 2, routing St. Peter's 28-0 behind three Royle touchdowns.

That was more like it and sent the Piners into league play with a confident feeling. They had no margin for error—with just four league games, they knew they needed to win every one in order to have a chance at maintaining their crown. Three more Royle touchdowns dismissed Neptune 28-0, but all knew Manasquan would be harder.[8]

The Big Blue scored early to take a 7-0 lead and held that lead into the second quarter. That's when Royle came to life. He tied the game with a touchdown pass to Andy Johnson, and then won it with an 18-yard touchdown run in the fourth quarter. By a 13-7 score, the Piners had seized control of the title race.[9] They refused to let up, ending the season unbeaten in the Shore with consecutive routs of Freehold and Toms River. Royle proved unstoppable, scoring four times in a 40-7 rout of the Indians. It was personally satisfying for the senior back, who set an area record with 116 points in a single season. Royle headed home a champion, enjoyed a turkey dinner and a long weekend, and then joined the U.S. Army. It was, after all, wartime.[10]

Royle was in the service training for almost a week before anyone knew if the Piners had won any titles at all. That was because both Shore and sectional titles were determined by mathematical formula, and it took time to work things out. Some years, the league champion was obvious; other years, it had to be calculated. In 1943, 5-1-1 Red Bank forced a calculation.

Nobody had known what to expect from the Bucs. Under Head Coach Dick Guest, the team had been totally unpredictable. The 1936 team lost its first seven games, then shocked Long Branch on Thanksgiving. The 1937 team had started 3-1, then skidded into a losing streak that didn't end until 1939. They broke the string with a CJ III title, which was followed by three straight losing seasons. It was like being on a roller coaster.

In 1943, the head job passed to a town fixture, Frank Pingitore. Pingitore had coached Red Bank's junior high teams for many years, and so knew his players well. He also had eleven returning letterwinners, two of whom (end Fred Bruno and halfback Walt "Babe" Jackson) would earn All-Shore honors. Still, the *Asbury Park Press* was cautious in its judgment—it saw Buc prospects as "fair," rather than outstanding.[11]

That image changed in the season opener when the Bucs invaded Manasquan and snatched a tie from the title favorites. Jackson was the hero, rushing for 132 yards and the tying touchdown. Although that wasn't a victory, it did signal a strong season.[12] The next three weeks may have been the most satisfying in the history of Red Bank football. First, they crushed their local rivals Rumson 26-0. Then they crossed the Navesink River and beat their Bayshore rivals Leonardo, 12-0. Finally, they turned their attentions to Asbury Park, one of their oldest foes and a team they had never beaten.

Although a nonconference game, this was still a huge attraction and drew 3,500 fans. The Bucs came out hot, scoring first on a 10-yard Jackson touchdown run. Asbury fumbled the ensuing kickoff, and Fred Bruno scooped up the loose ball and ran it in for a touchdown. Jackson scored again in the second and it was 18-0. Asbury got as close as 18-12, but thanks to the superb defensive efforts of Pete Prominski and Bart Gallagher, they got no closer. Afterward, Frank Pingitore was hoisted onto the shoulders of cheering fans, while 500 joyous students paraded down Broad Street.[13]

The Shore Conference title was now within Red Bank's grasp. Wins over Neptune and Keyport wrapped up their league slate, leaving them nothing to do but wait for the Dickinson ratings. That, and try to finish an undefeated season by beating Long Branch on Thanksgiving. A year's worth of bragging rights was on the line.

Four thousand fans, the biggest crowd to see a game at the Shore all season, packed into the bleachers at Long Branch. They saw an otherwise middling Brancher team turn in a vintage performance. The defense contained Walt Jackson, while Long Branch's unheralded fullback Eddie Coughlin turned in a vintage performance of his own, running for a touchdown and returning an interception for a second score. The final was 13-0.[14]

The game made Long Branch's Thanksgiving, but only partially spoiled Red Bank's. The Bucs went home knowing that they had a good shot at getting at least a share of the Shore Conference crown, and that's exactly what they received. Red Bank and Lakewood shared both the league title and the CJ II crown, making it a championship season for both (and making the Piners the first team in league history to repeat as champions).

Lakewood star Jim Royle's post-high school career was shaped by the war. In ordinary times, Royle (only a junior in 1943) would have returned for a final year of high school football as a highly touted recruit. Instead, he joined the Navy and spent what should have been his senior football season on an LST (a kind of wartime vessel called a landing ship, tank) in the Pacific. Although he made it through the war uninjured, and returned to Lakewood for his senior year (1946), he was too old to play high school football. Royle ended up playing a year at Penn Military College, then finished his athletic career playing semipro football for the Lakewood Athletic Club. This in no way suggests his life was a disappointment—Royle married his high school sweetheart, settled into his hometown, and became an insurance agent while raising five children. One of those sons, also named Jim, played football and baseball for the Piners.[15]

Another "what-might-have-been" story was Walter Jackson, who by the end of 1944 was clearly the best athlete in Red Bank High School. He starred in football, he starred in basketball, he set the school record in the javelin, and he even was the headliner of an exhibition boxing match held in the high school gymnasium.[16] But he never did compete in the Shore Conference track meet; his induction into the military came first. Jackson became one of the first African Americans to serve in the United States Marine Corps (which had been segregated as late as 1942). He saw action in the South Pacific, then returned to Red Bank High School.[17]

Like Royle, Jackson never did become a college star, and he also became a fixture on the local athletic circuit, playing softball, semipro football, and boxing in local venues. His name would reappear in local papers during the 1960s, when his son became one of the first athletic stars at the newly opened Monmouth Regional High School.

By the time football resumed in September 1944, the war looked very different. Whether or not the Allies would win was no longer in doubt. Italy had surrendered, the Western powers had re-established themselves in France and were driving inland, and Nazi Germany was crumbling under the weight of superior numbers pressing it from all sides and the air. In the Pacific, the United States controlled the sea and the skies, allowing American bombers to start blistering the home islands. Still, this didn't mean that Americans could stop following the war. Rationing still impinged on daily life, and although victory was certain, the day or the hour in which it arrived, or the form it would take, remained unclear. And those with loved ones overseas obviously had much to worry about.

The sports world continued to relieve the tension. The fall of 1944 would bring another heated, closely contested title race, one which once again came down to Thanksgiving Day. This time, though, the conference's two leading teams met in the regular season, providing the decisive showdown fans had been denied in 1942 and 1943. Another way that this race was different was that Lakewood, depleted by graduation and by Russ Wright's induction into the Navy, was not a factor. The 2-6 Piners instead watched the season turn into a three-way struggle between Toms River, Leonardo, and Red Bank.

Toms River was the most experienced team, and thus the early favorite. Bob Reigle's Indians had four starters returning on the offensive line and four more in the backfield. End Jim Tiner and tackle Matt Mincey were the best at their positions in the Shore Conference, and tailback Loreta "Junie" Sica was the next in a great line of Toms River athletes. Much like his older sibling, Loreta was an explosive runner and a dangerous ball-carrier. With him in the lineup, Toms River's offense would be hard to stop.[18]

Leonardo, meanwhile, had numbers on their side. Their sixty-five-man roster was one of the biggest in the Shore, and their line was anchored by tough players such as center Bob Hopler, end Dick Wackar, and guard Jim O'Shaughnessy. Their main ballcarriers, Gene McBride and Ed "88" Keyes, weren't as explosive as Sica, but both were good. The only concern was that McBride was likely to leave midseason to enter the military.[19]

The biggest team in the conference, though, belonged to the defending champions. Red Bank returned only three lettermen, but they had seventy players on their roster. Their talent was heavily concentrated along the line, which featured All-Conference tackle Pat D'Aloia and All-Conference end Bill Kaney.[20] The Bucs showed their stuff with season-opening wins over Manasquan and Rumson. Meanwhile, Leonardo was starting the season with equally impressive routs of Sayreville and Matawan. That set up the year's first big game—a showdown between these two 2-0 title contenders.

Red Bank jumped out to a 7-0 lead on a touchdown pass from Chick Murray to Kaney. They held that lead until the fourth quarter, when Keyes put the Lions on the board with a short touchdown run. Red Bank, still fighting, blocked the ensuing extra point, but the Lion defense held and forced a punt, which Keyes blocked. That gave Leonardo the ball at short range, setting up Dick Cooke for the decisive touchdown in Leonardo's 13-7 win.[21]

Two weeks later came another showdown—4-0 Leonardo against 4-0 Toms River. The Indians had been crushing everyone, outscoring their first four opponents by a margin of 126-13. However, Loreta Sica had injured his ankle a week before in the Freehold win and would be unavailable. That left the hosts favored.

In the first quarter, they lived up to that billing, taking a 6-0 lead on Tom Finnegan's touchdown run. However, the second quarter saw the injured Sica's teammates step up. First, Con Kahler returned a punt 80 yards for a touchdown, and then Irving Exel ran for a short touchdown of his own. Leonardo rallied to tie the game on a Keyes touchdown pass, so it was 13-13 at the half. Toms River gained the advantage in the third quarter when John Wirt blocked a punt and returned it for a touchdown. Fullback Bill Nicolini buried the extra point, putting the Indians ahead 20-13. That kick proved to be vital when Dick Cook ran for a fourth quarter touchdown. It all came down to the conversion attempt, a pass which sailed incomplete. Toms River escaped, 20-19.[22]

There was nothing left for the Lions to do but play out the season and hope Toms River slipped up. Although they no longer controlled their own destiny, they kept playing well and finished 7-1 after victories over Atlantic Highlands and Rumson. Red Bank also played well down the stretch, finishing the season with a Thanksgiving win over Long Branch. The Green Wave led 6-0 in the fourth, only for Ray Coreale to hit Jack Kaney for a 49-yard touchdown pass to tie the game. Pat D'Aloia then won it with an extra point. Whether they'd be champions or not, Red Bank at least had beaten their old rivals.[23]

In the end, though, Toms River refused to slip up. With or without Sica, the Indians were good enough to run through the year with a perfect 8-0 record. The Thanksgiving game against Lakewood got a little hairy, but the defense got the job done. Nicolini's late touchdown won it, 7-0, securing the league title. A few weeks later, Toms River was also awarded the CJ I crown by the NJSIAA. The Indians were on top of the world.[24]

The following summer, Toms River Head Coach Bob Reigle resigned to take a job at the Admiral Farragut Military Academy in St. Petersburg, Florida (it was a sister school to the academy of the same name in Beachwood). In eight years with the Indians, he had gone 46-18-10, winning three league titles and three sectional crowns. Not until Ron Signorino two decades later would Toms River have a more successful coach.

CHAPTER 7
THE T FORMATION ARRIVES

The 1945 football season was not played during wartime. Nazi Germany had surrendered in May, and Imperial Japan officially did the same in early September. Crowds, reported by the *Asbury Park Press* as the largest in history, were once again gathering at the Shore.[1] Yet 1945 was not quite peacetime yet either. Demobilization was a slow, gradual process, so most football players who had been in the military during the summer either played on service teams in the fall or not at all. Rationing, too, was lifted only gradually.

Even the anxieties of the war weren't totally gone. The struggle to defeat Nazi Germany had obscured the tensions between the Western Allies and their unlikely partners from the Soviet Union. Now that the great enemy was gone, those conflicts were coming into the open, laying the seeds for what would soon become the Cold War. So, the 1945 season occurred in an odd atmosphere that lay somewhere between peace and war.

That season was also unusual for the shape that its title race took. By midseason, it was clear that Point Pleasant was the frontrunner. Although the Shore's Group I schools were usually strong, schools the size of Point Pleasant didn't usually make serious runs at the conference title. Instead, they mostly focused their attention on the more manageable race for the CJ I crown. A Shore team with a decent record was always in the hunt for that title.

That's how it worked for Point Pleasant's 1942 team. The Gulls entered the season on a twenty-one-game losing streak, which was a daunting situation for First-Year Coach Stan "Tuffy" Baker. But Baker's team played with a new fire. They held Keyport and Toms River to scoreless ties to open the season, then upset Rumson 12-6 on touchdown runs by Tom Wilson and Pete Dunn.[2] That backfield tandem sparked a five-game winning streak and brought home a share of the CJ I title (Keyport, whom the Gulls had tied in the opener, won the other half).

The one thing they could not do was win the Shore Conference title. The two ties to open the season and a Thanksgiving loss to Manasquan put that out of reach. So, they ended the season with a 4-1-2 record. But the Gulls couldn't be too disappointed. They *never* beat Manasquan, and rarely beat any of the Group IIs. All they could do was make the best of it.

Except Head Coach Joe Pagano wanted more. A football star at New York University, Pagano had first arrived at the Shore in 1942 as the new head football coach at Atlantic Highlands. The war years were tough for the Tigers; their teams were small in the best of years, and with players regularly leaving the team to enter the military, the numbers plunged to unsustainable levels. They won just one game in two years. Still, Pagano's clubs won plaudits from the *Press* for the "spunk they have shown in launching the season" at all.[3]

In the spring of 1944, Pagano took a new job at Point Pleasant. Although the numbers there were small, the situation wasn't quite so dire. Pagano was able to field a full ballclub, and he was impressed with the running ability of his backs, particularly Bob Moore. His Point Pleasant team won its first game, a 19-0 shutout over Keyport. However, they lost their next two, to Toms River and Neptune, by shutout.

The losses didn't dishearten Pagano. Instead, they inspired him to make a momentous change. At this time, most teams in the Shore were running some variant of the single wing, and none of them had what a modern fan would recognize as a quarterback. Sure, each team had a player they called by that name, but he was a blocking back who called signals. No one was yet running the T formation.

That system, and its more modern method of quarterback play, had begun to take the football world by storm in 1940. The offense had been developed by Stanford Head Coach Clark Shaughnessy and Chicago Bears Head Coach George Halas. The two friends had similar quarterbacks (Frankie Albert for Stanford, Sid Luckman for the Bears). Neither was fast or strong enough to play tailback, but both were very effective passers and great at carrying out fakes. In order to maximize their strengths and minimize their weaknesses, the two coaches decided to have their quarterbacks take a direct hand-to-hand snap from center on every play. That would allow them to handle the ball without having to be the main running threat. Other players could do that; the quarterback would focus on passing.

The offense was an enormous success. Between 1939 and 1940, Stanford improved from 1-7-1 to 10-0, winning the Pacific Coast Conference and beating Nebraska in the Rose Bowl. The Bears, meanwhile, won back-to-back NFL championships, including a legendary 73-0 thrashing of Washington in the 1940 title game. Notre Dame's Frank Leahy and Texas's Dana Bible adopted the T formation soon after, and it paid off for them as well—the Longhorns won the 1942 Cotton Bowl, and the Irish won the 1943 national title.

The T formation began spreading across the nation like wildfire. It became the standard offense in the NFL, and today its concepts are the basis for just about every offense in current use at any level of football. In high schools, though, the T formation was slow to catch on. The Bears had claimed that the new offense allowed them to run over 1,000 possible plays, and the consensus was that the offense was just too complicated for high schoolers to learn.

Pagano, though, had some experience with the T formation, and did not think it was as difficult as all that. He had also seen enough Shore Conference action to believe that Point Pleasant would never win without finding an edge. He believed that the T formation, which was different than anything anyone else was running at the time, would give his boys that edge.

Joe Pagano: *"I had helped with the freshmen team at Rutgers, working with Harvey Harman. He taught the T formation. We had to do something different, and that loss to Toms River made me sure that the time was right for a change. We had nothing to lose."*[4]

Al Gray (Point Pleasant quarterback): *"The idea of the T was perfect for us. It was based on the idea of attacking the other team's weakness, of surprising them . . . I remember the playbook. It was two or three inches thick with our plays from every formation. As quarterback, coach had a rule for me. I was supposed to know what every player did on every play. I lived with that book for three years."*[5]

Point won their first four games in the new offense, running their record to 5-2 and setting up a Thanksgiving showdown with Manasquan. By now, the Thanksgiving rivalry had become a fixture. The dominance of the Big Blue did nothing to dampen the enthusiasm with which the two teams contested the rivalry, and their 1944 meeting drew over 3,000 fans.

This time, that crowd saw a Point Pleasant victory. Late in the first quarter, Bob Moore's 26-yard run put the ball deep in Manasquan territory, and his 10-yard touchdown pass to Joe Miller provided the Gulls with the game's only score. Bucky Johnson secured the 7-0 win with a late interception. The 6-2 Gulls roared into the offseason buoyed not just by a winning record, but by their first victory over Manasquan since 1934.[6]

That win spurred the Gulls toward high ambitions in 1945. Their schedule that year included games against Neptune, Toms River, and Manasquan (all Group II opponents). Wins in all three of those games would probably be enough to give the team a shot at the Shore Conference title. There was no margin for error, but it could be done.

It helped that the Gulls may have had their most talented team ever, placing four starters on the All-Shore team. Two of those starters were linemen, guard Bob O'Halleran and center Dick Wilson. Another was quarterback Al Gray, and the final was tailback Bob Moore, the hero of the Manasquan game from the year before.

The most obvious challenge would come from Toms River. The defending league champions had lost their coach, but they returned their best back, Loreto "Junie" Sica, as well as backs such as Irv Excel, who had stepped up to fill in for him when he had been injured. With sixty-eight players on the roster, new head man John Konowitz had every reason to hope for the future.[7]

Then there was Manasquan. John Schellenger was in his third year as head coach of the Big Blue, and with fifty players out for the team, he had high hopes of bringing home a title. Their roster featured a veteran line, anchored by All-Shore guard Nat McHenry, and an explosive backfield, anchored by All-Shore tailback Alf Morgan (the first of many athletes from that family to go through Manasquan High School). The Warriors were hungry to avenge 1944's Thanksgiving loss and get back to their familiar place near the top of the Shore.

Even hungrier were the fans; now that the war was over, they wanted to see action. Three thousand fans jammed the Deal Lake Stadium for Asbury Park's season opener against Lakewood, while Manasquan brought out its full marching band for the first time since Pearl Harbor.[8] They were especially excited for the season's first big game—a mid-October showdown between undefeated Toms River and undefeated Manasquan. The game was played in Ocean County, on a day when high winds put a premium on running the ball and throwing only short passes.

The game was scoreless into the third quarter, when Toms River took a 7-0 lead on Junie Sica's touchdown pass to Jack Pierce. That proved key when Jim Venerable answered with a 69-yard touchdown run, cutting the score to 7-6. Manasquan had a shot to tie, but the conversion pass was batted away and Toms River prevailed by that margin.[9]

That set up an even bigger game a week later—Toms River against Point Pleasant. The Indians were riding high after their Manasquan win and hoped to cement their place atop the league. Joe Pagano's Gulls, meanwhile, were a wild card. Their season opener with Keyport had been rained out, but they'd looked explosive in a 25-7 win over Neptune.

In front of a packed house at Clayton Field, the Indians went ahead 7-0 on a blocked punt that John Versnel recovered for a touchdown. Point immediately answered, tying the game in the second quarter when the effective passing of Don McIntyre set up a Dick Pearce touchdown run. Later that quarter, McIntyre's brilliance produced another score; he intercepted a pass deep in Toms River territory to set up his own short touchdown run. It was 14-7 Point Pleasant.

The defending champions didn't die easily. Junie Sica tied the game with a touchdown run. The fourth quarter, however, was all McIntyre. He slashed his way down the field for most of an 80-yard touchdown drive, scoring the winner with too little time left for a Toms River rally.[10] Point Pleasant was now the last unbeaten team in the Shore Conference.

Over the next several weeks, their potent T-formation attack continued to live up to its reputation. Opponents were baffled by the deceptive offense, and Gull runners were constantly breaking free for long gains. The team was the toast of the town. There wasn't money to throw around, but people contributed what they could—a local butcher provided fresh lamb chops after every game, and a local diner offered free banana splits with each victory.[11]

Even when they didn't play well, they won. That happened at Matawan, just one week before Thanksgiving. The underdog Huskies led 6-0 late, but Al Gray blocked a punt that Ed Smith recovered for a touchdown. Bob Moore than hit Gray on a conversion pass to win, 7-6.[12] So the Pointers rolled into Thanksgiving at 6-0. There they would face 5-1 Manasquan.

Ever since their early loss to Toms River, the Warriors had been clicking. Nobody could stop the outside runs of Alf Morgan, nor could they move on Manasquan's defense. And the Big Blue knew that they could be Shore Conference champions with a victory. On the other hand, if Point won or tied the rivalry game, they would claim the crown. This was indisputably the biggest game in the history of the Manasquan-Point Pleasant series, and it drew what was easily the biggest crowd in the history of the rivalry. Over 5,000 fans, including neutrals from around the Shore, turned out. Everyone wanted to see this game.

In the first half, both teams dodged bullets. Point's Don McIntyre fumbled at his own 7, setting up a dangerous Manasquan threat that was stopped only through superb defense. The Gulls then mounted a drive of their own, reaching the 'Squan 13 before Don Kenderman's interception ended the thrust and sent the two teams into the half tied at 0. The game of the year would come down to the second half.

The third quarter saw Manasquan take the lead on a trick play. They shifted guard Nat McHenry to end, and the Point defense neglected to guard him. Jim Venerable took the direct snap, faded back, and hit the wide-open McHenry for a 37-yard touchdown and a 6-0 lead. The Big Blue were in front, seemingly to stay. Point just couldn't move.

Their fortunes turned on an early fourth-quarter gamble by the Gulls. Bob Moore's lunge converted a fourth and inches from deep in Gull territory. Three other first-down conversions followed, ending in a touchdown pass from Moore to Dick Pearce. The game was tied at 6, but Pearce's lunge for the goal line on the conversion was stopped short. Knowing a tie was good enough for the title, Point played conservatively after that, and the game ended in a deadlock.[13]

> **Carl Barkalow (Point Pleasant center)**: *"Coach knew we had the championship as long as we didn't lose. But it's always bothered me a little that we tied. We were the better team."*[14]

The disappointment notwithstanding, Point Pleasant ended 1945 as both the Shore Conference and CJ I champions. More importantly, they became legends in their own community. There have been great teams since but Point Pleasant Beach has never again produced an unbeaten team. For that, the 1945 Gulls will always be remembered.

> **Bob Grace (Point Beach head coach, 1992)**: *"Those guys are legends. What they did is passed down from football generation to football generation."*[15]

Pagano left for Neptune after the season, but the Gull program remained strong, challenging for league titles again in both 1947 and 1949. Area teams, meanwhile, started adopting the T formation. Within ten years, it was unusual to run anything else. The Shore had taken some important steps into the future.

All over the Shore, there were signs that things were returning to normal. One of those signs came from Toms River's football star, Junie Sica. After starring on the Indians in 1944 and 1945, Sica was neither drafted into the military nor left to take a job in a factory. Instead, he accepted a scholarship to play football at Penn. He later transferred to Southwestern College in Kansas, where he played football and baseball. Sica was All-Conference for Southwestern in 1950, then enrolled in the Coast Guard. He spent three years teaching judo for the Cape May Coast Guard Receiving Station, and starred on its service football team, winning All-American honors in 1952. Like so many other Americans, he was enjoying the fruits of peace.[16]

CHAPTER 8
THE BAYSHORE BOYS

The existence of the Shore Conference didn't just benefit local powers. By helping to ensure that local teams were able to fill out full schedules and play natural rivals, the conference helped promote the sport's growth for all its members. This was especially the case at Matawan and Keyport, two of the smallest teams in the Shore throughout the 1940s.

Their story begins in the fall of 1939, a few years before American entry into World War II. Keyport was playing football for the very first season and struggling badly—they would finish with a final record of 0-6. Matawan, meanwhile, was under the direction of a new coach, former Rutgers star Paul Bednard. They would improve rapidly, but in this season were enjoying only a middling record. On the basis of record alone, neither team was having a memorable season. But Thanksgiving changed all that.

The two natural rivals agreed to a Thanksgiving game, and the towns embraced it; 1,500 fans came out for the season finale. They saw the teams play their best game of the year, competing in a contest that the *Long Branch Daily Record* compared to a miniature World War I battle. It was a heartbreaker for Keyport's winless Raiders. John Sellick intercepted an early Matawan pass and returned it 60 yards for a touchdown, but a missed extra point left the door open and the Huskies charged through it. In the fourth quarter, Frank LaMura's short touchdown run and Roy Veary's extra point won the game for Matawan. Their visiting fans stormed the field, tearing down Keyport's goalposts in their jubilation.[1]

Both programs soon benefited from the establishment of an annual classic. Keyport, in particular, established a reputation for playing its best football against the Huskies, something that Matawan would learn to its frustration in 1940 and 1941. In both seasons, Bednard's team used the running of Frank LaMura (and in 1941, the efforts of All-Shore end Walt Carey) to charge through the regular season. Both seasons ended with Keyport holding the Huskies to surprising ties (0-0 in 1940, 6-6 in 1941). Both games drew substantial crowds of over 2,000 fans (roughly 20 percent of the combined population of the two towns at that time).

The 1942 game turned out to be even bigger. By then the war was on, and Bednard was in the U.S. Army, where he would eventually rise to the rank of major. The Huskies were struggling through a disappointing 2-5 season, while Keyport was overcoming some turmoil to seek new glory. Head Coach Joe Barile was drafted midway through the season, leaving assistant Tommy Phipps in charge. Nonetheless, the Raiders kept winning behind the superb running of Frank Fragasso. They nearly upset Toms River and did beat Rumson 13-0, running their record to 4-2-1. A Thanksgiving win would give them a shot at a title.

The NJSIAA was awarding sectional titles to Group I teams for the first time in 1942, and one more victory would allow the Raiders to share the CJ I crown with Point Pleasant (whom they had tied earlier in the season). Matawan, meanwhile, had the incentive of denying their rivals all of that. It was an explosive mix. Just two minutes into the game, Keyport's Herb Spray fell on a fumble at the 22-yard line, setting up Frank Fragasso for a short touchdown run. That was all the scoring on the day. Keyport won, 6-0, and brought home the crown.[2]

The roles were reversed in 1943. Rationing curtailed the Keyport regular season, which the Red Raiders finished at just 2-2-1. Matawan, meanwhile, was rolling under the direction of Head Coach Tony Nuccio.

A backfield featuring Dutch Smith, Charlie Pike, and Al La Mura terrorized the Shore with an elite passing game, while a scrappy and determined line controlled most offenses. The Huskies went 4-0-2 through the regular season, upsetting Leonardo and tying Manasquan. They entered Thanksgiving one win from a CJ I title of their own.

They seized the opportunity, prevailing behind Dutch Smith. His effective passing orchestrated the game's lone drive, a 63-yard march that ended in a touchdown pass to Bill Baird. The final was 6-0, last year's score in reverse.[3]

Neither team was of championship caliber in 1944 and 1945, and in fact Keyport would slide into a multi-year losing streak. Thanksgiving, though, remained a rich and valued tradition in the two communities. The Raiders and Huskies would continue to play out their fierce holiday rivalry for decades to come; it wouldn't end until 1968, when rapid population growth in Matawan made the rivalry untenable. That, however, was a long way off. For now, the game was a fixture of Shore Conference football. And now that the war was over, Shore Conference football could take its place as a fixture of life in Monmouth and Ocean Counties.

PART 3:
THE AGE OF THE TITANS:
SHORE CONFERENCE
FOOTBALL FROM 1946-1961

CHAPTER 9
THE RIVALRY:
ASBURY PARK VS. LONG
BRANCH, 1932-1948

These were the darkest days of the Great Depression, with one out of four men out of work and relief nowhere in sight. Herbert Hoover, who offered no excuses and less hope, had just been turned out of office by a resounding margin, and no one was yet certain that President-Elect Franklin Roosevelt could do any better. These were the days of the Dust Bowl, of desperation, of high-powered stockbrokers turned apple-sellers, and of riches to rags.

It was no better at the Shore than it was anywhere else. Just four years before, Asbury Park mayor Clarence Hetrick had promised that the city's vast construction projects would shoot the resort past Atlantic City and make it the jewel of the Jersey Shore. Now, the convention hall and renovated boardwalk were empty white elephants, haunting reminders of a better time. But on this second Saturday in November, one of Hetrick's white elephants would be put to its intended use and would help to create a Shore legend to last a generation. Asbury Park was playing Long

Branch, and a crowd had formed early at the gates of Deal Lake Stadium. This was more than just another football Saturday in Monmouth County. This was the big one.

The two cities were born rivals. When James Bradley chose the site for the Methodist summer retreat that would one day become Asbury Park, he intentionally sited it so that woods, swamp, and an inlet separated it from ungodly Long Branch. The Branch was the premier resort spot on the Jersey Shore. Presidents, robber barons, and captains of industry gathered there for elegant, high class summer vacations. There, they could enjoy profane amusements such as band shells, coed bathing, and holding hands on the boardwalk . . . all things that Bradley wanted to keep out of Asbury Park. The rivalry grew further when Asbury Park abandoned the Methodist vision of a Shore utopia for the tourist dollars available to a resort town. Asbury and Long Branch were soon battling for summer visitors and the profits that came with them.

They were also competing, more directly, on the playing field. When Asbury Park High School began playing football in 1904, their first opponents were from Long Branch. The Branchers dominated the early years of the series, but it wasn't long before Asbury surpassed their hated rivals, growing into a state power that left the Green Wave far behind. Long years of frustration followed. What seemed like a lifetime passed, and every year without fail the Blue Bishops beat their archrivals like a drum. Rock bottom was hit in 1929, the year that Asbury Park won the first of four straight Central Jersey Group IV titles. The Green Wave, who ended up finishing winless, were humiliated 53-0.

That was Ted Bresset's first season as head coach at Long Branch, and the year that he set the school on the long, hard road to the top. Helping in his quest was a remarkable young athlete who had been a freshman on that winless team, Amadeo Ippolito. "Army" became the star quarterback and key player in Long Branch's turnaround, as they went from winless to 6-1-1 in a period of just three years. 1932 was Ippolito's senior season, and everyone in Long Branch had their sights set on bringing home the Central Jersey Group III crown, the school's first-ever sectional title. Even more important than that title, though, was the chance, *just once*, to get one over on those boys in blue. As Long Branch grimly marched through the regular season unbeaten, batting aside Neptune and New Brunswick and Woodbridge, one game remained circled in red on the calendar. And now it was here.

Ippolito and his teammates weren't the only ones for whom the game held special significance. Their Blue Bishop counterparts were equally motivated, because for them too this was the biggest game of the season. The Long Branch rivalry drew bigger crowds, was surrounded by more pageantry, and was covered in the press with more enthusiasm than any other single game anywhere in the Shore. Asbury played a statewide schedule, and Long Branch was their only local game. That alone made it a major event; with both teams as good as they were in 1932, it was the game of the year.

Besides, the host Bishops were also chasing a title, and history with it. Head Coach Bill Flynn had turned Asbury Park from a local power to a statewide terror in the late 1920s, and they solidified their reputation with every game they played. In five years under Flynn, the Bishops had run up a 33-4 record, won three straight Central Jersey Group IV titles, and finished with the overall number one ranking in the state in 1931. Now they were on the brink of a second straight undefeated season and second straight state championship. And while Long Branch had a star in Ippolito, Asbury had a star that shone just as brightly—Butch Bruno, their own star quarterback, currently being recruited by the University of Notre Dame.

For a few hours on that chilly Saturday afternoon in early November, the Great Depression was gone, and the only thing that mattered was the epic struggle playing out before the capacity crowd of over 5,000. The game would live long in Shore football lore, the story told and retold on the eve of the rivalry for years to come. Long Branch built an unlikely 6-0 lead when Vince Renzo found Ippolito wide open for a first-quarter touchdown, but Army missed what would prove to a crucial extra point. At first, the kick didn't seem to matter; the Green Wave defense was putting on one of the most impressive displays the locals had ever seen. Their efforts held the lead deep into the fourth quarter, and as the clock ticked away victory seemed all but certain. It was third down and three, and the Green Wave were coming to the line at their 28, preparing to attempt a quick kick, a punt that would leave Asbury Park with a full field to cover and almost no time in which to do it. And then, abruptly, things took a turn for the strange.

Punter Vernon Woolley seemingly got his quick kick away cleanly, but a gust of wind as strong as any that had ever blown through the stadium blew the ball *backward*. By the time he recovered it, it had rolled all the way back to his three. Still, the situation wasn't entirely bad; they could just kick again on fourth down. At least, they could have if the game officials hadn't made a colossal error. Forgetting that Long Branch had kicked on third down (and therefore had one more down to spare), they signaled for Asbury Park to take possession at the 4 going in.

Despite howls of protest from the Branchers, the Bishops had one more chance. Everyone in the stadium knew who was getting the ball— Bishop ace Butch Bruno. Bruno slammed into the line on five straight plays (Long Branch had jumped offside on one of them). On his final try, he sent the black and blue side of the bleachers into a frenzy by breaking through the line and into the end zone. As he crossed the goal line, Renzo smashed into him with the hardest tackle of the day, sending him sprawling. Brancher fans claimed for years that Bruno had been knocked unconscious, something he always denied.

Whether he had been unconscious or just dazed, Bruno picked himself up and joined his team for the vital extra point that would win the game. His first try at a drop kick was blocked by none other than Army Ippolito. Again, the Green and White jumped for joy, satisfied to come away with a tie, but a flag was down. Ippolito was ruled offside. Asbury would kick again. For the seventh straight play, the game rested on Bruno's shoulders. This time his kick was straight and true. The game ended moments later. Asbury Park 7, Long Branch 6.

No one was satisfied with the outcome. Asbury's victory was tainted, Long Branch's stolen. A storm of protests, photographs, and game films descended on the NJSIAA's state offices. Stunningly, the association bowed to the pressure. The game was declared a no-contest, the records expunged. It was as if the game had never been played. Officially, both teams finished the year undefeated sectional champions, the Bishops in CJ IV and the Wave in CJ III. Unofficially, the debate raged down through the years as to who had *really* won the 1932 classic. The two schools agreed to a brief cooling-off period, not playing for the next two years so that tensions could ease a bit (although the rivalry never really calmed down). Butch Bruno and Army Ippolito had taken the rivalry to new heights, and it wouldn't come down for decades.[1]

NOVEMBER 17, 1945

Thirteen years later, on another chilly November Saturday, Army Ippolito was back on the sidelines at Deal Lake Stadium, with only a date with Asbury Park standing between him and a Central Jersey Group III title for Long Branch. Now, though, the former star player was Long Branch's head coach. He had every reason to be confident. His team had every-thing a coach could ask for—two-time All-Shore halfback Langdon Viracola, All-State guard Len Palin, and inexhaustible defensive captain Bobby Acerra. It was a great day to be a Brancher.

Ippolito's road to this moment hadn't been a straight one. He had gone from Long Branch to Temple, playing end for legendary coach Pop Warner himself. When the Owls made the Sugar Bowl in 1934, Ippolito was their starting end. After college, he returned to the Garden State and played semipro football for three years with the Paterson Panthers. Shore fans eagerly followed Ippolito, sometimes even traveling up to North Jersey to watch him in action. When age and injuries finally caught up to the old star, he turned his energies to teaching and coaching, returning to the Shore in 1940 when a head coaching vacancy finally appeared.

That job was at little St. Rose in Belmar, where (ironically enough) Ippolito would be directly succeeding his old rival Butch Bruno. It would be a difficult task. The Roses were not known for taking sports particularly seriously. The school was small and lacked athletic facilities; it didn't even have a field within walking distance of the building. Yet the tiny student body loved football, and if the boys wanted to play, the priests and nuns of St. Rose were going to accommodate them. Ippolito's team played a four-game schedule that pitted them against large schools from North Jersey, and they gave a good account of themselves each week. In the season finale, the Roses grabbed their first win, upsetting North Arlington's Queen of Peace High School with two fourth-quarter touchdown passes.[2]

It was the last football game ever played at St. Rose. Between the lingering Great Depression and the approaching Second World War, maintaining a football team at a small, financially strapped Catholic school was too much to ask. St. Rose dropped the sport, eventually finding its athletic niche in basketball. Ippolito, meanwhile, was going back to his alma mater—in 1944, he became the head football coach at Long Branch.

Although the Green Wave struggled to a losing record in Ippolito's first season, they did accomplish something no other Brancher team had ever done—they beat Asbury Park twice in one season (war-time rationing had pushed the two teams into a home-and-home series). Neither game was a work of art, but both were thrillers.

The first game was a 6-4 slugfest in which junior Langdon Viracola starred. Long Branch took a 6-2 lead in the third on a hook-and-lateral play; Viracola both threw the hook and caught the lateral. Then, in the final seconds, he managed to dive on top of a bad punt snap and fall on it in the end zone for the game's second safety; had Asbury recovered, they would have won 8-6. The second game, a 13-12 Long Branch victory, was even more dramatic. The Wave defense held Asbury on the 1-yard-line as time expired. Both games ended with jubilant Long Branch fans pouring onto the field in celebration.

Now, one year later, the Green Wave needed a third straight victory over Asbury Park to crown the 1945 season. A near-capacity crowd of 4,000 fans, the biggest crowd since before the war, filled the bleachers for this one. It gave the event the atmosphere that the wartime games had lacked. The game was close, just 7-6 at the half, but Long Branch was cool, calm, and collected. Viracola scored three times in the second half as the Wave pulled away to win 28-6. Ten days later, he scored twice on Thanksgiving as Long Branch dispatched Red Bank 19-0 to clinch a sectional title. Viracola went on to star for a season at halfback for Fordham

University, while teammate Len Palin spent three years as the starting guard for Princeton.[3]

Fifty yards away from the wild Long Branch celebrations, on the home sideline, was an intense-looking young man in a military uniform. He stood at a respectful distance from the team, since Lachman Rinehart was still the coach, but he could nonetheless be seen pacing intensely as the game wore on. Butch Bruno had come home from the Navy, and was pretty clearly the head coach in waiting, expected to move right into the job at the end of the season.[4] His path to this moment had been even more winding than Ippolito's.

After graduating Asbury Park in the spring of 1933, Bruno had gone on to play at Notre Dame. Although never a starter, he *was* on the field when the Irish upset Ohio State in 1935 in what was then called the Game of the Century. After graduating in 1937, Bruno returned to the Shore, as an offensive line coach at Manasquan. This lasted two seasons before Bruno put his name in for the newly open head coaching job at his alma mater. He was turned down. Opportunity was knocking in a different place—St. Rose in Belmar.

Bruno was the only coach willing to take on the challenge of creating a new football program for the tiny parochial school. The same challenges that would eventually face Ippolito in 1940 were just as daunting for Bruno in 1939. He had no new equipment, only hand-me-downs scrounged from local schools. He had just eighteen players, none of them with any varsity experience. The team didn't even have a field. Dubbing his motley crew the "Dead End Kids," Butch Bruno took the job and began assembling a schedule.

The Roses were easy opponents for no one; they finished 2-2-1 in varsity action and beat Asbury Park's junior varsity in a scrimmage. Clearly, Bruno was doing something right. His time at St. Rose, however, was fated to be short. The Asbury job opened again in 1939, and Bruno applied for it again. He was once again passed over, but the school's choice, Bill "Clipper" Smith, decided to bring Bruno onboard as an assistant, hiring him to coach the offensive line. That unit helped power the Bishops to undefeated seasons in 1940 and 1941. When Asbury beat New

Brunswick on Thanksgiving morning in 1940, clinching the overall state championship and the school's first perfect season since 1932, Bruno got plenty of credit. [5]

All seemed to be going Butch Bruno's way. Just two or three more years as an assistant and the program he had always wanted would be his. Storm clouds, however, were gathering on the horizon, and the coming war would interrupt Bruno's story, as it would countless other stories. On December 7, 1941, less than two weeks after Asbury Park's second consecutive undefeated season, the Japanese attack on Pearl Harbor knocked high school football completely out of the public consciousness. All of America's attention was refocused on the Second World War. Bruno enlisted in the Navy and would not see New Jersey again until 1945. He was off to war, leaving his beloved Deal Lake Stadium and his coaching dream behind him.

The school administration, however, went out of its way to make arrangements for Bruno. When Clipper Smith stepped down in 1943, Lachman Rinehart was appointed to replace him, but only with the caveat that he was an *interim* head coach, and that the job would be Bruno's when he returned from the war.[6] Demobilization had come too late for Bruno to assume the job in 1945, but by the time the 1946 season started, he was home again and ready to take the reins. The golden age of Asbury Park football was about to begin.

NOVEMBER 13, 1948

The sky was gray and overcast and the wind was whipping at the Long Branch High School athletic field. While the crowd of 4,000 was still an overflow, with fans ringing the fence around the track, it was actually a disappointing turnout. That just showed how big the game had grown. For both teams, the 5-1-1 Bishops and the 4-2 Branchers, this was the game of the year. Since neither school was in a conference, their seasons were dominated by three main goals—win on Thanksgiving, win the sectional title, and win the Asbury Park-Long Branch game. This particular year, achieving the second goal required achieving the last one.[7]

By this point, Butch Bruno was used to the atmosphere. His official return three years ago had sparked a wave of excitement throughout Asbury Park, and it had never really broken. The city had immediately identified with his promise to provide "fiery, aggressive, cocky players" and to shake off the doldrums of three straight losing seasons. Players especially began buying into Bruno's rough and ready style.

> **Elliott Denman (Asbury Park Press sportswriter)**: *"Quite frequently his commands came down in gruff language. In the heat of athletic competition, Butch Bruno tended to rely on strong adjectives, but his messages were always understood. His athletes soon realized he had all of their interests at heart. This always turned into respect and frequently into adoration."*[8]

Expectations were high for both teams and their decorated coaches. People in Monmouth County expected the best in 1946. World War II was over, gasoline rationing was over, travel restrictions were lifted—for a tourist area such as the Jersey Shore, this was a godsend. Entertainment-starved Americans now had the time and disposable income to pour to the beach in huge numbers. Since there was no Garden State Parkway yet to speed travel from New York City, daily and weekend visitors tended to go no farther than Asbury Park, the practical limit of a morning's automobile travel. Others came by train, debarking right on the boardwalk and carrying their luggage to local hotels. Everywhere, there were crowds of summer revelers enjoying their vacation. Parades, fireworks, and movie shows projected on screens enlivened big holidays such as the Fourth of July and Labor Day Weekend. It was a good time to be at the Shore.

After the long summer days were over and beachfront visitors had departed, Asbury Park remained the hub of the Shore. People from all over Monmouth County spent their Saturday afternoons riding the trolley system and shopping at Steinbach's Department Store or gathering for special events at the Boardwalk's Convention Hall (home to trade shows, concerts, conventions, and the finals of the Shore Conference basketball tournament). When they weren't physically there, they read the *Asbury Park Press* for the daily news.[9]

Even on the oft-neglected West Side, there was still excitement and energy. Mainly home to Italian- and African-Americans, this neighborhood was poorer and more crowded than the rest of the city, but it nonetheless overflowed with promise of a better future. Its population was booming. Large numbers of African American soldiers had been posted to the city's ammunition depot or to the nearby Signal Corps lab at Fort Monmouth, and when they were discharged, they chose to stay in the city and send their sons and daughters to Asbury Park High School.[10]

For everyone in town, West Side or not, the high school stadium was the center of local entertainment in Asbury Park. Televisions were still a luxury, and Americans needed something to do on Friday nights and Saturday afternoons in the fall. They came to football games in huge numbers, with overflow crowds at almost every game. For big games, the Asbury Park Board of Education would rent floodlights, which drew even larger crowds (the 1946 season opener against Garfield drew 12,000 fans, a Shore Conference record for decades).[11]

Drawing crowds was easy. Winning titles was not. Butch Bruno's teams seemed to be cursed to suffer from near miss after near miss. In 1946, they finished 5-3, with all their losses coming by a touchdown or less. They shot for the title again in 1947, relying on Ralph Piscitello (an All-Shore end) and big John Williams (a sledgehammer of a fullback). However, the team started a deplorable 0-2-1, and although Bruno rallied the team to finish with another winning record, the title remained out of reach. Long Branch, meanwhile, was dealing with a different sort of frustration. They were good, with players such as Bubbie Acerra, Barry Rizzo, and Joe Oxley (the last two both future Shore Conference coaches), but they weren't good enough to beat South River. More frustrating, they weren't quite good enough to beat Asbury Park either.

In 1946, 6,000 fans saw Asbury avenge two years of frustration by winning 22-6 at their archrival's field. Piscitello clinched his All-Shore selection by catching two touchdown passes.[12] A year later, Joe Oxley's touchdown pass tied the game at 6-6 in the fourth quarter, but the Bishops rose up to score twice in the final four minutes to win 19-6.[13] It was becoming a point of pride with Bruno that he had never lost to any of Asbury's three main rivals (New Brunswick, Neptune, and Long Branch). A third straight win over Long Branch in 1948 would mean more than the other two combined, because it would mean winning that elusive CJ IV title.

Led by third-year fullback John Williams, Asbury Park seemed destined for greatness in 1948. But a slow start (including a preseason loss to West New York's Memorial High School and an injury to Williams) left the Bishops sitting at 1-1-1 in midseason. Bruno was so frustrated that he seriously considered resigning.[14] Then, the tide turned. Williams's ankle healed, the Bishops starting winning, and Asbury's sectional rivals dropped a few games. Provided they could beat Long Branch, they would be right back in the title race.

That wouldn't be easy. This was Army Ippolito's best team since the war, with Barry Rizzo and Eddie Edwards in the backfield and Mike Zoppi at end.[15] The Green Wave were on a three-game winning streak, and always took their game up another notch for Asbury. A Zoppi touchdown catch (in which he literally dragged a defender into the end zone with him) put the Wave up 6-0 at the half. A sudden rainstorm made their position even more secure; it turned the field into a sea of mud and stalled both offenses.

However, the Bishops just kept coming. One particularly vicious tackle knocked Rizzo unconscious and out of the game. Without him, the Brancher offense stalled, and when they turned the ball over on their own 13, the Bishops took advantage. Dick Smith found sophomore Mike Corbo for a touchdown, evening the score at 6-6. With the Brancher defense tiring, Smith added another touchdown pass to Dan Carrido, clinching Asbury's 12-6 triumph.[16]

That was enough to lift Asbury Park to the CJ IV title. In three years, Butch Bruno had brought home the ultimate prize and re-established Asbury Park's ancient superiority over Long Branch. Army Ippolito and his boys, meanwhile, had to be satisfied with another Thanksgiving win over Red Bank. Still, a frustration lingered—Army had beaten Asbury Park three times, but he had never beaten Butch Bruno. Breaking that jinx would have to wait at least another year.

CHAPTER 10
THE POSTWAR SHORE
CONFERENCE, 1946-49

It was the year of the "demobe"—demobilization. World War II had ended in August of 1945, but there was still much work to be done. Returning the over twelve million Americans still in uniformed service (including two-thirds of all men aged eighteen to forty-five) to civilian life was a massive project. So was phasing out years of rationing and converting factories back to civilian production. Throughout the winter of 1945, the United States hung in a strange kind of limbo. It was not until the first warm days of summer 1946 that the end of the war seemed real.

By then, prewar life was beginning to return. This was most obvious at the Jersey Shore, where the end of the blackout meant that the lights on the Boardwalk were literally coming back on. Once again, trainloads of happy beachgoers were crowding the roads and trains heading for the coast. When not vacationing, most Americans searched for something that was at once simpler and harder to define—normal. That meant everything from home-cooked food to weekly trips to the movie theater to a walk down Main Street. The search for normal, and the celebration of its return (whatever that meant) dominated 1946 and the years that followed. The search for entertainment, relaxation, and peace took center stage.

In that respect, the Jersey Shore was no different from the rest of the country. People found their normal by enjoying the sort of pastimes that had been denied them during the war. What followed was a golden age of local organizations, entertainment, and events. In the summertime, Freehold Racetrack was crowded to overflowing, American Legion baseball swelled with the ranks of new players, and the semipro Jersey Shore Baseball League drew large crowds and extensive media coverage. Then, when the weather cooled, they turned their attention to the king of local entertainment—Saturday afternoon high school football.

Even the Shore Conference's smallest schools could draw a few thousand fans for an important regular season game, and everyone played before a packed house on Thanksgiving Day. The excitement took many forms—coffee shop debates, marching band routines, victory parades. The *Asbury Park Press* not only ran game stories, but they also ran daily updates from each high school's practices and printed a weekly injury report. The biggest games were broadcast live on WJLK Radio, and eager ears across Monmouth and Ocean County tuned in.

On the playing field, the late 1940s saw established powers in their glory. First to the top were Arnie Truex's Leonardo Lions, who captured the 1946 Shore Conference crown in dominant style. It was typical Truex football—a punishing defense, disciplined offensive line, and a stable of backs. In the year's decisive game, Truex's Lions took on fellow league power Lakewood. Quarterback Bill Hemberger hit a 72-yard touchdown pass early in the game to give the Lions a 7-0 lead. Lakewood scored to cut it to 7-6, but in the final moments Tony Trezza stuffed Lakewood star Sterling Rozier's attempt to run for the tying conversion.[1] The Lions finished the year 7-1, clinching the title with shutout wins over Atlantic Highlands and Rumson.

In 1947, the torch passed to Manasquan. The Big Blue had been building for this season since 1946, when Head Coach Granville Magee returned from the army. After four years running POW camps in upstate

New York, Magee was ready to get back to the high school he loved.[2] The town was ready, too; Jack Schellenger's wartime teams had kept the Manasquan tradition alive, and Magee returned in 1946 to find a team stacked with talent.

The key was junior Alf Morgan, one of the greatest athletes the town had ever seen. A two-time All-Shore outfielder and a three-time Shore Conference sprint champion, he would have been a Manasquan legend even without football. On the gridiron, though, he was a force. Morgan demoralized teams with consistently effective outside runs, then broke their backs with a sudden and explosive burst for a big play.[3] The result was another long unbeaten streak.

The highlights of those two seasons were epic confrontations with Lakewood, and Morgan played a key role in both. The 1946 game pitted Morgan and his 2-0-2 Warriors against Sterling Rozier and his 4-1 Piners. In a fog so dense that spectators struggled to see the field, Morgan led his team back from a 6-0 fourth quarter deficit. His 38-yard run sparked a 92-yard drive to Frank Fairfax's tying score, and his extra point won the game.[4] Manasquan rolled through the rest of the season, completing an unbeaten year with a Thanksgiving win over Point Pleasant (played in front of 6,000 fans). The two ties cost Manasquan a share of the conference title, but their 7-0-2 record was good enough for the CJ II crown.

Morgan's senior year was even better. The Big Blue started fast, and by the time they met Lakewood for the inside track to the Shore Conference title, their winning streak had reached seventeen games. Well over 2,000 fans filled the bleachers at Ocean County Park for the game that would determine who had the inside track to the Shore Conference title.

The Piners led 7-0 in the fourth when quarterback Jack Anderson hit Morgan for a 39-yard touchdown, cutting the lead to 7-6. Following a defensive stop, the Warriors regained possession with one more chance to score and win. Anderson was the hero, slipping out of the backfield and hauling in a 5-yard touchdown catch to secure a 12-7 victory.[5] That ensured the winning streak extended into Thanksgiving Week, which the Warriors entered with every chance of winning their first league title since

1939. Excitement was at a boiling point, especially since the Garnet Gulls of archrival Point Pleasant were also unbeaten.

Led by triple-threat back Don McIntyre, the Garnet Gulls had baffled the Shore with something very rare for 1947—an all-out aerial assault. McIntyre was completing his passes at an incredible 78 percent clip and was involved in almost all his team's touchdowns. As long as the Point remained within a touchdown heading into the fourth quarter, McIntyre could usually find a way to save the day. Huge crowds filled Clayton Field almost every Saturday to see what their magical superstar would come up with next, and they were rarely disappointed.

Don McIntyre: *"Alfie Morgan was their guy. I was our guy. There were game stories every day leading up to Thanksgiving. . . . That game was everything to us and them."*[6]

In 1950, the combined population of Point Pleasant and Manasquan amounted to slightly over 9,000 people. On Thanksgiving Day 1947, almost that many fans (7,500) turned out for the big game, one of the biggest crowds ever gathered on the banks of the Manasquan. Those who came got their money's worth, since McIntyre and Morgan had both come to play.

McIntyre opened the game with seven straight completions, leading the Gulls down the field to a touchdown and a 6-0 lead. The Warriors answered, taking a 7-6 lead on Paul La Vance's touchdown run and Morgan's extra point. In the fourth, Morgan clinched the game with a dramatic 67-yard touchdown run. Manasquan won the game 14-6 and with it the Shore Conference title, the second in school history.[7]

At season's end, Morgan received both All-Shore and All-State honors, while the Warriors (now unbeaten in twenty-one straight games) were awarded another CJ II crown. Morgan's athletic career continued at North Carolina A&T, where he starred in both football and baseball. In the spring, he set school records for runs scored and stolen bases, while in the fall he led the Aggies to consecutive conference titles and the 1951 National Black College championship. The Morgan family, meanwhile, was just beginning to build its legacy. A long line of Morgans would follow Alf at Manasquan, each of them winning glory for the blue and gray.

Three more, in fact, joined the team the very next year—Meldon, Leonard, and Norman. Despite the loss of Mel to a broken leg, the Warriors still earned a winning record at 4-3-1. The 1948 season, though, belonged to Leonardo. Backs Tony Papa, Pete Trezza, and Ted Lauer had gained valuable experience during the 1947 season, and they broke out in 1948. Lauer, All-Shore in three sports, was a truly spectacular athlete. He followed the dominant Leonardo line to nineteen touchdowns and the Shore scoring title. The final week of the season was the best; Lauer scored six times in six days, as the Lions beat both Atlantic Highlands and Rumson to wrap up the Shore Conference title. Arnie Truex celebrated his fifth championship with a victory ride on the shoulders of his players, who marched him around the field to the cheers of 4,000 spectators. An impromptu parade through Middletown followed.[8]

Leonardo was now clearly the Shore Conference's dominant football power. They would stay near the top over the next three seasons, losing just four games and adding the 1950 CJ II title to their expanding list of honors. However, despite the brilliant play of halfback Pete Trezza, they couldn't bring home another league crown, coming up just short in consecutive seasons.

The 1949 and 1950 titles passed into the hands of two teams that were more typically Shore Conference dark horses. The first was Neptune, which had been waiting impatiently for a title team to come along. The school had excellent facilities and provided its teams with the fancy bright red-and-black uniforms that inspired the Scarlet Fliers nickname. They also had great athletes. Yet due to some bad breaks and strange losses, the Fliers had never put it all together. During the 1940s, those breakdowns became catastrophic and turned Neptune from a contender into a punching bag. By 1945, the Fliers were working on a string of six straight losing seasons, and there was no end in sight.

That November, a collection of parents and local boosters, all of them in agreement that the Neptune athletic program was underachieving, met to form the Red and Black Club. The club did everything from fundraising for a new football field to running a bus trip to Yankee Stadium to watch local hero Joe Vetrano kick for the San Francisco 49ers. They also wanted, and got, a new football coach—Point Pleasant's Joe Vetrano. Fresh off leading the Garnet Gulls to their first ever title, Pagano was rightly regarded as one of the Shore's finest coaches.

He also saw potential in Neptune and was eager to knew what potential Neptune held, and so he agreed to take the job for the 1947 season. At first, Pagano struggled. He was a demanding coach, and some objected to his often harsh, demanding style.[9] His first season was a struggle; the Fliers went 1-8 and lost 40-0 to Asbury Park on Thanksgiving.

It was also a turning point. During Thanksgiving Week, six players (including some starters) skipped a team workout. Pagano removed all six from the team. Neptune still lost, but the coach had made his point—no one was bigger than the team.[10] That issue never arose again. The Scarlet Fliers had taken their first steps on the long journey to the Shore Conference title.

They took more steps in 1947, following the lead of a remarkable end named Billy DeMidowitz. DeMidowitz was supposed to be the glue that held a young team together, and when he dislocated his shoulder late in the summer, Neptune's title hopes seemed to vanish. DeMidowitz, however, gamely rehabbed his shoulder and worked furiously at his kicking. He even managed to plead his way onto the field at the end of the game against title-bound Manasquan, catching two touchdown passes on two plays in Neptune's 27-14 loss to the Big Blue.[11]

It was the turning point of the season. Able only to play a few snaps each game, DeMidowitz made the most out of his limited time. He had two long catches to set up two touchdowns in a 13-7 upset of Leonardo, and he returned a punt to set up another touchdown against Red Bank.[12] His finest hour came on Thanksgiving against Asbury Park. The Bishops led 6-0 late in the game, but DeMidowitz tied the score with a late touchdown catch, holding on despite a jarring hit from an Asbury safety. The game ended in a 6-6 tie, and for once, the Fliers had impressed even their demanding coach.

Joe Pagano: *"I always knew they had it in them, but I never thought they'd be that terrific."*[13]

The late-season surge helped fuel a growing roster, and a growing roster fueled more success. In 1948, the Fliers finished 4-2-2 (their first winning season in a decade) and tied Asbury on Thanksgiving once more. That set the stage for a special 1949 season.

With four great backs in Joe Thoma, Tony Paudano, Walt Jaeger, and Jim Patterson, Neptune could finally run the T formation the way it was meant to be run. That quartet rambled behind an imposing line featuring All-Shore players Marv Atkinson, Lee Kirkpatrick, Tim Holly, and Steve "Tank" Santaniello. The result was the most prolific offense anyone at the Shore had ever seen. The Fliers averaged twenty-seven points per game and buried teams underneath an avalanche of fakes, end-arounds, and counters.

The title was decided in a midseason battle with Leonardo, which entered the game on a fourteen-game unbeaten run. With two minutes to play, Neptune trailed 14-13, and were pinned on their own 35. That's when end Marv Atkinson had a flash of inspiration. He suggested that the Fliers try the old sleeper play, a trick play in which Atkinson would pretend to leave the game for a substitute, but instead kneel in front of the Neptune bench, blending into the crowd on the sidelines. At the snap, he would jump up and race down the field, hopefully uncovered.

It worked perfectly. No one on the Leonardo defense saw Atkinson, who chugged into the end zone with the go-ahead score. Stunned at their sudden turn of bad luck, Leonardo fumbled the ensuing kickoff into the end zone, where Bob Applegate recovered it to cap a 25-13 victory.[14] One week later, the Scarlet Fliers completed their championship season by crushing Freehold Boro 32-0. Lee Kirkpatrick ran for two touchdowns and even Steve Santaniello managed to score on a tackle-around run.[15] Neptune was so dominant that many fans thought they had witnessed the birth of a new dynasty.

That was not to be. The 1949 team was senior heavy, and the 1950 team simply couldn't make up the loss of its stars. The roster shrunk to just thirty-five players (roughly half the size of Leonardo's), and only three of them were returning starters. The numbers shrank with each passing year, and by the mid-1950s, Neptune was only sporadically fielding a JV team. Pagano stepped down after two more losing seasons, and Neptune's wilderness years began; four coaches and eleven seasons lay between them and their next championship challenge.

CHAPTER 11
THE SHORE IN THE EARLY 1950s

NOVEMBER 10, 1951

A nother late autumn Saturday, another Long Branch-Asbury Park game, another capacity crowd at Deal Lake Stadium. This was the sixth straight year that Butch Bruno and Army Ippolito were squaring off, but it never grew old, even for the Green Wave, who frequently had their hearts broken. In 1949, explosive halfback Bob Roberto (the star of an upset win over South River) was injured just before the Asbury game, which the Bishops won, 27-7.[1] 1950 was even more frustrating—Asbury's easy win over Long Branch was the low point of a 1-7-1 season, the worst in Ippolito's career. Improvement in 1951 was a must. Ippolito put it modestly, noting that his team "wasn't great, but we are tougher than last year."[2]

He was wrong; the 1951 team was great. With speedster Howard "Brother" Williams joining All-State workhorse Tony Lubischer in the backfield and end Don D'Amico streaking downfield to catch passes, the Green Wave could score on anybody. They started quietly, tying South River and Plainfield before beating Carteret. Against Morristown, though, they broke out.

The Colonials had humiliated Long Branch three years running, beating them by a combined 117-12. In 1951, therefore, the Wave wanted blood. They got it in more ways than one. First, they had the better of a benches-clearing brawl that started when a Morristown player kicked a prone Brancher in the head. Then, they built a 20-0 lead behind the running of Williams and Tommy Marinelli before turning back a Colonial rally to win 20-19.[3] Having broken one jinx, the Green Wave turned immediately to break another. Asbury Park was next.

Although just 2-4, Asbury was still dangerous, with two explosive backs in Sam Apicelli and Norm Bleemer. Plus, they were playing at home, at Deal Lake Stadium, a traditional house of horrors for the Green Wave. If it weren't for Brother Williams, Long Branch might have crumpled under the pressure. His 37-yard touchdown run in the first half gave Long Branch a 6-0 lead, and his late interception stopped Asbury's final drive and secured the Green Wave's victory.[4] The Asbury jinx broken, the Green Wave brought home the CJ III title by winning their final two games over Red Bank and Princeton. At 7-0-2, they had also wrapped up the first undefeated season in school history. The Wave were the undisputed masters of the Shore.

LABOR DAY WEEKEND, 1950—FREEHOLD

The summer of 1950 had been the tensest and most nerve-wracking since the end of World War II. It was the summer that Korea went from being a difficult question on a high school geography test to a household name. The tension had started in June, when troops from the communist northern half of the peninsula poured across the border and invaded the American-aligned south. The United States responded by transferring men and weapons to the peninsula, supporting the south in their attempt to repel the invasion.

The shadow of war lingered all year. The draft was still in effect, and men from all walks of life were being shipped once again across the ocean to fight a war far from home. Every week, more telegrams arrived notifying the families that their son would not be returning. This more serious business reminded everyone of how small high school sports really were. The same weekend that the season began, news updates sent word that Douglas MacArthur's troops were launching a major counteroffensive into North Korea. Teams prepared for Thanksgiving rivalries the same week that American troops pressed toward the northern border of Korea and Manchuria. Just a few days after the season's end, the People's Republic of China entered the war and its army crossed the Yalu River, changing the tenor of the conflict entirely.

It was a time of anxiety and worry for the entire nation. Nonetheless, it was also a busy tourist season at the Shore. Even an inland town like Freehold grew crowded in the summer. From mid-May to late September, the downtown was jammed with traffic consisting of "beach-bound motorists," farm trucks carrying produce to market, and gamblers headed for the Freehold Raceway.[5] The traffic got worse every summer. People groused and complained about the difficulty of getting around, but still celebrated the business it was bringing to town. After all, times were good in Freehold.

In those days, the town's economy was based around the Karagheusian Rug Mill, which employed over 1,400 workers and shipped wall-to-wall carpeting to office buildings around the country. High prices and plentiful harvests meant that apple farmers in the nearby countryside were also feeling prosperous.[6] Outside of the downtown area, new housing developments were going up every day, as the suburban boom started to make its way to western Monmouth County. Freehold High School, which covered the whole area, was seeing its enrollment explode. Once one of the smallest schools in the Shore, by the end of the decade its graduating classes would top 600 students. With this population shift came a dramatic change in the balance of power across the Shore Conference—the Colonials would be doormats no more.

Since the founding of the league, the County Seaters had been hammered by everyone. The Colonials had not managed a winning season since 1936. Five coaches came and went without any success. One of them, Frank Mozeleski, would eventually become a Hall of Fame coach at Ridgewood High School, but even he was driven to despair at Freehold.

Frank Mozeleski (head coach, 1940): *"This is absolutely the worst situation I've ever seen. From all I can figure out, the kids here just don't care about football. It can't get much worse, but if it does, the school might as well just drop the sport altogether because the expense isn't worth it."*[7]

The tide began to turn under Head Coach Ed Cardner, who tirelessly recruited players out of every hallway and classroom in the school. His teams didn't manage any winning seasons, but he brought new enthusiasm to the program and expanded the size of its football family. The 1949 team had sixty-five players and drew 3,000 fans (the largest in school history) to their Thanksgiving finale.[8] The raw material was there. It was now just waiting for the right spark to ignite it.

As it turned out, the man with that spark was just a few miles south, coaching the Lakewood linemen. For more than a decade, Hal Schank had been learning to win from his own high school coach, Russ Wright. One of Wright's first great athletes, Schank had been a three-sport star for the Piners, a top lineman at Rutgers, and a longtime assistant under his old coach at Lakewood. By 1950, he was ready to build his own program. That year, Schank packed his bags and traveled the short way up Route 9 to his new home at Freehold High School. The Shore Conference would never be the same.

Schank's first look at his new team revealed a serious lack of size. Their best tailback, Dave Johnson, was only 5-4 and 130 pounds. His starting quarterback, Buddy Russell, was described in the *Asbury Park Press* as "diminutive." The line was called unimposing and inexperienced. Things looked bleak.[9] Schank, however, drilled his team carefully all offseason. By the time the season began against Frenchtown, the Colonials were ready. Thanks to two touchdown runs each from Buddy Russell and Willie Mott, Freehold crushed the Terriers 52-6.[10]

Freehold kept winning, and by late October they were undefeated and tied for first place in the Shore with Toms River. A standing-room-only crowd of 2,200 fans packed the Freehold athletic field that cool Saturday afternoon for the biggest game in school history. The air was abuzz with optimism for the future. Just a few days earlier, Allied forces had begun approaching what the press was calling their final positions on the border of Korea and China. The end of the war seemed in sight. There was a real chance that the boys would be home by Christmas.

On the field, meanwhile, the Colonials busied themselves with one of their finest games of the year. Carl Anderson tore off two touchdown runs, and Buddy Russell, the quarterback who was supposedly too small to lead his team to victory, added a crucial touchdown pass. Every time Toms River tried to close the gap, the Monmouth County boys answered with a big play of their own. The clock ran out with Freehold on top 28-14.[11]

Freehold was now on the inside track to the title, and they wouldn't get off it. On Thanksgiving against Neptune, 3,500 fans packed the bleachers with the hope of seeing the home team clinch its first ever Shore Conference championship. The Colonials took an early lead on Bob Kerwin's 25-yard touchdown run, then salted it away in the fourth as Buddy Russell bootlegged to a short score. In just one season, the Colonials had gone from laughingstock to champions.

As the cheering fans looked out at the many talented underclassmen happily milling about on the field, there was a definite feeling in the air that this celebration was a first, and not a last. After the game, the Freehold players made their way home to warm Thanksgiving dinners. Hope was in the air. The Korean War seemed all but over, with only a few short weeks before the boys came home again. It was Thanksgiving 1950, and things were good in Freehold.

LABOR DAY 1951—TOMS RIVER

Less than a year had passed since that happy Thanksgiving of 1950, but the American mood had shifted sharply. The shift had begun just a few days after the holiday, when the "unimaginably numerous" soldiers of the Chinese People's Liberation Army launched a devastating counterattack against the Allied armies. American forces went tumbling back to the 38th Parallel. The Korean War had entered a new and dangerous phase.[12]

As the war turned into something longer and more frustrating than most Americans had expected, the national mood soured, and partisan divides grew more intense (President Truman's decision to fire General MacArthur proved an especially intense flashpoint). The summer of 1951 was a sour one, with Americans fretting grimly over whether this prolonged, bloody war would ever end, and what would be gained from it.[13]

The stalemate also accelerated a fear gripping the United States—the Red Scare. Americans had been concerned about communism for decades, but the dawn of Cold War had intensified American anxieties. Now, many Americans feared that many of their neighbors were disloyal agents of the Soviet Union. Those fears had ebbed and flowed since 1945, often fueled by unscrupulous politicians.[14]

Wisconsin Senator Joe McCarthy was one such opportunist. He claimed to have lists of various lengths identifying known members of the Communist Party who worked in the State Department. He wasn't alone in sounding alarm bells. Evangelist Billy Graham warned that Communists controlled "over 1,100 social-sounding organizations," and a popular book called *Red Channels* warned that actors and entertainers of all kinds were subverting American values. Fears of external attacks also rose, as schools began holding air raid drills and the sales of backyard bomb shelters spiked. It was a very anxious summer.[15]

In that atmosphere, high school football was a welcome distraction, one to which Toms River Head Coach Jack Dalton was very much looking forward to. For the first time in six years, the Indians had a team that looked like they could win the Shore Conference. The excitement had started one year ago on Thanksgiving Day, when the Indians routed

Lakewood 38-0, beating their archrivals for the first time in five years. That allowed Toms River to finish the season 6-1-1, second in the Shore Conference only to Freehold. Best of all, the team's two best players, the Touchdown Twins, Butch Harvey and Carlton Hamilton, were coming back. As juniors, the duo had starred in every sport the high school offered—football, basketball, baseball, and track. They promised to be even better in 1951.

Toms River started 4-0, setting up another midseason showdown with Freehold. The favored Colonials went ahead 7-0 early, but the Touchdown Twins quickly answered with two touchdowns of their own. A goal-line stand preserved Toms River's 14-7 halftime lead, and the Indians went on from there to win 28-7. The wins just kept coming after that, most crucially against Leonardo. Harvey and Hamilton each scored to put Toms River up 13-0, and another late goal-line stand (this one coming on the 6-yard-line as time expired) ensured another victory.

That win left the Indians the Shore's lone remaining unbeaten team. A 28-0 rout of Lakewood, played out in front of 4,000 cheering fans at Ocean County Park, capped things off right. Hamilton scored to clinch his second straight Shore Conference scoring title. After the season, Toms River took home the Shore Conference crown, the CJ II crown, and individual All-Shore berths for Hamilton, end Jim Phillips, and tackle Jim Britton.[16] Butch Harvey went on to win All-Shore honors in baseball, later enjoying a long minor league career before appearing with the San Francisco Giants.

FADING INTO THE BACKGROUND: LAKEWOOD

During the 1930s and 1940s, the Lakewood Piners had been one of the Shore's strongest teams. Russ Wright's teams hit hard, scored via the big play, and drew large crowds of howling fans to every game. Although the postwar Piners won no titles, they were in the hunt in 1946, 1947, and 1948, producing an All-Shore back in each season (Sterling Rozier, Albie Maier, and Herb Kurinsky, respectively). Only a series of close losses to

Leonardo and Manasquan kept the Piners from what easily could have been three straight league championships.[17]

However, all was not well in Lakewood. The school had the worst facilities in the league and its size advantage was vanishing as the population of towns such as Leonardo, Toms River, and Freehold continued to grow. No longer could Lakewood overcome opponents with numbers. Finally, the town itself was in decline. Its days as a winter resort were long gone, and now that the local population was no longer swelled by wartime servicemen, the town's hotels and restaurants struggled to stay open. The poultry farms on the outskirts of towns were also struggling; the declining price of eggs left them in danger of going bust. As tough economic times closed in around the town, its overall athletic fortunes sank into a long decline.

In a different era, reporters would laugh when coaches such as Notre Dame's Lou Holtz professed to be "scared to death" of clearly outmanned opponents. Shore sports reporters made a similar ritual of dismissing Russ Wright's annual claims that Lakewood football was doomed. Every season, he gloomily claimed his team had no depth, then led them to eight victories. By 1949, though, the crisis was real. There were glaring holes in the Lakewood lineup, and only a remarkable season by junior back Bobby George got the Piners as far as a 5-4 record.[18] By 1950, the problems could no longer be hidden. George joined the Army, and a wave of injuries decimated the line.[19] The team finished 1-8, its worst record in many years. Wright resigned that offseason, which ended his problems, but it didn't end Lakewood's.

The number of players shrank (getting as low as twenty-five), and the number of losses grew. As the team's fortunes sank, so did attendance. Some games drew fewer than 500 fans.[20] It was obvious by Thanksgiving 1952 that the glory days were long gone. The Piners had lost twenty-one straight games, and Head Coach Dick Hoffmann had already announced that he planned to resign at season's end. The only thing left was a game against heavily favored Toms River.

Still, that meant a lot, and the Thanksgiving classic drew its usual large crowd of 3,000 fans. The Piners responded by playing their best game in two years and held the Indians scoreless for three quarters. Fred Morris threw a surprise jump pass to Roger Applegate, who then flipped to Walt Samuels on the old hook-and-lateral play. Samuels streaked down the field for the game's only touchdown and Lakewood's only win of the season, a 6-0 thriller.[21] The glory days might have been over, but the pride remained.

THE END OF AN ERA AND THE BIRTH OF DIVISIONS

By 1951, it was clear that enrollment disparities were becoming a serious problem for the Shore Conference. Back in 1936, all member schools had been roughly the same size. After World War II, however, the suburban boom began to create dramatic size differences, and the larger schools (Leonardo, Manasquan, Toms River, and Freehold) began to dominate. Realistically, only half the league was in competition for the Shore Conference title.

No one felt the plight of the small schools quite like tiny Atlantic Highlands. That tight-knit community had always come out in large numbers to watch the red and black. When the borough dedicated its new athletic field in 1949, no less than three marching bands took part in the parade.[22] Those fans cheered some great teams, too—the names Don Rackley and Charlie Mills still rang out in the Highlands. Rackley, the star back in 1945 and 1946, led the football team to consecutive wins over Leonardo (plus a statewide Group I title in basketball). Mills led the Tigers to a sectional title in football in 1948.

Unfortunately, such runs were growing more difficult. The gap between large and small schools was growing fast, and no amount of toughness or cleverness could make up the difference. In 1949, when Head Coach Vince "Roxy" Finn took over the program, the Tigers had thirty-six players on the roster. By 1953, that number was twenty-five.[23] Finn's teams compiled a total record of 6-43 between 1949 and 1955 and grew less competitive with each passing season. Their final victory came in 1954, when Don Loftus ran for two touchdowns in a 19-6 win over Allen-town.[24]

Loftus returned in 1955, the only veteran player on the final football team that would ever take the field for Atlantic Highlands High School. Injuries mounted early on, with Loftus suffering a concussion in a de-moralizing 41-7 loss to Keyport. The Tigers played their final game on October 23, at home against Point Pleasant, losing three more starters to injury and dropping the game 43-7. For Finn and the Board of Educa-tion, it was the last straw.[25]

> **Roxy Finn**: *"We never minded losing because we love to play foot-ball up here and we think that is the main thing. We want the sport and think that it is good, but we are not going to play it at the sacrifice of someone's health."*[26]

Highlands, later known as Henry Hudson Regional, had given up football, but not its proud sports tradition. They were especially com-petitive in basketball, winning a Shore Conference Tournament title in 1969. Roxy Finn's legacy, however, is much bigger than that. He actively coached multiple sports until 1962, when he stepped back to become a full-time athletic director, a job he held until 1984. He was a beloved fig-ure at Atlantic Highlands, and his players all admired and respected him. Perhaps the greatest tribute to the Highlands football program is that so many of its graduates went on to become educators themselves.

Charlie Mills spent sixteen years as the principal at Hempstead High School on Long Island and was so beloved they named the football field after him. He hired former Highlands running back Spencer Keys as one of his teachers; Keys also coached football, started the Hempstead lacrosse program, and eventually became the first African American superinten-dent of Baltimore Public Schools. Two other teachers, Jack Seeley and Joe Ash, became successful baseball coaches, with Ash spending fifteen years back at Highlands.

Herb Reed was another Highlands boy who came back to the Shore, although he had to go the long way to get there. After fighting in Korea, Reed used athletics to play his way through degree programs at Winston-Salem State and Shippensburg College. He returned to the Shore in the early 1960s, at a time when he was one of the only Black coaches in the area. He would spend thirty-two years as an assistant track and football coach at Red Bank. Then there was Dick Kleva, an All-Shore center for Finn who would go on to NYU before returning home to assemble some of the greatest teams ever seen in Middletown.

Atlantic Highlands was an extreme case. Their small-school compatriots, Point Pleasant and Matawan, were still able to enjoy success against schools of similar size. Under Coach Bill Stratton, Point Pleasant's daring passing attack made them one of the Shore's stronger teams. They finished 7-1 in 1947, winning a sectional crown and narrowly missing a Shore Conference title. The 1949 team rode dual-threat quarterback George Rennard and halfbacks Wes Gale and Billy Johnson to a share of the CJ I crown, upsetting Toms River and Freehold on their way to a 5-1-2 finish.[27] Johnson was All-Shore in both 1950 and 1951, and ensured that 1950's Thanksgiving turkey tasted right by scoring two touchdowns to beat Manasquan.[28]

Matawan too had a proud football identity, built by Head Coaches Paul Bednard and Tony Nuccio. The Huskies were known for playing punishing power football out of the single-wing formation. A string of great backs, most notably future Cleveland Brown Ed Weber ("the Laurence Harbor Flash") and Doug Marvel ("the Husky Whip") kept the team winning and competing.[29] After near misses in 1946 and 1947, they won the CJ I crown in 1948, with Marvel scoring two touchdowns in a Thanksgiving win over Keyport to clinch the title.[30]

At Keyport, Stan "Tuffy" Baker was doing the same thing. On Thanksgiving Day 1949, the Red Raiders upset Matawan 7-0. It was a golden moment in what was rapidly turning into one of the Shore's biggest holiday spectacles. Every year, the game drew over 3,000 fans, with both schools hosting pregame pep rallies and dances. The usually triumphant Matawan fans would celebrate by driving through downtown Keyport, waving banners and flags. The Red Raiders finally got one back when Bill Belleran's touchdown run sent Keyport home happy with a 7-0 victory. The tone was set for a rivalry that would only grow fiercer in the 1950s.

THE RETURN OF PAROCHIAL FOOTBALL—RED BANK CATHOLIC

In the earliest years of the United States, Catholics were a tiny minority, concentrated mostly in Maryland and Northern Virginia. Starting in the 1800s, that changed—huge waves of Irish and German immigrants came to the United States, bringing their religion with them. In the second half of that century, further waves of immigration from Eastern and Southern Europe brought an even more diverse population of Catholics onto American soil. They often faced overt religious discrimination and were accused of being sleeper agents for the Pope in Rome. In hopes of protecting themselves from bigotry and preserving their cultural traditions, they established a network of parochial schools, one which soon stretched from coast to coast.

By the 1940s, that sort of anti-Catholic prejudice was no longer institutionalized in the United States, especially not in immigrant-dominated New Jersey (where Catholicism represented the largest single religious denomination). The importance of Catholic education, however, remained. In those days, the hierarchy of the Catholic Church placed a high value on schools. Most parishes that could afford it were at least running an elementary school, and almost all the state's major cities were home to multiple Catholic high schools.

At that time, though, the Shore's Catholic population was (like everything else in the area) much smaller than it would one day become. When World War II ended, the only two Catholic high schools in the area were St. Rose (in Belmar) and Red Bank Catholic. Neither played football— RBC had briefly experimented with a team in the 1920s, and St. Rose (as we have seen) had done the same just before World War II. Both faced the same difficulties—small student bodies and low athletic budgets.

George Jones (RBC student, 1930s): *"Of course in those days, we didn't have any facilities for sporting events. We'd have to borrow the gymnasium at the River Street School for our basketball*

*. . . we didn't have a football team cause we were only paying ten
cents a week for book rent and the parishioners couldn't afford the
football and the uniforms and all that.*[31]

Things began to change in the fall of 1945. World War II was over,
high school football was booming statewide, and the students of Red
Bank Catholic wanted in on the fun. Monsignor James Byrnes decided to
provide the boys with an outlet and coached a few informal games. The
team was reasonably competitive, and occasionally drew a crowd, pulling
in 500 fans for a Thanksgiving game against Pope Pius (Passaic). The arrival of a new pastor, Monsignor James Casey, provided the impetus for
the team to take the next step.

Casey loved sports, especially football, and one of his dearest ambitions
was to bring a winning team to the high school. He sought out a coach
who could help build that team, eventually finding one in Holy Cross
football star and former Marine captain Adam Kretowicz. It seemed that
everyone who met Kretowicz was impressed by him; the *Asbury Park Press*
went so far as to dub him a "man of destiny." He was named head coach
and athletic director, and under his direction RBC players were pushed
to be the best. The school even arranged a training table that provided
a three-course meal after practice four nights a week. The games themselves, which were played on Sunday mornings, had a special atmosphere.
Crowds of parishioners on their way home from Mass would stop to cheer
on the home team. Monsignor Casey was also present, filming the game
so that the team could review the "pictures" during the week.[32]

RBC's energetic building program, however, made it difficult to find
games. Some local teams feared that the Caseys (unbounded by any geo-
graphic limits to their student population) would start recruiting athletes
from across Monmouth County and turn into a powerhouse. Very few
Shore Conference schools were willing to play the newcomers. The team
was forced to wander the state, scheduling what Kretowicz bitterly called
a "suicide card" against established North Jersey parochial powers.[33] To
everyone's surprise, the Caseys handled it fairly well, finishing 4-4-1 and
claiming a major upset over powerful Trenton Catholic.

Leading the way in that late season surge was a rugged freshman back named Jack Keelen. Keelen, a fan favorite, would star for the Caseys over the next two years. Newspapers loved to report on the season's enduring image—Keelen stiff-arming defenders as he rumbled down the field for another 7-yard gain.[34] His sophomore year, 1947, saw the Caseys improve to 4-3-1, with another notable win over Trenton Catholic and an upset of defending CJ I champions Sayreville. The Caseys claimed the Parochial B South crown, their first football title.

They had also played a Monmouth County foe for the first time—Rumson. The game was a scoreless tie, but the natural rivalry nonetheless drew almost 1,000 fans.[35] It would be nearly a decade before the rivalry turned into a Thanksgiving classic, but the groundwork was already being laid. It was also seemingly being laid for a 1948 season that promised glory.

The 1948 calendar year started with great promise. Sports-mad RBC students cheered a competitive basketball team and a sectional champion baseball team. When football started in the fall, the roster swelled to seventy-five players and drew ever-larger crowds for its home game. After victories over Seton Hall Prep and St. Mary's of Rutherford, the fighting Caseys were 3-1 and well on their way to a second consecutive title. But trouble was brewing.

Those bruising wins generated hostility, which proved to be RBC's undoing. St. Mary's coach Frank Ruggerio filed a complaint with the NJSIAA that Keelen was overage. The resulting investigation disproved that but did reveal that Keelen was academically ineligible.[36] The Caseys forfeited all three of their wins and without Keelen lost their next five.

The *Asbury Park Press* had little sympathy for the Caseys, cheerfully describing the losses that followed Keelen's ineligibility. After one loss, the *Press* reported that "a Casey team without Jack Keelen is no team at all" and dubbed the team "disorganized and inept."[37] Chastened, RBC backed off its pursuit of football glory. The next three seasons were all losing campaigns. It was obvious that the Caseys were not going to be a football power just yet.

They had, however, established themselves as a fixture in the Shore sports world. Kretowicz stayed on as a multisport coach for two more competitive seasons before leaving for Sayreville. By then, RBC was a member of the NJSIAA and had gotten an annual game with Red Bank High School on the schedule. The first game was played on the first day of the 1951 season, starting a tradition that would last for thirty years. RBC football was not at the top of the heap, but they weren't about to disappear anytime soon.

CHAPTER 12
THE SHORE IN THE MIDDLE
1950s

Although it was only noon and the gates of Long Branch's Ted Bressett Field were not scheduled to open for another half hour, a crowd was already forming. By the time the game kicked off the bleachers would be jam-packed with 5,500 fans, most of them wrapped in blankets to ward off the cold. A new chapter was about to be written in the epic, seemingly unending war between Long Branch and Asbury Park. Over the past four years, the two teams had pushed each other to new heights—sectional honors, state honors, and the pursuit of the mythical state championship of New Jersey were all becoming regular occurrences. This year, the two teams had but a loss and a tie between them, and both were in the hunt for sectional and state honors. Everything was possible and only one thing was certain for the eager spectators, lining the bleachers and track—these were the glory days.

Joe Valenti (Long Branch resident): *"You went to the games. Everybody went to the games. It was the thing to do . . . I never missed a home game. I joined the band in the seventh and eighth* *grade just to see the games. My clarinet got me to the night games at New Brunswick."[1]*

Bill Bruno (son of Butch Bruno): *"I grew up on the bus rides and in my dad's locker rooms. My buddies and I all remember being in the locker room smelling my dad's smoke come out of his office under the Asbury Park Stadium. We all understand now how great it was to be a part of that. I remember traveling up the Parkway to places like Perth Amboy, New Brunswick, Thomas Jefferson, Trenton Central. I had the pleasure of walking the sidelines and I remember every Saturday morning when Asbury Park played at home, my dad would send me over to pick up chewing gum and cigars from his favorite deli, three blocks from the stadium. So, I'd run down to the deli, pick up my dad's water, bring it back to him . . . life was good."[2]*

Throughout the 1950s, summer attendance records were repeatedly broken as happy crowds filled the boardwalks and hotels of the Shore. The streets were lined with cars filling every available spot, the beaches packed with eager bathers, and the boardwalk noisy from the sounds from the pinball machines, bumper cars, and roller coasters. The opening of expressways across the state only promised better times to come. Although the New Jersey Turnpike (opened in 1951) did not run directly to the Shore, it did herald a new age of travel. Instead of fighting traffic jams through town after town, one could zip along the highway at sixty miles an hour. For New Jerseyans, it was a totally new way to drive.

Asa Hall: *"'Before the Turnpike . . . it was a drag—you'd go up and down Route 1, you'd have to stop for lights and there were all sorts of delays. The first time [we drove on the Turnpike] I thought we must be taking the same trip but in heaven. You could just get on it and run."[3]*

The Garden State Parkway soon followed. Governor Alfred Driscoll spearheaded the project, which began in 1952. By August 1954, the road stretched from Union County into Southern Ocean County. At first, it seemed like a blessing for Asbury Park—more Shore visitors. As years went by, however, it became clear that the town had suffered a serious blow. Asbury Park was essentially a conservative, nostalgic town. The staid boardwalk resisted adding the wilder rides and louder games of places like Seaside and Wildwood. And now, for the first time, those places could compete with Asbury for daily visitors.

A sign of the times came in 1955, when Frankie Lymon and the Teenagers performed at Convention Hall. The concert turned into a riot when teenagers (the spectators, not the band) abruptly began fighting each other and spilled out into the streets. The city's police blamed the bad influence of rock music, which the city council briefly banned from the Boardwalk. It was not the sort of move that attracted many young visitors.

Asbury's resistance to change was starting to undermine it from within, as well. The West Side was hurting badly, and nothing was really being done about it. Even integration was slow and mostly symbolic. The two major moves since the war had been the end of segregation at the Bangs Avenue Elementary School and the hiring of a single Black patrolman for the police department. Meanwhile, residential segregation continued to worsen. Much of the city's white population was leaving, moving out to the suburban housing developments of nearby Ocean Township. The same pattern could be seen in Long Branch, where many white families departed for new developments in West Long Branch.

Still, the impact of those shifts was a few years away. In 1956, Asbury remained the shopping hub of the northern shore, the jewel of the Jersey Coast, and Long Branch ran not far behind. Their respective football teams remained the class of Monmouth and Ocean County because the booming suburban towns still sent their students to the city high schools. The ground was shifting beneath their feet, but the summer was still summer, the Boardwalk was still the Boardwalk, and on fall afternoons, football was still football.

Both teams had their tried-and-true formulas. Army Ippolito's Long Branch teams ran some of the most intricate offenses in the Shore, mixing and matching various formations to hide a single superstar back who could explode for three or four touchdowns on any given afternoon. Butch Bruno's teams, meanwhile, ran a stable of backs behind the toughest linemen in the Shore, whipped into shape by Veteran Assistant Coach Lachman Rinehart. What the two teams had in common, though, was that they always played with heart, and frequently found that extra spark late in the game as they rallied past a tired foe.

After a rare losing season in 1951, Bruno's Bishops bounced back in 1952, running up a 5-3-1 record. Guard George Wilson and tailback Sam Apicelli both were named to the All-Shore team, while the coach's nephew, Jim Bruno, played a key role on defense, returning a fumble 30 yards for the winning touchdown against New Brunswick.[4] Only a narrow 7-2 loss to Plainfield kept the Bishops from winning the CJ IV title (that Plainfield team featured future Olympic decathlete and gold medalist Milt Campbell).[5]

The game of the season was, as usual, against Long Branch. Army's 1952 edition was thinner than the 1951 team of destiny but was still talented and with a stable of backs that included Brother Williams, Buck Loftland, and quarterback Ward Britton. Britton, though, broke his jaw against Linden, seemingly dooming the Green Wave's hopes for a CJ III title. They had no quarterback, and South River was waiting.[6] The Green Wave, though, were mentally and physically tougher than most teams. Army Ippolito's intensity and training methods had the team well-prepared for any adversity.

> **Elliott Denman (Asbury Park Press sportswriter)**: *"The original 'Burma Road' remained half a planet away but the essence of it was transported to Monmouth County in the 1950s. It evolved into a jogging path around the perimeter of the Long Branch High School property and was capped by two laps around the school's quarter mile track. The Burma Road trek became a Thursday afternoon tradition."*[7]

Bill George (former Long Branch captain): *"It was one way he got everybody hustling. A lot of times, he hustled right along with the team. We worked hard but we had fun along the way."*[8]

It all paid off against South River. The Rams led 7-0 early, but backup quarterback Eddie Bruno rallied the Wave. In the words of the *Asbury Park Press,* their determination to win the game for Britton had "welded [them] into a cold fury." Bruno threw two touchdown passes and ran for another as the Branchers rallied for a narrow 26-20 victory.[9] It was this rolling Wave team that did battle with Asbury Park in 1952 on a rainy afternoon in Long Branch.

That was when the Green Wave magic ran out. The Branchers suffered through a miserable afternoon that saw their CJ III title hopes collapse in rain and muck. Touchdown runs by Sam Apicelli and Bill Mayes helped the Bishops build an early lead, then hang on for a 16-13 victory.[10] The Branchers had to settle for a 6-3 finish and another Thanksgiving rout of Red Bank (a game in which Brother Williams capped his brilliant career with two touchdown runs).[11] Asbury Park, meanwhile, accepted their 5-3-1 finish with some satisfaction. They had beaten Long Branch, and the team's future looked bright.

The year 1953 was a good one to be in Asbury Park. A broiling summer drew record-breaking crowds to the Shore, cheering all the locals. Those same locals were treated that fall to one of the greatest of all Asbury Park teams. The 1953 Bishops had one of the most powerful lines in their history, featuring two All-Shore ends (Tony DeAngelis and sophomore George Stephenson), an All-Shore guard (James Leone), and an All-Shore center (James Albano). The backfield starred Bill Myers at fullback, Andy Garrity and Barry Stewart at halfback, and Harry Grodberg at quarterback. This was a team, the locals thought, that could go all the way.

The North Jersey papers didn't think that way at first, instead tabbing traditional powers, such as Montclair, Clifton, Hackensack, Memorial (West New York), and Jersey City's St. Peter's Prep as the main title contenders.[12] As the season went on, however, it became clear that the Blue Bishops were the equal and perhaps the superior of all those teams. They started with overwhelming victories over Garfield and New Brunswick, thunderous routs that allowed the Bishops to "barge into the front ranks of New Jersey High school football."[13]

Irvington was tougher, but the churning legs of Meyers pushed the team down the field for the game-winning touchdown midway through the third quarter. Stewart had scored in every game, and Harry Grodberg had piled up six touchdowns in less than a month.[14] As the Long Branch game approached, Asbury continued to climb in the state rankings, and by November it was clear that the still-undefeated Bishops had a rare shot at a state title.

If things were going as well as they could have in Asbury, they were going as poorly as possible in Long Branch. Injuries had ended the season of halfback Buck Loftland and forced end Mike Ippolito into limited duty. The undermanned Branchers fought bravely against Asbury Park, putting on a show for almost a half, but in the end the capacity crowd at Deal Lake Stadium saw what it really wanted. Barry Stewart's 75-yard interception return for a touchdown and two scoring runs by Bill Meyers helped Asbury pull away for a 41-7 victory.[15] Meanwhile, the North Jersey powers were falling like dominoes—undefeated East Orange beat previously undefeated Montclair, then lost themselves to an underdog Orange team. That last upset occurred the same day that the Blue Bishops crushed Newark South Side 38-7, and it allowed them to take the top spot in the state polls. It was the first time since 1940 that they'd held that spot, and comparisons to the great teams of the past quickly began.

On Thanksgiving 1953, 5,500 fans filled Deal Lake Stadium to watch the Bishops dispatch 5-3 Woodbridge. Barry Stewart caught a touchdown pass and ran for another, giving him touchdowns in all nine games. The score was just 13-0, but the outcome had never been in doubt. For the first time since the days of Jack Netcher, Asbury Park had finished with a perfect record. They were No. 1 in all of New Jersey. Butch Bruno had returned his alma mater to the mountaintop.[16] The honors kept pouring in. Grodberg was first-team All-State, tackle Tony DeAngelis second team, and sophomore end George Stephenson second-team All-Group IV.

Bruno's next challenge was to keep his team at the top. He had a lot of talent back (Stewart, Garritty, and Meyers were all in the backfield), but they also had to face a schedule full of old rivals gunning for them. The 1954 season-opener saw New Brunswick upset the Bishops, ending their thirteen-game winning streak and sending quarterback Garritty to the reserves with an injury.[17] Even that didn't rattle the defending champions, though. Bruno introduced Tommy Steckbeck into the lineup, and Asbury was soon back on the winning track. Thanks to some unexpected help from their archrivals, the Bishops were soon back in the CJ IV race as well.

Long Branch was young that season, built around a remarkable sophomore talent named Avan "Bobo" Reeves. Their record was a misleading 4-4-1; the team was anything but average. When the Branchers were playing well, they could beat anybody. They proved that in midseason, upending South River and New Brunswick in consecutive weeks. The New Brunswick game, in which the Wave ambushed the undefeated Zebras 33-6, was especially wild.

Two weeks after the New Brunswick upset, an overflow crowd of 5,000 fans ringed the Long Branch athletic field, anticipating a duel between "Bobo" Reeves and the Asbury backfield. They saw a classic. Long Branch struck first, with Reeves setting up a Bob Robinson touchdown run with his 48-yard dash. Meyers answered the bell for Asbury on the ensuing kickoff, following perfect blocking on his way to an electrifying 94-yard score and a 7-6 lead. Robinson and Reeves led the counterattack, smashing into the line on a 64-yard drive to a Robinson touchdown run of 16 yards. Meyers responded in the third quarter with a performance that pushed the *Asbury Park Press* to describe it in unusually dramatic terms.

> **Asbury Park Press:** *"His performance was brutish. On each play he was directed through guard or tackle, and he made no pretense at cleverness, just put his head down and plowed, dragging four or five Wave tacklers."[18]*

He tied the game with a short run, and in the fourth quarter, when Long Branch went to the air, he came up with the game's key interception. It set up Garritty's 38-yard run to the goal line and allowed Meyers to win the game with his third touchdown. Asbury was now back in command of the CJ IV race.[19] Wins over Middletown and Woodbridge finished the job, and for the first time since 1940-41, Asbury Park had won consecutive titles. Long Branch gained some consolation by routing Red Bank, 29-0, a game in which Reeves led the way and clinched his first All-Shore appearance.[20]

Butch Bruno had his eyes on a third straight title, a feat not achieved since his own high school days. The stars of previous years were off to college—Bill Meyers would play fullback at Syracuse, Andy Garrity baseball at Fordham, and Joe Kremer three years at tackle for Albright—but a new group had emerged to replace them. Frank Wojciehowicz, son of Fordham football legend Alex Wojciehowicz, was the quarterback in an explosive backfield that featured Steckbeck and speedster Nate Bruno (the head coach's nephew). Lachman Rinehart had turned out another one of his traditionally powerful lines, anchored by guard Richie Napolitani, tackle Dave Feeney, and end Clarence Holland.

Army Ippolito, too, was chomping at the bit. Halfback Bobo Reeves was back, as were fullback Mike Ippolito (the coach's son), quarterback Arnie Elmore, scatback "Little Joe" Graziano, and outstanding tackle Frank Mazza. The Green Wave had a rare opportunity, and Ippolito felt that if the team stayed together, they had a real chance to go all the way.[21]

A slow 1-1-1 start left Asbury with plenty of ground to make up in the CJ IV race, but Tommy Steckbeck's touchdown run powered a 6-0 win over Plainfield and put them right back into it. Routs of Perth Amboy and Freehold (which had won twenty-one straight games coming in) kept the momentum going and set the stage for a showdown with undefeated Long Branch. Reeves provided the Green Wave with their scoring punch, while Mazza anchored an impenetrable defense. The more they won, the faster they climbed the statewide polls. Many of the state's top teams were picking up losses and ties, and if the Branchers could beat Asbury Park, there was a good chance that they could finish the year as the state's top team.

Butch Bruno: *"Long Branch had better have plenty of respect for Asbury Park. If my team plays like it did against Plainfield, we'll beat them. We beat Plainfield in the line, and we're ready to do the same thing to Long Branch."*[22]

An overflow crowd of 8,000 fans mobbed Deal Lake Stadium for the year's biggest game. As Bruno had predicted, the Blue Bishops dominated on the line, and Tommy Steckbeck stood out among a crowded field of talented backs, running for 139 yards. Up front, Holland and Napolitani carved holes in the Brancher line on offense and contained Reeves and Ippolito on defense. Long Branch's only threat of the day crested and broke at the 24-yard line, and Reeves could never seem to find a way into the clear. "Bobo," however, was too talented a player to go quietly. His play at safety kept the Bishops from getting any big plays, and when Steckbeck broke free late in the game, Reeves ran him down from behind at the 18. The inspired Brancher defense, led by linebacker Alex Saharic and his vicious tackling, held the line from there. The game ended in a bitterly fought 0-0 tie.[23]

The tie cost both teams. Asbury finished 5-1-3, a strong record, but not quite strong enough to retain the CJ IV crown.[24] Long Branch finished 8-0-1 and won the CJ III title, but they narrowly missed out on a state crown that ultimately went to Montclair. Still, both teams could be proud of both the season they had enjoyed and the future success of their graduates.[25] Asbury's Dave Feeney went on to Cornell, where he started three years at guard and won All-Ivy honors as a senior in 1959. His Long Branch rival Mike Ippolito went to Princeton, playing football and baseball for the Tigers. Ippolito capped his athletic career in 1960 by winning the Roper Award, given each year to the university's outstanding scholar-athlete.[26]

And thus back to 1956. Long Branch had unfinished business from the year before, trying to knock off Asbury Park and bring in the school's first overall state title. They had a fantastic backfield, starring Reeves (now in his third year as a starter and on his way to scoring twenty touchdowns) and Joe Graziano.

Mike Ippolito: *"He wouldn't go down. He was just relentless . . . He'd bowl you over. Defensive players would pay the price."*[27]

Reeves had only one rival that year—Asbury Park's junior halfback Frank Budd. The Shore had only rarely seen anyone like him. Budd was born in Long Branch in 1939 to two former runners, but in the early years of his life it didn't seem like Frank would ever run. A childhood illness left his right leg weak and smaller than his healthy left leg. A combination of will, determination, and his mother's homemade remedy (a special oil made from goose grease, nutmeg, mutton fat, and witch hazel) allowed him to overcome the issue. By the time Budd was in high school, he was running everywhere.[28] It wasn't long before his classmates took notice.

John Morton (classmate and friend of Frank Budd): *We used to have a high school Olympics at Asbury Park, and he would win [the team title] . . . all by himself. . . . Many of us are still so proud of him because he was such a nice guy, a nice person. He was very, very quiet, no braggadocio about him. He was only cocky when he participated in sports."*[29]

Budd's best sport was track, where as a junior he won Shore Conference championships in three separate events. During his senior year, he became the first high schooler in the area to run the 100-yard dash in under ten seconds. He went on to win state championships in the 100 and 220. That blazing speed would eventually take him to the 1960 Rome Olympics. His favorite sport in high school, though, was football.

Bill Bruno (son of Asbury Park Head Coach Butch Bruno): *"Frank Budd actually used to come over on Thanksgiving and have dinner with us. My dad and his dad were fast friends. Frank and his family would come over for Thanksgiving, just prior to the years that he went to the Olympics, when he was still at Villanova. They'd come over, and we'd break bread together. Frank was just a great young person. Very personable, and a very talented athlete."*[30]

In the fall of 1956, the lightning-quick Budd ran wild in season-opening wins over South River and New Brunswick, tearing off three exhilarating touchdown sprints in two dominant victories over respected opponents.[31] And then, surprisingly, the Bishops temporarily lost their footing with a loss to Union and a tie with Plainfield. They recovered to crunch Perth Amboy and overwhelm Freehold, but they were out of the sectional title race. The only consolation prize remaining for them was a potential victory over Long Branch.

Nobody really thought they could do it. Bobo was scoring at will, and the Brancher defense was stifling every opponent. Not since Army Ippolito himself had played quarterback had the town seen a team like this. As the weather cooled, and opponents fell one by one, it became clear that the last team with a chance to stop the Green Wave was Asbury Park. Who else could it have been? The entire season came down to the Shore's greatest rivalry.

Asbury Park Press: *"For 48 hysterical minutes, 5,500 screaming, stomping grownups and teenagers rocked the high school athletic field. The victory was as victory should be. Hard fought, at times uncertain, and finally an intoxicating reward for students who believed unwaveringly in their teams."*[32]

Asbury Park threatened first, driving to the Long Branch 1, where they faced fourth and goal. The decisive play was a meeting of two legendary athletes—Bruno called for a dive to Frank Budd, only for Bobo Reeves to meet him in the hole and stuff him short of the goal line. Long Branch answered by driving to the Asbury 26 before a fumble halted their drive. Asbury immediately took advantage—Nate Bruno tore off a 30-yard run into Long Branch territory, then carried the ball twice more to the Asbury 2. On the next play, a double reverse to Budd resulted in a touchdown and put the Bishops ahead 6-0.

Long Branch tied the game on defense; Bill George stripped Budd at the 30, and John Carroll scooped it up and ran for a touchdown to even the score at 6-6. It stayed that way deep into the fourth, when special teams decided the game. With two minutes to go, Asbury was punting.

Reeves, deep in Long Branch territory and trying to make something happen, ran up to try to return a bouncer. He couldn't field it cleanly, and instead the Bishops recovered at the 13 going in. The Green Wave defense made the Bishops fight for every inch of ground, but the outcome seemed inevitable to everyone who knew the way this rivalry always went. On fourth and goal from the 2, Nate Bruno powered into the end zone for the winning touchdown.[33]

The loss was devastating, but it didn't ruin Long Branch's season. The Green Wave finished 8-1 by beating Red Bank on Thanksgiving Day, a win that wrapped up the CJ III title. Avan Reeves scored twice that day, giving him a Shore-area single-season record with 122 points. He played football at Indiana, then left to join the Marines, serving two tours of duty in Vietnam. After returning home, he became a Long Branch community leader for many years.

Asbury, meanwhile, won their final two games, beating Woodbridge and Middletown on Thanksgiving. Although they did not win the CJ IV crown, a 7-1-1 record and victory over Long Branch gave the Bishops plenty to celebrate.[34] On Thanksgiving 1956, the turkey tasted good in both Long Branch and Asbury Park, home to the kings of the Shore.[35]

THE SHORE CONFERENCE FROM 1952 TO 1956

While Asbury Park and Long Branch were enjoying their most glorious of glory days, the Shore's smaller towns were also in high spirits. The 1952 presidential election saw Dwight Eisenhower, the hero of World War II, sweep to a landslide electoral victory for the Republican Party. His popularity crossed party lines; his genial smile and glowing record inspired many Democrats to split their tickets and vote "Ike" for President. He carried New Jersey easily, winning over 70 percent of the vote at the Shore. Eisenhower's eight years in office proved to be good times for the area. The Korean War ended, and the economy boomed.[36] So did the population—Monmouth County's population increased by almost half, while Ocean County's nearly doubled. The area's sleepy farm towns were giving way to the suburbs.

The changes in Middletown were typical. At the end of World War II, Middletown was not one cohesive township but instead a collection of little villages separated by long stretches of farmland. Even the name of its high school, Leonardo, was a reminder that the town's sections were very much distinct. By the early 1950s, though, housing developments were beginning to fill in the gaps between neighborhoods, and a single identity was emerging. In 1952, the Board of Education officially dropped the Leonardo name and asked the papers to do the same.

When the school did appear in the paper, it was usually for high school sports, and in 1952 Middletown High School sports meant Arnie Truex. The gruff, hard-driving Truex had produced winning teams in football, basketball, and baseball, claiming seven Shore Conference championships (four in football, three in baseball). He found success using the old ways. Other teams might embrace the deceptive new T formation, but Truex preferred to stick to straight-ahead power plays out of his favored Notre Dame Box formation. Usually, Middletown's opponents simply crumbled beneath the Lions relentless onslaught.

Matawan Independent: *"While other mentors bring in the fast-moving T or other types of deception, 'Uncle Arnie' uses the same old box formation. He storms and rants and raves, but he wins ball games."*[37]

In 1952, Truex knew that he had another title contender. The Lions had a tremendous line featuring guard John Trezza and All-Shore ends Ernie "Nipper" Vaughan and Al Ecklof. When they wanted to run the ball, they handed off to punishing fullback John Schultheis.[38] They rolled to a 9-0 record and won the Shore's first ever Class A title. In most games, Middletown's defense was simply so dominant that teams were psychologically beaten before the half. They won their final three games of the season by shutout, capping one of their most impressive title seasons yet. After the season, Vaughan accepted a football scholarship to Syracuse, starting on the Orange's 1959 national title team.

Many of Vaughan's teammates returned in 1953, and Truex hoped that his team would become the first in league history to win consecutive championships. Instead, Freehold's football program was about to reach heights that no Shore Conference program had ever reached. The borough of Freehold and the towns that surrounded it were booming in the 1950s, as huge new housing tracts began to replace the old farmland of Western Monmouth County. The packed school building, with its lunch line spilling out of the cafeteria and into its narrow hallways, was a testament to the area's rapid growth. So were the dominant Colonial teams.[39]

It helped that their head coach was an innovator. At a time when most teams had their best players going both ways, Hal Schank not only used separate offensive and defensive units, but he also rushed new sets of players on for special teams as well. Colonial players were both fresher and more specialized than their opponents, a major advantage on game day.[40] The football team may have changed for practice in the high school's old agricultural building (sitting on feed bags and dodging tractors while they dressed), but their method of victory was all new.[41]

Not everyone loved Schanck's teams, though. Frustrated opponents grumbled that his Colonials teams employed dirty play (an accusation thrown at the Lakewood teams coached by Schank's mentor, Russ Wright). Others accused him of holding illegal summer practices and secretly enrolling athletes from outside the Freehold school district.[42] But there also may have been darker motives for the accusations.

In 1953, Schanck moved halfback Jackie Mayes to quarterback, making him the first African American quarterback in the history of the Shore Conference. That alone would have raised eyebrows, but Freehold's team that year went a step further by fielding the Shore's first all-Black backfield—Mayes at quarterback, Nalton Goode and Danny Lewis at halfback, and Stan Nixon at fullback.[43] The Shore Conference had never been a segregated league, but the Jersey Shore was not free of racial prejudice, and this move drew some ugly reactions from Colonial opponents. Years later, Freehold players would recall racial comments made by opposing fans, players, and even coaches. Schanck, however, never wavered or backed down in supporting his players. Neither did the people of

Freehold, who were thoroughly enjoying the novel experience of being home to a football powerhouse.[44]

It was fun to root for the Colonials in 1953. They were the clear pre-season favorite, and they were deep at every position, from that standout backfield to a massive line anchored by towering tackle Pollard Stanford. The star, though, was Danny Lewis. Lewis had emerged as a junior, showing flashes of brilliance with the occasional long touchdown run. Although he was passed over for a place on the All-Shore team that year, intelligent observers knew just how good he was. As a senior, he made so much noise that it was impossible to ignore him.

> **Hal Schank**: *"Of course we had a lot of good athletes come out of Freehold, but Danny Lewis was as good as they came. He had everything. He was a big guy who had the speed, too, and he was a great team player."*[45]

In 1953, Lewis scored touchdowns at an unprecedented clip, while the Colonial defense kept their opponents from scoring at all; the combined score of Freehold's first five games was 110-0. In midseason, undefeated Freehold met undefeated Middletown in a game that was fated to decide the league title. Five thousand fans came out to see a clash of backs—Lewis and company against Middletown stars Sal DeSalvo and Jon Schultheis.[46] At first, it was all Middletown; the Lions led 7-6 at the half and Mayes limped off with a twisted ankle.

Just when it looked like Truex's sheer power would win out again, though, Freehold rose to the occasion. Mayes shook off the pain in his ankle to tear off a run deep into Middletown territory. Then Lewis, who had been contained all game, broke out of the pile for a 32-yard touchdown run to put Freehold in front. Late Lion drives were turned away by the solid Colonial defense, and the hometown fans cheered their heroes, victorious by a 13-7 score.[47]

By now, the Colonials were local celebrities. After each victory, the team would parade through downtown Freehold, waving to cheering pedestrians from the back of their convertibles. The local soda shop offered free sundaes to any player who scored in that week's game. The hungry football stars loved that; when Lewis scored multiple times, his linemen would accompany him, hoping to get their hands on his extra scoops of ice cream.

Walt Freeman (split end, 1953): *"[The town] was all blue and gold. Everyone supported us 100 percent."*

Jackie Mayes: *"It was Freehold football. Everyone was a part of it."* [48]

The season's decisive game was played at Manasquan, where the 6-0 Warriors had become the toast of their own town. Temporary bleachers were built to accommodate the expected huge crowd, and a long caravan of Freehold faithful followed their team to the big game. Little Manasquan "wore the mantle of a college town" that Saturday, and the game more than lived up to the atmosphere.[49] Lewis started the fireworks with a 45-yard run deep into Manasquan territory. Then, with the Big Blue packing the line to stop Lewis, Jackie Mayes went to the air and found Freehold's talented but seldom-used end, Walter Freeman.

Jackie Mayes: *"Walt was like a train. It was hard to get him down once he got the ball."* [50]

Freeman caught the ball and rumbled for a 32-yard touchdown, putting Freehold up 6-0. He had two more long catches in the second quarter, setting up a Lewis touchdown run and sending the Colonials into the locker room with a two-score lead. Freehold ended up hanging on for a hard-fought 13-6 victory. At game's end, a jubilant Schanck was hoisted onto his players' shoulders and paraded around the field.[51] A Thanksgiving win over Neptune, in which Lewis scored twice more to set the Shore scoring record, made it official. After the game, the gridiron heroes piled into convertibles one more time to parade through downtown Freehold.[52]

It had been a glorious year for the Colonials. Danny Lewis, Jackie Mayes, and Pollard Stanford were easy choices for the All-Shore team, while guard Tony Fowler and end Walter Freeman earned second- and third-team honors. Stanford went on to play four years of football at

North Carolina A&T, one of the largest historically Black colleges in the United States. This started a tradition that lasted into the 1960s—at least six other Freehold graduates (including Stanford's brothers, Lorenzo and Carl) would become starters for the Aggies. The most successful of the 1953 Freehold football stars, though, was Danny Lewis.

He had scored 20 touchdowns and 120 total points, smashing the Shore scoring record and winning the attention of major college scouts from across the country. He went to Wisconsin, where he started for two years and won the 1957 Big 10 rushing title. The Detroit Lions took him in the sixth round of the 1958 NFL Draft. He played in the NFL until 1966, finishing his career with 3,000 yards and 24 touchdowns.[53]

The loss of Lewis and his classmates would have crippled most teams, but with Schank's machine running at full steam, there was no drop off coming. Ninety boys turned out for the first practice of 1954, with full-back/linebacker Stan Nixon looming largest. The only two-way player on the team, Nixon anchored the Colonial defense alongside smaller, scrappy defenders such as Skip Thompson, Fred Frick, John Walker, and Fred Quinn. At fullback, he followed towering tackles Lorenzo Stanford and Amadeo Bianchini on devastating line plunges. And with Walt Freeman back at end, teams that jammed the line found themselves giving up long touchdown passes.[54]

The Colonials went undefeated again, finishing 8-0-1. Even the tie was to their credit; they went up to Roosevelt Stadium to play Jersey City's larger Lincoln High School and emerged with honors even. In the season finale, Freehold thrilled its 3,500 fans with a 25-6 Thanksgiving win over Neptune. They had now won three titles in five years and become the first team in Shore Conference history to repeat as outright champions.[55] The Colonials had finished undefeated in consecutive seasons, placed two starters (Freeman and Nixon) on the All-Shore team, and won back-to-back CJ II titles. Their eyes now turned to the next season. Freehold was the Shore Conference's reigning power, and they had another year of Stan Nixon—why not win a third straight title?

That would be harder in 1955 than ever before. Freehold's enrollment was growing, but its schedule was also getting tougher. Schanck added games against Trenton and Asbury Park, the two largest schools Freehold had ever faced. And league games were getting tougher, too—Manasquan and Middletown were always dangerous, but the revival of Red Bank football was what really made the league so strong in 1955.

The postwar era had not been kind to Red Bank, whose long slide down the standings had culminated in a winless 1953 season. Adding to the frustration of that season was the team's first-ever loss to Red Bank Catholic. It was a stressful time to be a Red Bank football fan. But then, that was expected. This was a stressful time to be in Red Bank.

In 1953, it was the height of the Second Red Scare, and the entire country seemed to be gripped by fear of Communist spies. Wisconsin Senator Joe McCarthy dominated headlines nationwide with accusations that Reds had infiltrated the State Department, had infiltrated the universities, had infiltrated the atomic bomb program, and had infiltrated the Army and the Navy. The Russians, he charged, were everywhere. Only constant vigilance could root them out.

A favorite McCarthy tactic was to come into a smaller town and make a wild accusation about local subversives. Out-of-town reporters, who lacked the context or time to investigate, would report the story, which would then become national news. The accuracy of the charges mattered little; by the time any real investigating was done, McCarthy and the media had moved on. Meanwhile, the town unfortunate enough to be the target of McCarthy's whims would be torn apart by suspicion and recrimination for years to come.[56]

In 1953, Red Bank was that unlucky town. Nearby Fort Monmouth was an anchor of the borough's economy, providing employment for hundreds of residents and drawing business from all over Monmouth County. Any goings on at the Fort and any news about the Army Signal Corps, which was based there, were of immediate interest to the residents and would be headline news in both the *Red Bank Register* and *Asbury Park Press*.[57] Naturally, a visit to the base by McCarthy on October 6 made headline news. So did his charges that the Signal Corps included as many as thirty Communist spies. Since the recently executed spy Julius

Rosenberg had worked at Fort Monmouth during World War II, that charge caused immediate panic. [58]

McCarthy didn't stay long; within a week, he was in sunny San Diego investigating rumors of a KGB plot. Workers at the Fort didn't have that luxury. They had to stay and sweat their way through an increasingly paranoid security crackdown. Employees were fired or lost their security clearances on the flimsiest of pretexts. One came under suspicion because he graduated the City College of New York in the same year as a known spy. Another was investigated because he read the liberal-leaning *New York Post*. A third lost his clearance for carpooling with other suspects. Adding to the fear was that the identities of those investigated were not random; the vast majority of the engineers who were fired as security threats were Jewish.

In total, thirty-one engineers were suspended pending the results of an investigation. During that time, the suspended men found themselves isolated. Friends avoided them in the streets and uninvited their families from parties. Red Bank had suddenly become very hostile indeed. In the end, not a single spy was identified, and all suspects were cleared. Still, the scars lingered.

Fort Monmouth Engineer (still insisting on anonymity in 1974): *"Once you've gone through what we have, you never feel safe again. . . . Even after two decades, I still feel the anger."*[59]

McCarthy was long gone by the summer of 1954, but the feelings were still raw. Red Bank was a town divided, and the bitterness wouldn't go away quickly. It was a relief, therefore, to have anything other than politics to talk about. Football filled that need nicely. For most of the summer, the local football talk was about Red Bank's new Head Coach Bob Glisson. Glisson had built a winning reputation at Williamstown High School in Pennsylvania, where his tricky "double-winged T" offense had propelled the team to two conference titles.[60]

His first season saw the team improve to 3-6, and with seven starters returning in 1955 (most notably explosive quarterback Angelo Scotti), they were expected to provide a real challenge for Freehold in 1955.[61] But long before summer practice began, Freehold's football program exploded in scandal. It all started with a wedding.

Stan Nixon got married in May of 1955, which under Freehold school policy made him ineligible for sports. Nixon, however, had a chance at a college scholarship, and so his parents asked the Freehold Board of Education for an exemption that would allow their son to continue playing. Instead, they received an incredibly draconian response from the NJSIAA. The state association declared that they had discovered that Nixon's parents lived in Middlesex County, and that the family had improperly used his aunt's address to register him as a student at Freehold High School. The state therefore declared him ineligible. The Board of Education showed even less mercy, sending the family a bill for three years' worth of tuition.[62]

The story now became badly tangled. The Nixon family lawyer argued that Nixon had transferred from Monroe to Freehold, with the approval of the Monroe school board, and charged the board and superintendent with pursuing a personal vendetta against Stan Nixon. During the course of charges and countercharges, it came out that it was the district itself that had turned the star fullback into the NJSIAA. Why?

It appears that the Nixon case was driven by the intersection of football and race. Nixon was African American, part of that same backfield that had starred Jackie Mayes. The same board meeting that declared Nixon ineligible also criticized the football booster association for overemphasizing the sport (their sin was buying a set of jackets for the team).[63] Hal Schanck was a major booster of his football program and was highly respected by his players for pushing integration. It seems possible that the Board of Education felt that he was pushing both too hard, and used Nixon as an object lesson to rein him in. If that was the plan, it didn't work.

The Nixon story was front-page news in the *Asbury Park Press* all summer long, and the August board meeting drew crowds of protestors from the Blue and Gold Booster Association. Meanwhile, the Shore Conference, in a vengeful mood, voted to suspend the Colonials from the league for two full seasons, rendering them ineligible to win titles in *any* sports. It took the personal intervention of Schanck's old mentor Russ Wright to overturn the suspension; the vacated titles, though, stood. The Colonial program would be taking the field under a bitter cloud of resentment and suspicion, and the loss of Nixon, their workhorse back, made their quest to retain the Shore Conference title even harder.[64]

Nixon won his court battle against the suspension, but the Freehold Board of Education responded by threatening to cancel the season, and so he dropped the fight. Although he briefly enrolled at Delaware State, he never did play college football, instead spending a decade playing semipro football for teams such as the Bayshore Redwings and the Jersey Generals. In 1956, he would have to watch from the sidelines.

Even with the loss of Nixon, though, Schanck remained confident. The line was anchored by three All-Shore linemen (Lorenzo Stanford, Walter Brown, and Emery Pudder), and the backfield powered by Nixon's replacement, Cal Wilson.[65] Wilson made his presence felt in the season opener, scoring in a 6-6 tie with Trenton. That was a great result against a Group IV power.[66] Things went even better in the Shore; Wilson scored in wins over Lakewood, Toms River, and Middletown. Meanwhile, the Colonial defense pitched three more shutouts in a ruthless display of defensive efficiency.

That set up a showdown with 4-0 Red Bank. No one seemed able to solve Red Bank's tricky double-winged T or move the ball against the swarming Maroon defense. The Bucs' most impressive performance had come in Middletown, where Joe Ellison's 101-yard interception return for a touchdown had allowed Red Bank to beat the Lions for the first time since 1946.[67] They followed that victory up with a 40-0 rout of Toms River, one of their most impressive performances in recent memory. It was the best Red Bank team in many a year, and the Bucs seemed to have as good a shot as anyone in the Shore at dethroning Freehold.

For a half, it looked like they just might. Down 7-0 in the second, the Bucs mounted a steady, determined drive toward the Freehold goal. However, even as that long drive wore on, Red Bank's weakness was becoming apparent. Freehold had a seemingly endless supply of players and was running fresh defenders on the field constantly. The Bucs could not match those numbers, and their drive finally ran out of steam at the nine.

The attrition mounted in the second half, and Freehold ultimately pulled away for a 20-0 victory, their fourth straight shutout.[68]

That all but wrapped up the Shore Conference title race. The Colonials even gave a good accounting of themselves in a narrow loss at mighty Asbury Park (where Butch Bruno graciously noted that Freehold could play with anybody.)[69] That ended the twenty-one game Colonial winning streak, but it did not end their dominance of the Shore Conference. Freehold officially sealed their third title with a 21-6 win over Neptune. For all the controversy of the summer, Freehold was still atop the Shore Conference.[70] Wilson, the league scoring champion, went on to star at halfback for Delaware State (where he is now in the school's athletic Hall of Fame).

Freehold's football machine, meanwhile, reached its peak in 1956, when an unheard-of 112 players went out for the team. With a senior class that had never lost a Shore Conference game, the Colonials had high hopes of winning a fourth consecutive title. Their football spirit was running so high that even the usually quiet Schank couldn't help but crow about it. "The students at Freehold Regional have the desire and spirit to play football. Some of the boys would like to work to buy cars, but football comes first and cars come second," he said.

The *Asbury Park Press*, meanwhile, could only marvel at Freehold's talent. Their annual preview started with a disclaimer for other Shore coaches— "don't torture yourself reading about a team that has half a dozen men at every position." A look at their practice told the tale. Here was Lorenzo Stanford, now in his third year as a starting tackle and weighing in at 230 pounds. There was Emery Pudder, the other tackle, a hefty 210 pounds. At the end of the field stood ends John Muly and Mike Ogborne, who "would start at any team in the Shore." Running through drills in the far end zone was bullish halfback Joe Henderson.[71]

And yet for all that talent, by mid-October the Colonials found themselves just 2-2-1, having lost to Trenton and Long Branch and tied Middletown. The Long Branch loss, a 47-6 beating, was their worst defeat since the end of World War II. The favorite now seemed to be Red Bank. Behind fullback Tony Christiano ("an express train behind schedule") and slippery quarterback Angelo Scotti ("a 120-pound package of atomic energy"), the Bucs were off and running, seemingly on their way to a Shore Conference title.[72]

Wins over RBC and Middletown had thrilled fans and won the loyalty of the once-dormant borough fanbase. Crowds of 5,000 and 6,000 were no longer unusual.[73] Everyone knew that if the Bucs beat Freehold, they would have an insurmountable lead in the league race. With his team up against the wall, Hal Schanck knew he needed something special to even the odds.

He decided to move 220-pound Lorenzo Stanford from tackle to fullback. The plan was to send the big man straight into the teeth of the Red Bank defense, wearing them down with waves of attacks. It turned out to be exactly the right strategy. Stanford scored twice in the first quarter against a Buc squad that couldn't seem to find a way to drag him down. By the time Red Bank adjusted to contain Stanford, it was too late. Freehold hung on for a 14-7 victory and moved into first place in the league.[74]

Two weeks later, the Colonials wrapped up the league crown by routing Manasquan, 20-0. They capped the season with a 25-0 Thanksgiving victory over Neptune. Four different players scored that morning—Francis Carter, Phil Hayes, Lorenzo Stanford, and John Muly on a touchdown pass from Stu Robinson. Over 3,000 fans cheered them as they walked off the field with their fourth straight title.[75] The Freehold Class of 1957 had conquered everything.

They'd won four Shore Conference titles and had never once lost a league game. Their athletic glory continued even after high school. Mike Ogborne went to Wake Forest, while Joe Henderson and Lorenzo Stanford kept a school tradition alive by heading south to North Carolina A&T. Stanford later played for the Dallas Cowboys, New York Giants, and the CFL's Hamilton Tiger-Cats. Their team had built a dynasty unlike any that the conference had ever seen, establishing their school as one of the most feared football powers in Monmouth County. With three more huge classes on their way, it seemed that the Colonials run would continue indefinitely into the future.

THE B SIDE: LIFE IN THE SHORE'S SMALLER DIVISION

While Freehold was dominating Class A, Matawan was emerging as the cream of the crop in Class B. In 1952, the Huskies finished second in the division, behind only Point Beach. The Garnet Gulls, led by All-Shore tackle Jack Stephenson, had downed Matawan 14-7 in the season opener. They never looked back, bullying the rest of the division into submission and clinching the title with a 7-0 victory over Rumson.

Matawan, however, had recovered well, winning six straight games behind tailback Don Marvel. The team couldn't take the Class B title, but they did win the CJ I crown, while Marvel won the Shore scoring title.[76] In 1953, Marvel was joined in the backfield by sophomore speedster Steve Fedele.[77] The addition of another back made all the difference; the Huskies crushed Point Pleasant 26-0 and rolled to the division title. Only a loss to mighty Freehold separated them from an undefeated season.

The highlight of the year remained the annual Keyport rivalry. During the mid-1950s, that Thanksgiving game became an annual Bayshore event, bringing out the best in both teams. The 1953 game was a fine example. Keyport almost denied the Huskies the title, taking a 12-7 halftime lead after two Hal Schumock touchdown runs. In the end, though, Marvel led a Matawan rally and the Huskies escaped with the division crown, 25-12.[78]

The Huskies changed coaches and backs in 1954 (basketball coach Jud Evans took over for Tony Nuccio and Steve Fedele replaced Don Marvel), but the results were the same. Matawan thundered through their division schedule and claimed their second straight crown by beating Keyport 6-0 on Thanksgiving. This was another classic, a mud bowl decided only in the fourth quarter when Ken Bruder blocked a Keyport punt at the Raider 25-yard line. Pete Vina wasted no time finding Stan Parrish for the only touchdown of Matawan's victory.[79]

In 1955, Keyport felt they finally had a team capable of avenging years of losses to Matawan. After eight years of careful building, Tuffy Baker had assembled a powerhouse. A jumbo-sized line featuring 260-pound center George Walling and third-team All-Shore tackle Harold Craft led the way, but the strength of the team was the backfield, which featured Hank Cleary and George "Babe" Ruth.[80]

That backfield combination shredded their opponents as Keyport tore off to a 6-1 start. Ruth had the biggest touchdowns of the year, scoring twice to defeat Point Pleasant and returning the opening kickoff 81 yards for a touchdown in a 13-7 win over Rumson. Once again, though, Matawan managed to thwart Keyport on Thanksgiving. Steve Fedele scored two first-half touchdowns as Matawan won 13-0 and claimed their third division title in three years. A huge crowd of 4,000 home fans went home disappointed.[81]

That only drove Keyport to new heights. The Red Raider seniors of 1955 wanted one championship before they graduated, and they trained furiously to do it. The combination of the crafty Cleary and speedy Ruth gave the Raiders a powerful backfield punch, especially when Baker redesigned the offense to suit their strengths. He shifted the team to the wide-open Split T, and frequently called quarterback options for Cleary. If teams forced Cleary to give up the ball, he simply pitched it back to Ruth. No one could stop it.

The Raiders routed their first three opponents, then managed a thrilling comeback win over Point Pleasant. After trailing 20-6 at the half, Keyport got long touchdown runs from Ray LoPresto, Ruth, and Cleary as they rallied to win, 32-26.[82] That set up (once again) a holiday showdown for the Class B title against Matawan.

A capacity crowd of 4,500 fans ignored the wind and rain to watch the annual classic. The difference, fittingly, was Keyport's big-play backs. Cleary's 60-yard touchdown run in the third quarter and Ruth's 46-yard sprint in the fourth were the only scores in Keyport's 14-0 victory, their first over their neighbors since 1949.[83] With that victory came undisputed possession of the Red Raiders' first-ever division championship, and perhaps most treasured of all, bragging rights. At least for the next 364 days.

There weren't many times in Barry Rizzo's life when he had to concede bragging rights to someone else. Rizzo had been a second-team All-Shore tailback at Long Branch and a scholarship football player at the University of North Carolina. His first year as the head coach at Matawan, though, was a humbling one. The year before he arrived in Matawan, the Huskies had won championships in football, baseball, basketball, and track. Victory was an expectation. Rizzo, however, didn't inherit a championship team—the roster size was down and returning starters were few. His early problems were only made worse by one of the few coaching mistakes that Barry Rizzo would ever make. Impressed by the speed of his backfield, Rizzo took the Huskies out of the single wing they had been running and installed an orthodox T formation. It didn't work, and the Huskies were pummeled by Neptune in the season opener.

Rizzo quickly scrapped the T and put the single wing back into operation. The Huskies used the old-fashioned attack to grind Point Pleasant into submission, and the satisfied head coach never changed his offense again. Matawan wouldn't win the Class B title that season, but they would establish a pattern. The sight of Rizzo coaching Huskies out of the single wing . . . that was something that Monmouth County fans would simply have to get used to.[84]

RED BANK CATHOLIC RISES AGAIN

Red Bank Catholic finished the 1952 season without a single win. Ever since the Jack Keelen affair in 1948, the Caseys had struggled badly. That futility would end with the arrival of a new coach—George "Snuffy" Stirnweiss. Stirnweiss had what was in those days the typical upbringing of a middle-class American Catholic. The son of a New York City police officer, he had spent his childhood in Catholic schools. What wasn't typical was his athletic ability.

He had gone to high school at Fordham Prep, in the Bronx, where he was an outstanding three-sport star. In 1935-36, he quarterbacked the Rams to a winning season and a Thanksgiving win over their archrivals from Xavier, played point guard on a city championship basketball team, and hit the home run that lifted the Rams to the city baseball crown.[85] And that was just the beginning—he captained the football and baseball teams at North Carolina, and was offered contracts by both professional football and baseball teams.

Stirnweiss ultimately settled on baseball, signing up with the New York Yankees. Unable to serve in the military due to illness, Stirnweiss spent World War II playing baseball and rose rapidly through the war-depleted minor leagues. He reached the bigs in 1943, a year in which the Yankees (due to wartime travel restrictions) held their spring training at Asbury Park High School. Former Asbury football coach Clipper Smith would put the team through calisthenics each morning. It was Stirnweiss's first exposure to Monmouth County, and he apparently enjoyed it enough to make his permanent home not far to the north in Red Bank.[86]

That was where he lived for all of his successful major league career, during which he won the 1945 batting crown and earned three World Series rings, all with the Yankees (1943, 1947, and 1949). Stirnweiss retired in 1952 and began settling into his role as the head of a growing household (he had five children then and would eventually have seven). The former major leaguer had some extra time on his hands, and so he became an eager fundraiser and volunteer at the local parochial school— Red Bank Catholic.[87] When the head football coaching position became open for the 1953 season, Stirnweiss agreed to fill in.

He saw potential. Frank Caprioni was a bruiser at tailback, basketball star George Saxenmeyer was a force at end, and Ray Dobson was a bulldozer at fullback. With that array of talent, Stirnweiss felt the Caseys were ready to win the Borough Rivalry against Red Bank (something they hadn't done in their first two tries).[88] This was the biggest attraction of the Shore's opening week of football, drawing 2,000 fans into downtown Red Bank. Although the Bucs scored first, this was George Saxenmeyer's game. He took a double reverse into the end zone for one touchdown, then threw off of another double reverse to Jim Sigler for the win.[89]

It was the beginning of an up-and-down season. The Caseys won most of the games they were supposed to win, lost most of the games they were supposed to lose, and stunningly tied a heavily favored Trenton Catholic team when Saxenmeyer pulled down a Hail Mary pass from Sigler as time expired.[90] RBC's season turned on that moment. They beat Point

Pleasant a week later, and then shut down St. Peter's of New Brunswick on Thanksgiving to cap the school's first winning season since 1947. A cheering crowd of Casey faithful rose to applaud a team that had finally finished a season stronger than it started.

Stirnweiss stepped aside in 1954, taking a job as a minor league manager in Schenectady.[91] Still, his one-year stint had made an impact. The Caseys were now a well-drilled, well-balanced, dangerous *team*. This was something different than even the successful 1946 and 1947 teams, which had relied almost entirely on the talents of Jack Keelen. Tackle Frank Maloney and guard Lou Mustillo formed the heart of a veteran front line that would confidently run interference for seasoned backs Dick Largey and Bucky Moran. In the experienced hands of Stirnweiss's successor, former Leonardo halfback Joe Bolger, this Casey team would achieve more than any RBC team that had come before.[92]

The team started the year with four straight shutouts, including a win over Red Bank in front of 3,000 fans and broadcast on local television. They traveled to Sayreville, St. Joseph's of West New York, and even Prendergast High School of Philadelphia, trailed by six busloads of loyal Casey fans. They won that game 38-0, with Bucky Moran running for two touchdowns.[93] They beat Matawan 14-0, tied Trenton Catholic, and routed Allentown to finish the job. Just two years after going winless, the Caseys were unbeaten Parochial B South champs.

At season's end, Lou Mustillo became RBC's first-ever All-Shore player, while linemen Frank Maloney and Richard Breslin joined Dick Largey on the third team. It was a great season, and it left Casey faithful beaming with pride. Although several years would pass before RBC approached that level of success again, the 1953-54 teams had shown the heights that Casey football program could attain.

Bolger, who also coached the Caseys to a state baseball championship in 1953, stayed at the school as coach and athletic director until 1957. In later years, he became a principal in Atlantic Highlands and the superintendent of the Keansburg school district, where he was working when the school opened its first high school. He is today in RBC's athletic Hall of Fame for his contributions.

Stirnweiss, meanwhile, remained a loyal booster and volunteer for RBC even as he wrapped up his career in major league baseball. He spent a few more years as a minor league coach and manager before retiring in 1954 to spend more time with his growing family. He ran a sandlot baseball program and worked as a purchasing agent for a freight company in New York City, commuting by train each day from Red Bank to Manhattan. It should have been the beginning of a long and happy life. Instead, it ended all too soon.

In 1958, the 3314 train of the Central Railroad of New Jersey missed its stop signals and plunged off an open drawbridge into the Raritan Bay. George Stirnweiss was one of the forty-four people killed in the tragedy. A host of former Yankees, including Phil Rizzuto, made the trip to St. James in Red Bank for his funeral. His memory lived on in the hearts of those who knew him, and in the name of Red Bank Catholic's original gymnasium, the George Stirnweiss Building.[94]

THE DREAM GAME OF THE CENTURY

Deal Lake Stadium had a special buzz on Thanksgiving morning 1957, although the noise wouldn't have penetrated the thick doors leading down the stairs to where the aspiring champions were sitting, standing, or laying around. Clad in their black and orange jerseys, the Middletown Lions were scattered about the visiting locker room. Arnie Truex was the longest tenured coach in the Shore Conference, and this might have been his best team. First-team All-Shore guard Dan Esposito carved holes alongside three second-team All-Shore choices, center Dick Kirk, guard Bob Babcock, and tackle Bob Foster.

Truex didn't often ask these linemen to pull, trap, or even to change formations. He preferred pure power plays, and pure power was what they gave him. They opened holes for three straight-ahead runners, quarterback Gene Bibaud and halfbacks Bob Breunig and Pete Boyd. Those three, nicknamed the Bee Boys, did not rely on deception. They plowed directly into the line, either running over tacklers or charging like freight trains through the holes that their teammates had opened for them.

This team was good, but they were also on edge. They were preparing for perhaps the biggest game in school history. One more win and the undefeated Lions would turn back the clock, back to the days before the Freehold juggernaut had rewritten the power structure of the Shore Conference, back to when Middletown had ruled the roost. To claim this title, though, would require every ounce of discipline, luck, and skill that the Lions could muster. For the first time in league history, the road to the title ran through Deal Lake Stadium in Asbury Park. The undefeated Blue Bishops had finally joined the league and were determined to prove that what they had always said was true—the best football in Monmouth County was played in Asbury.

It isn't likely that anyone in that locker room knew about the earliest meetings between Middletown and Asbury Park, back in 1921 and 1922, when the Blue Bishops won by scores of 55-0 and 110-0. That was ancient history. The past three years, though, were not. The Lions had resumed their series with the Bishops in 1954, moving it to Thanksgiving the following year. In those three meetings, Asbury had been the better team, but not by much. The scores had gotten closer each time—26-6, 14-0, and 6-2. That last game saw the Lions lead for a significant part of the game, falling only when Natie Bruno hit a late touchdown pass to Joe Major.[95]

The gap between Asbury and its smaller rivals was shrinking every year. With 1,600 students walking its hallways, Asbury Park was big, but it was no longer the biggest school in Monmouth County.[96] Maybe, some Blue Bishop fans thought, it was time to join the Shore Conference and see what these local schools were made of. There were other reasons, too.

Although the Bishops continued to win and win big, high school football was no longer the moneymaker it once was. In an age of television and easy sightseeing, attendance had plummeted. Sports fans could settle in to watch a big college football game instead of trekking over to the local stadium, while restless souls could travel to New York City or out to any of New Jersey's many state parks. On one Saturday, the Asbury Park-New Brunswick game found itself competing with the television broadcast of the World Series, and it lost badly. Less than 1,000 fans turned out to see a game that once regularly drew more than 5,000.[97]

By joining the Shore Conference, Asbury hoped to increase local interest and draw bigger crowds. The Shore athletic directors were also eager for Asbury Park to join the circuit; not only would playing the Bishops help sell a few tickets, it would provide the more ambitious schools the chance to challenge the Bishops for the Shore's first true football championship. In 1957, Asbury Park became a full member of the Shore Conference for the first time. Long Branch, which was in a similar situation, would follow in 1958.[98] Thanksgiving 1957 showed the wisdom of that move. Deal Lake Stadium was sold out for the first time in years, and the crowd was roaring. Everyone wanted to see this game.

Asbury Park and Middletown were the last two teams standing from what had been a tough bunch of Shore Conference opponents. The toughest opposition came from the Freehold football machine, which was aiming for an incredible fifth straight championship. The Colonials had eighty-two fresh bodies, most notably another set of towering linemen—tackle Emery Pudder, guard Joe Henderson, and Carl Stanford, the third of the Stanford brothers to earn All-Shore honors.[99] That team had started 3-0, but their hopes of another crown had been derailed in the season's fifth game against Middletown.

The Lions hadn't been expected to win that game. They were also 3-0, but they hadn't looked dominant and were still wobbly from an outbreak of the flu. None of that mattered, as the Bee Boys shredded Freehold's vaunted front wall and romped to a 19-6 victory.[100] Middletown didn't take center stage, though, because everyone in the Shore Conference was turning their heads to catch a glance of something or someone moving very quickly.

The year 1957 was a good one for speed. In the fall, *Sputnik* had flashed dramatically across the October sky. This Soviet satellite startled the United States and provoked fears that the Russians had somehow gained a technological edge over their capitalist counterparts. In the halls of government, harried officials debated what exactly to do about this challenge, while science classrooms hummed with excited conversations about the burgeoning space race. The anxiety *Sputnik* provoked in the halls of government was matched only by the concern that Asbury Park's own speedster produced in opposing locker rooms.

His name was Frank Budd, and he played football for Asbury Park. It began in the spring, when as a junior he won Shore Conference track championships in three events (the 100, 220, and high jump), and claimed state titles in the 100 and 220. After setting the New Jersey track world on fire, Budd turned his attentions to football, and by November he was without question the best back in the Shore Conference.

There seemed to be no stopping him. He ran for two touchdowns against Manasquan, then two more against New Brunswick.[101] Even Neptune, which geared their entire defensive efforts to stopping Budd, couldn't keep him from running for a 60-yard touchdown. That was the one game in which he did not play the hero, turning the main efforts over to the indomitable Joe Major, enjoying one momentous day in the spotlight by running for 236 yards in a 24-6 rout.[102] Then, against Red Bank, Budd ran for three touchdowns in the first four minutes, sparking a stunning blitzkrieg that left Red Bank down 20-0 before they ran an offensive play and coasting from there to a 39-6 victory.[103]

Budd wasn't alone, either. This was one of the best teams that Butch Bruno had ever coached, and they were within spitting distance of the ultimate prize. As Bruno looked around his locker room, he would have seen a hefty group of starting linemen, averaging 216 pounds to a man. He would have seen blocking back extraordinaire Joe Major, stretching in a corner. He would have seen a team that was just one victory from a perfect season, the Class A title, the CJ IV title, and maybe the No. 1 ranking in all of New Jersey. In his long tenure at Asbury Park, dating back to his playing days in the early 1930s, he had only been involved in three teams to reach that lofty peak. He wanted badly to return there for a fourth visit.

The local press realized this showdown was a possibility by mid-October. Once both teams emerged victorious over Long Branch, it became clear—the "dream game of the century" was really going to happen. Of course, those Long Branch games were no joke. The Asbury Park-

Long Branch game was another exciting entry in that long series. The Green Wave defense gave the Bishops a hard time, choking off their running game and forcing them to the air. Only the accurate passing of Frank Holland and the soft hands of Frank Budd kept the Asbury offense from stalling completely. Holland hit Budd for touchdowns in the first and third quarters, giving Asbury a 13-6 lead that they would not relinquish.[104]

The Middletown-Long Branch game a week later was very similar. Down 6-0 in the third, the Lions rallied behind the passing of Gene Bibaud. He hit two long touchdown passes to Bob Breunig for a 12-6 lead with time running out.[105] So it was time for the game that seemed to have it all. Two great offensive lines from two schools known for producing great linemen. The "Bee Boys" of Middletown against Frank Budd and Joe Major of Asbury Park. The Shore's traditional small-school power feeling its oats and challenging the Shore's traditional representative among the state powers, a battle that was at last being fought on even terms.

Things started fast, as Middletown's Dick Kirk ran the opening kickoff back into Asbury territory. With the Bishop defense geared to stop the Lion power game, Truex decided to employ a little misdirection. Bibaud faked a handoff and bootlegged around end for 21 yards, deep into Asbury territory. After that, the Lions returned to their typical power plays. Guards Bob Babcock and Dan Esposito carved enough space for Pete Boyd's short touchdown. It was the first time a Lion had ever crossed the Asbury goal line. Middletown led, 7-0.

In the second quarter, Bob Breunig's punt return to the Asbury 33 set up another series of line plunges. Seven plays later, Bibaud was crossing the goal line for a touchdown and a 14-0 lead. Things looked dark for the Bishops. The Asbury line was being pushed around, and Frank Budd could find no space against the swarming Lion defense. Casting about for an answer, Butch Bruno called for a double reverse. It turned out to be just what Asbury needed and allowed Budd to outrun the entire Middletown defense for a touchdown that cut the lead to 14-7. After a decent kick pinned the visitors at their own 32-yard line, all the pressure rested on the shoulders of the Bee Boys. The crowd was starting to come back into the game, and there was a real threat that the momentum would suddenly start to swing Asbury Park's way.

The Lions ponderous offense, however, was able to ignore the roaring crowd. Again and again their backs slammed into the line. There was only one big play on this drive, a 22-yard run by Bibaud on an inside handoff. Most of the plays were short, hammering runs. It all came down to fourth down and goal. An Asbury Park stop would give them the ball back down just one score, and with the greatest sprinter in the state of New Jersey waiting in the wings, a long field made no difference. A Middletown touchdown, however, would put them up two scores and leave the Bishops without enough time for a comeback.

Gene Bibaud took the handoff and went around right end. The Middletown line opened the way, and he crossed the goal line untouched. Middletown was ahead 21-7 and had now scored more points than Asbury's previous four opponents combined. The Blue Bishops still had plenty of fight in them, but the clock was not on their side. In the game's final minute, Asbury scored on a touchdown pass from Taft Dimmock to Budd, but the Lions fell on the onside kick and ran out the clock. When the clock ran out, Butch Bruno's chances of a second overall state championship ran out with it. Cruelly, so did their chances of a Central Jersey Group IV title, which went to Union.

On the Middletown side, meanwhile, wild celebrations erupted. Arnie Truex was hoisted onto the shoulders of his players as they began to celebrate their first Shore Conference title since 1952. A week later, the NJSIAA would crown them CJ III champions. What really mattered was bragging rights. For the first time in as long as anyone could remember, the undisputed football king of the Shore wasn't Long Branch and it wasn't Asbury Park. It was Middletown.[106]

That one of the original members of the Shore Conference would finally slay the giant that was Asbury Park would have been unthinkable in 1936. Equally unthinkable was the flood of new residents that had made that upset possible. The combination of Baby Boom and suburban boom was changing the Jersey Shore faster and faster with each passing year. Two days after Thanksgiving, the Shore Conference voted to accept the membership application of four new schools, located in Brick, Wall, Bay-ville (Central Regional), and Manahawkin (Southern Regional). Confer-ence athletic directors already were beginning to draw up new divisional structures in preparation for the new schools. The times were truly chang-ing, often in ways different than anyone could have expected.[107]

CHAPTER 13
GOLDEN HOUR

NOVEMBER 11, 1961

"Golden hour" is a photography term that refers to the first lights of the morning, or last part of late afternoon when the sun sits low in the sky. Because of the angle of the sun's rays, shadows are small, and the landscape is brilliantly illuminated in soft light. Photographs taken at this time seem to glow, the entire landscape lit up with color. Golden hour, though, is short, and its onset means that dusk is coming soon. It means the day is almost over.

By 1961, the sun had sunk low in the sky for both Asbury Park and Long Branch. Although the beaches still filled up each summer, there was more nostalgia and less energy about it than ever before. The Parkway was funneling tourists further down the Shore, and Asbury Park's once-rollicking boardwalk now seemed "ho-hum" compared to places such as Seaside.[1] The real damage, though, was happening away from the board-walk. The suburban populations of towns such as Ocean, West Long Branch, and Eatontown were exploding as white families continued their exodus out of the Shore's two oldest cities. Left behind were those who could not afford to move and the black families who couldn't get anyone to sell them a house. Also left behind were Asbury Park and Long Branch.[2]

The Asbury Park trolleys were by now out of date and out of service, and major businesses such as Sears and Bamberger's were starting to relocate to the suburbs. The death knells were sounded in 1959 and 1960, by the opening of two massive suburban malls—Monmouth Mall and the Eatontown Shopping Center. Monmouth Mall drew 100,000 customers on its very first day.[3] Asbury's fading downtown could not possibly hope to compete with that.

The cities themselves were changing in unsettling ways. Racial tensions were starting to divide the high schools, especially Asbury Park. A few years earlier, after one of Butch Bruno's grueling preseason practices, a scuffle had erupted between white and Black players. The next morning, city police pulled over a car driven by two unfamiliar men, each about twenty years old. The backseat was filled with five students (four of them football players) from the previous day's fight, heading toward the school to clean up yesterday's business. One of them was carrying a switchblade. The school was rocked. The athletes were thrown off the team, and extra police patrols watched the streets around the school. No trouble developed, but tension hung in the air for some time to come.[4]

Even the games themselves had an edge to them now. Fans were growing rowdier, and profanity was hurled from the stands with increasing frequency. Sometimes, rocks and bottles were hurled instead. At a 1961 game against Freehold, Colonial Coach Hal Schank was knocked down by a rock thrown from the stands. Enraged, a dozen or so Freehold players charged into the bleachers at Deal Lake Stadium, where they began fighting with local fans until police managed to pull the combatants apart. Frustrated at Asbury's inability to identify any specific individuals as responsible, the Freehold Board of Education passed a resolution vowing that no local teams would play at Asbury until changes were made.[5]

That was the reason for an unusual guardedness in the air at the stadium on this particular Saturday, as the over 7,000 fans began finding their seats. It was the largest crowd in several years, which made sense because this was easily the biggest game in several years. Both Asbury Park and Long Branch were undefeated, and both the division and Central Jersey Group IV titles were on the line. The same eager discussions as in past years buzzed through the air—questions of who would make All-Shore, if this was finally Long Branch's year, if the Wave could handle Lachman Rinehart's line or if the Bishops could find a way to defend Army Ippolito's tricky offense—but there were now interruptions.

At regular intervals, a stern voice came over the public address system, reminding fans that anyone throwing objects or going onto the field would be ejected from the stadium and arrested. A sharp-eyed observer might even have noted the unusually large number of uniforms down on the track. While a typical game might be patrolled by five or six police officers, there were twenty-two at this game, including police reserves called up to provide a few extra bodies. The game was the same. The stakes were the same. It was the times that were changing.[6]

They were changing even for the Shore's two most legendary coaches. Asbury Park and Long Branch no longer ruled the roost as they once had. The two schools had joined the Shore Conference to great fanfare in 1957, but they soon found that dominating it was not as easy as they might have expected. The standard of football around Monmouth County had risen dramatically, and now every Class A school was capable of beating their more established rivals. Even Red Bank had managed to beat Asbury Park twice in three years. The *Asbury Park Press* even did what would once have been unthinkable and questioned Asbury's play-calling at the end of a 1959 loss to Long Branch.[7]

There were some brash parents who even dared to suggest that the game had passed Army and Butch by. Ippolito and Bruno were of the old school and issued only general instructions, allowing the quarterback to call the plays on the field. Their successes were not based on their own in-game tactics, but instead on their ability to instill an indomitable spirit in their team, to teach their offenses and defenses well, and to cultivate smart, quick-thinking quarterbacks. The idea that high school students would occasionally make a mistake and call the wrong play was something that both men accepted as part of the game, and as part of the learning experience for young athletes.

That would never have happened at the *Asbury Park Press's* new favorite school, Brick Township. The Green Dragons roamed Ocean County, where they had begun to dominate the Shore Conference's B Division. Brick's quarterbacks never called the wrong plays because Brick's quarterbacks didn't call the plays. Their head coach, Warren Wolf, did. Assistant coaches using walkie-talkies passed advice down to Wolf, who shuttled the plays in and out of the game with messengers.[8] Headlines and pictures from Green Dragon victories were pushing updates on the Green Wave and the Blue Bishops into smaller and smaller corners of the page. Sometimes, the old powers were even pushed to the *second* page of the sports section. The old legends of the 1932 game were told with less frequency until finally they were not told at all.

A new era had arrived, and in it, the wins didn't come as easily as they once did. Long Branch went 4-4 in 1957 and 4-3-2 in 1958; Asbury Park lost more games in 1958 and 1959 than they had in the previous six years combined. One thing remained the same—Long Branch still couldn't beat Asbury Park. Two more losses made it seven long years since the Wave's last victory over the Bishops. Frustration continued to mount.

Army Ippolito, however, never lost faith. By 1959, his patience and development of young players paid off. The Wave unveiled a seasoned team, featuring quarterback Dewey Moser, halfback Vinnie Muscillo, and the talented DeSheplo brothers (shifty Joe and powerful "Frank the Tank"). The Green Wave came into the Asbury Park game with an unimpressive overall record of 4-3, but an undefeated Shore Conference record and a chance at the Class A title. The Bishops were also back on their feet, having won three straight games behind Brian Barrabee, a relentless battering ram of a runner who would later play fullback at Delaware.[9]

The game was a classic, as usual. After a scoreless first half, the Long Branch offense took command in the third quarter. Frank "The Tank" DeSheplo ran for one score and his brother Joe DeSheplo ran for another as the Green Wave built a 14-0 lead. Asbury rallied with two scores of their own, but the Wave stopped a late conversion try to hold on, 14-13.

Ten days later, nearly 7,000 fans watched as Muscillo and the DeSheplos combined to overwhelm Red Bank 40-0 and clinch their first-ever Shore Conference division title.[10]

In 1960, the Class A title passed from Long Branch to Red Bank, eluding the frustrated grasp of Asbury Park. That set up a scrap between those three teams for the crown in 1961. Red Bank, the defending champions, was favored because they returned eleven starters. They had one of the Shore's best lines, quarterback Willie Davis, and his favorite downfield passing target, massive end Utah Scott.[11] Asbury Park, featuring a great two-way lineman in Ken Saunders, plus powerful backs in Bill Athans and Hal Crenshaw, was not far behind. They also had a sense of urgency—in 1962, the Bishops would be leaving the Shore Conference to join the newly formed Central Jersey Group IV Conference. This was their last chance at a Shore title.

Long Branch was generally rated third. With fifteen seniors, they were by far the most experienced team, but no one of their athletes was rated as highly as the stars for Asbury or Red Bank. Perceptive observers, though, might have noticed All-Shore back Randy Phillips, his backfield mate Grayland "Musty" Newman, and rugged tackle Bill Sullivan. However, their real strength lay in their depth, not their individual ability. Ippolito and his assistants could substitute frequently in order to wear down their opponents, allowing the team to dominate late in games.[12]

Both Asbury and Long Branch quickly established themselves as title contenders. The Bishops started 3-0 with wins over Perth Amboy, Trenton, and Union. Crenshaw and Athans ran wild, scoring like crazy.[13] Long Branch, meanwhile, was also running hot. Randy Phillips and Musty Newman combined for three touchdowns in a 19-7 win over Neptune, and the swarming Brancher defense pitched shutouts in wins over Middletown and Freehold.[14]

Outside of conference play, the Wave were even more impressive. Randy Phillips ran for over 100 yards and two touchdowns in a 28-0 rout of a tough Union team, then scored the only touchdown in a hard-fought 7-0 victory over South River.[15] Total team efforts led to dominating wins over Paulsboro and Princeton, triumphs that lifted the Long Branch record to

7-0, earning them mentions alongside some of New Jersey's elite teams. They were in the title mix. However, before they could climb that mountain, they still needed to get past Asbury Park.

The Bishops had proven their worth by dispatching two old rivals. First, they buried Neptune under a "stampede of backs" in a 47-12 win. Then, they sprang Hal Crenshaw for three touchdowns in a convincing 28-14 win over a tough 3-1 Red Bank team. The next week, Asbury grabbed its most impressive victory in years, going up to New Brunswick on a Saturday night and routing the Zebras 41-7. The size of that win shocked the Shore, earning front page coverage in the *Asbury Park Press*. Next came a wild, come-from-behind win over a tough Freehold team. Crenshaw's steady running helped the Bishops overturn an early 6-0 Freehold lead, taking a 14-12 advantage for themselves. Even then, the Asbury faithful couldn't breathe easy until a desperation field goal sailed wide right.[16]

Now the stage was set—Asbury and Long Branch, grappling for the Shore Conference championship, as they always had and seemingly always would. Once the actual game began, that crowd of 7,000 fans was well-behaved. The game was played without incident, and even the twenty-two police officers on hand were able to turn their eyes to the field and watch one more chapter in the epic rivalry between Butch Bruno and Army Ippolito. It was, perhaps, the best game in a long line of great games, a perfect display of everything that the Long Branch-Asbury Park rivalry had ever been. And when it came to a display of talent and passion, well . . .

> **The Asbury Park Press**: *"Randy Phillips is a threat every time he handles the ball. He has plenty of speed running the ends. He can hit up the middle and he has the power to pick up extra yardage after being hit. He is adept at broken field running, and he can throw long and accurate passes."*[17]

> **Butch Bruno**: *"I think we're going to explode. The boys would like to play Long Branch nine times a year."*[18]

Joe Valenti: *"That week was bedlam. There were never pep rallies. There were for this. A Friday afternoon on a football field. You had the band out there. You didn't do that for every game."[19]*

Asbury Park did explode, seizing the initiative on the game's first play from scrimmage. Long Branch's Bob Mazza was hit hard going into the line, and the ball popped loose, into the hands of Asbury's great end George Plasteras, who returned the bobble 18 yards for a touchdown and a 6-0 Asbury lead. That was all the action for most of the first half. Both teams were feeling each other out, with neither team able to gain an upper hand.

Butch Bruno must have sensed that a 6-0 lead wasn't enough, because late in the second quarter, he decided to roll the dice and put the ball in the air. Deep in his own territory, Asbury's Hal Crenshaw dropped back to try a pass. Terry Johnson, one of Long Branch's best defensive players, came hard off the edge, stripped Crenshaw of the ball, and fell on it. Now the Branchers had ball in striking distance of the Asbury goal and could not be stopped. They fed the ball to Randy Phillips, who forced his way over with just seconds left in the half. The point was good and now it was Long Branch in front, 7-6. As the teams headed to their locker rooms beneath the stadium, the championship was still up in the air.

Asbury regained the lead soon after the break. Bill Athans forced the Green Wave defense back on their heels by threading the needle on a few short, accurate passes to Pete Tomaino. That set up Crenshaw for the go-ahead score, a 35-yard touchdown run. It was 12-7, Asbury. Long Branch, pinned at their own 35 after the kickoff, was hungry for an answer. All eyes were on Randy Phillips, which was exactly where the Green Wave wanted them.

The ball went to Long Branch's *other* star back, Musty Newman. Newman broke into the clear, sprinting down the sideline as the green-and-white clad faithful exploded in joy. Sixty-five yards later, Newman could pause to take a breath and look up at the scoreboard that now had his team in front, 13-12. It was the play of the season, and it had turned the game on its head.

Now it was Asbury with their backs to the wall, and with time running short, the Bishops had to throw. Long Branch knew it, and Fred Vitola's interception regained possession for the Wave. This time, there was no need for trickery or deception—it was just Phillips, plowing the middle of the line with rugged determination. He scored to make it 20-12, and Long Branch was in front by eight, a two-touchdown lead (there were no two-point conversions in 1961). The Blue Bishops mounted a series of drives, but the clock was not on their side. Phillips' touchdown was the last score of the game. Long Branch had won it.

The good kind of pandemonium followed. Jubilant Brancher players scooped up Army Ippolito and tossed him into the chilly waters of Deal Lake. When he emerged from his dunking, they hoisted him onto their shoulders and paraded him back toward the bus, through a throng of overjoyed supporters, shouting congratulations to players and coaches alike. Beneath the stadium, meanwhile, the despondent Blue Bishops had retired to their gloomy locker room, where Butch Bruno sadly congratulated the Green Wave on taking advantage of the breaks that had been offered to them.[20]

For Long Branch, the journey was not over. They still needed to beat Red Bank on Thanksgiving Day. Red Bank was tough, but the Wave weren't about to slip up now. Ray Reed tore off a 40-yard touchdown run in the second quarter, and Randy Phillips added a short run right before the half. That was enough for a 13-6 Green Wave victory.[21] They had done it. The elusive perfect season, never before achieved by any Long Branch team in the history of the high school, had been brought home. On top of that, they claimed the Shore Conference Class A crown and the Central Jersey Group IV title. A glorious year had ended in glorious fashion.

Just up Route 35, Hal Crenshaw was putting together a grand finale to his season, scoring three touchdowns in Asbury Park's 33-7 road victory over the Middletown Lions. The news that they really wanted, though, word of a Red Bank victory, never arrived. By evening, the Asbury Park football team would have heard the score of the Long Branch-Red Bank game reported on WJLK Radio. For the second year in a row, the Bishops had finished with eight wins, one loss, and no championships.[22]

To any of the thousands of the fans who saw the two best teams in the Shore play in 1961, it would have seemed like it was going to go on forever. Who knew what 1962 would hold? Maybe it would be another undefeated clash. Maybe just one team would be in contention, with the other playing spoiler. Maybe it would just be a game for pride between two good, but not great teams. Anything was possible, but one thing was certain—this game would be played on its traditional date (two Saturdays before Thanksgiving) for years to come.

Only that wasn't certain. Asbury's return to the Central Jersey Group IV Conference forced them to rearrange their schedule, and the traditional date of the Long Branch game was one of the sacrifices. The 1962 game would be played in mid-October. More changes were coming. Within five years, both Bruno and Ippolito would be gone. Of the two games that they had left to play against each other, neither had the drama or significance of the 1961 game. Within ten years, the old Asbury Park and the old Long Branch, to whom that pre-Thanksgiving showdown had meant so much and who had turned out in such numbers to see it, would be gone, washed away as completely as if they were sandcastles crushed by a crashing wave.

That, though, was all for the future. On November 11, 1961, 7,000 fans saw Long Branch beat Asbury Park, playing out another chapter in their epic rivalry. As Army rode his players shoulders through that admiring Long Branch crowd, heading toward the buses after his greatest victory as a head coach, the sun hung low in that late afternoon sky. It was a cloudless and beautiful, if chilly, day and the Asbury Park stadium would have been lit by a soft, golden light, shining brightly on the Wave in their green and white uniforms. None of it—the losses and the leavings, the unoccupied seats at the stadiums and the vacant storefronts, the riots and the emptiness—none of it had happened yet. All that could be heard that day were joyous teenage boys belting out the song that had become Long Branch's fight song that season, "O When the Wave Goes Marching In." Over that happy chorus, Army Ippolito's voice could clearly be heard, shouting back to a supporter offering him congratulations. "They're great kids, aren't they?" It was November 11, 1961, and Long Branch was on top of the world.

EPILOGUE: THE END OF AN ERA

Butch Bruno and Army Ippolito faced each other twice more. Both times, the Green Wave won by a touchdown—Army Ippolito started his coaching career with three straight wins over Asbury Park, and he would finish his time at Long Branch the same way. There were still thrills left to be had, but something was missing. Now that Asbury Park was no longer in the Shore Conference, the only way for them to get press coverage was to compete for sectional titles, and they simply didn't have the depth to do it. The school's falling population made the decision to join the Central Jersey Group IV conference a mistake; the Bishops just couldn't keep up with the bigger schools that they now had to play week in and week out.

Consecutive losing seasons followed, and in 1963 the Bishops finished 1-6-2, their worst record since Bruno had become head coach (the team even lost to Neptune on Thanksgiving, something that hadn't happened since the legend was in grade school). The *Asbury Park Press*, which had once run a daily report on the team's doings in practice, could barely be bothered to cover the declining fortunes of the team that had once been kings of the Shore. That year, the paper didn't even run a photograph of the annual Long Branch-Asbury Park game.

Bruno would coach two years after 1963, winning one more championship (a sweep of Mercer County foes won them a CJ IV Conference Southern Division Title) but would not get back above .500 or beat Neptune again. Health problems stemming from diabetes were beginning to dog him, and he even blacked out during several games. In September of 1965, Bruno announced that he would be retiring at the end of the season, an announcement that gave his old friends and supporters one last chance to demonstrate how much he meant to them.

He coached Asbury to one more victory over Long Branch, a narrow 13-0 victory, celebrated with one last victory ride on the shoulders of his players.[23] He also enjoyed one more homecoming game, a 45-7 rout of

Linden. An enormous crowd of alumni and friends came out for a half-time ceremony honoring every Asbury Park captain from 1915 to 1945.[24] On Thanksgiving, all eyes turned again to Deal Lake Stadium. For the first time since the 1961 Long Branch struggle, the Blue Bishops were playing in the premier game at the Shore, this time against a favored Neptune team.

A throwback crowd of 7,000 fans, ringing the track three and four deep, came out to see what they knew was the end of an era. The year 1965 had been filled with the symbolic breaking of ties to the past. That summer, the Casino, a Boardwalk landmark since the 1920s, had been severely damaged in a fire and would not be rebuilt. In September, the long-promised Ocean Township High School opened its doors for the first time, a move that would eventually cut the city's already shrinking student population in half. And now it was the iconic coach's last game. The Blue Bishops played with the old heart and desire, but in the end, Neptune just had too much, winning 20-6. And so, after twenty years and 105 wins, Butch Bruno's career ended.[25]

Army Ippolito's career was also ending that very day, although under surprising circumstances—on a normal Thanksgiving, he would have been preparing to coach against Red Bank. Instead, he was at the Middletown High School Athletic Field, coaching his Mater Dei Seraphs against his nephew Joe Oxley's Raritan team. His 1962 and 1963 editions of the Green Wave had remained a force in the Shore Conference, going 7-2 and 6-3. Only two narrow losses to Brick kept them from sharing the Class A title. To all outside appearances, the future was bright. The 1963 season ended the same way that the previous eighteen had ended, as the Branchers crushed Red Bank to maintain their stranglehold on their ancient rivals.

Then came a falling out between the coach and the Board of Education. Ippolito was abruptly fired and replaced with assistant coach Hugh Mendez. Still a Spanish teacher at the high school, he took a year off from football before returning to coaching in a situation oddly similar to his very first job at St. Rose. He was once again the coach of a young football program at a tiny Catholic school, this time at Middletown's Mater Dei

High School. Although the Seraphs won just two games that year, they gave a creditable account of themselves, and Ippolito retired with the program in good shape.

The end of their football careers did not signal the end of Bruno's and Ippolito's service to their communities. Bruno taught at Asbury Park until 1968 and acted as an assistant coach with the football team until 1970. He spent several years as the director of the Asbury Park boardwalk before retiring for good in 1973. Ippolito continued to teach Spanish in Long Branch. He ran for city council in 1965 and won, serving until 1970. He continued to teach at the high school until retiring (like Butch Bruno) in 1973.

Army Ippolito died on June 29, 1980. Almost exactly a year later, on June 27, 1981, his great rival Butch Bruno passed away. These two giants of the Shore Conference, forever linked by history, ended their stories in the most appropriate way possible—together.

Bill George (Long Branch player and graduate): *"Ipp would give everybody a chance. He'd call a child who couldn't break a balloon a tiger and gave him his shot on the kick return or punt return or somewhere. And some day, when we had a tight game and that kid was in, he'd be ready, be prepared. He knew how to fire you up, too, and he never let you forget that playing football for Long Branch was something special."[26]*

Elliott Denman (Asbury Park Press Sportswriter): *"Even by the standards of the 1930s when he played football for Asbury Park and Notre Dame, Butch Bruno was a man of everyday stature. But those who were touched by this man and saw him in action will deny the facts of the matter. Those who knew Butch Bruno will forever say he stood high above the crowd."[27]*

CHAPTER 14
SHORE CONFERENCE FOOTBALL, 1957-1961

"They even got themselves a football team already . . ."
Ed Roberts, Football Comes to Central Regional

There was a time when "almost every field in rural Ocean County was a pastoral scene of cows grazing in fields, hogs snorting in pens, horses grazing on pastureland and chicken farmyards littered with white chickens pecking and scratching."[1] By 1957, that time was gone. The opening of the Garden State Parkway connected the county to the northern part of the state, making it possible for commuters work there or in New York City, all while living Ocean County. At the same time, suburban housing was growing more affordable nationwide.

In the years after World War II, the Federal Housing Administration and Veterans Administration made home loans available on terms much more generous than had ever been available before. The Levitt Brothers, meanwhile, were pioneering an astonishingly cheap way to build tract housing—and they were only the best known of a host of similar builders. Between 1940 and 1960, the percentage of Americans living in the suburbs rose from 40 percent to 60 percent.[2]

It is important to note, though, that the adventures of the suburbs were not available to everyone. FHA and VA loans were extremely difficult for African Americans to acquire, and even if they could get loans, restrictive covenants often made it impossible for them to buy in the new developments. When they could, they were often met with hostility—a Black family that sought to move into Levittown, Pennsylvania, in 1957 was greeted only with rock throwing. The result was a society that was often more segregated than the one that had come before—cities became increasingly Black, while the new suburbs were predominantly white. No African Americans were able to buy a Levittown house until 1960, and as late as 1990, Long Island's Levittown (the largest suburban development of the era) had just 127 African Americans out of a population that topped 400,000.[3]

Housing discrimination created neighborhoods and towns that may not have been segregated by law but were segregated in fact. This, in turn, created segregated schools. By the 1990s, "more than two-thirds of minority schoolchildren in the United States attended public schools in which they exceeded 50 percent of the enrollment." And the schools of the rapidly expanding suburbs were funded more generously than the schools of New Jersey's cities.[4] As white residents departed for the suburbs, those cities faced rapidly declining tax bases and living conditions. This would have dire consequences for the state in the very near future.

The suburban boom may have been driven by general trends, but local conditions could be very important, and in Ocean County those conditions were very favorable. At the start of the decade, the area's two main industries were poultry farming and cranberry harvesting. A crash in the price of both eggs and cranberries suddenly rendered them unprofitable for small farmers, and many of them began selling their farms. Developers, seeing an opportunity, quickly began converting them into housing lots. Young families, seeing an opportunity to purchase a new home at a much better price than they would ever get in North Jersey, quickly moved in.[5]

The result was a population explosion, which left local schools bursting at the seams. Traditionally, towns such as Toms River and Point Pleasant had taken students from surrounding areas into their small high schools, but now it was becoming difficult for them to accommodate even their own residents. It was obvious that more schools were needed, and fast. The first one to open was Central Regional, created in 1956 to serve all the small towns of Ocean County from Brick to Lacey (a sister school, Southern Regional, opened two years later). The new buildings were thrown up in a hurry, with little time for planning and preparing. When *Asbury Park Press* reporter Ed Roberts made his first trip down to Berkeley to write a preview of Central's first football team, he found the area a study in contrasts. The high school had seemingly been dropped in "the pine belt . . . a wilds roamed only by animals lost from the pack" in a part of the state once home to nothing but "spittin' clams and a few Republicans."

Not everyone liked the changes, especially not the old-timers whose once quiet region was rapidly being swallowed up. On his visit to practice, Roberts described a weather-beaten old farmer pausing momentarily to watch the Eagles go through their workouts, then growling, "They even got themselves a football team already," before motoring off on his tractor.

There were challenges for the students as well. Central was a sprawling district in 1956, and some students didn't end their bus ride home until 5:30 in the evening.[6] There was no sense of community, no camaraderie, and no tradition. That made the athletic programs especially important. Fortunately for the Golden Eagles, they had quite a football coach.

Joe Boyd was a football lifer. He had been a high school and college star in Philadelphia, first at Northeast Catholic and then Temple. During World War II, he was assigned to the North Carolina Pre-Flight Cloudbusters, a service team coached by college football legend "Sleepy Jim" Crowley (one of Notre Dame's famed Four Horsemen and the architect of Fordham's Seven Blocks of Granite). After the war, Boyd became an assistant coach at South Jersey power Atlantic City and waited patiently for an opportunity to take over a program of his own.

Boyd's place in the history of Shore Conference football is not as prominent as it should be. Central Regional never grew as big as Brick Township, and so Boyd's Eagles never received the media attention that came with playing against the Shore's largest schools in Class A. His greatest team, the 1971 squad, came along too early for NJSIAA playoffs and so never had the opportunity to etch itself into the lore of the Shore Conference that way either. Nonetheless, his accomplishments at Central were great. None were greater than what he achieved in the first two years of the new school, with his players new to him and each other, and their practice time severely limited by the long bus ride that awaited so much of his team at the end of the day.

What the team had were talented and dedicated players, none more so than halfback Frank Copeland. Copeland, a speedster who would win the state championship in the 440 that spring, was the Eagles' first workhorse back.[7] Helped by his running, the Eagles were able to win four of their final five games, including a 7-6 upset of Matawan. Copeland scored the winner in that game, lifting Central to a winning record and the CJ I crown in its first season.[8]

The new high school had caught football fever, and in 1957 nearly a third of its male students came out for the team. There was talent in that bunch as well, most notably power back Larry Way and explosive outside runner Ed Benson. Boyd also had two equally capable quarterbacks, Bud Suharsky and Ray Roe. Instead of naming one starter and the other the backup, he alternated them on every down, allowing him to send in a new play every time. Judging by the *Asbury Park Press's* surprised and approving reaction, Boyd was probably the first coach in the history of the Shore Conference to call all of his own plays.[9]

That year, most of those plays worked. The Eagles routed Lakewood, upset Class A Neptune, and shut out Toms River South in front of 2,000 fans. The biggest game was once again against Matawan, and in that battle Central prevailed again. This time, they won 6-0, with Paul Wilbersheid high-stepping 40 yards for the game's only touchdown.[10] That win vaulted the Eagles into first place in Class B, a position they held all through a rainy and cold November.

Benson provided the exclamation point to the season by returning the second-half kickoff 73 yards for a touchdown to beat Keyport, picking his way to the end zone on a field so muddy that neither team could threaten the rest of the game.[11] In just their second season, the Eagles had finished 8-0 and won the Shore Conference Class B title. Two years before, nothing but scrub pines had covered the football field, and now it was home to a championship team.

THE RISE OF BARRY RIZZO

Central's unexpected championship may have brought celebrations to Ocean County, but it just brought frustration to Matawan. After winning three straight Class B titles from 1953-55, the Huskies had seen the crown slip through their fingers in 1956 and 1957. First, they had lost it on Thanksgiving Day to Keyport, and then Paul Wilbersheid's long touchdown run had ripped the title out of their hands and handed it to Central. As the 1958 season approached, young coach Barry Rizzo, his players, and the people of Matawan were hungry to regain the crown.

Most of the key players from those two near misses were back for another run in 1958, but two, backs Purvis Peeler and Davey Jones, stood above the rest. Both were lightning fast—Peeler had won a state title in the 440 as a freshman, and Jones was the defending champion in the 100. In Matawan's tricky single wing, both would often have big-play opportunities. Peeler scored four touchdowns in a 47-12 season-opening rout of Lambertville, while Jones returned a punt for a touchdown in a 47-6 win over Point Pleasant.[12] The "Touchdown Twins" had been born, and over the first three games they would combine for a total of sixteen touchdowns.[13]

In the season's decisive game against Toms River, Peeler returned the second-half kickoff for a touchdown, helping the Huskies clinch the Class B title. He also set a new Shore Conference scoring record with 140 points. Now all that stood between Matawan and a CJ II title was a Thanksgiving win over Keyport. The Red Raiders were a mediocre 4-4 in 1958 and had no shot of winning or sharing the division title, but Thanksgiving was always dangerous. Alone among Matawan's opponents in the second half of the season, they found a way to contain Peeler, limiting him to just one touchdown and holding Jones to nothing at all.

Matawan led 6-0 in the fourth, only for Keyport to steadily drive to a first down at the 2-yard line. Matawan's title hopes now depended on their ability to defend six feet of real estate over four plays. Three runs (by quarterback Gene Fleming and fullbacks Larry Dane and Russ Zilinski) gained just 1 yard. Both crowds rose to their feet for fourth down and goal. Zilinski tried again, plowing into a massive pile of players from both teams. When the referees finished tearing bodies off the pile, the nose of the ball was inches across the goal line. Keyport's celebrations were cut short, however, by the referee's ruling that Zilinski's knee had touched before the ball crossed. Keyport fans were furious and could only watch in frustration as Peeler fell on the ball for an intentional safety. Matawan survived, 6-2.[14]

The third time had proved to be the charm for Rizzo's Huskies. Peeler, meanwhile, joined the ranks of great backs gone before by earning a place on the statewide All-Group II team. However, his legacy was bigger than that. By helping the Huskies to their 1958 championship, he had solidified Barry Rizzo as head coach, and the single wing as his offense. Both the coach and the system would remain Matawan staples for decades to come, and those decades would be bright indeed.

BACK TO THE TOP: MANASQUAN IN THE 1950s

Fans of Manasquan's Big Blue Warriors had grown spoiled in the 1940s. From 1945 to 1947, the Warriors lost just once in 23 games while winning two CJ II crowns and a Shore Conference championship. Their 1949 team, which featured Leonard and Norman Morgan, won no championships but it added more lines to the growing legend of Big Blue football and the illustrious Morgan clan. Norm was the defensive ace while Len (an All-Shore and statewide All Group II selection) was the big-play back, running for long touchdowns regularly. Only a loss to eventual champions Neptune and a tie with Point Pleasant blemished 'Squan's record.[15]

That 0-0 tie, seen by an enthusiastic crowd of 7,000 people, was the end of an era. Granville Magee stepped down as football coach at the end of the school year to take on new responsibilities as the vice principal, leaving his post with a 57-14-1 record, three undefeated seasons, and two Shore Conference titles. Winning was now firmly established as a Manasquan tradition. The challenge for the new coach would be to keep that tradition alive.

Magee's choice for his successor was his top assistant, 29-year-old Hal Manson. Manson was just one year out of Kentucky's Murray State Teachers' College, but to those who knew him it was obvious that he was the right man for the job. Manson was a Navy man, a former football and baseball star at Asbury Park, and an ex-football player at Murray State. He may have been young, but he knew his football and related well to his players. He was also patient, something he needed as the Warriors went 0-8 in 1950 and lost their first three games of the 1951 season.

Manson kept at it, and by midseason 1951 he had found a workhorse fullback in sophomore Bill Hewitson. The Big Blue won three out of their last five games, including a 20-0 victory on Thanksgiving over Point Pleasant. As a junior and a senior, Hewitson was even better, and Manasquan surged to consecutive winning seasons. Their 7-2 season in 1953 included a 13-0 upset of Long Branch and announced to the world that the Warriors were back. As the program gained momentum, the team grew in numbers, and over fifty players came out for the summer practice in 1954. That was the largest squad assembled in Manasquan in many years, and it had the talent to make a serious title run. Football fever was running high. Unfortunately, the talented Warriors were never really able to show what they could do, thanks to the outbreak of a different kind of sickness—polio.

The summer season that year had been a good one, with the newly opened Garden State Parkway drawing record crowds to beaches up and down the coast.[16] The trouble started as the weather cooled, and the crowds began to head home. A nine-year-old boy named Roger White died suddenly that September, and the dreaded word polio was associated with it. Seven more cases appeared that week, and by October the number had risen to thirty-six.[17] Once again the Jersey Shore was living with a nightmare. Poliomyelitis had been a fact of life in the United States ever since the summer of 1916, when a major outbreak swept New York and New Jersey, infecting 9,000 and killing over 2,000. Ever since that horrible August, the words "polio outbreak" were among the most feared in the English language.[18]

In 95 percent of cases, individuals who contracted polio suffered no symptoms at all. Most of the remaining 5 percent of victims suffered only very mild symptoms—a stiff neck, nausea, and fleeting episodes of paralysis. In a tiny percentage of cases, however, the paralysis was not temporary. Those people suffered permanent muscle weakness at best, and in some cases were disabled for life. A small percentage of those who contracted the paralyzing form of what was called paralytic polio did not survive.

The odds may have been on the side of the infected, but the disease was nonetheless terrifying. It was impossible to prevent, there were no advance warnings, and children were especially vulnerable. Parents could only wait for the late summer months to pass before the illness was out of season. The standard treatment for a child was total isolation; if parents could see their sick children at all, it would be through a window. Most made a full recovery, but there was no predicting that, and as late as the 1950s there was no real knowledge of the cause. The only thing that people knew for sure was that one could catch it from close contact with an infected person, and that many of the infected showed no symptoms. Any large gatherings of children, at places such as swimming pools and summer camps, thus became suspicious.[19]

> **Larry Alexander:** *"The fear of polio was the fear of something you had no defense against, something that struck with no logic or reason. Yesterday it was the man down the block. Tomorrow it could be you or your children."*[20]

Clouded as it was by worry, life at the Shore went on, and at first football season went on with it. Manson's team started the year 2-1, and with a game against first-place Freehold still on the schedule, the Warriors were in a strong position to make a run at the title. Then, just a few days before Manasquan's scheduled game with Neptune, team captain Robert Livingston was brought by his parents to Monmouth Medical Center with what the doctors recognized as polio. Soon afterward, Livingston was joined in the hospital by defensive tackle Orrie Clayton and fullback Charlie Ormsbee. Since no one knew for sure where Livingston had contracted the disease or who he had already spread it to, the Manasquan school district had little choice. Schools were closed for the remainder of the week, and the Neptune game postponed.[21]

The schedule started to fall like a row of dominoes. Lakewood, Middletown, and Freehold all refused to play a team that might be carrying polio. Only a game with Neptune and the Thanksgiving classic with Point Pleasant could be salvaged. The seniors of 1954, who had carried such high hopes of a title, would have to settle for a five-game season.[22]

They certainly made the most of the football they had left. First, Bruce Beckman ran for three touchdowns in a thick fog, enough to beat Neptune 19-0.[23] Then came Thanksgiving. Even in the crowded records of the Point Pleasant-Manasquan rivalry, the 1954 clash would go down as one of the classics. All the disappointments, all the heartbreak, and all the frustration of a season cut in half would come down to this one Thanksgiving morning.

> **Asbury Park Press:** *"At the final whistle, the Manasquan rooters went wild. On the Point Pleasant side, grown men wept. Both teams stumbled wearily from the field seemingly unconscious of the roaring thousands. The 6,000 spectators were quick to know they had watched something more than boys at play."*[24]

Bill Stratton's 3-4 Gulls came out firing. Leigh Millar threw one touchdown pass to Joe Lynch and then ran for another, putting the Point ahead 12-0 in the fourth. It was almost more; on the last play of the first half, Ray Hulse had fired a halfback pass to an open Tom Morris. Morris had hauled the ball in, but the Manasquan defense managed to tackle him at the 5-yard-line, and the clock ran out before the Gulls could run another play.

That saving tackle proved crucial as the Big Blue rallied, starting with the kickoff after Millar's touchdown run. Manasquan speedster Dave Chafey returned that kick 95 yards for a touchdown, cutting the score to 12-7. Point Pleasant fans were beginning to whisper nervously about the 5-yard line and about missed extra points. Beckman, Chafey, and Charlie Sherwood were now hitting the line like piledrivers, and the Gull defense was tiring. With five minutes to play in the game, Chafey plunged over from a short distance away. The Pointers never managed another threat, and the final stood at Manasquan 14, Point Pleasant 12. There would be no championship for the boys of 1954, but on that chill Thanksgiving morning, it certainly felt like they had something that meant just a little bit more.

As the years went by, the missed opportunity that 1954 represented slowly started to loom larger and larger. Manasquan's student population was rapidly falling behind the populations of its Shore Conference rivals, making it increasingly difficult to compete in the Shore Conference's A Division.[25] Although Manasquan kept winning on Thanksgiving, they were unable to mount a serious challenge for the league title, even with the brilliant Bruce Beckman in the backfield. That showed how large the gap had grown.

The "Gray Ghost" was one of the finest athletes to ever come through Manasquan High School. He was a two-time All-Shore basketball player, a record-setting sprinter, and an incredibly versatile football player who could run, pass, and kick. His final Thanksgiving Day game was the perfect showcase for his incredible talents; he ran for two touchdowns and dropkicked two extra points in a 20-19 win over Point Pleasant.[26] And yet for all his ability, Manasquan finished no higher than fourth in Class A his senior year. If the Warriors couldn't compete even with Beckman, what chance did they have without him?

In 1956 and 1957, the answer was not much. In 1958, though, things were different. Hal Manson finally had a line good enough to stand up to the best in the Shore. In fact, it was one of the best of the decade. Three linemen (Jay LaSala, Mel Wood, and Bill Osborn) would earn places on the All-Shore team at season's end. Veteran *Asbury Park Press* sportswriter

Jim Sullivan rated Osborn as one of the best centers in the history of the high school.[27] What made them especially dangerous, though, was that they had a great backfield to block for.

That backfield had first started to emerge during the otherwise unremarkable 1957 season, during an otherwise unremarkable game against Red Bank Catholic. The miserable weather, the middling records of both teams, and a lingering Asian flu epidemic kept the crowd down to a paltry 650. Hal Manson was experimenting with his lineup, tinkering with an all-underclassmen backfield. There were a few youngsters he wanted to give a look. One was junior back John Kenney, a physical inside runner. Then there was the lanky sophomore with breakaway speed, Doug Deicke. And finally, there was the sophomore quarterback. His name was Vic Kubu.

Kubu wasn't the best athlete on the team, but he was perfect for the quarterback role. Skilled at faking and ballhandling, he called plays well, and his teammates followed him. He loved his high school and its traditions, he had a relentless work ethic, and he had a sharp football mind. That mind was sharpened by his unusually close relationship with his head coach. Kubu's father, a railroad worker, was often gone for weeks at a time, and the young quarterback would often stay at Hal Manson's house, where the coach and his wife treated him almost as a second son. From 1957 to 1959 he started at quarterback, and both he and his team improved with every passing year. Something great was beginning.[28]

The Warriors earned their first win of the season in impressive style, annihilating RBC 51-0. Kenney scored three times, Deicke twice, and Kubu once.[29] Manson stuck with that backfield the rest of the season as the Warriors won half of their remaining games to finish 3-4-1. More importantly, the three backs had gained crucial experience that they would use in 1958.

They were tested early that year, in the wind and the rain against Asbury Park. The Warriors, hoping to avenge a lopsided 1957 loss, came out fired up in front of their usually passionate home crowd. An early Bishop turnover gave Manasquan an opportunity, and a quick halfback pass from Kenney to Kubu put the Warriors in striking distance. On fourth and goal from the 4, Deicke slogged through thick mud to score the game's first touchdown. A fumbled punt allowed Asbury to retake the lead 7-6 in the third, but the Big Blue refused to fold. Deicke ripped off a 23-yard run, sparking a 60-yard drive that turned the field position back in favor of the Big Blue. It eventually led to a Kenney touchdown and a 13-7 Manasquan win.[30]

Two weeks later, Manasquan took on Long Branch in a key league game. They trailed in the fourth quarter of that game, too, this time 13-7. It took a Kenney-to-Kubu connection to get them moving. Kubu caught the ball for a 16-yard gain but was stripped of the ball while trying to fight for extra yardage. A massive pileup ensued, with Kubu alone underneath a mountain of Branchers. Somehow, he got it back. One play later, Kenney was free into the Long Branch secondary for a 29-yard touchdown run. Deicke's second extra point then won the game, 14-13.

Now the Warriors were really going. Kubu scrambled for two touchdowns against Neptune, and Kenney shredded the RBC defense for three of his own. Middletown was shut out, and Freehold was dominated. Kenney, Deicke, and Larry Morgan (another Morgan!) all scored as the Warriors rolled to a 20-0 victory and clinched the Shore Conference title. Celebrations erupted across town.[31] The Thanksgiving game, a 19-0 victory over Point Pleasant played before 4,000 fans, was an extended farewell for Kenney and his fellow seniors. He carried the ball on almost every play, rushing for 294 yards and scoring twice.[32]

It completed an incredible season, maybe the most dominant in Manasquan history. The Big Blue pitched seven shutouts in nine games, outscored their opponents 197 to 20, won both the Class A and CJ III titles, and placed four players on the All-Shore team. Stretching back to the end of the 1958 season, they had won eleven straight. Their stars would go on to further greatness. Jay LaSalle started three years on the line at Lafayette, while John Kenney became a running back at Tennessee A&I. End Dave Lewis played at Delaware State.

One who did not play college football was Bill Osborn. He was originally supposed to attend Murray State (Hal Manson's alma mater), but in late summer he developed what was thought to be a bone infection and was hospitalized at Monmouth Medical Center.[33] It turned out to be more than that. In November of 1959, he passed away of leukemia at the age of eighteen. He was not forgotten. A group of students and former teammates organized an award that would be given in his honor—the William Osborn Memorial Award, presented each year to Manasquan High School's outstanding offensive lineman.

The traditions built by the 1958 team continued into 1959. Kubu and Deicke were back, and with them running wild the Warriors finished 7-2, losing only to Brick and Long Branch. The Big Blue defense finished the year with five more shutouts, placed two more players (Kubu and guard Bob Leonard) on the All-Shore team, and crushed Point Pleasant on Thanksgiving. Kubu closed his high school career in the finest way possible, throwing three touchdowns and returning an interception for another score.[34]

Kubu became the next in a long line of Manasquan athletes to head to Murray State. Originally a walk-on, he earned a scholarship by his sophomore year and was a star by his junior year. His best year was 1963, when in consecutive weeks he caught the winning touchdown pass against Tennessee Tech and then returned two kickoffs for touchdowns against Arkansas State. His football career didn't end when he graduated, and his name would soon ring out again in the halls of the Shore Conference. Kubu's fellow backfield star, Doug Deicke, also went on to enjoy great success in college football, playing at Albright. A three-year starter and workhorse back, he was the leading scorer on the undefeated Lions team of 1961.

The finale of Kubu and Deicke's high school careers also represented the end of Manasquan's impressive run in Class A. Starting in 1960, the Shore Conference was divided into three divisions, and Manasquan was realigned into the newly created B North. The Big Blue began the new decade in a new division, with new rivals. Hal Manson's next challenge would be to keep the momentum going.

RED BANK RISES AGAIN

In three years, Bob Glisson and his double-winged T had restored Red Bank football to respectability. The Bucs had challenged for league titles in 1956, 1957, and 1958 and seemed to be bound to win a title soon or later. Then, in 1959, the roof suddenly caved in. It was a tough time for Red Bank High School. With the population of the nearby suburbs of Eatontown, Shrewsbury, and Tinton Falls exploding, the high school was at full capacity. Delays in the construction of a new high school (Monmouth Regional) forced Red Bank onto double sessions.

No matter how the school board attempted to split up the student body, that put an immense strain on the school's resources, and all the athletic teams suffered, football included. Since younger players had evening sessions and couldn't participate in sports, the team's depth was cut in half. The team was inexperienced as it was, and they ended up stumbling to a 1-8 season, which ended in an ugly 40-0 loss to Long Branch.

More trouble came that summer. Glisson, who was paid a relatively low coaching stipend, asked for a salary increase. When the Board of Education denied him that, he stepped down just before the start of practice.[35] With no time left to find a coach, the board had no choice but to promote assistant Lee Walsky to the head spot. Walsky was an experienced coach who had enjoyed success as the head man at Highland Park and Garfield, but he was taking over a team from which not very much was expected. After the Bucs lost their first three games (all by blowouts, the worst of them a 31-0 loss to RBC), expectations dropped even lower.

The Bucs finally won a game by beating Middletown, but since the Lions hadn't won a game yet either no one was all that impressed. Certainly, no one expected them to beat Asbury Park. The Blue Bishops were 3-0-1, ranked No. 1 in the Shore, and featured an offensive machine that starred All-Shore tackle Bill Savage and future Yale halfback Ralph Vandersloot. Perhaps the only people in Monmouth County who expected Red Bank to even compete with Asbury were the team's coaches and players themselves.

They knew what few other people did—that the Bucs had a wealth of talent in their own right. Junior end Walter "Utah" Scott was a physical blocker, sure-handed receiver, and tenacious defender. New quarterback Willie Davis was gaining confidence handling the ball, and Wendell Brown was emerging as a reliable runner who could play quarterback in a pinch. That was important since Davis struggled all season with a wrenched back. The week of the Asbury game, Davis was in so much pain that he was unable to play at all. Fortunately for Red Bank, they had Brown.[36]

The Bucs gained confidence by holding the Bishops scoreless in the first half, and they stayed calm even after Asbury took a 7-0 lead in the third quarter. Brown's long pass to Scott set up his own touchdown sneak and cut the score to 7-6, but Red Bank missed the conversion. Butch Bruno's teams were always good at milking the clock and sitting on a lead, and they spent much of the fourth quarter pounding the line. They didn't give the ball up until the game's final moments, and when they did, they left Red Bank pinned on their own 20-yard line.

The season's biggest play came like a bolt from the blue. Richard Robinson was a backfield regular, but he didn't carry the ball very often. On the first play of this drive, however, Robinson took a handoff up the middle and found a seam. He went through it with "electrifying swiftness," leaving the stunned Asbury defenders without an angle to catch him. Eighty yards later, he was celebrating in the end zone with his teammates. Red Bank led 13-7, and the shocked Bishops were behind for the first time all year.

Asbury mounted a desperation drive, and reached the 11-yard-line with forty seconds left. The Buc defense, however, came up with two sacks to end the game and complete the upset. Somehow, Red Bank had knocked off Asbury Park. Now, despite their mediocre 2-3 overall record, the Bucs were undefeated in Class A and tied with Long Branch for first in the standings. It was a spot they simply refused to relinquish. Willie Davis came back from his injury to throw two touchdown passes (one to Scott) in a 26-19 win over Freehold, and Robinson ran for two more touchdowns in a 29-14 victory against a talented Neptune team.[37]

It was almost cruel to Asbury Park. The 7-1-1 Blue Bishops had enjoyed a magnificent season, which would finish on Thanksgiving with a 27-6 rout of Middletown. Their bruising defense allowed just 32 points in total, and they had proven themselves on a par with just about any team in the state. Yet their destiny was completely out of their control. Unless Union lost, they had no hopes of even winning a share of the CJ IV crown, and unless Red Bank lost, they'd be frozen out of the Class A title as well. Asbury's only hope lay with their own hated rival, Long Branch. Only a Green Wave victory over the Bankers would gain Butch Bruno's boys a split of the title. Anything less and it would be Red Bank's alone.

The chance to win a title for the first time in sixteen years was motivation enough for the Buccaneers, but there were other factors thrown in to sweeten the pot. The Bucs hadn't beaten Long Branch since 1944 and only rarely were the games even close. The *Asbury Park Press* was so certain that the Green Wave would win that they had billed the Long Branch-Asbury Park game a week earlier as a title decider.[38] Red Bank had no intention of sharing the title with anyone and had even less intention of conceding any superiority to a 3-5 Long Branch team.

The stage was set for a Thanksgiving epic. Six thousand fans saw it happen live. Robinson ran for a touchdown, while Eddie Winrow threw one to Utah Scott and returned an interception for another. That, plus a critical extra point from Scott, staked the Bucs to a 19-6 lead midway through the second. Then, as it always did on Thanksgiving morning, the tide turned Long Branch's way. The Wave cut the lead to 19-12 at the half, and then Winrow limped off with an injury. The Bucs offense was stalling, and they were starting to turn the ball over. Early in the fourth, they fumbled at their own 31 and the Branchers recovered. A few foolish penalties set up Moser for a short touchdown sneak, and Phillips buried the extra point to tie the game at 19.

That was how the game ended. Neither team could get possession with good field position, and neither coach was willing to take any unnecessary risks. The game ended with Long Branch's quarterback falling on the ball to run out the clock.[39] It was a fittingly odd ending to one of the strangest Class A title races the Shore Conference would ever see. Asbury Park, with a 7-1-1 record and one of the greatest defensive seasons in their history, won nothing. Red Bank won the crown at 4-4-1, undefeated in their league games and winless outside of them. They hadn't won them all; they had won the right ones, and that was enough. From doormats in August to champions in November, Red Bank had seen it all.

THE RISE OF RUMSON

From 1937 to 1941, Joe Rosati had been the chief assistant to Lou Jacoubs at Rumson. During those years, Jacoubs (the founder of football at Rumson) and Rosati had seen their team steadily rise from a doormat to a competitive force in the Shore Conference. All that came to a sudden halt with Pearl Harbor. Jacoubs stepped down as head coach, Rosati went into the Army, and the all-encompassing war knocked football down to the bottom of the priority list. More and more of Rumson's young men set off for war with each passing year, and the on-field results steadily declined. The Bulldogs hit their low point in 1945, when a still-depleted team struggled through an ugly 0-7-1 campaign, scoring just one touchdown all season.

It was to these diminished football fortunes that Joe Rosati returned in the summer of 1946. Things weren't easy at first. In his first fifteen games as head coach, the Bulldogs won just once. However, Rosati was confident that with time and continuity, he would be able to rebuild the program. Never one for elaborate trick plays or intricate offensive systems, the Rumson mentor relied on a simple formula—continuity, fundamentals, and supreme effort.[40]

The team steadily improved, and in 1948, they enjoyed their first winning season in eight years. These were the days of star quarterback Bill "Apple" Rountree, a junior on that team.[41] Rountree was even better in 1949, winning the Shore Conference scoring title and leading Rumson to their best record yet, 5-2-1.[42] The most meaningful of those wins was the last, a 13-7 Thanksgiving Day victory over Leonardo, their first win in the series since 1941. The Bulldogs trailed into the fourth quarter, but a fumble recovery set them up at the 23-yard-line going in, and Rountree broke free on a sweep around right end that won him the scoring title and Rumson the game.[43]

In 1950 and 1951, the Bulldogs used another Rosati specialty, disciplined linemen, to stay in contention against a tough schedule. Three linemen (Walter "Eggy" Brown, Bill Parker, and future Brown captain Jim McGuiness) won All-Shore honors as Rumson enjoyed two more strong seasons. When the B Division of the Shore Conference debuted in 1952, Rumson had a reputation as a highly competitive program and was expected to contend for titles every year. Instead, they hit a dry spell. Cursed by low numbers and bad luck, the Bulldogs won just five games in four years. Some of those years, Rumson wasn't even able to field a JV team.[44]

Rosati, however, took a longer view than most and saw that the tide was turning. In the fall of 1955, 118 freshmen entered the school, the first Rumson High School class to hit triple digits. The next year, 146 more arrived. While this meant overcrowded hallways and classrooms, it also gave Rosati enough bodies to restore JV football and even add a freshman team.[45] It all paid off in 1957, when the backfield combination of Bill Lewis and JC Williams turned the Bulldogs back into contenders. They upset Lakewood and Matawan on their way to an impressive 7-2 finish. A 27-7 loss to Central kept them from a division title, but they were good enough to win the CJ II crown and capped their season with a 50-14 Thanksgiving rout of a new rival—Red Bank Catholic.

COLLISION COURSE: RUMSON, RED BANK CATHOLIC, AND THE BIRTH OF A THANKSGIVING DAY RIVALRY

Rumson and Red Bank had always been natural rivals; Red Bank was the shopping hub of the Bayshore, and Rumson was its upscale suburb. Rumson-Fair Haven High School and Red Bank High School had a bitter rivalry of their own, the annual early season Battle of Ridge Road. What Rumson lacked, and Red Bank had, however, was a Thanksgiving rival. Middletown's rapid growth took them out of Rumson's class and led to the end of that series in 1952. That left Rumson casting about for a Thanksgiving opponent, which in those days was no small thing.

Those annual rivalry games were the central attraction of high school football in the state. It wasn't unusual to see rivalry games attract 10,000 fans; some of the biggest drew over 20,000. As many as 200,000 people watched high school football every Thanksgiving morning. Rumson didn't just lack a rival. They were left out of New Jersey's single largest annual community event. Fortunately, there was another school nearby that was in the same boat.

Red Bank Catholic had never managed to establish a permanent holiday series either, although they did want one. The Catholic school was receptive to the idea of playing Rumson; saving travel time by adding local games was always a winner with the Caseys, who often had to wander the state in search of games. The two schools also had some history together, having played annually from 1947 until 1951. Their first Thanksgiving Day meeting in 1957 was a mismatch. RBC's first-year Head Coach Al Forte was in the middle of a major rebuilding job, and it showed on the field. Rumson crushed the Caseys, 51-14, with Bill Lewis scoring four times to clinch the Shore scoring title.[46] In the long run, though, that only fueled the rivalry, giving the Caseys even more motivation for 1958.

That was the year that Forte's rebuilding efforts first started to bear fruit. The 1958 Casey team didn't win many games, but they had more steel to them than the teams that had taken the field in the past several years. In large part, that was due to Forte's young line coach, recent Atlantic Highlands graduate Dick Kleva. Lacking bulk and numbers, Kleva managed to turn his linemen into disciplined, technically sound overachievers. The Caseys nearly upset Red Bank in the season opener and closed the gap on Rumson, losing a hard-fought 13-0 game to a strong 5-2-2 Bulldogs team. Over the course of that game, the undersized RBC line outperformed everyone's expectations by containing the Bulldogs' All-Shore back, Terry Sieg.[47]

That Thanksgiving win, Rumson's seventh against Red Bank Catholic without defeat, was also the fifth game in a season-ending winning streak.

That momentum carried over into 1959, a year for which the Bulldogs had high expectations. Sieg, back for his senior year, was the headliner, but he was far from a one-man gang. Rumson had ninety-nine players that year and plenty of talent. The backfield, which featured Sieg, Lou DeGeorge, and Bill Jackubecy, was loaded with speed. Up front, there was center/linebacker George Fallon, guard Bill Kelly, and physically imposing tackle James "JV" McCarthy. The goal for the season was to win the B Division and a sectional title, and the team started fast toward that goal.

Sieg was the star, finishing the season with fifteen touchdowns in nine games, including a 75-yard interception return for a touchdown against Keyport that clinched the Class B title, Rumson's first-ever football championship. Only the Thanksgiving game stood between them and another first—an unbeaten season. Rumson had never lost to RBC, but this Casey team was different than any that had come before. They too were undefeated, and arguably even better than the 1954 state title team. They too had assembled a great offensive line, whipped carefully into shape by Kleva—tackles Frank Manzi and Ted Bremmekamp, guards Matt Husson and Joe Miele, and two versatile ends who could catch passes just as well as they could throw crushing body blocks, Ralph "Doc" Corley and Jay Abbes.

The Caseys beat all comers—Red Bank, Sayreville, Neptune, and even traditionally strong parochial powers such as Holy Cross and Trenton Catholic. Routing Trenton Catholic clinched the Parochial A South title for the Caseys and added spice to the game against Rumson. A huge crowd of 7,000 fans filed into the Rumson bleachers, the biggest crowd that either team had ever played before. They had high hopes of seeing a classic, and they were not disappointed. This was a game of "vicious tackling, bone-crunching blocking, and savage collisions."[48]

The tackling was so jarring, in fact, that the usually sure-handed rivals combined to fumble the ball thirteen times before game's end. Rumson, which had a significant size advantage, grabbed the upper hand early. JV McCarthy blocked a punt that Bill Kelly recovered for a touchdown and a 6-0 lead. The RBC defense, however, set the tone for the rest of the game by coming up with a crucial play on the extra point. Rumson tried a dive with fullback Jim Jackubecy, but he was met in the hole by Spencer Hoos and stopped short of the line.

That proved crucial. In the third quarter, the undersized Casey defense forced a fumble and fell on it deep in Rumson territory. Bob Bossone carried the ball twice, finding the end zone on the second try. It was 6-6. Now it was the turn of the Rumson defense to come up with a crucial stop on the point after, forcing Bossone into an incomplete pass and keeping the game tied. That was how it ended.[49] Both teams finished with 7-0-2 records and a reputation as the best in the history of their respective school. The quality of play displayed by both schools had also secured the RBC-Rumson classic a prominent place among the Shore's Thanksgiving Day attractions.

Two of Rumson's players would continue their careers in the Atlantic Coast Conference—Terry Sieg at Virginia and JV McCarthy at Duke (where he started from 1962-64, winning a spot in the North South College All-Star Game after his senior year). While the graduates were beginning their college careers, both Bulldogs and Caseys were reloading for what they intended to be another fine season. Graduation had badly thinned Rumson's ranks in 1960, but the few and proud veterans of the prior year gave a good account of themselves. The Bulldogs managed to extend their unbeaten streak to seventeen games before losing to Matawan, and they rolled into Thanksgiving Day with a respectable 4-2-1 record. Yet even that paled in comparison to the magic happening over at Red Bank Catholic.

Before the season started, Forte and Kleva saw that they had a team with great talent. Bob Bossone had matured into one of the best quarterbacks seen at the Shore in some years, and he'd have a towering, reliable target in end Jay Abbes. When the Caseys needed to run the ball, they could turn to bone-crunching halfbacks Doc Corley and Eric Donath. Still, the coaches were concerned that the young line was not particularly polished, and they wanted their team to come together as a tight-knit unit. Knowing that their team needed some seasoning if they were to achieve their full potential, the two coaches came up with a creative way to do it.[50]

In 1960, much of Monmouth County was still farmland. Just west of Holmdel lay a Farmers and Garden Association Labor Project Camp, a collection of cabins for migrant workers during the summertime. For two weeks in September, the Casey football team moved into the vacant cabins. Each day began with a light workout at six a.m., followed by a hearty breakfast, two full-contact practices separated by a lunch break, a dinner, and team meetings interspersed with New York Giants game films. In all, it was eight hours' worth of football each day.[51] By any possible measure, the camp was an enormous success.

The Caseys charged into their season opener against Red Bank a prepared team. Bob Bossone threw for three touchdowns and ran for a fourth as RBC routed their crosstown rivals 31-0.[52] They routed two other Class A schools that year, burying Neptune and Middletown. Bossone had four touchdowns over the course of the two games, and Doc Corley polished off Middletown with a 55-yard touchdown run.[53] By the time Thanksgiving rolled around, the Caseys were unbeaten in seventeen straight games and had clinched the Parochial A South title. They were regularly drawing crowds of over 2,000 fans, and when they faced Rumson on Thanksgiving, an overflow crowd of 7,000 came out to see it.

Joe Rosati's team, always meticulously prepared, fought hard, but the Caseys had too much talent. Kleva's superbly drilled line carved huge holes for Corley, who scored twice, and Eric Donath, who scored once. RBC slowly but surely ground out an 18-0 victory. When the clock ran out, the cheering only got louder.[54] It had been an incredible run. Red Bank Catholic had pitched six shutouts and outscored their opponents 198-38 en route to finishing the season at 9-0-0. It was the first time in school history that they had finished with an unblemished record, and although the Broad Street School has produced many fine teams since, none have been perfect. The 1960 team was perfect.

PART 4:
THE RISE OF THE SHORE CONFERENCE, 1960 TO 1974

CHAPTER 15
THE BIRTH OF BRICK

Friday, December 6, 1974, was a red-letter day in the history of New Jersey high school football. That was the day of the first-ever state championship playoff game, which pitted Brick Township against Camden for the South Jersey Group IV crown. The instant classic, played in front of a roaring crowd at Convention Hall in Atlantic City, captured much of what was changing in New Jersey—the decline of the state's cities, the rise of its suburbs, and the emergence of the Shore as a year-round residential community. Appropriately, it featured two schools that could not have been more different.

Camden was one of the state's traditional athletic powers. They were urban, predominantly African American, and eager to add another plaque to their high school's crowded trophy case. The glory days of World War II might have been gone, but Camden was still one of the largest cities in New Jersey and it still carried some of the glow from its days as an industrial powerhouse. In those golden years, the city had been home to Campbell's Soup, to the world's largest record company, and to the world's busiest shipyards. Locals swelled with pride as they recalled those important days when they had built the ships that helped win the Pacific War for the United States Navy.

Many Brick residents would have felt that this game was the most exciting event in the town's history. Their suburban community was as new as Camden's was old, and in their search for a tradition to call their own, they had turned to football. Between the football team, the cheerleaders, the band, and the massive convoy of fans that had followed them, it seemed as though the entire town had made the trip to Atlantic City.

Some of those who had come were not even from Brick, but from its neighboring towns. This game was a chance to prove that the Shore's football teams were as good as any in the state, and fans from across the area were there to cheer for the Dragons. Among the crowd was Red Bank's entire football team; the Bucs, who had been denied a spot in the CJ II playoffs, were there cheering for Brick in the hopes that a Shore victory would prove the state association wrong for leaving them out of the playoffs.

Red Bank's anger showed how far the Shore had come in the crowded, glorious fifteen years since 1960. Once a lightly regarded local league, self-conscious of its inferiority, the Shore Conference had grown to feel that it was as good as any other league in the state. Its goal now was to prove that to everyone else, and on this night in Atlantic City, it was Brick carrying the banner. For once, the whole Shore was united behind one team, chasing one dream. It was a football game unlike any other.[1]

Warren Wolf (Brick Township head coach): *"There was such unity in Brick Township at that time. There was such a community spirit that went down and filled the whole sideline and half of Convention Hall. It was a great thrill to be able to play there."*[2]

Dan Duddy (Brick Township Class of 1973, former Green Dragon quarterback): *"I went with a bunch of guys as freshmen at Glassboro State, now Rowan. It was unbelievable."*[3]

Tony Graham (Asbury Park Press sportswriter): *"Brick was the flagship football team of the Jersey Shore and had been for some time. The pride of Shore football was wrapped up in this game. Never before or since have I been as psyched up for a high school football game as I was for that one. I've seen some big ones since but that was king in my mind."[4]*

For Brick Township, this was the pinnacle. This was a town whose passion rivaled that of any other in New Jersey. The rituals of the fall—the first day of practice, the season opener, the Homecoming game, and the Thanksgiving Day finale—all were civic holidays in Brick. Crowds at Green Dragon games were always huge. From the youngest children to the oldest grandparents, from recent alumni to childless adults, all of Brick buzzed with Dragon fever. The remarkable thing was that all that passion had emerged from virtually nothing. Just twenty years before, almost everyone in the stands on that chilly December evening was from somewhere else, and most of them had never even heard of Brick. Brick Township High School wasn't even a ballot item, and Brick Township football wasn't even a dream.

DECEMBER 6, 1954

What was Brick in 1954? Well, that depended on who you asked. To an Ocean County local, it was a quiet rural town east of Lakewood. To boy scouts, it was a place to go to summer camp and stay in lodges with long Native American names. To a few vacationers, it was a nice place to rent a bungalow for the summer on the shady shores of the Metedeconk River. To the *Asbury Park Press*, it was "three housing developments linked by a few dirt roads." If it had a community center, it was a country store where "old men went and sat around a potbellied stove, drinking coffee and telling stories."[5]

The small population didn't require much of a school system and certainly didn't need a high school; the few teenagers attended Point Pleasant. Building a high school would have been dismissed as a completely unnecessary luxury. That would mean more taxes, which nobody wanted. Brick residents were content to live in a quiet, quaint corner of a quiet, quaint county. There was no need for anything to change.[6]

It seemed ridiculous to suggest that this little town would win the attention of the state for anything, let alone football. There was a clear hierarchy in New Jersey football in those years, and within it, Ocean County might as well not even have existed. The Newark papers compiled the state rankings, and their sports editors *knew* that the best football was played in North Jersey. These were the glory years for the big city high schools, and for no school were these years more glorious than for Memorial High School of West New York, the colossus of Hudson County.

> **Al Saner (former Memorial player):** *"At that time, Memorial High School was the cream of the crop. We had a great system; we had a great coach. I think about Coach Coviello often . . . my whole philosophy of football comes from him."*[7]

Under the great Joe Coviello, Memorial had emerged as a state power, losing just four games between 1946 and 1954. In 1954, they enjoyed their second straight unbeaten season, their third straight North I Group IV championship, and their seventh straight Hudson County title. Memorial had ascended to heights that no school in the state had ever reached. Few enjoyed the ride more than a young assistant coach named Warren Wolf.

Wolf, a 1944 graduate of Memorial, had gone to college and then returned to his hometown as a teacher. He enjoyed football, and so in order to pick up a little extra money he began spending nights coaching a local semipro team. Like everyone else in Hudson County, he was awestruck by what Joe Coviello was doing with the high school squad, and so was overjoyed in the summer of 1948 when Coviello invited him to join the staff at Memorial.

> **Warren Wolf:** *"My wife Peggy [had been] in his social studies class at Memorial . . . and Coach asked Peggy to ask me if I would be interested in coaching at Memorial. Well, that hit me like a bombshell. . . . That request was like a message from God. It stands out*

in my mind, that I was now starting my career in the footsteps of an immortal. The three most influential people in my life were my dad, my pastor, and Joe Coviello. He taught me about life and how to handle things. . . . Whenever I had a problem, he was the first person I called."[8]

Wolf wanted to one day run a program of his own, but in 1954 he was more than happy to be a part of Coviello's staff, helping to coach the greatest team in all of New Jersey for the greatest coach in all of New Jersey. There was really no need for anything to change.

BRICK TOWNSHIP, SUMMER 1958

What a difference four years could make. There were still dirt roads, and it was still a small town, but now there were housing developments springing up here, there, and everywhere. The arrival of the Garden State Parkway had seen to that. People were starting to move down in record numbers. The town's population quadrupled from 4,000 in 1950 to 16,000 in 1960. More of everything was needed—more roads, more firemen, and most of all, more schools.

This was the height of the Baby Boom, and the number of school-age children in Brick was skyrocketing. It was clear that the town would need a high school of its own, and soon. Construction on the building started in the spring of 1957, and by the summer of 1958, the building was complete.[9] Meanwhile, the school's new administrators were busily searching for secretaries, teachers . . . and coaches.

Football was considered the most important coaching position. It was the most popular sport, and it was the easiest way for a school to show itself off to the entire town. A good team would put the school on display every Saturday for a host of curious onlookers, and everyone associated with Brick wanted to represent themselves well. The Board of Education wanted immediate success, so they wanted an experienced football coach.

Their first choice was George Conti, the architect of successful teams at both Newark West Side and Metuchen. He mulled it over, then declined.

Conti was still new at Metuchen and didn't want to change schools again so quickly.[10] Now the summer was getting late.

That same summer saw Warren Wolf in a pickle of his own. He loved working under Joe Coviello and Memorial had lost just once in six years. Teaching at Public School #4 in West New York was just as good. But housing was a problem. His apartment in West New York couldn't comfortably house his growing family, and larger homes in Hudson County were just too expensive. The summer was getting late.

> **Warren Wolf Jr. (son of the head coach)**: *"My grandmother and grandpa on my father's side had a house down on Point Pleasant. They would come down here, and my parents would come down here during the summer. My Dad was approached at our church."*[11]

That church, the Harvey Memorial Methodist Church, was also attended by Brick's principal, Joseph Nixon. It just so happened that the church's pastor had somehow learned about these respective problems and realized that introducing them to each other might just provide the solution. On a "clear, bright, sunny, blue-sky" Sunday morning at Harvey Memorial, the pastor introduced the principal to the coach, who proceeded to offer him a job. It was the first time Warren Wolf learned of the high school where he would spend the next fifty years.

Naturally, he hesitated. Leaving Memorial meant leaving West New York, leaving his coaching mentor, and uprooting his entire family. Wolf wouldn't even be able to tell Joe Coviello in person, since the head coach was away working at a summer camp in New Hampshire. On top of that, it meant leaving for a completely unknown situation.

> **Warren Wolf Jr.**: *"[My dad] goes back up to have dinner on a Sunday with my family on my mother's side. My father goes 'Well, I took a job at Brick High School to be a head coach and gym teacher,' and my uncle Ted goes 'Where the hell is that?' That was his first introduction to the way people would respond."*

On the other hand, an opportunity like this one, to not only become a head coach but to build a program completely from scratch, might not come again. He had to do it. One day in late July, Wolf sat down and wrote a letter to Coviello. Then he drove to Brick and signed a contract to become a physical education teacher and head football coach.

Warren Wolf: *"Of course, my knees were shaking and my heart was beating, but my wife gave me great confidence that we could do it. [It] reminded me of Brigham Young on his trip to Utah."[12]*

In moving to Brick, the Wolfs were taking part in a truly enormous population movement. Suburbanization was sweeping the country, and it was completely reshaping the Jersey Shore. Monmouth and Ocean Counties, where farmland was every day being converted into new housing developments, were now the two fastest growing counties in the state. Meanwhile, the state's largest cities were shrinking or stagnating.

In that way, the growth of Brick represented a perfect storm of trends nationwide. City housing was in in short supply, and what was available was not cheap or designed for children. During the Baby Boom, when new birth rate records were set every year from 1946 to 1963, the number of families was growing fast. The most affordable family homes could be found in the suburbs, where tract housing was cheap, and the land was available. Without these two trends coming together, Brick High School would never have existed.[13]

The boom would feed on itself. A large permanent population meant a need for more services, and that meant more jobs at supermarkets, restaurants, gas stations, toy stores, and, crucially for young college graduates hoping to embark on a teaching career, schools. Between 1950 and 1980, twenty-four new high schools would open at the Shore. The flood of new arrivals was creating what we would recognize today as the modern Shore Conference.

The impact of this population tide can best be seen among the Shore's head football coaches. During this era, there were eleven Shore head coaches who had originally lived in Hudson County. Five more came from equally urban Essex County, and another four came over from Brooklyn. Like the families of their players, they were all building something new.

ENTER THE DRAGONS

On September 1, 1958, the very first Brick Green Dragon football team assembled on the field behind the high school for their very first practice. At least, one day it would be a field; right now, it was just black sand and high reeds. There were no lights, so evening practices would be lit by the headlights of cars, school buses, and even an airport search light that the mayor had borrowed from a nearby landing strip.[14] It was fitting that the field was so raw—of the fifty-five boys on the roster, only one of them (Jack McGrath, a transfer from Dumont High School in Bergen County) had ever earned a varsity letter.[15] Warren Wolf knew he had work to do.

From those very first weeks of practice, a Warren Wolf trademark emerged—he would take his team anywhere and play anyone if it would help them improve. The Dragons traveled to North Jersey for scrimmages with St. Joseph's of West New York and Pascack Valley. More locally, they scrimmaged Asbury Park and the postgraduates of Admiral Farragut Academy.

> **Denny Toddings (Brick player and future Shore head coach)**: *"He knew all the tough schools [in New Jersey] and that's what he wanted. He wanted to win. . . . We didn't know that. We just thought this was normal. Then you look back and you go, 'Holy Christ, Montclair! We scrimmage Montclair!' One of the best schools in the state for a hundred years, and here we are, coming up, bunch of little guys, the Dragons, the Green Dragons."[16]*

> **Kevin Williams (longtime Ocean County sports reporter)**: *"When Warren started growing that program, he started playing teams from out of the area. North Jersey teams. Going to their place . . . they'd go to the North Bergens and Bayonnes and all these perennial powers who thought of Ocean County as this little dump in the woods. They went up there, and they won."[17]*

Meanwhile, Wolf and his coaches were working furiously to bring their inexperienced team up to the high standards that they had set. They needed every minute available in order to install their chosen offensive system—the wing-T. That was the offense that Joe Coviello ran at Memorial, and it was what Wolf wanted his team to run. Now a standard among high school offenses, the wing-T was new in 1958. Brick may have been the first school to use it at the Shore. This was a deceptively complex offense, relying on perfect technique and timing.

Tubby Raymond (former head coach at Delaware and architect of the wing-T offense): *"The wing-T made up for a lot of things you didn't have. By hiding the ball and using misdirection, you catch up with any deficiencies you have physically,"*[18]

A wing-T coach looks to find a defensive player with incompatible responsibilities, and then attacks that player with plays that put those responsibilities in conflict. If the defense tried to provide help to the targeted man, a good wing-T coach (and Warren Wolf was good at what he did) would have plays ready to attack newly emerging weaknesses. The key was execution. If the plays are run sloppily, all that fancy backfield action achieves nothing. Run properly, though, they could be devastatingly effective.

After just under a month of preparation, Brick's new team took to their unfinished field to face North Hunterdon. For this first game, the team was clad in white helmets with a green stripe, not their later, iconic winged white and green helmets. Still, it was recognizably Brick football. The Green Dragons were running the wing-T, and Warren Wolf was pacing the sidelines in the gray suit that would become his trademark. A large crowd came out, eager to see what the new coach would put on the field to represent their home.

Dan Duddy: *"Coach Wolf came down from North Jersey and everybody in our neighborhoods were transplants from North Jersey. They all kind of knew about Coach Wolf and his background with Coach Coviello, so the whole town was abuzz about this new coach from North Jersey who was coaching our very first football team in our brand-new high school."*[19]

Brick was not yet a powerhouse, and North Hunterdon proved it. The visitors took a 20-0 lead and never looked like losing the game. Still, Brick showed potential. Late in the game, quarterback John Gant perfectly executed a play-action fake and found Jack McGrath all alone in the end zone for the first touchdown in Brick history. The *Asbury Park Press* noted that while Brick's offense "either sparked or sputtered," at times it "showed the same slashing ground game that has made Memorial tops in Hudson County." Something special was starting.[20]

The smartest ones noticed a diminutive freshman named Sam Riello. Riello's story was common to Brick—he had been born in Newark, then moved with his parents to Ocean County as they traded their apartment for a house with bedrooms for each of their five children. A successful runner in CYO meets in Newark, Riello decided to try out for the football team at his new school. Almost immediately, he questioned his decision.

> **Sam Riello**: *"It was the first day of football, and I was in line to get my equipment. The guy ahead of me was a senior, Jack Mc-Grath. He was 6-2, 220 pounds. He was a man. I weighed about 130 pounds at the time, so I looked at him and wondered if I should try this game."* [21]

Warren Wolf looked past Riello's small size and saw instead his ability to make rapid cuts and evade tacklers. Although just a freshman, he soon electrified the Shore, running for two touchdowns in Brick's first-ever victory (against Bordentown). The Dragons didn't look back, winning three of their next four games. They entered their first-ever Thanksgiving Game against Central Regional with plenty of momentum.[22]

Enthusiasm was at high tide in Brick. Most of the high school's students had gone to Central in 1957, making this a natural rivalry. They held a Thanksgiving Eve bonfire, at which they burned a dummy representing a Central football player.[23] The game itself was a tooth-and-nail struggle, fought in the spirit of all great Thanksgiving Day games. Central managed to snatch a 13-12 victory, but the Dragons had acquitted themselves well.[24]

Their final record of 4-4 could be fairly counted as a success. A young team had bought into Wolf's system, and with so many players returning for 1959, the future looked bright. Linemen such as All-Shore tackle Tony Hennessey and junior center Denny Toddings were that much more instinctive in their blocking assignments, quarterback John Gant that much more deceptive in his fakes, and little sophomore Sammy Riello that much faster to the hole.

They would need all those advantages. In order to prepare his team for its entry into the Shore Conference in 1960, Warren Wolf had booked a tough slate that included games against Class A champions Manasquan and Class B champions Matawan. These weren't challenges to be feared, though. Instead, they were opportunities to establish Brick football's reputation by playing and beating the best.

Warren Wolf: *"We like winning as much as anyone else, but we are much more interested in playing interesting football."*[25]

The Dragons beat Matawan 14-13 in their season opener, displaying for the first time what later generations of Brick fans would call Brick magic. It was the third quarter, and the Dragons had just tied the game at 6-6 on Bill Geldhauser's touchdown run. The extra point snap was low and rolled back to holder Jack Osborne, who alertly scooped it up and scrambled into the end zone for the extra point and a 7-6 lead. Riello's later touchdown and extra point proved the difference in Brick's narrow 14-13 victory.

Their next performance was even more astounding. It was the grand opening of Brick's new football field, complete with shining bleachers on each side. The opponent was Manasquan, and the Warriors hadn't lost a game in almost two years. This was the upstart against the established power, something highlighted by the state of the gridiron.

Richard Bonelli (Manasquan player): *"They'd just put a new field in. They didn't have a blade of grass on it. We played on dried dirt . . . it was very dusty. There was no moisture. We'd rinse our* *face off with a wet rag or something so we could see who the hell we were.*[26]

Rudimentary field and all, Brick prevailed, 14-0. The impressed *Asbury Park Press* rated them even with Long Branch as the best team in the area. When Riello opened the Toms River South game with a 69-yard touchdown run, the Brick crowd roared, and possibilities of an undefeated season danced before their eyes. It wasn't quite time for that yet. South rallied to win, 19-7.[27] A few weeks later, the Dragons missed their chance to win a CJ II title when they lost 6-0 in the rain and mud at Sayreville. However, the team still rolled to a 7-2 finish, routing Central 31-0 on Thanksgiving. A tradition was being born.

The Sayreville game was a sign of what was to come. The game might have been played in a miserable freezing rain, but there were still 600 Brick fans willing to make the trip. They traveled by caravan, riding eleven buses and countless cars, and although they shivered, they cheered each play that went Brick's way and heckled each call that went against them.[28] Those crowds grew with each week, peaking with a huge crowd on Thanksgiving. Warren Wolf was laying the permanent foundation for a program, one that could win over the long term and rival the achievements of any football dynasty the state had ever seen.

Brick's newness was more opportunity than challenge. With no established way of doing things, Wolf had almost complete freedom to organize his program as he saw fit. He would use that freedom and his considerable force of personality to convince people to join with him in the dream of a Brick football dynasty.

> **Dan Duddy**: *"It was this fresh, new, budding town. It was wet clay, just waiting to be molded. He had a strong personality, and he knew how to intrigue, interest, motivate, and inspire people and bring them to levels they otherwise never could have imagined."*[29]

One of the first things that Wolf set out to do at Brick was to establish strong freshmen and junior varsity teams, complete with quality coaches and a challenging schedule. By the end of the 1960s, it was not unusual for Brick's freshmen teams to top eighty players. Just like the varsity team, they also would go anywhere for a game—the 1958 team even went to Hudson County to face Memorial. Those early sub-varsity teams won plenty of games, developing an expectation of victory right from the start.[30] As the town grew, a Pop Warner program was founded, bringing grade schoolers into the pipeline.

Therefore, the Dragons were never really young. Starters graduated, but the newcomers were well prepared. They had been running the same offense and defense since they were eight years old; they knew it all by heart.[31] Besides, they'd been watching the Green Dragons for as long as they could remember. Football was everywhere in the fall. Monday afternoons were for junior varsity games, weekdays for youth games, and Friday belonged to the freshmen. It all built up to the varsity game on Saturday afternoon. Home games were a major public event, and away games meant a caravan of buses to whatever distant town the mighty Dragons were bound for next. Football had become the glue that held the entire town together.

Dan Duddy: *"It was on the streets of our neighborhoods that we learned what Brick football was. We were all kind of raised on football. . . . We played football in the street all day long, every day. Everybody on our street became a Brick football player or a big fan. Of course, everybody was at the games. You could hear the horns blaring at about 4:30, 5:00 on Saturday afternoons all over town that we had won the football game. You were either there or wished you were there. So, I was raised to be a Brick football player.*

I started playing in the Pop Warner Program. I think I was ten years old. . . . I was mesmerized by the other end of the field, looking at senior football players practicing while we were practicing. There were about seventy-five to eighty freshmen, there were more than a hundred varsity players. Some kids wore jersey number 101, 102, 103 on their jerseys. It was this huge, glorious football factory that I had become a part of."[32]

The year 1960 was Brick's third season, and the first real chance to display what they were becoming. It was also their first year as a full-fledged member of the Shore Conference, a league that would never be the same again. The Dragons hit Class B South like a hurricane.

It started with a 31-0 rout of a strong Matawan team to open the season. All-Shore end Bob Bittenbinder caved in the Husky line, All-Shore halfback Sam Riello ran through their defense, and star linebacker Denny Toddings stifled their offense. A series of routs followed, as Riello scored a combined seven touchdowns in wins over Neptune and Toms River.[33] Shutouts of Freehold, Point Pleasant, and Southern followed. Sayreville managed to score a touchdown, but they came no closer to stopping the Green Dragons than anyone else.

Thanksgiving saw Brick in Bayville, taking on Central. Four-thousand fans came to see if the Dragons could complete an undefeated season, and they were not disappointed. The hero was Riello, who ran for 118 yards on 20 carries and just wore out the Eagles. When the final gun sounded, Warren Wolf and his team were celebrating a 9-0 finish. To the residents of Brick, this was all something entirely new (as if to symbolize how new, Central's temporary bleachers collapsed during the game). The little coach from West New York in his battered old gray suit had brought his new town a perfect football team.[34]

Awards fell on the team—B South champions, CJ II champions, and No. 1 in Ocean County. Wolf, now a vice principal and one of the town's most celebrated citizens, received the student body's highest possible honor—the yearbook dedication. The book was appropriately titled *The Challenge,* and the dedication was inscribed "We work for him because he works tirelessly for what he believes . . . may the spirit and desire that are his become ours."[35]

In 1961, the Dragons matched 1960—they went undefeated again. This team may have been even better. Riello, now a senior, was the terror of the Shore, earning All-Shore and second-team All-State honors while leading his team to division and sectional titles. Brick won every game by at least two scores and drew at least 3,000 fans each Saturday.[36] After every game, swarms of grammar school children crowded the gate to shake the hands of their heroes. Brick's youngsters were dreaming of the day when they too would don the Green and White.[37]

The conclusion came at home, on Thanksgiving against Central. Eight-thousand fans saw Riello run for a touchdown in his final game for the Dragons, a 13-0 victory (their twentieth consecutive). Riello became the first Dragon player to win first-team All-State honors, while both he and end Dick Hudak won consensus places on the All-Shore team.[38]

Hudak went on to Harvard, starting at nose guard as a senior. Riello played at Hofstra and Glassboro State, later returning to the Shore as a coach and longtime referee. Denny Toddings, meanwhile, spent a post-grad year at Bordentown Military Institute and then went to Delaware, where he became a starting center on one of the nation's strongest small college teams. Like Riello, he returned to Ocean County, coaching and eventually becoming the athletic director at Monsignor Donovan High School.

The first era of Brick's football history was over. Brick's population was growing with incredible speed, and with each eighth grade class bigger than the next, the high school was soon growing larger than all of its small-school rivals. When the Shore Conference realigned in 1962, the Dragons were placed into Class A, where they would do battle with the league's established powers. They arrived just in time to play a key role in a glorious decade of Shore football.

CHAPTER 16
THE RISING TIDE:
CLASS A IN THE 1960s

B rick may have been on the rise, but the Shore Conference was still only rarely attracting statewide attention. A team from Asbury Park, Long Branch, or Freehold might grab an occasional headline, but everyone, even the local *Asbury Park Press*, perceived the North Jersey schools as being "farther ahead" than their Shore rivals. It was during the 1960s that this image finally changed. By the time Brick took the field against Camden in 1974, Shore players, coaches, and fans felt that they were the equals of anyone in the state and were determined to win the respect that they believed they deserved.

There were a number of factors that caused that change. The booming population flooded the high schools with talent and allowed the creation of Pop Warner leagues to develop young players. It also attracted a wave of ambitious young coaches. The 1960s saw a new generation of Shore Conference coaches build on the legacy left by their predecessors. Finally, local interest in the league was growing. New residents of Monmouth and

Ocean County wanted to be a part of the community in their new homes, and football games attracted them in large numbers.

They certainly got their money's worth. The 1960s were filled with exciting title races, decided by some of the greatest games ever played at the Shore. In nonleague games, local teams challenged some of the state's traditional powers, proving themselves across the length and breadth of the state. Caravans of local fans eagerly followed, cheering their sons and neighbors as they proved that boys with sand between their toes really could play football.

> **Skip Edwards (Long Branch resident and player)**: *"I always knew the Shore Conference. Red Bank, Long Branch, Manasquan, Middletown, Neptune. . . . I seemed like every week was a big game for Long Branch when I was in school . . . my father and my mother used to take me to Long Branch every Saturday in the fall, no matter where they were."*[1]

The spotlight fell mostly on the Shore's largest division, Class A. Between 1962 and 1969, that division was as wide open as it ever had been—four schools (Brick, Neptune, Toms River, and Middletown) won the crown, while three more (Long Branch, Monmouth, and Red Bank) regularly challenged them. Huge crowds filled the bleachers for games, and the clashes between the titans usually exceeded the hype. Each program had an identity of its own, often built around their colorful teams and iconic coaches.

The four teams that did win Shore Conference championships during the 1960s all had a few things in common. Their suburban location allowed them to benefit from the new housing developments springing up around the Shore. This meant a growing population, a broader tax base, and more students in the hallways. With those growing enrollment numbers came new teaching jobs, which could be filled by young assistant coaches. As a result, these relative upstarts were able to surpass established powers, such as Asbury Park and Long Branch, who saw their funding stagnate and their student populations decline.

Middletown was the most established of the decade's four championship contenders. The Lions had been the great power of the Shore Conference's early years, winning six Shore Conference championships for
Head Coach Arnie Truex. After 1957, however, the Lions began to struggle. Truex's preferred offensive system, the straight-ahead Notre Dame
Box, had gone out of style. Its simple blocking schemes and reliance on
the quarterback calling his own plays gave way to more complex offenses
in which plays were signaled in from the sidelines. Truex, who wanted
no part of that, stepped down in 1959 to become the school's athletic
director.

Arnie Truex (speaking in 1972 to the Red Bank Register):
*"We used to teach the basics . . . but today, they are big time with
their varying defenses, shooting linebackers, and rotating backfields
instead of focusing on simple things which the kids can execute . . .
it's too complex for kids to enjoy it. . . . If we made a mistake in the
old days with our one or two ways of doing the job, we didn't get
hit with an evaluation by the coaching staff and belittled in front
of everybody else and given a numerical rating on our play for the
day after a film review. To me, it takes the pleasure out of the game
for a high school boy."[2]*

After the coach's retirement, Middletown suffered through a series of
losing seasons and struggled to find a new identity. They got it in 1963,
when Truex hired Dick Kleva to serve as the school's head football and
head wrestling coach. Kleva, an all-state center at Atlantic Highlands, was
an excellent choice. Before arriving at Middletown, he had been a college
football player at NYU, a Marine drill instructor at Camp Lejeune, and an
assistant football and head wrestling coach at Red Bank Catholic.[3]

Gary Foulks: *"My father played for Coach Kleva. My dad said
he was a tough ex-Marine son of a gun. Every practice was five
quarters so that when you played in a game, and everybody else was
getting tired in the fourth quarter, you had another quarter left in
you."[4]*

Year in and year out, Kleva's linemen were the best in the Shore. They were seasoned by his gridiron drills, and also by their wrestling experience (he also coached that sport at Middletown, and his teams won five division titles). The Lions were a workmanlike team, rarely flashy but always in the mix. You took them lightly at your peril.

Neptune's Scarlet Fliers were very different—they were the glamor team of the Shore Conference. Flier football in some ways emulated Flier basketball (which had at one point won six straight Shore Conference titles). More than any of their local foes, they relied on individual brilliance and team speed. Even during the barren 1950s, they had produced fine individual stars, such as Nate Ramsey, who played first at Indiana and then with the Philadelphia Eagles.

Their football revival started in 1960, with the return of Joe Vetrano. An All-Shore player during his high school days, Vetrano had later kicked for five years for the San Francisco 49ers. His return brought excitement back to a team that had lost fifteen straight football games. Two hundred fans turned out for a dinner to celebrate his appointment as head coach, and 4,000 more turned out for his first game in charge, a 13-12 upset of Long Branch.[5] With sophomore quarterback Bob Davis running wild, the Fliers finished 5-4, their first winning season in over a decade. Vetrano left after the season to return to California, but the future was bright.

Leading the way into that future was John Bednarik. The brother of Philadelphia Eagles legend and NFL Hall of Famer Chuck Bednarik, the younger Bednarik was no football slouch himself. He had starred at William & Mary, then served as an assistant at Pennsylvania power Easton High School.[6] At Neptune, he built on Vetrano's foundation and translated the town's great athletic talent into football success. It was perhaps the decade's most impressive turnaround, rivaled only by what Ron Signorino was doing in Toms River.

Toms River had hit rock bottom in the early 1960s, losing seventeen out of eighteen games. Football was rapidly becoming an exercise in futility. That changed in 1964, when Signorino arrived in town. The thirty-year-old had played at Penn State and already enjoyed coaching success at Bald Eagle High School in Central Pennsylvania, where his teams lost just once in two seasons.[7] There, he began to develop the trademarks that would mark him as one of the Shore's most exciting characters. He was a disciplinarian, obsessed with conditioning and game fitness. He ran a fast-paced offense, and he was unafraid to use trick plays. Above all else, he was a fiery speaker and a master at inspiriting his teams with his own visible passion.

Gary Dyke (Bald Eagle defensive back, 1962-63): *"I have heard it said that Sig was like a Marine, with that flat-top haircut. I have some friends who are Marines, and he fits that description to a T. He was a fantastic motivator."*

After two winning seasons at Bald Eagle, Signorino was tipped off to a vacancy at Toms River by a friend on the Penn State coaching staff. He had never heard of the place. That wasn't unusual; many lifelong New Jerseyans knew nothing about little Toms River, a town so small that many of its roads were still unpaved.

Ron Signorino: *"I drove to my brother's house in Valley Forge, and we pulled out the atlas. We couldn't find the town. I thought I was going to a place called Palms River."*

Mistaken identity notwithstanding, Signorino jumped on the job. He was hired on a Sunday and began the process of moving to Ocean County the very next day. The job proved to be even bigger than he had first expected.

Joe Adelizzi (Toms River graduate): *"I went to Sig's first practice in 1964. There were about a hundred guys out for football. On the first day, the players had to meet times in a distance run. The previous two years, the players were given a pass when they didn't make the required times. But not under Sig. The second day of practice there were only sixty guys left."*[8]

Ron Signorino: *"The resources were not here. The coaching staffs were very, very small. The resources were very, very limited. They* *didn't film road games. . . . The language that I spoke to the players was like speaking Greek to them. That was what I noticed most. The emphasis, the intensity, the preparation in practice—wasn't there. We were playing Monmouth Regional [in the second week of the season]. They kicked us around. We went into the fourth quarter, and we were behind 25-0. I don't recall if they put the JVs in, I don't remember that, but we scored. So, we lost 27-7. Next thing I know, the band is marching down Main Street, and they're having a parade. I said, 'What's this?' They said, 'We're celebrating, we're having a parade, we scored a touchdown.' That's when I knew that maybe I had made a mistake."[9]*

But rather than accept defeat or give up, Signorino simply continued to work at building the program. He continued to demand the most of his players, expanded the staff and acquired quality assistant coaches, and began to run legendarily demanding practices. He wanted this teams to play with passion, enthusiasm, discipline, and a commitment to vicious hitting. It didn't take long before South's identity began to change.

One month into the season, the Indians won their first game, beating Freehold Regional 3-0 on a late Don Lewis field goal. The victory bell rang out for the first time in Signorino's Toms River career. And although the Indians won only one game that first year, the work they did that off-season ensured that there would be many more victories to come.[10]

Ron Signorino: *"I knew, after that first year, there was some encouragement. We got better at the end. . . . Between the first and second year, I got some very good assistant coaches. And we came up with the name, Hitting Indians. That's one thing I'm very proud of, because that has stuck. We're not the Indians. We're the Hitting Indians. And that name has stuck. The second thing we did was come up with a name for our defense. The players thought about it, the coaches thought about it, and one of the players suggested 'Coach, why don't we call the defense the War Lords?' That sounded pretty good. So that year, the Hitting Indians were born, and the War Lords were born. And we did play good defense. We won four, lost* *four, and tied one. But all the games were competitive. We began to build dedication. . . . We gradually got better. The third year we were 5-4, and the next year we were 6-3, and we started what became a nineteen-game winning streak."*[11]

Wolf. Bednarik. Kleva. And now Signorino. The formula was nothing short of explosive. Four fiery, innovative, larger-than-life coaches, in charge of programs at rapidly growing high schools blessed with great athletic talent and passionate fan bases. With all the pieces now in place, Class A of the Shore Conference was ready to move into its golden age.

THE EIGHT-YEAR WAR

Brick Township entered Class A in 1962. The *Asbury Park Press* predicted trouble; the Dragons were facing the toughest schedule in school history with a young team. Warren Wolf, however, remained confident. His team had come up through the Brick system, and they knew it inside and out. They also were playing for a great coaching staff—offensive coordinator George Jeck, line coaches Bill Keeney and George Spada, and defensive coach Bob Auriemma (the founding father of Brick's hockey program). A year later, the staff would get even deeper when Wolf turned the defense over to Manasquan graduate Vic Kubu, another young assistant with a very bright future. And all of them were constantly striving to learn more.

Warren Wolf Jr.: *"My Dad started preparing for the next season the day after Thanksgiving. . . . He was always a learner. Every year he'd go somewhere and learn something new on offense. In the 1960s, he used to go to Arkansas, or Texas, or Texas A&M. In the 1970s, when I was a sophomore, we went to the University of Houston. We went to Colorado one year. When I started coaching with him, we did a lot of different excursions to different colleges in order to learn. He never felt he knew enough. That's what made him successful."*[12]

Two new backfield stars, quarterback Carl Lamberson and halfback George Hennessey, took up key roles, while three linemen named Scott (Jim, Bob, and Joel) carved holes in opposition defenses. For all that, though, the season still came down to a single play. It was a Tuesday afternoon, a makeup of a rain-delayed game against undefeated Red Bank.

Although played in midweek, the game still drew 5,000 fans. Brick led 6-0 early, but Red Bank evened the score with a late touchdown. It all came down to the conversion. A host of Dragons dragged Eddie Winrow to the ground shy of the goal line. The game ended in a tie.[13] Brick won its final three games, extending their unbeaten streak to twenty-nine and clinching the CJ III crown. Meanwhile, Red Bank was upset by Long Branch on Thanksgiving, 13-6.

> **Joe Valenti**: *"Red Bank had not beat Long Branch for many years. My junior year, Red Bank was undefeated. They were so confident they were going to beat Long Branch they already had Monday off [to celebrate the victory]. Richie Caldwell threw an unheard-of halfback option pass to Tommy Olivadotti and scored the go-ahead touchdown. Big upset. Big upset."[14]*

That left Brick as the undisputed Class A Champions. While the Dragons were celebrating, Neptune fans were tearing their hair out. Asbury Park beat the Fliers, leaving them 4-5 and without a win in the rivalry since 1927. Even with one of the finest athletes in school history, All-Shore quarterback Bob Davis, Neptune hadn't been able to turn it around.

Davis was an outstanding, once-in-a-lifetime athlete. He had been a force of nature on the football field and a 1,000-point scorer on the basketball court. He attended the University of Virginia on a football scholarship, starting for three years and setting thirteen ACC records. He was chosen thirtieth overall in the 1967 NFL draft, then played a total of five years of professional football, three with the Jets and two in the World Football League.[15]

Dick Kleva: *"If there's such a thing as a triple-threat guy in high school, he was it. He could run the ball, throw the ball, handle the ball. He was a Roger Staubach-type guy. He made plays that weren't supposed to be made."*[16]

And yet with Davis, Neptune had won just four games. What could they do without him? A 20-0 loss to Long Branch in the 1963 season opener was a negative sign. Still, John Bednarik was unwilling to give up hope. The Fliers had athletes, great ones. Halfback Ricardo Hopkins was the fastest man in the Shore, and Bednarik felt that end Ted Beekman was "the most outstanding linemen I have ever coached." Both would earn first-team All-Shore honors.[17]

As the season went on, Long Branch stumbled, and Neptune surged to three straight wins. When Brick beat Long Branch 19-14, it eliminated the Green Wave and set up a showdown between the Dragons and Fliers for the division title. Brick, their unbeaten streak now at thirty-two games, was heavily favored to retain their crown. Their big star was two-way end Art Thoms, who would later start at Syracuse and play eight years in the NFL for the Oakland Raiders.

With the title on the line, a huge crowd was expected, so Neptune moved their home game to spacious Asbury Park Stadium. Those who came saw one of the most physical games of the decade. Thoms was hit so hard on one play that his facemask was driven back into his face, causing a severe cut and lots of bleeding. He was rushed to the nearest hospital, where he received twelve stitches. The procedure was barely finished before Thoms was back on his feet and rushing back to the stadium; he arrived in time for the game's final possession.[18]

By then, two Hopkins touchdown runs (one of 75 yards) had swung the game in Neptune's favor. The Fliers led 14-12, needing just one stop to win the game. The newly arrived Thoms took the field and lined up at end, participating in a furious drive down the field. They got close enough for one shot into the end zone, an option pass from George Hennessey. Thoms was open for a brief second, but the pass was batted down. Mighty Brick had been slain, and the Scarlet Fliers were a Shore Conference power at last. A banner unfurled as the clock hit 0:00 captured the spirit perfectly, reading "Neptune and Football: Just Married."[19]

The Fliers won all their remaining league games, clinching a share of the Class A title after a 34-7 win over Red Bank. Brick stayed right on their heels. Their final division game, against winless Manasquan, was to be played on November 25, 1963, the Saturday before Thanksgiving. It looked to be the week's most important event. Then the real world intervened.

At 12:30 p.m. on Thursday, November 23, President John F. Kennedy was shot by Lee Harvey Oswald while riding in a motorcade through Dallas, Texas. The newsflash startled the nation, and millions across the nation raced to their televisions and radios, hanging on every word to learn the fate of the president. They watched Edward R. Murrow wipe away tears announcing the President's death and witnessed Lyndon Johnson take the oath of office aboard Air Force One. They were glued to their televisions all weekend long, watching the bizarre and confusing murder of Oswald by Jack Ruby. When Kennedy's funeral was held on Monday, over 90 percent of the nation either watched or heard a broadcast.[20]

Compared to the national grief, high school football couldn't have been less important. Brick's game with Manasquan was simply canceled. As a result, Neptune finished with one more division win than the Dragons and laid claim to sole possession of the crown. No one protested too loudly; it just didn't seem to matter. Brick's season ended with a 20-7 loss to Central on Thanksgiving. Still, the Dragons had much to be proud of. They had gone 14-2-1 over their first two seasons in Class A and established themselves as a force to be reckoned with.

A big part of that success was quarterback Carl Lamberson. In many respects the All-American boy, Lamberson had been a four-sport star at Brick (baseball, basketball, and track were his other pastimes), and was an all-around solid student and citizen. He graduated Upsala College in East Orange, then volunteered for the Army. In 1966, Lamberson was commissioned a lieutenant and assigned to the 199th Infantry, stationed outside of Saigon, in Vietnam. On July 2, 1969, Lieutenant Carl Lamberson was crossing a rope bridge when the ropes became entangled, throwing him into the river, where he drowned. He was twenty-two years old when he died in the service of his country.[21]

Lamberson's life was one of too many cut short by the Vietnam War. By the time of his death in 1969, the conflict had seeped into everything, leaving a nation divided and embittered. On Thanksgiving 1963, that hadn't happened yet. The country was still in grief from the death of President Kennedy (200,000 people filed past his grave in Arlington National Ceremony that day), but there was room for frivolous and joyous things, like Thanksgiving football. The crowds came out across New Jersey that holiday, and they packed into the bleachers as they always had to see the traditional rivalry games that dominated the day.

The biggest game in the Shore was played at Deal Lake Stadium, between Neptune and Asbury Park. The Scarlet Fliers already had the Class A title, but Bednarik nonetheless dubbed the game "the one that means everything." Neptune had a real chance to beat Asbury for the first time since 1927. The town was energized, and the booster club paid for a huge fold-out poster in the *Asbury Park Press* urging fans to attend the game.[22] Attend they did; 5,000 fans turned out.

LeRoy Hayes (Asbury Park player, graduate, and coach): *"With Asbury, nothing was bigger than the Neptune game. Back then we were averaging 5,000 people just about for the Neptune game. It was a biggie."* [23]

Asbury was just 1-5-2, but strange things often happened on Thanksgiving. The Bishops led 7-0 at the half and were tied 7-7 until late in the fourth. With just four minutes left to play, Neptune was pinned back at its own 32. They drove until they reached the 15 with time for one more play. Jim O'Connor fired a pass for Arnie Morgan at the goal line. The ball arrived at the same time as an Asbury defender, who leveled Morgan as the ball arrived. At the same moment that the Asbury crowd began to cheer, flags flew, and officials signaled for pass interference.

The game would come down to one play. Neptune put the ball in the hands of Ricky Hopkins, who took a pitch to the outside and raced untouched into the end zone with the winning touchdown. As the final gun sounded to end the game, chaos erupted. Fans in the stands began brawling each other, while the players duked it out on the field. The battle only ended when a few Neptune players and cheerleaders grabbed John Bednarik and threw him into Sunset Lake in celebration. That was enough to pull the Neptune faithful away from the melee and join the cheers. The Scarlet Fliers had finally conquered the Shore.[24]

The dramatic end to the 1963 season led nicely into 1964. Neptune returned twenty lettermen, including Hopkins and Beekman, and so was the clear favorite to repeat. They held that status for just two weeks before losing to a surprising Middletown team.[25] Dick Kleva's team had talent of its own—guard Tom DeMarks was one of the strongest men in the Shore (he was a champion wrestler and the conference shot put champion), while quarterback Dave "Dixie" Abdella commanded the field like few other quarterbacks in the state. He was a smart, strong-armed quarterback who always gave his team a chance to win.

> **Dick Kleva:** *"[Dixie Abdella] was about 6-3, 215 pounds. He had the size, the great arm, just a good, level-headed kid, mature for that age bracket. He was very strong. He'd roll out and carry a few tacklers with him . . . he could throw long ball and keep everybody loose."*[26]

Thanks to Abdella's game management and DeMarks's versatility (he played both ways on the line and even scored a touchdown from the fullback position), Middletown upset Neptune 7-6. One week later, the Lions went on the road and upset Brick, 9-6. Once again, it was DeMarks who scored the winning touchdown, although the credit really went to the Middletown defense, which forced two fourth-quarter turnovers. A month later, Middletown clinched the Class A crown with a thrilling win over Long Branch. The Green Wave led 13-6 at the start of the fourth, which was when Abdella came to life. He threw a 33-yard touchdown pass to Jim Jenkins to tie the game and then scrambled for the winning score himself.[27]

With the title clinched, all that was left was the celebration. The Lions did that in front of 6,000 fans on Thanksgiving morning, thrashing Freehold 45-0. It was a fine sendoff to a great team. Dixie Abdella went to Duke, where he played football and baseball for four seasons, while Tom DeMarks went on to play football at South Carolina. The Lions were back. A similarly joyful mood prevailed at the home fields of their two main division rivals. After a poor start, Brick had gotten hot and their 27-6 win over Central capped a seven-game winning streak to end the season. The Class A crown was out of reach, but their record was good enough to win the CJ III title. Neptune, meanwhile, was busy beating Asbury Park for the second year in a row.

Ricky Hopkins capped his brilliant season by scoring all three touchdowns in a 20-0 victory.[28] He finished his high school career by winning both Shore Conference sprint championships, then accepted a football scholarship to Arizona State. A bout with pneumonia destroyed his freshman season and he ended up joining the Air Force instead. His teammate Ted Beekman played football and baseball at Colgate (captaining the 1969 baseball team).

A new wave of Neptune athletes emerged in 1965. There was guard/middle linebacker Jeff Ruby (who later started for Cornell), end Bill Findler, and running back Fred Warren (another championship sprinter), all of whom won All-Shore honors. They all shone in a 12-0 win over Middletown, snapping a ten-game Lion winning streak. Brick fell too, with Findler catching a touchdown pass and batting down a late Dragon Hail Mary in a 7-0 victory.

Then came a challenge from the year's biggest surprise—Monmouth Regional. The Eatontown high school was just four years old and drew its student population mostly from the families who worked at the Fort Monmouth military base. Coach Cy Benson had his team running a system that played to their strengths. The Falcons spread the field and filled the air with passes, using the arm of quarterback Pete Tuck to open up the inside for fast junior halfback Walt Jackson. Behind that aerial assault, the Falcons upset Brick 34-12 (with Tuck throwing three touchdown passes) and gave themselves a shot at the Shore Conference title.[29] To do it, they just needed one more upset, this time over Neptune.

About 4,500 fans saw the showdown at Neptune, many of them Monmouth fans who had made the short trip down the road for the game. Tuck put on a brilliant performance, throwing one touchdown pass and connecting with Ed Kennedy on a 37-yard strike to set up another, but two missed extra points forced them to settle for a 12-12 tie.[30] That clinched the title for Neptune. The Fliers finished their season undefeated by beating Asbury Park on Thanksgiving in front of 7,000 fans. Fred Warren starred, running for 149 yards and a touchdown.[31]

Down in Ocean County, a similarly sized crowd packed itself into Keller Memorial Field. They left unhappy, as Central Regional rallied for an upset 12-7 victory, knocking Brick's record down to a disappointing 4-3-2. More worrying was the rumor that Warren Wolf was stepping down as head coach to enter administration.[32] Had the Brick magic actually run out? With Wolf leaving, it certainly seemed possible. Perhaps the Brick glory days really were over.

In fact, Brick's glory days were just beginning. The rumors that Wolf was gone were untrue, and good times were coming fast. The years to come wouldn't just be glory days for the Green Dragons, either—times were good all along the Jersey Shore. The strong economy meant that the suburban boom just kept booming and that beaches stayed crowded up and down the coast.[33] The summer of 1966 was filled with optimism—it even ended with the successful Gemini space mission, another American victory in the space race.

There was, however, another current running beneath the surface like a riptide at the Jersey Shore. New Jersey's cities were struggling, their urban cores crumbling and growing increasingly decrepit. Their large African American populations felt trapped, felt like the heralded gains of the civil rights movement had not improved their lives at all, and began to join a groundswell of frustration and anger. There were riots in 1964 in New York, Philadelphia, Chicago, and, locally, in Jersey City, Paterson, and Elizabeth. Watts burned in Los Angeles in 1965, while parts of Cleveland, Chicago, and Atlanta erupted in the summer of 1966. All this only accelerated the exodus of white residents to places like the Shore.

They could afford to leave, knew they could find a home in a new town, and were doing it as fast as possible.

The frustration that caused those riots was not as far from the Shore as people wanted to believe. Residents of the African American side of Neptune complained bitterly that all of the town's junkyards and dumps were concentrated in their neighborhoods, where the streets were barely maintained and the police rarely went. Asbury Park's beach front was decaying, and race relations were growing tenser, unemployment was rising in Freehold, and Lakewood's overcrowded and underfunded neighborhoods looked more like slums with each passing season.[34] The white population of those towns could move out to Ocean, Toms River, Freehold Township, and Howell. Black residents had fewer options. Many could not afford to leave, and even those who could were often denied housing loans.

And then there was Vietnam. At the start of the decade, most Americans had never heard of that country. Now, no American could ignore it. The war and the draft that came with it were becoming increasingly hot political issues. When Martin Luther King Jr. spoke at Monmouth University in October, he caused a stir by declaring his opposition to the war; there was a smattering of applause among the students, while Monmouth County freeholder Marcus Daly rose to boo. A few days later, during a local political debate at Rumson High School, anti-war third-party candidate Marcus Watkins (who was not invited to the debate) tried to crash the stage. He was tackled by a local police sergeant, falling into the crowd as he shouted anti-war slogans.[35] Most of the Shore still supported the war, but tempers were getting hotter.

Nonetheless, life went on, and an important part of that life was football. In Brick, people were getting excited for another season. Fueled by a rich pipeline of talent (the freshmen team hadn't lost a game in five years), the Dragons were loaded in 1966. The key to the team was halfback Billy Hess, the next in a long line of undersized but big-hearted runners. One of the fastest sprinters in the Shore, Hess would earn All-Shore honors as a junior and again as a senior. Together with backfield mate Bob

Donofrio, he would follow All-Shore linemen Wayne Reeves and Gary Bronson to glory in 1966.[36]

Brick's main challenger that year would be the Hitting Indians of Toms River South. Ron Signorino's rebuilding program was starting to take effect, and third-year starting quarterback Mickey Carroll and center/defensive tackle Chuck Avery gave the team some veteran steel. With experience on their side, the Indians had high hopes of winning the school its first football championship in fifteen years.[37] The first step to doing that was beating Brick, a team that had already broken Signorino's heart once before. In his first season in charge, the one-win Indians had Brick on the ropes, leading 18-13 with the clock running out.

> **Ron Signorino**: *"There were fourteen seconds left. Brick had no timeouts and one of my players started grandstanding and didn't get up off the ground. The referee stopped the clock for an injury. Brick regrouped, called a screen pass, and scored."*[38]

The two rivals met again in the 1966 season opener. Brick jumped out to an early 13-0 lead, helped by a 94-yard interception return for a touchdown by Dan Seme. Toms River answered with an aerial assault, taking a 14-13 lead on Mickey Carroll's 12-yard touchdown pass to LeRoy Thaxton. In the fourth, however, Brick rallied behind the passing of Steve Sendzik and the running of Bob Donofrio. Donofrio's fourth-quarter touchdown secured Brick's 20-14 victory, breaking Toms River hearts once more.[39]

Still, the team bounced back, fighting their way to a 6-3 record, the school's first winning season in a decade. After the final game, a 27-7 Thanksgiving win over Lakewood, the Toms River players hoisted Signorino on their shoulders and carried him off the field.[40] Their anchor, Chuck Avery, went on to the University of Delaware, where he started for three years at defensive tackle. And considering what Brick did that year, their narrow loss was no shame.

One week after the Toms River win, Brick set out to take on an opponent that would become an important part of the school's football mythology—Phillipsburg. The Stateliners had a mystique unlike any other team in the state. Even their regular Friday night home games drew huge crowds, and their fabled Thanksgiving rivalry with Easton was seen annually by over 20,000 fans. Warren Wolf loved the idea of exposing his team to a tradition like that, and Phillipsburg games soon became an essential part of the Brick schedule.

> **Dan Duddy**: *"The Phillipsburg games were great to play. They were huge, a great football program, wrestling program. The field is a bowl setting, an old school with a lot of history, and it was tremendous. I remember listening on the radio and I hear the broadcaster saying 'Here comes Brick Township on to the field. They just won't stop coming. There's gotta be 300 of those guys coming through that gate.'"[41]*

Brick's first meeting with Phillipsburg ended in a 34-13 defeat, but the second meeting (back in Ocean County) saw the Dragons battle to a tie. Their return to Warren County in 1966 was a major local event—a caravan of buses and a full broadcast team from WJLK radio followed the team. All who came witnessed a dominating Dragon performance. Bruce Puglisi and Bill Hess each scored touchdowns, while defensive linemen Bill Bauer, Howard Doherty, and Gary Bronson totally shut down the Stateliners in a 27-6 win.[42] The rest of the schedule played out with little drama, as Hess and company overwhelmed their remaining Class A opponents. The undefeated season ended with a rout of Central on Thanksgiving morning.

Hess and Bronson both became starters at Murray State, with Hess setting the school's receiving record. Donofrio played at Lafayette and set *their* receiving record. The word was spreading among college recruiters— you could find quality football players at Brick.

Off the field, the real world was closing in. The pandemonium at the Rumson debate was only the start of a particularly tense election season. It felt like the good times of the past decade were unraveling, and someone had to take the blame.[43] Amid it all, the shadows of Vietnam just kept growing. On October 24, General William Westmoreland told reporters at a briefing that the end of the war was far off, dashing American hopes of an early peace.[44] Ten days later, a Marine from Neptune named Robert Johnson was killed in action. He wasn't the first resident of the Jersey Shore to fall in combat, and he wouldn't be the last.[45]

The following summer was no easier. Riots rocked Newark in August, and easily could have hit Monmouth County as well. Municipal workers in Long Branch and Asbury Park (including former Long Branch half-back Randy Phillips) worked furiously to keep teenagers busy with jobs and recreation, but no one breathed easily until the weather began to cool.[46] And the Vietnam War went on. Every day, there were new head-lines in the paper, and every family was touched by the conflict in some way. It showed no signs of letting up.

The football games that fall offered a valuable distraction, one of the few places where the superheated political issues of the day could be set aside. It helped that the Class A race offered a lot to talk about. There were three main contenders—Brick, Neptune, and Red Bank—and all had varying strengths and weaknesses.

The Dragons had a huge roster but were starting an unusually large number of sophomores. Neptune had experienced ball-carriers in quar-terback Kim Coleman and halfback Ed Calderon but was also breaking in a new head coach. After thirty-four wins and two Shore Conference titles, John Bednarik was moving back to Northeast Pennsylvania to become the head coach at Allentown's Dieruff High School. His replacement was Cy Benson, the successful coach of Monmouth Regional.[47] Benson liked the roster he was inheriting but knew that it was never easy to succeed a legend such as Bednarik. Compared to the problems facing Bob Morris at Red Bank, though, these issues were just a walk in the park.

Morris's predecessor, Tom Karlo, had been successful with the Bucs, leading the team to three winning seasons and three victories over Long Branch. In 1967, he had a team that everyone thought had a chance to contend—All-Shore guard Tony Mazza, veteran quarterback Tom Mot-tine, and talented halfbacks Al Griffin and Gary Sergeant were all re-turning. Karlo, however, wasn't. He had spent years butting heads over funding with the Red Bank Board of Education, and when they refused that summer to pay for any stipends for new assistant coaches, he abruptly resigned with just a week left before the season opener. That left Morris, his top assistant, in charge of a team that could easily descend into chaos.[48]

Morris faced the difficulties calmly and kept the team together. They opened the season with a 54-0 rout of Red Bank Catholic, setting the tone for an opening month in which the Buc defense allowed just one touchdown. Against Toms River, in a hard-fought 12-6 game, that defense saved the day when cornerback Charlie Taylor recovered a fumble to set up Griffin for the winning touchdown run.[49] Meanwhile, the rest of the division was stumbling.

Middletown upset Neptune 15-13, then promptly lost to Brick. The Dragons held the division lead for less than a week before losing to Neptune on a 74-yard touchdown run by Ed Calderone.[50] Brick lost again a few weeks later, bowing 19-7 to the Miracle Bucs. Charles Carter and Al Sergeant tore apart the Brick line, and the swarming Buccaneer defense came up with some key stands. Emotional Buccaneer fans poured onto the field in celebration after the game, carrying Carter off the field to chants of "We're number one!" Red Bank was just one win away from clinching the Shore Conference title.[51]

Neptune, meanwhile, saw their own season melting away. A sophomore buzzsaw named Tony Williams ran for two touchdowns as winless Monmouth Regional shocked the Fliers 12-7. Now 4-2 in Class A play, Neptune no longer controlled its own destiny.[52] Even if they beat Red Bank, they would still need the Bucs to lose again on Thanksgiving. Brick, their Class A schedule finished, was in the same boat. All they could do was wait and watch.

The second Saturday in November brought hope to the Fliers and Dragons, as Neptune beat Red Bank 19-7 behind touchdowns from Coleman and Calderon.[53] Red Bank had used up their extra chance. Now they had to beat Long Branch, or they would fall from first to third in the division. The Green Wave were 3-5, but they were still dangerous, and everyone expected a classic. Heavy rains postponed all the games twenty-four hours, and the fields were still soggy when the teams took the field on Friday. With Brick and Neptune playing nonleague games (and winning both handily) all eyes were on the Wave and the Bucs.

Both teams traded long drives early. The Branchers reached the 11-yard line before Glen Covin was stopped on fourth and 1 from the 11, while Tom Mottine was stuffed on a fourth-down quarterback sneak from the 1-yard line. Red Bank's offense did most of the moving after that, but four turnovers undid any chance they had to score. The key play of the game came in the third, when Long Branch partially blocked a punt to set up Covin for the game's only touchdown run. Red Bank's last desperate efforts all failed, and the Green Wave hung on for a 6-0 win.[54]

It was a glorious win for Long Branch. Mayor Paul Anastasio even visited the team in the locker room to offer congratulations. The joy was bigger in Neptune and Brick, where the players came home to learn that they had emerged as Class A Champions. In Red Bank, there was pure frustration. They had had the title in their grasp, and it had still slipped away.

The fall of 1967 saw the pressure of the real world continue to mount. The Vietnam War dominated the news now. American special forces had spent the first week in November under siege in Loc Ninh, repulsing four full-scale Viet Cong attacks in desperate fighting.[55] Anti-war Democrats, seeing no end to the war in sight, began contemplating the unthinkable—a primary challenge to a sitting president. Temperatures were continuing to rise.[56]

In January 1968, the Tet Offensive sent them spiraling higher. All of Vietnam was engulfed by this Viet Cong offensive, which provoked some of the war's bloodiest fighting. Although the American and South Vietnamese armies soon recovered, the credibility of the federal government had been fatally damaged. Confident press releases from the Pentagon no longer carried much weight with anyone. Walter Cronkite, the most trusted newsman in America, summed up the disillusioned feelings of many Americans when he said, "It seems more certain than ever that the bloody experience of Vietnam is to end in a stalemate."

All through that calendar year, there was a general feeling that something was seriously wrong in the United States. Incumbent President Lyndon Johnson chose not to seek reelection. Martin Luther King Jr. was murdered outside of a Memphis hotel, sparking rioting in 130 cities.

College students took over their campuses from the Atlantic to the Pacific protesting segregation, racial discrimination, and the war. Presidential hopeful Bobby Kennedy was assassinated in Los Angeles in June, crime across the nation spiked, and the Democratic National Convention was racked by riots inside and outside the event. The presidential campaign, pitting Hubert Humphrey against Richard Nixon, was as nasty as anyone could remember.[57]

It was also incredibly close, and New Jersey, with seventeen electoral votes, was a crucial swing state. Both Humphrey and Nixon visited the Shore to make speeches.[58] High school hallways, cafeterias, and lunchrooms rang out with heated debates about the election, the war, and the draft. In many towns, sports were pushed to the background. The exception was Toms River, where the Hitting Indians were on a quest to win the Shore Conference championship.

Ron Signorino's team that year had over 200 players, more than any in the Shore. Their roster featured some of the greatest athletes in the history of the town. There was All-Shore end Harry Walter, halfback Bob Hermanni, All-Shore defensive tackle Pete Bush, and All-Shore defensive back Steve Costello. Bush even won a place on the All-State team. Before they could take the title, though, they'd have to find a way to get past Brick.

Brick was once again the favorite to win Class A, something that seemed to bore the *Asbury Park Press*. They abandoned their usual punning headlines to flatly state that "Brick Should Have Usual Powerhouse."[59] There was no reason to believe any team in the Shore could challenge them, let alone Toms River, which hadn't beaten the Dragons since 1959. That didn't faze the Indians, who worked harder that offseason than they ever had before. It paid off.

Pete Bush (Toms River defensive tackle): *"After the 1967 season, all the players on the Toms River football team got calendars. We counted off the days until the opening game against Brick Township. We were a group of young men dedicated to playing football and going unbeaten."*[60]

Ron Signorino: *"In 1968, which was the last year of Toms River High School, we waltzed to a 9-0 season. And when I say waltz, I think our closest game was 30-0. Arguably the best team I was ever associated with."*[61]

The victory procession started in the opener, a 30-13 win over Brick Township. That was an emotional win, a triumph over a team that had frequently tormented Toms River, and it had gone so well. The Indians hadn't just beaten Brick, they had overwhelmed them, thrashing them in every phase of the game.[62] Every other game was a blowout, including a 69-14 rout of Lakewood on Thanksgiving. It seemed like they could do everything. Opposing offenses couldn't move, opposing defenses couldn't stop them.

All-State lineman Pete Bush became a star at New Mexico, later earning a tryout with the Kansas City Chiefs. However, he was one of only a few of the Hitting Indians who graduated that year. Hermanni, was back, as was his backfield partner, Dave Bloom. So was Scherer and his favorite target, end Harry Walter. South had a team that looked loaded for years to come.

Ron Signorino: *"We dedicated ourselves to an impossible dream but achieved the goal."*[63]

By then, the election of 1968 was over. Richard Nixon had won a tense but clear victory over Hubert Humphrey. Nixon continually claimed that he was supported by a "silent majority"—people tired of the chaos of the 1960s, of causes, and of the anti-war movement. Above all else, Nixon's "silent majority" wanted peace and quiet in 1969. They wouldn't get it.

CHAPTER 17
THE GREATEST SEASON
EVER PLAYED

A chaotic and dramatic year such as 1969 was the only appropriate way to end a chaotic and dramatic decade like the 1960s. There was the youthful optimism of Woodstock, the continuing political divide over Vietnam, victories for two iconic underdogs (the New York Jets and New York Mets), and the American triumph of the Apollo 11 moon landing. In the Shore Conference, too, 1969 provided the appropriate cap to the decade. It was the most dramatic and memorable season in an era full of them, one that would never be forgotten.

The season climaxed with a game almost immediately dubbed "the greatest game ever played in the Shore Conference," an epic confrontation between undefeated Middletown and undefeated Toms River, with the winner claiming both the Class A title and the overall number one ranking in the state of New Jersey. But there was much more to the 1969 season than just one game. It was a thrilling season, one in which the conference asserted itself on a statewide stage in a way it had never done before.

It had taken many years of building to get to this point. For a decade, the teams of Monmouth and Ocean County had been proving that their football was as good as that played anywhere else. Brick, which had already contributed to that effort with their games against Phillipsburg, added another piece to the puzzle on Thanksgiving Day 1968 by taking down one of Philadelphia's strongest Catholic powers.

Bishop Egan High School was, like Brick, a school built from the Baby Boom. It drew its students from the rapidly expanding Philadelphia suburbs, and with that growing population they won consecutive city championships and a reputation as one of Pennsylvania's best teams. Brick, although 6-2 and bound for no titles that season, proved more than a match for the mighty Eagles, upsetting them 6-0 thanks to a fourth-quarter goal-line stand. Warren Wolf dubbed it "Brick's most glorious victory."[1] He had reason to hope for more glory in 1969. The Dragons returned both quarterback John Meyer and towering lineman Ken Scott (who would earn All-State honors at season's end).[2] There was, however, another team with a championship dream.

The 1969 Toms River Indians had a chance to be the most talented in school history. The *Asbury Park Press* compared them to a "handcrafted Rolls Royce," capable of moving faster and with more style than any team in the Shore. The backfield featured quarterback Rip Scherer (so dedicated to the team that he had stayed in Toms River after his family moved to Pennsylvania) and halfbacks Dave Bloom and Bobby Herrmanni. The line featured All-State end Harry Walters and All-State center John Pedone. Guards Rich Longo and Bill Malast were two of the strongest linemen in the county. The defense, which featured All-Shore defensive tackle John Peterson and safety Butch Brunson, was just as good.[3]

Rip Scherer: *"We had probably the best eleven people together I had ever seen on a team."*[4]

Toms River's 9-0 record in 1968 had already earned them some statewide attention, and Ron Signorino felt that another perfect season would give his team a shot at the state's No. 1 ranking. To that end, he added a game with Hudson County power Bayonne. Yet even as Signorino was making up the schedule, doubt was growing that the 1969 Indians would even be able to take the field as one team. The same population boom that had fueled the football program now threatened to destroy it.

Toms River High School had originally been built for 600 students; by 1968, it held 2,000, with more coming every year. The building simply couldn't handle the strain; a new school was needed. The original school would become Toms River South, while an enormous modern one would be constructed and opened as Toms River North. That brought up a key question—what would happen to the seniors, the Class of 1970? Some wanted to open North with all four grades, splitting the senior class in two. That would alleviate overcrowding at the old high school, but it would also wreck South's chances of a perfect season.

It might have happened if not for the Toms River Booster Association, which assembled over a hundred football parents and other supporters to protest the move. That pressure persuaded the Board of Education to keep the entire senior class at their original school.[5] South's undefeated dream was alive. To Ron Signorino, it had always been the obvious choice.

Ron Signorino: *"It was a very controversial decision to hold the seniors at South, but I didn't think it had to be. . . . You just don't take a kid who has been at a high school for three years and make him a senior at a new high school in his last year. Almost all schools have done it this way, at Brick Memorial, Point Boro, Manchester, and elsewhere."*[6]

While Toms River was at the center of a media storm, Middletown was flying under the radar. Dick Kleva's Lions entered 1969 with a talented, veteran offensive line led by All-State center Ray Veth and guard Kenny Hallgring, a state champion wrestler. The backfield featured halfbacks Ron Carhart and John Kauffmann, plus fullbacks John Gill and Rich Mikla. The entire system would be orchestrated by veteran quarterback Bob Abbott. On defense, they were equally tough. As Ron Signorino would later write in his weekly column, "Middletown doesn't make mistakes. They hang in there and wait for you to make one instead."[7]

In addition to players, they also had a system. Dick Kleva hadn't been a fan of the team's offense in 1968, and during the offseason he began a search for a strategy that would work more effectively the next year. It came to him on New Year's Day.

> **Dick Kleva**: *"In 1968, we were sort of a multiple nothing, but we did have some success with the option. We had cracked off some long gains with it in '68 and evaluated it as being the way to go . . . I had no one to look at for the wishbone except the University of Texas. I was watching them play in a bowl game in '68, and I called Bobby Abbott on the phone. I said to him 'Watch the second half of the game. I think we have an offense for next year.' . . . In 1969, we became the first team at the Shore and one of the first in the state to run the wishbone offense."[8]*

The 'bone made its Shore debut on opening day, September 27. Middletown looked great, piling up 297 yards of total offense in a 37-22 rout of a strong Long Branch team. The defensive line, led by Mike Monaco and Don Peters, was just as good, keeping the vaunted Long Branch backfield under wraps all day.[9] Still, the spotlight that Saturday shone elsewhere, on Keller Memorial Field, where 5,000 fans had gathered to watch Brick vs. Toms River South.

Brick's Ken Scott threw people around in the trenches all day, but it wasn't enough to stop South's explosive offense. Dave Bloom scored twice and Bobby Herrmanni broke Brick's back with a 91-yard touchdown run in the third quarter. South won convincingly, 26-6. Wins over Freehold and Raritan followed, setting up the much-anticipated showdown with Bayonne.[10] That would be harder. Led by star tailback Gary Danback and Syracuse-bound quarterback Walter Dalikat, the Bees had state title designs of their own.[11] The meeting of the two powers was New Jersey's Game of the Week.

Ironically, it came in a week when not many people were thinking about high school football. That Wednesday, October 15, was Moratorium Day. The newest tactic of the anti-war movement, Moratorium Day called for everyday people to demonstrate against the Vietnam War in their own hometowns. There were gatherings at Fort Dix, Fort Monmouth, Monmouth University, and Brookdale Community College. Black armbands (a symbol of the protest) were everywhere. Moratorium Day drew strong reactions from everyone, whether they were for or against the war. At the Shore, hawks were in the majority, but there was no shortage of doves or black armbands in the area. Day-long debates were held at most of the area's high schools. No matter one's feeling on the war, Moratorium Day was unavoidable.[12]

In Ocean County, however, Moratorium Day paled in comparison to Bayonne fever. Toms River fans followed their team up to the game in larger numbers than ever before. Even the *Jersey Journal*, which had seen crowds of over 20,000 turn up for Thanksgiving Day games, was impressed. The Indians didn't just bring a team, they brought a marching band, fifteen fan buses, the broadcast teams of three different radio stations, and even a fire engine. A full forty minutes before game time, every parking spot in the lot at Bayonne's field was taken. In total, 8,000 fans jammed their way into Veterans Stadium for the biggest test yet of Shore football.[13]

> **Ron Signorino**: *"We slaughtered them. 40-0, 28-0 at the half. We were just dominant. It was no game. They had this great running back, and we smothered him. That put the Shore Conference on the map, and it put Toms River on the map."* [14]

Rip Scherer's passing picked Bayonne to pieces, while Bill Malast and Bob Currie blew huge holes in the Bayonne defense. Hermanni and Bloom ran for two touchdowns each, while linebacker John Salerno led a relentless defense in shutting out the Bees. Harry Walters starred on both sides of the ball, catching a touchdown pass and harassing Delikat all day. The Shore Conference had not just proven itself the equal of North Jersey football, it had proven itself superior (Bayonne's 8-1 finish only strengthened that claim). It was well after midnight when the caravan of buses finally arrived back at Toms River South, but despite the late hour, a crowd of faithful supporters were already lining the streets to cheer the conquering heroes on their return. The Indians were well on their way to ruling the state.[15]

Middletown, meanwhile, was marching along. Bruce Abbott was continuing to prove himself at quarterback, and his performance in Week 3 against Brick helped establish him and his team as among the best in the Shore. Middletown won 12-0, with Abbott running for one scoring and throwing for another. The Lion defense held Brick to just two first downs all day.[16] It was a performance to remember, and it fit Middletown's style—quietly effective. One week later, the Lions beat Linden 29-0, an impressive win to match South's victory over Bayonne. It was around now that fans first began eyeing November 15, the day that Middletown visited Toms River South, and imagining a potential showdown between unbeatens. With each passing week, that showdown became more and more likely.

Bruce Abbott: *"Coming into the season, we knew we'd be very solid, but it wasn't until we beat Brick in our third game that we knew we had the opportunity to go all the way. From that point on, we began to believe that we could be contenders for the Shore Conference."[17]*

Abbott was running the wishbone to perfection and the Lion defense was putting on a clinic; the Lions held Lakewood, Raritan, and South Plainfield scoreless in eleven of twelve quarters. South's offense was just as impressive. Even after Bob Hermanni went down with a knee injury in a 43-0 rout of Ocean, Scherer and Bloom stepped up to carry the load. Scherer's family (whom he hadn't seen since they moved to Pennsylvania over the summer) paid a surprise visit for the Neptune game, and the quarterback responded by throwing three touchdown passes against the Fliers in a 36-6 win.[18] The ultimate showdown was just two weeks away.

That's when Long Branch intervened. Ken Schroeck's Green Wave had recovered from their opening-day loss to Middletown with five straight wins, rising to No. 3 in the *Asbury Park Press* Top 10 and keeping their own title hopes alive. An upset of Toms River would vault them right back into the title race.

Ken Schroeck (Long Branch head coach): *"This has to rate as one of the greatest Long Branch football performances in years. . . . Covin is an All-American kid if there ever was one. He did everything any coach could ever ask for."*[19]

A week of rain had turned the gridiron into a sea of mud, but it didn't slow down either offense. No matter how many times the Indians scored, they could not seem to shake the Wave, who trailed just 26-22 at the start of the fourth. Midway through the fourth, Glenn Covin's fake froze the South defense and sprang Darrell Willis for a 56-yard touchdown run and a 29-26 lead.

Their backs to the wall, the Indians answered with their finest performance of the year. Jon Kuntz ran the kickoff out to the 33, and then Dave Bloom took over. He converted two third downs, then served as a decoy when Steve Jobson converted a vital fourth down. With time running down, South had earned a first and goal from the 9. Jobson gained a yard, Bloom gained three. On third down, Bloom hit a seam in the Long Branch defense for the winning touchdown. Toms River South 32, Long Branch 29.

Ron Signorino: *"The mark of a champion is his ability to come back when the going looks roughest. These boys want to be state champions, and they want it bad. I think they showed what they really can do when the pressure was greatest.*[20]

The Indians had no time to celebrate. It was now time for the ultimate showdown between undefeated Middletown and undefeated Toms River South. The game was front page news all week long, stealing space not only from college and professional sports but also the Apollo 12 moon mission. Not even the second Vietnam War Moratorium Day, scheduled for that same Saturday, could compete. A movement that drew busloads of protestors to Washington, DC, drew just a hundred people to the local march in Shrewsbury.[21] Everyone was heading for Toms River.

And why not? The consensus had both teams in the statewide top five, and one Newark paper had them ranked number one and two. A crew from WJLK Radio would be there to broadcast the game. So would a massive crowd, estimated at somewhere between 10,000 and 15,000 people.

Nicholas Campanile (Middletown High School Principal):
"The buildup was phenomenal. It was touted as the game for the mythical state championship. At the time, Shore teams were still striving for state recognition. . . . The entire community was up for that game. We sent a dozen or more buses. I think anyone who lived in Middletown remembers that."

Both coaches had their opponent well-scouted, and both had some tricks up their sleeves. Signorino went with some psychological warfare, insisting all week long that Bob Hermanni's knee wasn't healing quickly enough and that the great halfback wouldn't play. The plan was to keep him in street clothes until the last minute, then put him out on the field.

Dick Kleva, meanwhile, was making adjustments on both sides of the ball. Worried about South's explosive offense, he designed his defense to prevent the big play, even at the expense of allowing the Indians to drive up and down the field—bend, but don't break. Offensively, Kleva unveiled a play he'd been keeping in his pocket all season long.

Dick Kleva: *"We had four special plays for the season. One of them was the quarterback draw. It was designed to work against the type of defense Toms River was playing. We really didn't see that defense all year until the Toms River game, and we didn't use the quarterback draw until the last drive."*[22]

On game day, nothing moved in either town. Stores were shut down, with handmade "Gone to game" signs hung on them. The bitterly cold weather didn't deter them. Detwiler Stadium was mobbed. Both teams had played in big games before, and Signorino had played major college football at Penn State. Still, no one there that day had yet seen anything like this.

Susan Abbot (Middletown cheerleader, now Bob Abbot's wife): *"We as cheerleaders were behind the fence, but the track area in front of the fence was just packed with people, standing ten deep. My family was there on top of fences. There were people hanging in the trees and people standing on top of cars."*[23]

Kevin Williams (Ocean County resident): *"We got there three hours before to get a seat. People were climbing trees and everything to get in and see it. It was off the chart."*[24]

Ron Signorino: *"People were on roofs, on trees, on the water tower. They were everywhere."*[25]

The tension resulted in a quiet first quarter, but by the second period both teams were settled in. Toms River hit first, as the offensive line opened some holes and Dave Bloom started finding traction. He carried the ball eight times on an 83-yard drive, scoring from the two. After Scherer's two-point pass to Harry Walters, South was ahead 8-0.

It took Middletown just three plays to answer. Ed Jones fielded the Toms River kickoff at his own 26-yard line, cut across the field, and began picking up blockers. He made it to the 5, setting up Abbot's quarterback sneak for a touchdown. South, however, stopped Middletown's two-point play, and stayed out front by an 8-6 score. Stalemate followed. Middletown couldn't move the ball, but South couldn't hang on to it, committing five turnovers (three fumbles and two interceptions). The score stayed 8-6 into the second half, but while Middletown was just barely hanging on, South was constantly threatening to expand their lead.

Dick Kleva: *"They were blowing holes in us a mile wide. We were closing them just as fast. We were trying to save our lives in the first part of the game, trying to stay in the game."*[26]

They couldn't hold out forever. Early in the fourth quarter, the running of Bloom and Hermanni began to take its toll, as the Indians drove from their 24 to the Middletown 11. A touchdown and an extra point were all

South needed to take a likely insurmountable two-score lead. Looking for the knockout punch, Scherer called for one more pass.

> **Rip Scherer (Toms River quarterback):** *"I don't remember many of the interceptions I've thrown, but I remember that one. As a coach, I refer to it as a panic throw. . . . I got a little bit of pressure, tried to get it out early, and made a bad throw."*[27]

> **Jack Kauffman (Middletown defensive back):** *"It was an out-and-up for one of their ends. He released off of the corner. I came over and picked him. For sure, that was the biggest interception I ever made."*[28]

Kauffman's pick got the Lions the ball back, but they were still in deep trouble, at their own 4 with under ten minutes to play. If they were going to score, it needed to be now. Richie Steward earned his team some breathing space with three carries for 24 yards, then Ron Carhart and Ed Jones combined to gain another first down. Middletown was moving, but not quickly enough. With the clock continuing to wind down, Kleva unveiled the quarterback draw that his team had been preparing all week.

> **Bob Abbot:** *"Our scouts had seen the linebackers dropped off very quickly when the other teams showed pass.*[29] *If I just took a step back, I could run. . . . It got yardage every time. It was coaching genius."*[30]

Abbot took that first quarterback draw for 14 yards, then handed off to Steve Wiltshire for 12 more. They were in Toms River territory now. The Indians defense stiffened, holding Jones to 3 yards on two carries and forcing third and 7. Middletown went back to the draw, and Abbot scampered for 9 more yards and a first down.

> **Rip Scherer:** *"I remember sitting there with a sick feeling of it slipping away."*

Abbot carried the ball on the next three plays, for 6 yards, for 3 yards, and for 1 yard and a first down at the 15 going in. The goal line was in sight, but the Toms River defenders were contesting every yard. Wiltshire gained 2. Jones gained 2. Steward gained 3. It was fourth and 3 from the 8, with just five minutes remained. The temperature was dropping, and snow flurries were starting to form. The season had come down to just one play. Dick Kleva called time out to talk over his options. One thing he knew he did not want to do was try for a field goal.

> **Dick Kleva**: *"Maybe we have a shot at the field goal, which would have made the score 9-8. . . . We looked at our sophomore kicker, Sean Pattwell. You've got yourself a fifteen-year-old kid who has been freezing in seven-degree weather, and we're going to put the game on his shoulders?"[31]*

Having decided to go for it, Kleva walked over to Bruce Abbot to discuss their options. Toms River South had started to close down on the draw, so that was out. The coach trusted his veteran quarterback and wanted to know what he thought.

> **Dick Kleva**: *"I didn't know what the hell to do. Everyone thought we coaches were so damn smart. You've got 27 million people screaming at you, and the whole thing is up for grabs. You've got all the assistant coaches yelling at you, they've all got 1,000 plays. I said to Bobby, 'What the hell do you think we ought to do?'"*

> **Bob Abbot**: *"I went over to Kleva, and I really thought we could spring Eddie Jones on the option to the outside."*

Middletown came to the line. South's defense dug in. The few members of the crowd who weren't already standing rose to their feet. This was it. Abbot took the snap and came down the line on the option, his eyes locked on South defensive end Harry Walters.

> **Bob Abbot**: *"When I went down the line of scrimmage to run the option or to pitch, Harry Walters was the defensive end. He covered outside. I turned it up inside. I dragged a guy into the end zone."[32]*

That would-be tackler was John Salerno, who had come flying across the field to make a desperate attempt at a game-saving tackle. It wasn't to be. He could only manage to get a piece of Abbot's leg as the quarterback crossed the goal line (a perfectly timed photograph of that moment appeared the next morning on the front page of the *Asbury Park Press*). The Middletown crowd erupted. With just 4:48 to go, the Lions had taken their first lead. The cheers continued as Richie Steward converted the two-point attempt with a short run to make the score 14-8 in favor of the visitors. Middletown's dream was about to come true.

South responded like the defending champions they were. Three quick passes by Rip Scherer got the Indians down to the 25, only for Middletown to force and recover a fumble, thwarting the drive. Still South refused to fold, forcing a quick three-and-out to get one more chance with thirty seconds to play. Now, though, everyone knew the Indians were going to the air. Scherer could find no one open and had to force the ball down the field, where Middletown safety Ed Jones was able to pluck it out of the air. Now it was truly over. Abbott took a knee, bringing the game of the century to its end. Middletown 14, Toms River 8.[33]

It was heartbreak for South. Their nineteen-game winning streak was over, their chances of a state championship gone. Worse, some feared that Toms River would never see such a team again. Starting with the 1970-71 school year, the town's gridiron talents would be divided, which would make it difficult to ever assemble such a juggernaut again. The *Ocean County Observer*'s sports columnist, Ed Schiff, gave voice to that fear.

> **Ed Schiff**: *"Never again will 10,000 football fans from all over New Jersey park into the aged stadium behind the four-block area that for nearly a century made up the school complex for Toms River. . . . There was never joy so great in the hundred years of Toms River High School as that brief, shining moment that spanned nineteen games and had the one-time whipping boy floating with greatness."*[34]

The Indians finished the season 8-1 by routing Lakewood 50-18. Still, the split was coming, and no one knew what it would mean. Toms River

South was headed for an uncertain future, with dark clouds on the horizon.

Not far up Hooper Avenue, all was bright sunshine. Brick's Green Dragons had recovered to finish 7-2. After the Toms River Loss, Vic Kubu's defense had allowed just one touchdown, sparking a long streak that included wins over both Phillipsburg and Bishop Egan. The Egan game (again on Thanksgiving) was a Brick classic, a 13-9 victory. Eight thousand fans watched quarterback John Meyer drag three Eagles defenders with him into the end zone for a last-minute, game-winning touchdown. Brick's era of greatest glory was about to dawn.[35]

That lay in the future. The present belonged to Middletown. The night of the Toms River game, a group of Lion starters had gathered at Trezza's Deli, where they talked and ate until the Sunday papers arrived. Then they celebrated by reading the newest edition of the *Asbury Park Press,* whose headlines proclaimed their victory. Mayor Harold Foulks joined the fun, proclaiming it to be the "The Week of the Roaring Lion."[36] A 61-0 Thanksgiving rout of Freehold clinched the Shore Conference title. As the state's only Group IV team with a perfect record, they were also chosen by the *Star Ledger* as the number-one team in all New Jersey.

The glory year marked the end of an era for Middletown. Dick Kleva hung up his whistle at the end of the 1969-70 school year. After guiding the Middletown wrestling team to its fifth straight division crown, he retired from coaching to become a professor of physical education at Brookdale Community College (where he helped start a certification program in scuba diving).[37] Ron Signorino was also out of the division, although only temporarily—the split had dropped Toms River South into Class B, where they would stay for two seasons. By the time they came back up in 1972, they were entering a different world of Shore sports.

Many of the players from Middletown and Toms River South went on to further greatness in their athletic careers. The most impressive college career belonged to South's Harry Walters, who starred at defensive end for the University of Maryland. The Denver Broncos drafted him in the spring of 1974, but he passed up the NFL to cross the border into Canada, becoming an All-Star linebacker for the Winnipeg Blue Bombers.[38]

One of his opposite numbers, Middletown's Ed Jones, also ended up in the CFL. Jones was an All-East safety at Rutgers, and after brief runs with the Dallas Cowboys and Buffalo Bills, he also crossed to the frozen north, winning five Grey Cups with the Edmonton Eskimos.

South lineman Bill Malast played at Villanova, later making a training camp with the Philadelphia Eagles. Rip Scherer played quarterback for Lou Holtz at William & Mary, then got into coaching himself. His long career included two stops in the NFL and runs as the head coach at James Madison and Memphis. Scherer's counterpart, Bob Abbot, was one of the many players in that game to also enjoy a college football career. Along with teammate Ron Carhart, Abbot played four years of football at Ursinus College, just outside of Philadelphia. Three other Lion graduates (Frank Kuhl, Jack Kaufmann, and Rich Steward) became standout Division II players at Slippery Rock College.

Montclair State took the remainder of the game's college players. There, former opponents became not just teammates, but roommates—South guard Rich Longo found himself paired up with Middletown tackle Kenny Hallgring. Both blocked for Bobby Hermanni, who proved just as great a college player as he was a high school one. He was a two-time All-NJAC player and helped Montclair State win three league titles in four years. Longtime Montclair State Coach Clary Anderson would later dub Hermanni the toughest player he had ever coached.[39]

All would always treasure the day on which their teams came together to write Shore Conference history. Years would pass, coaches would come and go, and yellowing yearbook pages would slowly fade, but memories of that game remained fresh and special. The outcome brought joy to Middletown and pain to Toms River, but that was far less important than the event itself. The real magic of what happened on that bitterly cold day in November 1969 is that two teams of high schoolers met at Detwiler Stadium in Toms River, and the game that they played remains etched on the hearts of all who were there.

Bob Abbot: *"It was the highlight of my athletic career."*[40]

Jack Kaufmann (Middletown safety): *"Athletically, it's the biggest moment of my career, and one of the biggest moments of my life aside from getting married and watching my kids be born."*[41]

Bill Malast (Toms River lineman): *"That game? Do I remember that game? Oh my God, of course. Of course."*[42]

CHAPTER 18
CLASS B FOOTBALL
IN THE 1960s

S hore Conference football fans enjoyed a feast in the 1960s; there were fierce rivalries and exciting title races in no less than three divisions. As exciting as Class A football was, the schools of Class B matched their larger counterparts in both enthusiasm and excitement. No matter the size of the town or its student body, no matter how many championships were won or lost, football *mattered* at the Shore.

> **Joe Dunne (Point Pleasant resident and player)**: *"It seemed to me like everybody in town went to those games. Those bleachers were packed. I remember the sounds of that. I was small enough that I wouldn't be at the game, but I was right across the street. If I stood in my backyard, I was only 300 yards from the 50-yard line. When the home team was running for a touchdown, it was an amazing sound, a roar. The band would be playing . . . the whole thing. The neighbors would all talk about it. And when I was older, you just didn't miss a game. It was a big thing. And you knew a lot*

of the people because they lived around you. These were our stars, these were our heroes. That's what everybody talked about."[1]

The headline rivalry in the 1960s was between Matawan and Manasquan, two Shore Conference originals who combined for six division titles in ten years. These two close-knit, football-loving towns went down very different paths in the 1960s, highlighting the changes that the suburban boom was bringing to the Jersey Shore.

Manasquan's roots ran deep, and even as the population of the Shore boomed, the town remained much the same as it had always been. It was dominated by the beach, the docks, and the fishing boats. Families stayed in the area for generations. The high school building, in use since 1933, had been expanded, but not replaced. Times changed, and people changed with them, but Manasquan remained, essentially, Manasquan.

Ginnie Vidola (lifelong resident): *"Part of the reason Manasquan High School is so deep in tradition is that we were raised in a tight-knit community. We all aspired to be a Warrior."[2]*

Richard Bonelli (Manasquan football player, 1957-59): *"Manasquan did not have a big stadium, but we always had a big crowd here [at football games]. They used to hang around the outside of the field and cheer us on. . . . It was an important part of the town because the band would parade through the town, playing our music. That would bring the crowd out."[3]*

Matawan's community was also close-knit but was in most other ways very different. Firstly, it wasn't actually one town—Matawan Borough was the downtown, citified section, bordered on three sides by the more rural Matawan Township. Traditionally, the township had been home to farmers, who would head to the borough each weekend to do their shopping and to sell their wares.[4]

That farmland had rapidly disappeared during the 1950s. Right off the Parkway and an easy commute to North Jersey, Matawan was a developer's dream, and soon massive housing developments began springing up across the township. Its population boomed from 7,000 to 17,000 in a decade.[5] The borough, on the other hand, lacked room to grow like that. Worse, local shoppers began bypassing the downtown in favor of suburban shopping centers closer to the highway. Separate identities began to develop. The township was primarily white and predominantly transplants. The borough had more old-timers, had a larger Black population, and with the business district struggling was facing rising unemployment.

> **Sarah Ellison (local resident):** *"All these developments coming in made it more people than farms, you know what I mean? Matawan is no longer the center because people do their shopping out on the highway."*[6]

One section of the township was further separated from the rest of the community—Cliffwood Beach. The only part of Matawan to front the ocean, it had once been a resort area with a boardwalk, amusement park, and hotels. That ended in 1960, when Hurricane Donna destroyed the amusements and eroded the beach. After that, Cliffwood Beach began to struggle. It was geographically isolated, blue collar, and easily ignored. The streets were narrow, the houses small. There were no nearby schools, no busing, and no sidewalks, so children had to walk to class down the shoulder of Route 35.[7] It was easy for Cliffwood Beach residents to feel like the forgotten men and women of Matawan.

The one force that linked these three disparate places together was Matawan High School, where few things were as important as Huskie football. Under the direction of Head Coach Barry Rizzo, Matawan played a smashmouth game, running the ball out of the increasingly old-fashioned single-wing formation and playing punishing defense. One of the few other things that the three sections had in common was a hard-working, blue-collar identity, and the single wing fit that self-image perfectly. Boys of all backgrounds watched their Huskies win games and dreamed of donning the maroon and steel.

Matawan and Manasquan first collided in 1960, when both teams were placed in the Shore's new Class B North. Both teams had outstanding backfields that year. The Big Blue used sophomores Ray Harvey and

Butch Maccanico, while the Huskies relied on the Wathington brothers, Charley and Bill. Their game was in in early November, with the division on the line.

Matawan dominated the game, piling up thirteen first downs, but they couldn't seem to find the end zone. Maccanico starred on defense and helped shut down the Wathingtons, while Harvey's two touchdown runs keyed Manasquan's 19-6 victory. The division was Manasquan's, and they celebrated by beating Point Pleasant on Thanksgiving, 26-0.[8] Matawan, meanwhile, ended their season in a funk by losing their own holiday game to Keyport.

The return of Harvey and Maccanico left Manasquan favored to repeat in 1961, especially after they started a dominant 6-0. Matawan, who was 4-2, entered the game as a huge underdog, with even the local paper dubbing the game "a grim assignment."[9] But the Huskies were no pushover. Experienced players filled every position on the team, most notably the Wathington brothers.[10] A year older, a year more talented and out for revenge, Matawan was strong indeed.

Charley Wathington's early touchdown run gave the Huskies a 6-0 lead that they spent four quarters defending. The key moment came in the final quarter, when Manasquan mounted a threatening drive and reached fourth and 2 from the 8. A poor handoff broke the Manasquan fullback's momentum, and he was swarmed in the backfield by the Huskie defense. After that, the Huskies controlled the ball and ran out the clock.[11]

Matawan secured the division in a wild game against Keyport. The underdog Raiders took a 13-6 fourth quarter lead, but Charley Wathington's brilliant effort led the Huskies back. He twice got the Huskies out of long yardage situations with perfect passes to his brother Bill, scrambled to the 8 on a draw, and found Bill once more for the tying touchdown.[12] The 13-13 tie was good enough for a 6-2-1 record and the B North crown. Manasquan, which beat Point Pleasant on Thanksgiving, had to settle for second place despite their 7-2 record. To everyone's disappointment, there would be no rubber match between the rivals, thanks to the Shore Conference's regular realignment of its divisions.

In 1962, Manasquan moved up into Class A, where they became the smallest school in the largest division. The outmatched Warriors struggled all year long, finishing 3-6 with a Thanksgiving loss to Point Pleasant. The end of the season also saw the Warriors lose their coach. After ten years in charge of the school's football program, Hal Manson stepped down and became a vice principal, leaving behind a legacy that included two division titles and one spectacular four-year run of thirty wins in thirty-six tries.

Manasquan struggled in 1963, the Warriors were shut out six times and finished 1-7. However, the Manasquan spirit lived on, thanks to the efforts of players such as halfback Jake Landfried. The son of two deaf-mute parents, Landfried had grown up in Western Pennsylvania, where he dreamed of playing on Friday nights for powerful Ambridge High School. The move to Manasquan was a tough adjustment—the Warriors were losing, and their Saturday afternoon crowds had become comparatively small.

Landfried nonetheless bought into the Warrior tradition and became the star of a struggling team. He went on to play at Montclair State, earning two NFL tryouts before a knee injury ended his professional career. He then returned to Manasquan, where he became a fixture as a football assistant and head baseball coach.[13] Decades later, in the 1990s, his sons would carry the family legacy on as Manasquan stars.

While the Big Blue was wandering in the wilderness, Matawan was finding the now unified Class B harder than expected. Central Regional, led by sophomore tailback Dewey Marvin, quarterback Richie Norcross, and end Len Walencikowski, mounted an unexpected challenge. They upset Matawan in the season opener, then roared to a 6-0 start. Joe Bauer's team was on the verge of a Class B title, with only equally surprising Wall in their way.[14]

Like Central, Wall was a child of the Parkway boom and a newcomer to the Shore scene. Until 1955, the town had sent its children to Manasquan, and its high school still carried some legacies from its older neighbor. Manasquan legend Granville Magee was Wall's first superintendent, and when he chose the new high school's colors, he selected red as a tribute to

Rutgers and blue as a tribute to Manasquan.[15] That was the easy part. Establishing a winning tradition was hard. The early days of Knights football saw small teams, gimmicky offenses, and blowout losses. They won just twice in three years.

That changed in 1961, when Charlie Harding became head coach. He arrived just in time to take advantage of two underclass stars, junior quarterback John Eckman and sophomore end Bill McGowan. The Knights' started the year 5-1, best in school history, and gave Central quite a fright. In the end, though, the Eagles were too good, clinching a 32-21 win on Norcross's 80-yard touchdown run.[16] The Golden Eagles were division champions, and even a Thanksgiving loss to mighty Brick couldn't change that. Their 8-1 finish was the best in school history.

Matawan did not win the division title, but they had plenty to celebrate. Junior halfback George Morrell (the Shore scoring champion) led the Huskies to a 7-2 finish. His return for 1963 made the Huskies early division favorites. However, he injured his leg in the preseason and Matawan dropped out of the race early. Wall, too, failed to get off the ground, as an inconsistent defense undid the aerial brilliance of Eckman (1,600 yards passing, 14 touchdowns) and McGowan (a league record 68 receptions). Central, was equally inconsistent, finishing 4-2-2. They, at least, were able to highlight their season with a Thanksgiving upset of Brick.

There was Monmouth Regional, just two years old and built around hard-charging fullback Mike Lucarelli and quarterback Ralphie Mango.[17] There was Rumson, going to the air behind veteran quarterback Vern Paulson. Paulson loved to pick defenses apart with short, accurate passes to end Jay Benedict. Then there was Point Pleasant, which under Second-Year Head Coach John Kelley was enjoying a sudden football renaissance. The tiny school had one of its largest rosters ever, seventy-six players, and featured explosive backfield stars Bob Pourchier, Dan Nemeth, and Bob Harris.[18] A 1962 win over Manasquan sent them into 1963 with high hopes.

> **Joe Dunne**: *"I'll never forget that day [when Point beat Manasquan]. Here I'm an eighth grader, in the pouring rain, everybody is just mired in mud, and the town marched back to*

the high school. Everybody celebrated for days. Nobody could sleep. They had lost to Manasquan so many years prior. . . . It seemed like forever. In my lifetime, I don't know if I ever witnessed it, until that moment."[19]

The title race was tight all year. Rumson beat Point Pleasant, then lost to Monmouth. Monmouth went out and lost to Central, leaving the division in a three-way tie that would be settled the Saturday before Thanksgiving. Then President Kennedy was assassinated, and the games were postponed until the Tuesday after Thanksgiving. Point Pleasant would win a share of the division crown if they could beat Monmouth and if winless Raritan could upset Rumson. The Gulls won, and briefly celebrated after hearing rumors that Raritan had pulled it out. The rumors were wrong. Vern Paulson's booming punts tilted the field position in Rumson's favor and set up Robert Moncrief's 18-yard touchdown run. Rumson won the division at 7-1-1.[20]

> **Joe Dunne**: *"The Asbury Park Press was broadcasting the Rumson–Raritan game. At one point, Raritan was beating Rumson. It was late. Rumson was losing late. At the end of the game, everybody thought Rumson had lost that game. They got on the bus, and Coach Kelly comes on the bus and tells them Rumson pulled it out. I remember being there when the bus pulled up at the high school. You would've thought they had lost badly. There was no joy."[21]*

Point Pleasant High School's moment had come and gone. Point Boro opened in 1964, splitting the student population in half and turning the old school (now known as Point Beach) into one of the smallest football-playing schools in the state.[22] Winning with such tiny numbers would prove to be a near-impossible task.

> **Joe Dunne**: *"My junior year we were a completely group I high school. We were the smallest public high school fielding a football team. No one of our size was playing football. We were down to 300 and some kids overall, in the building."[23]*

Considering how talented Class B was, that low level of enrollment was a major handicap. The division produced a bumper crop of college athletes in the early 1960s, ranging from Rumson's Bob Moncrief and Jay Benedict (Colgate) to Point Pleasant's Dan Nemeth (Cornell) and Monmouth's Mike Luccarelli (Sioux Falls College in South Dakota). The most unique career belonged to Wall quarterback John Eckman, who went on to Wichita State and led the nation in passing with 2,339 yards in 1966. Unfortunately, he also threw 34 interceptions against only 7 touchdowns and the Shockers finished 2-8. Point Pleasant's Bob Harris made it to the highest level of all, playing at South Carolina. No one, however, was as good as Harris's younger brother Dick, possibly the greatest athlete in the history of Point Pleasant High School.

The Shore Conference first saw Dick Harris in 1964, when he was just a freshman on an 0-4 Point Pleasant team. In desperate need of a spark, John Kelley started Harris against Jackson. He was an immediate sensation, playing a key role in a 39-6 victory. He never looked back.[24] Although the Gulls enjoyed only one winning season during Harris's time, they were always competitive and grabbed their fair share of glory. Harris won the Shore scoring title his senior year, scoring 119 points as Beach won three of its final four games. On his last Thanksgiving in a Beach uniform, Harris ignored a painful ankle injury to run for a 31-yard touchdown that forced a 6-6 tie against Manasquan.[25]

Like his brother, Harris went on to South Carolina, starring from 1969 to 1971 as a defensive back and kick returner. He earned All-American honors his senior year, then spurned a contract offer from the New York Jets to instead join the Canadian Football League's Montreal Alouettes. Harris was an immediate star, winning All-CFL honors seven times and setting a franchise record with 38 career interceptions. The Alouettes reached the Grey Cup final five times during his career, winning it twice. In 2006, when Canada's national sports network ranked the best fifty players in the history of the Canadian Football League, Harris was listed at No. 33, high honors for a kid from Point Pleasant Beach.

THE TRIUMPH OF SOUTHERN FREEHOLD

The Shore Conference grew with incredible speed during the 1960s. The year 1964 alone saw the addition of four schools—Point Boro, Jackson, Shore Regional (which had opened in 1962 but spent two years as an independent), and Southern Freehold (now known as Howell). Realignment was once again in the cards, and so Class B was again split into northern and southern divisions. In these wide-open divisions, any newcomer had a chance to make a splash, and that's exactly what Southern Freehold did.

Another product of the housing boom, Southern Freehold had been built to serve the growing number of families in Howell, all of whom were tired of making the long haul to downtown Freehold every day. In its search for a new identity, the school embraced the "Southern" aspect of its name. Its teams were nicknamed the Rebels, and Confederate flags flew at home games, a tradition that lasted until the 1980s. Their coach, Jack Van Etten, had a wealth of experience. He had played at Lakewood and coached the line for Hal Schank at Freehold. When the school split in 1963 (the first of four splits that would eventually give birth to Freehold Township, Manalapan, and Marlboro), Schank stopped coaching and became the district's athletic director. The newly opened coaching jobs went to his old assistants—Al Berlin at Freehold and Jack Van Etten at Southern Freehold.[26]

Van Etten had come to the right place because Southern Freehold was home to the Hill family. They would quickly make names for themselves as some of Howell's greatest athletes.[27] Doug Hill had been an All-Shore back at Freehold in 1962, and Herman Hill was a sophomore sensation there in 1963. Now he was a Rebel at Southern Freehold. Due to age limits, he had only one season left, but he would make the most of it in 1964.

In Hill's very first game in a Rebel uniform, he ran for two touchdowns in an upset victory against Matawan. After scoring the winning touchdowns against both Raritan and Rumson, he put up an all-time great performance against Manasquan, scoring five touchdowns in a 32-13 win that clinched the B North title for Southern Freehold. Hill said his grid-iron farewells on Thanksgiving, scoring five more touchdowns in a 56-0 rout of Jackson.[28] That gave him 108 points on the season, earning him a spot on the All-Shore team and tied for the scoring title.

Southern Freehold finished 6-1-1, good for anyone but special for a first-year program. Hill, who was even better at baseball than he was at football, was just getting started. He signed a minor league contract with the Minnesota Twins, quickly earning a reputation as the best base-stealer in the Minnesota farm system. By 1970, he was starting to make major league appearances as a pinch runner and was expected to push for a roster spot in 1971. Hill was in Venezuela playing winter ball to prepare for spring training when tragedy struck. While swimming on the Caribbean coast with some fellow ballplayers, he was caught in a rip current and sucked out to sea. Those present tried to jump in and rescue him, but they were unsuccessful. Herman Hill drowned on October 14, 1970, at the age of twenty-five years old.[29]

The tragic loss was devastating. Hill had been well-remembered in Howell and was loved by his teachers and classmates alike. On word of his untimely death, Howell principal Walter Zuber declared that Hill "was one of the finest gentlemen I have come in contact with. . . . He was polite, an exceptional leader, and respected by everyone in the school."[30] His family's legacy at Howell would continue into the 1970s.

THE ROCKETS' RED GLARE

Raritan was another child of the Parkway boom. Named for the nearby Raritan River, the high school was created to serve Hazlet and its surrounding towns. Making this area distinct was that its growth was not entirely due to the Parkway. Instead, its rapid growth was fueled by transplants from Staten Island and Brooklyn, who had come over the newly opened Outerbridge Crossing.[31] It didn't take long before the once-rural area became suburbia.

Raritan football had a lot going for it in those early years. The population was growing fast, and it was already closely knit due to the Staten Island/Brooklyn connection. They also had a fine coach in Joe Oxley. Oxley had deep Shore roots—a native of Long Branch, he had played at that high school for his uncle, the legendary Army Ippolito. He was a former star athlete (a member of the Lebanon Valley College Hall of Fame) and an experienced coach. He showed patience through some early struggles and in 1964 rode junior halfback Loften Swenger to Raritan's first winning season.

In 1965, Raritan returned both Swenger and two-way end Joe Barth, but they were not expected to contend for the B North title. The favorites instead were from Southern Freehold, led by champion wrestler Orlando Fontanez and halfback Jack Hill. If not them, then Matawan, with its massive 117-man roster and winning tradition. And if not Matawan, then Manasquan, returning to glory under second-year coach Fred Lockenmeyer. In Lockenmeyer's first season, 1964, the Big Blue had started a host of sophomores. The youngsters took their lumps, then came of age on Thanksgiving against Point Beach.

The Gulls had beaten Manasquan two years running and were closing in on a third as they held a 13-0 lead into the fourth quarter. The tide turned on Manasquan freshman John Ferreira's 12-yard touchdown run. Ray Salkeld then broke three tackles on his way to a 47-yard run to tie the game. On the next possession, sophomore quarterback Jim Roper found Bob Segall for a 32-yard pass down to the goal line, setting up Roper for the winning touchdown, a fourth-down quarterback sneak. Manasquan escaped, 19-13.[32]

Ferreira, Roper, and six linemen returned for the 1965 season, and the Warriors were clear favorites for the division title. They beat Rumson to start the season, only to run into trouble against Raritan. Mark Howard threw two touchdowns and ran for another, while Swenger tore off an 80-yard run. The Rockets led 25-7 at the half, leaving the stands abuzz and the broadcasting WJLK Radio crew in shock. But 'Squan wasn't finished.

They recovered because Jim Roper had one of the greatest second halves a quarterback at the Shore had ever had. He completed his first seven passes of the third quarter, including a 43-yard touchdown pass to John Ferreira to cut the score to 25-13. Mike Momousis made it 25-19 by returning a Rocket fumble for a touchdown, and then Roper tied the game with a 30-yard strike to end Glen Ditzenberger. Roper's extra point made the score 26-25 and won the game.[33]

The stunning comeback left Manasquan on top of the world, but there was a weakness. Perceptive *Asbury Park Press* sportswriter Marty Fischbein noted the victors had struggled against Lofton Swenger's outside running.[34] Southern Freehold noticed it too, and they used Jack Hill to punish that weakness with a 25-0 upset of the Big Blue. Hill intercepted two passes, ran for a touchdown, and caught another.[35] That upset and Raritan's own comeback victory over Matawan (Swenger ran for two second-half touchdowns) left the division in a tie.[36] That was how it stayed through to the end of the year, as both teams won out to finish co-champions.

Thanksgiving was happy for both teams. Raritan's 7-6 victory over Mater Dei was especially meaningful to their head coach, who prevailed in his first and only on-field battle against his uncle, Army Ippolito. Manasquan, meanwhile, enjoyed another comeback to beat Point Beach. John Ferreira returned a kickoff 95 yards for a touchdown, while Jim Roper threw two more touchdown passes in another clutch performance. Since both were underclassmen, Manasquan fans were excited that the best was yet to come.[37]

While Raritan and Manasquan were enjoying their turkeys, Matawan was wondering where it all had gone wrong. The Huskies had stumbled to a 4-5 record and only narrowly managed to beat winless Keyport. After the game, brawls broke out in the stands and had to be broken up by the police. It was not the way that the season was supposed to have gone.[38]

Bouncing back in 1966 would be difficult, especially since the schedule was getting more challenging. B North and B South unified again, which brought Ocean County powers Central and Lakewood onto the schedule. Joining them was Ocean Township, new to the Shore but very talented. Barry Rizzo, though, found more than a few reasons to be optimistic. He had another 117 players on his roster, including versatile single-wing tailback Chick Geran, bulldozing fullback Edmund Jones, quarterback Frank Devino, and hard-nosed center Curtis Washington. On defense, ends Bill Bond and Robert Truiar and middle guard Joe Martucci filled out a rock-solid defensive line.[39] And then there was Randy Davis.

Although only a junior, Davis was clearly Matawan's best athlete. He starred on the basketball team in the winter, he hurdled for the track team in the spring, and he was a successful amateur boxer in the summertime. It was on the gridiron, though, that he was at his best. An explosive wing-back, Davis was the division's most dangerous breakaway threat. After the season, Rizzo would dub Davis the best back he had ever coached. With him, the team's potential seemed limitless.[40]

Matawan opened the season by showing how high they could reach in a 51-0 rout of Southern Regional. After the game, awed Southern coach William Scherer sighed, "They just had too many guns." He wouldn't be the last coach to feel that way.[41] Matawan hung 45 on Ocean, 41 on Southern Freehold, 33 on Raritan, and 38 on Freehold Regional. By mid-season, Davis had scored nineteen touchdowns and Geran had thrown fifteen touchdown passes. The Huskies rose to number two in the Shore, behind only undefeated Brick Township. They were just one win away from the Class B title. They also still weren't necessarily clear favorites.

That was because Manasquan had it all. Quarterback Jim Roper was an exceptional deep passer, throwing for five touchdowns against Ocean. Halfback John Ferreira could also score at will, and led Davis in the Shore scoring race, twenty touchdowns to nineteen. They too had run up big scores, savaging Ocean for fifty-one points behind five Roper touchdown passes.[42] Their early November collision was the biggest game of the 1966 season. Barry Rizzo called it "the game of my life," and Lockenmeyer predicted "a whale of a ball game."

A cold November rain fell that Saturday, but it didn't deter a caravan of twenty-one buses full of Manasquan fans from following the team up to Matawan. In all, 8,000 fans braved the elements to listen in, and many more listened live on WJLK Radio.[43] The Big Blue jumped ahead 12-0 on two Ken Bill touchdowns, only for Randy Davis to rally the Huskies with a 65-yard touchdown run in the second quarter. Now it was a ball game.

After Manasquan's next possession stalled, the Huskies blocked the ensuing punt, and took over in Big Blue territory. Davis carried the ball on almost every play of a 40-yard drive and scored on a short burst up the middle for a 13-12 lead. Manasquan regained the lead, 18-13, on Bill's third score, but the loss of Ferreira to a badly twisted ankle crippled their offense. Meanwhile, Matawan kept coming. A perfectly executed screen pass from Geran to Randy Davis went 76 yards for a touchdown, with Davis stutter-stepping the last 'Squan defender on his way to a brilliant score. Billy Bond's third-quarter touchdown run extended Matawan's lead to nine and all but finished the Warriors. On the game's final play, Barry Rizzo intended to let the clock run out, but Randy Davis wanted one more shot at the end zone.

He took a short snap and dashed up the middle, weaving his way through the defeated Warrior defense on his way to his fourth touchdown that afternoon. The final was 33-18, and Matawan had won the Class B championship. Fans poured onto the field in celebration, while the Huskie team hoisted Rizzo onto their shoulders and paraded him around the field. It was one of the veteran coach's greatest victories.[44] Davis scored four more touchdowns on Thanksgiving against Keyport, giving him 163 points, the state scoring title, and the Shore scoring record.[45] So ended the first perfect season in school history.

The 1967 team had a chance to be even better. Davis, quarterback Chick Geran, fullback Curtis Washington, linemen Joe Martucci and Walt White, end Larry Shaw, linebacker Mike Phelan . . . they were all back.[46] Their chief rivals, meanwhile, were down. Manasquan had lost Roper, Bill, and Ferreira and started the year with a mediocre 0-1-2 record. While they struggled, Matawan was obliterating people.

Barry Rizzo (Matawan head coach): *"Not only is Randy Davis the best back I have ever coached, he is the finest high school back I have ever seen. He's a much stronger runner this year, and he still has never been caught from behind. . . . Two and three players hit him on every play, and everybody runs after him even when he doesn't have the ball."[47]*

Davis totaled eight touchdowns in the season's first three games and by the halfway point of the season, had scored 120 points, well on pace for another Shore Conference record. Matawan started 5-0 and was ranked No. 1 in the Shore. The crowds were getting bigger every week, and a midseason clash with 4-1 Raritan drew the biggest crowd yet.

The Rockets, after losing their opener to Central, were playing well. Backs Don Russomanno and Stan Piorkowski powered a tough running game, while linebacker Glenn Waltsak led a defense that posted four consecutive shutouts, including one against Manasquan. The *Red Bank Register* called the game "Memorial Day, Flag Day, and Election Day all rolled into one big gridiron package." It drew a standing-room only crowd of 4,000 fans.

Davis's touchdown run put Matawan ahead 6-0, and although Raritan was fighting hard, it was clear that they were just barely hanging on. Worse, an injury to Russomanno and the ejection of Piorkowski left them without their stars. Then, abruptly, the game turned. Davis had twisted his ankle in the second quarter, and although he played on, he was not his usual explosive self. Raritan, meanwhile, rallied. Reserve back Barry McBride broke free for 25 yards, setting up quarterback Bill Fleming to tie the game with a touchdown pass to Jim Mason. Bill Heinzer's extra point untied it, giving the Rockets a 7-6 lead. Raritan's defense held on from there, clinching a 7-6 upset.[48] Raritan had won.

The division was now deadlocked, and streaking Manasquan was coming up fast. The Big Blue had a new backfield combination, featuring Gene Landis, Lenny Warwick, and explosive sophomore Skip Whitman. Ocean's upset of Raritan put them right back in the race.

> **Joe Oxley (Raritan coach)**: *"We just couldn't get going. They were fired up for us the same way we were for Matawan, and those pass interceptions and other mistakes stopped us early in the game. Actually, the only big mistake we made was on the first play of the game."*[49]

That mistake was a big one. On the game's first play, no one covered Ocean end Joe Simon, who proceeded to catch a 75-yard touchdown pass from Brian Fitzgerald. Raritan fought back on offense, but the best they could manage was a 7-7 tie. That closed the books on their division schedule with a 4-1-1 record.[50] Now all eyes turned to the Matawan-Manasquan showdown. The Huskies could claim an outright Class B title with a win, while Manasquan would share it with Raritan if they could manage the upset.

Another 4,000 turned up to Warrior Field to watch the game. This time, it was Matawan's turn to deal with the injury jinx, as Davis's nagging injury forced him to the sideline. Still, the Huskies led 7-6 lead into the fourth, and Manasquan's offense wasn't moving. It took a big play on special teams to save the Big Blue. Skip Whitman blocked a Matawan punt, giving the Warriors the ball at the 28 going in. That set up Warwick for the winning touchdown run.[51] It was Matawan's second division heartbreak, and this time it had cost them a title. Raritan and Manasquan would share the crown for the second time in three years.

Thanksgiving provided an odd epilogue to the season. Raritan was upset by Mater Dei and finished 6-2-1, while Manasquan finished with the unusual final record of 4-1-3 after tying Point Beach. Matawan managed to blast Keyport 46-14 and finished 7-2, but still had to settle for third place in the division. Davis's leg injury kept him out of that game as well and cost him a chance to break his own scoring record. Still, it didn't scare off the college scouts. He earned a football scholarship to Michigan State and spent three years as a flanker for the Spartans.

Davis had forged another link in Matawan's long chain of exceptional tailbacks, which only continued to grow after Davis's graduation. His successor was Tony Russell, who ran for over 1,000 yards in 1969 and won the league scoring title. He also won county, Shore, and state championships in the long jump. Russell played two years of football at the Naval Academy, eventually reaching the rank of captain before retiring from the military.[52]

Russell would be doing his running in a Class B that looked very different in 1968. Raritan was moving out for Class A, while Red Bank and Asbury Park were moving in. Manasquan wasn't moving, but they were breaking in a new head coach. The biggest change of all, though, was a challenge coming from one of the Shore's youngest football programs.

THE HIGH TIDE

The fall of 1968 was filled with promise at Ocean Township High School. That year's senior class was going to be the first to spend all of its high school career at Ocean. When the Class of 1969 had been born, Ocean had been nothing more than a small collection of houses on the border of Asbury Park. And then the boom hit. Housing developments mushroomed all over the town, and the population nearly doubled.[53]

Many of Ocean's families were closely connected to Asbury Park—the new houses in the township were often occupied by longtime Asbury residents that were leaving city for the large, affordable houses they could open in the suburbs. However, as years went by and Ocean's population continued to grow, the town's connection to Asbury Park began to fade. There were already elementary schools in Ocean, and starting in 1965, there was a high school as well. This totally changed the composition of both school systems.

The split also completely changed the composition of the local school system. Once, Asbury Park had been one of the most integrated schools at the Shore; now, it was predominantly Black, while Ocean's student population was almost entirely white. Deprived of a valuable tax base, Asbury Park High School started to decline physically. Meanwhile, Ocean was able to support beautiful new athletic facilities, drawing large crowds of local fans. As the town's longtime mayor, Joseph Palaia, put it, Ocean was "an involved town . . . a place where everyone basically pulls together."[54]

The split also altered the sports fortunes of Asbury Park. Some of the city's best athletic families were now going elsewhere, and a whole generation that would have starred at Asbury Park made their name in the red and white of the Ocean Spartans. The Villapianos were just one of several examples—brothers Phil and John were multisport stars at Ocean and quickly established the new school as a local sports power. Phil, in particular, stood out. At first, he was none too thrilled about having to change schools. As a sophomore in 1964, he had started at linebacker for Asbury, which meant playing in front of 5,000 fans against Neptune on Thanksgiving. Transferring to Ocean as a junior in 1965 meant giving up varsity football; the Spartans played only a JV schedule that year.

Still, Phil emerged to become a two-year team captain, earning second-team All-Shore honors as a senior in 1966. He was a two-time All-MAC linebacker at Bowling Green, which attracted the attention of the Oakland Raiders. He was their second-round draft choice in 1971, and he didn't disappoint. By the time Villapiano's fourteen-year career ended, he had made the trip to four Pro Bowls and started for the victorious Raiders in Super Bowl XI.

Such players would prove valuable to Head Coach Jack Tighe, who arrived at Ocean in 1967. Tighe was the third Shore Conference head coach to come out of West New York (the other two were Brick's Warren Wolf and Point Boro's Al Saner), and like those two he found immediate success. Large roster numbers, plentiful community support, and the fine play of halfback Matty Tomo helped lift Ocean to a 6-2-1 record in his first year. Tighe's second year looked to be even better, as the return of nose tackle Randy Rose; ends Joe Falco and Toby Husserl; guard Bob Fromer; and backs John Villiapiano, Syd Stitely, and Jamie Henneberry marked Ocean as a serious title contender.[55] Ocean started 3-1 (their only loss coming to Toms River) setting up a midseason showdown with Manasquan.

'Squan was still the favorite to win the division. The Warriors had roared to a 4-0-1 start behind junior guard Skip Whitman, junior halfback Bill McKelvey, and All-Shore end Norm Hall. The Warriors led 16-13 in the fourth, but Ocean rallied behind backup quarterback Ed Busch. He found Joe Falco for two long passes, setting up Jamie Henneberry's go-ahead touchdown run. Now behind and with the clock ticking, the Big Blue went to the air. It backfired. Bob Frommer returned an interception for a touchdown to secure Ocean's 25-16 victory.[56]

The Spartans rolled from there, clinching the Class B title. While the Spartans celebrated, opposing coaches worried, not least about Jamie Henneberry. Only a junior, he had scored eight touchdowns in the season's final month. His return in 1969 would power the Spartans and set up one of the most exciting Class B races of the decade.

Fred Lockenmeyer stepped down as Manasquan head coach after the 1967 season, turning the reigns over to assistant Jack Hawkins. It didn't take Hawkins long to become a legend; in some ways he already was, having won All-State honors at Princeton High School and started at quarterback for Pennsylvania's West Chester State. As a coach at Manasquan, he won eighty-one games and four division titles in football, plus a hundred games and four more division championships in baseball (as well as an overall Group II state title). It is not the wins, though, for which "the Hawk" is most warmly remembered. In his decade of coaching, he molded the character of countless Manasquan athletes, leaving a mark on their lives and the lives of many others with the sheer joy he brought to the sports and the love he showed for his athletes.

Jack Hawkins: *"I thought of Manasquan as the Notre Dame of high school football. Cheerleaders were out on Thursday at our practices to pump us up. There was a pep rally every Friday, and the cheerleaders would decorate our meeting room. There was nothing like it."*[57]

In 1968 (his first season), the Warriors went 7-1-1, finishing second in Class B and placing two starters (Hall and McKelvey) on the All-Shore team. The 1969 team was even better. Hall was off playing at Gettysburg College, but McKelvey, running back Len Warwick, and lineman Skip Whitman were all back. Whitman, a three-sport star and second-year starter at guard, was the clear choice for team captain. Even a void at quarterback came up roses—when appendicitis forced Bill Applegate to the sideline, Hawkins turned to sophomore John Ervin. Ervin would win twenty-two games as a three-year starting quarterback.

Hawkins' Warriors were tested right from the start. The season opener against Wall came down to a late two-point conversion. Linebacker Jimmy Van Schoick stuffed Knight back Mark Roberts on the critical two-point run to preserve the victory. A week later, the Big Blue downed Red Bank behind a great performance from their undersized defense. Next, they conquered Tony Russell and an undefeated Matawan team. With the game tied 8-8 late, John Ervin showed his coolness under fire by leading his team 75 yards to the winning touchdown.[58]

That set up a showdown with the team that had denied Manasquan the title last year—Jamie Henneberry and the Ocean Spartans. The game was scoreless until the second-half kickoff, which McKelvey returned 90 yards for the first touchdown. On the ensuing two-point conversion, Ervin rolled out, read the defense, and scrambled for an 8-0 lead. The Manasquan defense fought tooth and nail, making that score stand up only by tremendous effort. Three times Henneberry and the Spartans drove inside the Manasquan 20, and three times Skip Whitman and the Warriors defense held them. When Ocean finally did score on John Villapiano's 20-yard touchdown run, the Big Blue managed to bat down their two-point conversion pass to preserve the victory.[59]

One week later, Manasquan made their title official by crushing Jackson 49-0. All that was left to do was celebrate, which they did by thrashing Point Beach on Thanksgiving. Even Whitman got the chance to score a touchdown, capping his Manasquan career with a comfortable 36-16 win over the old rivals. The Big Blue ended the year as one of only nine undefeated, untied teams in all of New Jersey and brought home the CJ II title (their first since 1958).[60]

The legend of the 1969 team, however, did not end there. Team captain Skip Whitman had a bright athletic future in front of him. That December, he was honored as an All-Shore, All-State, and High School All-American offensive linemen. He captained the wrestling team that winter and the baseball team that spring (winning All-Shore, All-State, and New York Daily News All-Star honors as a catcher). By the time he graduated, the saying around Manasquan was that "Skip Whitman's the man who can do anything."[61] Whitman chose to attend West Point, where he was a two-year starting linebacker and team captain in 1973. It was after his time at the academy that Whitman would truly make his mark, however—he became a surgeon with the 82nd Airborne, serving during the first Gulf War. During that service, he performed the first combat zone orthopedic surgery in the history of the United States Army.[62]

A BRIEF HISTORY OF A SHORT-LIVED DIVISION: B SOUTH FOOTBALL

From 1964-65, Class B of the Shore Conference was divided into northern and southern divisions. The northern division got most of the attention, but the southern division produced one of the Shore Conference's overlooked rivalries and one of its great stories—the resurrection of Lakewood football. The Piners hadn't won anything of note since Russ Wright's retirement in 1950, and it took the return of an old grad to yank them out of virtual irrelevance.

The returning graduate was Ed Brandt, a senior guard on the 1949 team. During his time away, he had played football at West Virginia Tech, served in the Army, and coached the offensive line at Ewing High School. His number one mission was to restore the pride he had known as a student. That would be a challenge. The team and its fans had grown accustomed to losing and the town's passion had migrated from the gridiron to the basketball court, where Lakewood's best athletes now won glory. Football was an afterthought. Brandt, however, was undeterred. Not only would he succeed, but he would also become a Lakewood fixture for decades to come.

The first hint of something special came in the 1962 season finale, held two days after Thanksgiving. Winless Lakewood was visiting Detwiler Stadium to face equally winless Toms River. It marked the final game in a long, frustrating season. An outside observer, who didn't understand the weight that Thanksgiving football carried, would have dubbed it one of the year's most meaningless games. That would have been an enormous mistake.

Despite the bitter cold and howling wind, 2,000 fans turned out for the game. Toms River led most of the way, but the Piners kept coming back. Late in the fourth quarter, Jay Burdge scored on a 5-yard touchdown to tie the game at 19. Brandt elected to run for the decisive point and put the ball in the hands of fullback Frank Iraci's hands. He was met in the backfield by four Toms River defenders, but refused to go down, dragging the pile into the end zone with him. Lakewood 20, Toms River 19. Brandt could be seen "jumping up and down as though his team had completed a perfect season." Such was the power of Thanksgiving.[63]

The Piners had turned the corner. They improved to 4-5 the next year, led by a talented junior class. That group included tackle Dan DeCausey, the Brown brothers (John and Joe), and two strong defensive linemen in Moe Hill and Isaac Grodzinski. They also had a stable of big-play threats—backs Bill Riva, Mel Sharpe, and Andy Sebris, and end John Brown. As the team entered 1964, that group was reaching its athletic peak, and the impressed *Asbury Park Press* concluded that "This Could Be Lakewood's Year."[64]

Sharpe's touchdown run helped the Piners survive a 7-6 challenge from Point Beach, and after that the team got rolling.[65] They won each of their next four games by at least thirty points. They were 5-0 and thumping everyone. Sebris was at quarterback, conducting the offense like an old pro. The three backs were running wild, and no one could cover John Brown. Then, much to their surprise, they literally hit the Wall.

The Crimson Knights, led by quarterback Ken Fortier, halfback Dick Przyblewski, and end Bill McGowan, had one of the best passing offenses in the Shore Conference. Moving the ball effectively through the air, they managed to hold Lakewood to a surprising 13-13 tie.[66] That opened the door for a surging second-place Central team and turned up the pressure on the Piners, who had to play the Eagles the very next week. Four lost fumbles left Lakewood down 20-19 at the start of the fourth. Central drove to the 21 in the fourth, looking to put the game out of reach, only to fumble themselves. Now Lakewood had it, but the clock was ebbing away, and they had shown no signs of any offensive explosion.

It was time for Mel Sharpe to become a hero. On second and 7 from his own 24, Sharpe hit the line and found a seam, racing 76 yards to the end zone for the game-winning touchdown. The Piners were still unbeaten at 6-0-1.[67] One week later, Sharpe's three touchdowns powered his team to a 25-0 win over a depleted Point Boro team. Shortly after the final whistle blew, word reached the Lakewood players that Central had overpowered Wall, giving the Piners sole possession of the Class B South title. They scooped Brandt up on their shoulders and carried him around the field. For the first time since 1942, Lakewood football had won a Shore Conference championship.[68]

It finished where it had started two years earlier, on Thanksgiving. This time, there was very little drama. Lakewood simply had too many athletes for an outmatched Toms River team, rolling to a 42-13 victory. For the first time since 1936, Lakewood had finished a season undefeated. Even Ron Signorino (in his first year at Toms River) was left in awe of what the Piners had accomplished.[69]

> **Ron Signorino**: *"That was maybe the greatest team in Lakewood history. They were undefeated, and I think they beat us 41-0. . . . They were just dynamic."*[70]

The glow of the unbeaten season lasted all winter, but once the weather began to warm, the burning question of 1965 started to form: Could Lakewood repeat? One projected starter quit to focus on basketball, and another moved to Neptune, leaving only four returning regulars for the upcoming season. Meanwhile, newspaper previews of Central Regional and Point Boro carried word that the Golden Eagles had eighty players on their roster and that the Panthers had eighteen returning lettermen. There was every reason for Lakewood to be daunted. Still, there was talent, most notably in the person of two-sport star Pierre DeCausey, the basketball guard who was taking over at quarterback.[71]

The Piners didn't have the same level of explosiveness that they had enjoyed in 1964, but they still managed to grind their way to a 4-0 start, with DeCausey and Brown running the ball effectively. In midseason, though, the Piners slipped in a rivalry game with Southern Freehold. The Rebels, eager to knock off their nearest neighbors, drew 1,500 fans to their homecoming. Then they rallied from 6-0 down to beat the Piners on a fourth-quarter touchdown run by Jack Hill and a conversion pass from Orlando Fontanez to Jim Perry.[72]

The loss snapped Lakewood's fifteen-game winning streak, but since it wasn't a division loss, the Piners were still atop Class B South. However, the team had not played well, and that concerned Ed Brandt. A 12-0 loss to Central, though, allowed the upstarts from Point Boro to tie Lakewood for the division lead. The Panthers were just in their second year of varsity competition, but they were also 8-0 and on the verge of a title themselves.

Under the Shore Conference's modern rules, Al Saner's Panthers would have already won part of the B South crown and Lakewood would be playing for a share; the league no longer has tiebreakers for division titles and instead just awards split titles. In 1965, though, the Shore Conference did use head-to-head record as a tiebreaker. That meant the winner of the Boro-Lakewood game would get everything, and the loser nothing.

The high stakes, and the talent level of the two teams involved, drew plenty of press attention, including a broadcast crew from WJLK Radio. They saw a good one. Early on, the Piners jumped ahead when Buddy Goldman tore off a 69-yard touchdown run. Vitally, Pierre DeCausey added an extra point to make it 7-0. The rest of the game saw Point Boro on the attack. They opened the second half with a classic Panther infantry assault; Gene Monahan carried twelve times on a 15-play drive and the Panthers worked their way to the 7-yard line before stalling. In the fourth quarter, they went outside, with quarterback Bob Houlihan slashing for 12, 16, 19, and 8 yards before running for a 13-yard touchdown. DeCausey, however, blocked the extra point. It was 7-6 and the clock was running down.

Thanks to a bad punt snap, Boro got the ball back on the Lakewood 25 with under four minutes to play. With the clock ticking away, they had no choice but to go to the air—it didn't work. Defensive tackle Harold Sutton hurried Houlihan into an errant throw that DeCausey intercepted. Lakewood ran out the clock from there, after which wild celebrations ensued and Ed Brandt was carried off the field in triumph. It was their second straight division title.[73]

Ten days later, the champions played their annual season finale in front of 4,500 fans at the field behind Lakewood High School. The visitors from Toms River acquitted themselves well, challenging the Piners in a game that Ed Brandt called "the toughest we have played all season." Both defenses were punishing, and neither offense could find the goal line in a 0-0 tie. So, Lakewood's season ended at 6-2-1.[74]

DeCausey earned All-Shore honors at season's end. He also earned All-Shore honors that winter, helping the Piner basketball team win division and state titles. Lakewood's athletic glory continued into the spring, when the baseball team won the prestigious Monmouth College Tournament (at that time the equivalent of the Shore Conference Tournament).

The Piners continued to enjoy success in basketball and baseball, but their football fortunes declined after 1965. They wouldn't win another title until their 1985 state crown, and they wouldn't win another division title until 2000. Worse, the annual Thanksgiving rivalry with Toms River shifted decisively toward the Indians. For all those reasons, the 1964-65 run was important—it proved that there would always be a chance that the Piners could rise again.

CHAPTER 19
CLASS C FOOTBALL:
FROM 1966 TO 1969

By the mid-1960s, it was obvious that the Shore Conference needed a third division. The smallest schools in Class B were being worn down by weight of numbers. Southern Regional, which opened in 1958, was typical. Created by the merger of two tiny schools, the original Barnegat High and the one-room Tuckerton High School, Southern was one of the smallest schools in the league and its football program was far from imposing.

> **Asbury Park Press**: *"While every school appreciated playing the Rams because it was a sure victory, there was still a problem with playing on the Southern gridiron. . . . Coaches would come down to Manahawkin to scout the Rams and return in utter confusion. The newcomers lined up in formations that no one had ever dreamed up, including the coach."[1]*

Over its first eight years, Southern football averaged less than two wins a season. That was the way things were for the Shore's smallest schools.

Wall, Point Beach, and Jackson (which opened in 1964) all faced similar difficulties. The most vivid example of the problem, though, could be found at Shore Regional. The West Long Branch school opened in 1962 with no senior class, and so chose to spend its first two years as an independent, operating outside the Shore Conference. That choice paid off for Head Coach Dave Wachter and his team. In 1963, the school's second year, halfback Eric Swenson and junior quarterback Merv Eastwick helped the Blue Devils to an undefeated 8-0-1 record.

The final game of that season was a classic battle with 6-1 Monmouth Regional. The two schools were natural rivals, and their Thanksgiving rivalry would run for thirty-three years. Their first game, which pitted Swenson against Monmouth's star quarterback Ralphie Mango, set the standard for all to follow. Ultimately, Shore's special teams won the game, as Blue Devil Tony DeMarco scooped up a fumbled kickoff and returned it for what proved to be the deciding touchdown.[2]

When Shore Regional joined the Shore Conference, however, they found wins much harder to come by, especially in the difficult Class B North. Not even a program that had experienced immediate success could fend off the weight of numbers. It was obvious that something needed to be done, and in 1966 the Shore Conference created a new Class C for the smallest schools. The immediate favorite in that division was one small school that *had* fought off those numbers—Point Pleasant Boro.

Until the early 1960s, students from the Boro had attended high school over the canal bridge, at Point Pleasant Beach. That had made sense for years, when this was an undeveloped, open stretch of land to the west of the populated Beach.

Joe Dunne (Point Pleasant resident): *"Point Pleasant Beach is only a square mile town, and the population during the winter was somewhere around 2,500 people. During the summer, it would go to between 8,000 and 10,000 people. Most of those people were from Jersey City, who summered in Point Beach. . . . After Labor Day, everything would shut down. There was a big parade the week after Labor Day, called the Big Sea Day Parade . . . and after,*

*that they practically turned the traffic lights off. It became a quiet,
small town. . . . Over in the Boro, there was a lot of undeveloped
area. Where the high school is now was a big junkyard . . . that was
all vacant land."[3]*

That changed with astonishing speed during the Parkway boom. As
commuters poured farther and farther south, new housing developments started springing up and its population skyrocketed. In ten years,
the town's population went from 4,000 to 10,000. When the new high
school opened, it immediately started developing a football program under the direction of fiery Head Coach Al Saner. The Panthers very nearly
snatched the B South title from Lakewood in 1966 and were eager to
compete against schools their own size.

Saner had been part of rich football traditions all his life. He had played
high school football for the great Joe Coviello at Memorial in West New
York, prep football for the legendary Joe Kasberger at. St. Benedict's Prep,
and college football at Gettysburg under future Harvard coach John
Yovicsin. He had served a stint in the army and then coached for sev-
en years at Hawthorne High School (five as an assistant, two as a head
coach). The Boro job, though, offered an opportunity to create a tradition
of his own. He also had an existing Shore connection—Warren Wolf had
been an assistant when he was a player in high school.

> **Al Saner**: *"I applied for three head coaching jobs down here at the
> Shore, and I used Warren Wolf's name. I took the Point Pleasant
> job because nobody had ever been there. It was a brand-new school.
> Whatever tradition was established would be established by me. I
> didn't have to look over my shoulder or anything like that."[4]*

Creating a new tradition was an opportunity, but it was also a challenge. In 1964, the Panthers played a full varsity schedule without a senior
class; Saner was taking what was essentially a JV team into a tough Class
B schedule. Knowing the challenge ahead, he drilled his team relentlessly
over the summer. Their mission was to perfect the straight-ahead, physical I-formation offense that would become synonymous with Point Boro

football. Generations of Panthers backs would follow a legion of tough-as-nails linemen straight up the middle.

Denny Toddings (longtime area coach and friend of Al Saner's): *"He is one of the most intense individuals I've ever been around. And one of the most basic coaches ... when you're in trouble, give it to your best back, go to your best linemen, and pray to God."[5]*

Al Saner: *"I looked at football in a simple way. Don't get too complex. Don't get too complex. And be tough. A physical type of game. We ran the ball more than we passed. That was a criticism of me that I didn't throw very much. We maybe passed three or four times a game, sometimes. We'd run right at you and dig you out. We ran an I, which at that time was the thing to do. Fullback leading and a tailback running behind."[6]*

The first of those teams began to emerge that summer—big tackle Bob DeVoto, lighting-quick end Pete Hatch, and workhorse tailback John Burd. The boy drawing the most attention was the tireless Gene Monahan, the team's best runner and best tackler. Monahan never wanted to come off the field, and by the time he graduated the whole Shore would know his name.[7]

Considering the difficulties that the 1964 Panthers faced, their 3-6 record was quite impressive. And the entire Panther team would be back in 1965, a year older, stronger, and wiser. They wanted a league title, and they almost won one. With a big line clearing the way for the thundering runs of Burd and Monahan, the Panthers won their first seven games by a combined 212-27. Only a heartbreaking loss to Lakewood kept them from finishing undefeated and winning a division title. The Panthers still finished the year 8-1 and ranked fourth in the Shore, while Monahan and DeVoto both earned first-team All-Shore honors. Monahan went on to the University of Vermont, where he set several school receiving records from his end position.[8]

Point Boro entered Class C in 1966 with just one returning starter—two-way tackle Chuck Shaffer. But he was a good one, earning All-Shore honors that year. There was also a key addition, junior Dave Rola, a transfer from CBA. Although just five-foot-five and 145 pounds, he was lightning-quick and had the heart of a lion.[9]

> **Dave Rola**: *"The lead back would go into the hole, and nobody could see where I was. By the time they found me I was in the secondary. . . . Some games I carried the ball forty-five times."*[10]

> **Al Saner**: *"Tough as nails. Played with his heart. He was the perfect tailback for us because he was always going forward."*[11]

Rola's running and Shaffer's defense rocketed the Panthers to an undefeated start, and for the first half of the season they looked invincible. Then, in October, they ran into Shore Regional. Led by quarterback/linebacker Jay Franks, who scored on both offense and defense, the Blue Devils romped to a 32-7 victory and took control of the Class C race.[12]

Shore students were renowned for their school spirit, which helped to fuel wins like that one. There were seventy-five players on the team, and large crowds of students in the stands at every game. Much of the credit belonged to Head Coach Jake Jeffrey. A 1946 graduate of Red Bank Catholic, Jeffrey had been one of the first teachers hired at Shore and became a winning head coach in football, basketball, and baseball. Shore's young athletes were all eager to play for him.

> **Fred Kampf (baseball player and later coach at Shore Regional)**: *"Jake was the type of coach who was very inspirational and commanded respect. If we got on the bus and he said we were all going to jump off the Empire State Building, we would all jump off it."*[13]

With Franks playing both ways and halfback John Demaree running wild, Shore was one of the strongest teams in Monmouth County. They upset RBC and then crushed Southern to move within one game of their first ever division title. On November 5, a chilly autumn day, the Devils invaded Wall in pursuit of a championship. Dwain Painter's Crimson Knights, also thriving in Class C, had other ideas. The Knights had won four straight games behind quarterback Pete Tonks and runners Elwood Smith and Mark D'Andrea. A win over Shore would earn them a share of their first-ever division championship.

It was the second quarter, the finest that Wall had played in its short football history, which did the trick. Over the span of twelve minutes, Wall scored four times. That avalanche made all the difference as the Knights coasted home to a 32-7 victory.[14] Wall and Shore, their league seasons finished, were now guaranteed a tie for the division crown. Point Boro could win their own share by beating Jackson on Thanksgiving.

That wasn't easy. Rola was on the bench due to a head injury suffered against Lower Cape May, and the Jaguars were fired up. It all came down to the final minute, with Boro ahead 20-19 and Jackson lining up for an extra point. A tie would end their title hopes, so the kick had to be blocked. Boro's best lineman, Chuck Shaffer, came hurtling up the middle and deflected the ball with both hands. He was ruled offsides. Jackson would get another chance. Again, Shaffer came hurtling up the middle, this time accompanied by Jack Carter. Once again, the kick deflected harmlessly away, and this time there were no flags. The Panthers had won a share of their first-ever division crown. Their winning streak now stood at two games. No one knew then that it would last almost four years.[15]

In 1967, the return of Rola and a stout defensive line featuring Jim West, Steve Hatch, and Mark Van Beveran turned a streak into *the* streak.[16] The Panthers scored early and often, usually through a long Rola touchdown run. Only Lakewood managed to challenge them, and even that game ended in a comfortable 21-7 Panther victory. On Thanksgiving Day against Jackson, Rola rumbled through the slop and mud for two touchdowns, powering the Boro to a 13-0 victory and their first outright Class C championship.[17] Saner had enjoyed his first undefeated season and the streak was now eleven games long.

Then, 1968 brought a new challenge—Rola and Van Beveren were off to play football at Gettysburg College, leaving their old teammates behind to defend the crown. Fortunately, some key pieces were back, such as tackle Steve Hatch and quarterback Roy Cole, while Jack Vitale stepped enthusiastically into the key spot at tailback. The Panthers were challenged early in the season by a tough Wall team, but Cole's touchdown pass and two touchdown runs helped the Panthers build a lead that Hatch and the defensive line preserved with two goal-line stands.[18] With their toughest challenge behind them, nothing was stopping the Panthers now.

They clobbered their remaining division opponents by at least thirty points in every game. Hatch wreaked havoc on defense, while Vitale ran for over 1,000 yards and 22 touchdowns (both earned All-Shore honors). The Panthers finished No. 3 in the Shore. After graduation, Vitale moved onto Wagner College, where he set the school's single-game rushing record by carrying the ball 42 times for 207 yards in a 28-3 win over Kings Point.[19]

> **Al Saner**: *"Vitale was sensational. Played both ways. He was a great running back. . . . Tough, tough guy. . . . The best running back I ever coached was Jack Vitale."*[20]

The winning streak was now at twenty games, and the town was rallying behind them. Talent was emerging from every corner—tackle Rich Hoffman (also a star wrestler and champion shot putter), linebacker Mickey Hart, and nose guard Tim Dwyer. In the backfield, Saner had two super sophomores, quarterback Rich Leibfried and halfback Mike Swigon.[21] Those two would be tested early against a vastly improved Southern team.

The more favorable Class C schedule allowed Southern coach William "Rip" Scherer to rebuild the Rams over the course of a three-year stint, ending with a winning record in 1968. Scherer moved back to Pennsylvania after that season, but assistant Ken Arndt kept the program running. The key player was senior tailback/linebacker Brian Sprague, who helped power the Rams to a 7-2 finish. They also claimed their first-ever Thanksgiving win, beating Central Regional. They weren't, however, good enough to beat Point Boro.

The Panthers survived, 8-0, scoring on a touchdown pass from Mickey Hart to Bill Windle.[22] They won another classic a week later, fending off a talented Wall team, 14-12. That game wasn't decided until the fourth quarter, when Rich Liebfried hit Ray Jantusch for the winning two-point conversion. Three weeks later, Boro secured their twenty-fifth consecutive win and their third consecutive outright division title by beating Central. Over the final four weeks, the Panthers outscored their remaining opponents 134-12, extending the winning streak to twenty-nine games and finishing undefeated once more. They showed no signs of stopping.

CHAPTER 20
THE INDEPENDENTS: RBC, RUMSON, AND ASBURY PARK

During the 1960s, there were three Monmouth County schools that left the Shore Conference. The first, Red Bank Catholic, was a true independent. The Caseys had won consecutive titles in 1959 and 1960, earning a reputation as one of the tougher teams in Central Jersey. The first part of the 1960s saw them defend that reputation and continue their high-profile rivalry with Rumson. The 1961 Caseys finished the year with a respectable 5-3-1 record, holding off Rumson, 25-12, thanks to a late pick six from safety Tom Lally.[1]

A disappointing 1962 season proved a learning experience for a junior-dominated squad. Most of the starters returned for 1963, most notably quarterback Pete Stirnweiss (son of the late coach Snuffy Stirnweiss). Stirnweiss started the season with a star performance against Red Bank, scoring three touchdowns in a 37-7 romp. He then saved a tie against powerful Seton Hall Prep with a late touchdown.[2] When opposing defenses ganged up on Stirnweiss, it only opened opportunities for teammates Joe Largey, Mike Keagle, and Joe Thompson.

Those teammates came through in a big way in one of the season's biggest games, against Catholic rival St. Peter's (New Brunswick). With Stirnweiss out and the Cardinals ahead 13-7, the Casey line took command. Rich Laggan blocked a punt that Sohl scooped up and returned for the tying touchdown. Backup quarterback Joe Hochreiter then found Ed Thompson for the winning point in RBC's 14-13 victory.[3] That kept the Caseys alive in the Parochial A South race and set up an exciting Thanksgiving game with 6-1 Rumson, on their way to winning a Shore Conference Class B crown.

Less than a week before Thanksgiving, though, the game was thrown into the background by outside events. On November 22, 1963, President John F. Kennedy was assassinated by Lee Harvey Oswald while riding in a motorcade through downtown Dallas. The assassination shocked the nation—Kennedy had been a youthful and popular president, and his sudden death made him into a martyr. Millions of Americans felt the assassination as a personal loss. They watched the events of the ensuing week intently. They felt fear when the assassin Lee Harvey Oswald was himself killed by Jack Ruby and they cried as the Kennedy children watched their father's coffin process toward Arlington National Cemetery.[4]

The assassination was felt especially deeply by Catholics, Irish Catholics most of all. Conventional wisdom had long held that no Catholic could be elected president, and when Kennedy ran in 1960 there were many adults who remembered well the humiliation and bigotry to which Al Smith (the first major Catholic candidate for president) had been subjected in 1928. Kennedy's victory over Nixon in 1960 seemed a repudiation of that, a triumphant declaration that one could be both Catholic and American. His death, therefore, was crushing.

In many Catholic schools nationwide, word of Kennedy's assassination trickled into classrooms during a school day. At RBC, the entire student body had already been gathered in the school auditorium for a musical program put on by the Fort Monmouth Band. When word of the assassination arrived, the assembly became an impromptu prayer service, after which the students were taken to pray in nearby St. James's Church.[5]

Although 5,000 fans still came out for the final game against Rumson, the festivities were somewhat muted by a nation still in mourning. Before the game, the RBC band honored the fallen president with a rendition of "Hail to the Chief." The game was equally subdued; neither team could score in a 0-0 tie.[6] It was enough for RBC to bring home a third Parochial A South crown. That was a fitting end to Al Forte's final season at RBC. He left to become the head football coach at Monsignor Farrell on Staten Island, later returning to New Jersey at DePaul (in Wayne) and St. Joseph's Regional (in Montvale).

After Forte's departure, RBC's athletic fortunes took a bit of a dip. The opening of Christian Brothers Academy in Lincroft and Mater Dei in New Monmouth meant that the older school faced increased competition for students. Even within the school, the football program faced growing competition for athletes, as legendary cross country and track coach Jack Rafter began to turn RBC into a running powerhouse. Victories in football became scarce, and the Caseys would not return to glory until the arrival of an alumnus, John McNamara, in 1967.

Meanwhile, RBC's great rival Rumson was beginning its own adventure beyond the boundaries of the Shore Conference. Irritated by the Shore's constant realignment, in the spring of 1965 the Bulldogs decided to defect. Rumson left the Shore Conference in favor of the newly formed Garden State League. There, they would play other small schools from Middlesex, Union, and Essex Counties, teams such as Roselle, Carteret, and South Brunswick.[7]

Rumson never did manage to win this highly competitive league's football title, although they did come close in 1966. They finished 7-2 that year, winning the CJ II crown behind the passing combination of quarterback Dave Hammond and end Ashley Bell. The season finale on Thanksgiving against RBC was a celebration, with Hammond throwing four touchdown passes in a 46-0 romp.[8] After high school, end Ashley Bell went to Purdue, starting for three years and leading the 1969 Boilermakers in receptions. He was later drafted by the Miami Dolphins.

The Bulldogs continued to win, extending their Thanksgiving unbeaten streak to seven games with two more wins over RBC. These games continued to draw large crowds and were always the highlight of the season. The intensity of that rivalry, though, showed the biggest problem with the

Garden State Conference—no such rivalries were developing. Neutral fans cared little for the GSC, and newspapers devoted little coverage to a league that was so thinly spread across four counties. In 1970, Rumson officially applied for readmission to the Shore Conference, which was granted for 1972.[9] The Bulldogs were back where they belonged.

The other statewide adventure of the 1960s was undertaken by Asbury Park. The community was in transition in 1966. The city was fighting a losing battle against its slow decline as a resort destination, while the high school was struggling to adjust to the withdrawal of Ocean Township students, which left it with a significantly smaller enrollment. Adding to that difficult adjustment was the retirement of Butch Bruno, which left the Bishops searching for a new head coach for the first time since World War II. On top of that, the disbanding of the Central Jersey Group IV Conference left the Bishops an independent once again.

Bruno's replacement, Tony Frey, resigned after going 2-7 in both 1966 and 1967. The alumni grumbled at consecutive losses to Neptune, and the locals just stopped showing up. Following his resignation after the 1967 season, Frey returned to Northeast Pennsylvania and coached successfully there for many years.[10]

Asbury was forced to accept that times had changed. Now a Group II school, they just didn't have enough players to compete against a Group IV schedule.[11] Besides, the players they did have were nowhere near as seasoned as their opponents. Asbury was one of the last towns in the Shore to adopt Pop Warner football. With no feeder program, the high school team suffered for years to come.[12] There was a time when football was king in Asbury Park, and a single glare from the head coach could shatter the ego of a high schooler. No more. Attendance and participation were down in all sports. It was emblematic of the city's difficult situation.

On one hot afternoon in 1967, the same year as the Newark riots, it looked like Asbury Park might burn as well. Fighting between teenagers had escalated into rock throwing, and a car was set on fire. Only the timely arrival of committed workers from the Monmouth Community Action Project managed to keep things from spiraling out of control.[13]

Rebuilding the Asbury Park football program was going to take serious work. Fortunately, the school district had a serious man on hand—line coach Ed Hudson. He quickly began the hard work of reconstruction. However, the team, its school, and the schedule it played were almost unrecognizable to those who had followed Asbury through its 1950s glory days. When Blue Bishop football rose again in the 1970s, it rose as something almost completely different from what had come before.

CHAPTER 21
BRICK AT THE TOP

By 1970, the Shore Conference's top division looked very different than it had in 1960. Old coaches had retired, and fixtures such as Freehold, Long Branch, and Toms River had dropped into Class B. The one constant was Warren Wolf's Brick, winning as always. Not only did the team have tremendous players, but it also had an expert staff (Vic Kubu on defense, George Jeck on offense, Bob Spada on the line, and Sam Riello with the freshmen).

> **Dan Duddy (freshman football player, 1970):** "*I was mesmerized by the other end of the field, looking at senior football players practicing while we were practicing. There were about seventy-five to eighty freshmen, there were more than a hundred varsity players. Some kids wore jersey number 101, 102, 103 on their jerseys. It was this huge, glorious football factory that I had become a part of. . . . We were coached by ex-Brick football players, legends. . . . One of our coaches was first-team All-State running back Sam Riello, and I don't think he lost a football game in his career. So, we were all expecting to win.*"[1]

In 1970, Brick was loaded with talent, especially on the line, where they had All-Shore tackle Lou Vocaturo, end Don Rutherford, and center Ken Matusewicz. The Dragons opened their season with the eyes of the state upon them for a trip to Jersey City's Roosevelt Stadium. It was a homecoming for Warren Wolf, who was facing his mentor, Joe Coviello, for the very first time. Coviello was now at North Bergen, and he had his Bruins playing at a level as high as his old Memorial teams. The clash between the North Jersey and Central Jersey powers drew 10,000 fans, many of them who had made the long trip up from the Shore.[2]

> **Dennis Filippone (Brick player, 1970-73)**: *"I remember playing North Bergen, which is quite a ride, and seeing people walking down Journal Square. Coach Wolf stopped the bus and picked up a couple of people who had gotten off the commuter bus and were walking to the game."*[3]

Brick jumped out to an 18-0 lead but couldn't hold it against a furious North Bergen rally. The Bruins scored three unanswered touchdowns, the last coming with two minutes to play, and won 22-18.[4] Although disappointed, the Dragons bounced back and completed their North Jersey tour with impressive victories against Phillipsburg and East Orange. Back in the Shore, they rolled past Matawan and Lakewood, rising back to the top of the Shore.

Their path to the Class A crown, however, was unexpectedly blocked by Joe Oxley's Raritan team. The Rockets returned fifteen lettermen, most notably quarterback Brian Brady and a trio of runners with speed to burn. They were halfbacks Ronnie Gordon and Jeff Herman (both track stars) and fullback John Iacouzzi. Defensively, the team was anchored by Howard Crow, a true sideline-to-sideline defender. The Rockets won three of their first four games, then boarded buses for a trip to the Delaware Water Gap. Like Brick, Raritan was taking on Phillipsburg.

Down 14-7 at the half, Raritan rallied in the third. Brian Brady hit Jeff Herman for 54 yards, setting up Jeff Iacouzzi's second touchdown run of the night. As an underdog on the road, Joe Oxley liked to play it aggressively, and he called for a two-point play. Brady's completion to Herman put Raritan ahead 15-14. Touchdown runs by Herman and Iacouzzi finished the job, and Raritan went home with a 27-14 victory.[5] Now 4-1, the Rockets were ready to face Brick.

On Halloween afternoon, the Rockets arrived at Keller Memorial Field for the biggest game in school history. Brick led 7-0 in the third quarter, but Mike Flynn's fumble recovery led to an Iacouzzi touchdown and cut it back to 7-6. Oxley was aggressive once again, calling for a fake kick. Brian Brady took the short snap, sprang up from his holder position, and rolled out. Seeing no one open, he tucked the ball and ran in for the two points and an 8-7 Raritan lead. The Rocket defense turned back Brick's final two drives, completing a stunning upset.[6]

There were two undefeated teams left in the division, Raritan and Matawan, trailed by two one-loss teams, Brick and Lakewood. All met on the first Saturday in November, with Brick invading Matawan and Raritan returning to Ocean County to face Lakewood. It all came down to one weekend. By evening, the title picture would be a lot clearer.

For 5-1 Matawan, this was the easy part. The Huskies were battling their way through a season unlike any other. The year 1970 had been a tough one at the Shore, as the destructive Asbury Park race riots raised anxieties around the regions. In Matawan, nerves were already frayed. Two years prior, the school had seen a number of students walk out in protest over the low number of Black teachers in the school district. The walkout ended, but tensions remained high.[7]

It didn't help that the area's rapid population growth left the high school badly overcrowded. Heated encounters between students in the jam-packed hallways and cafeterias weren't uncommon. The critical moment came on Friday, September 25, at a school dance the night before the season opener against Middletown. Fights broke out and the event had to be ended early. Fears of another Asbury Park were obvious in reporting of local newspapers like the *Matawan Independent*.[8] The season opener against Middletown, Matawan's Class A debut, was a much-needed relief. Workhorse tailback Curtis Edwards led the Huskies to victory by running for two touchdowns.[9] By Monday, however, the community was at odds once more.

Teenage hangouts all over Matawan were plagued by scuffles, and police stopped carloads of hotheaded students looking for action. By the week's end, twenty-eight students had been suspended and three arrested for carrying concealed weapons. The Jewish holidays closed schools for two days and created a valuable cooling-off period, but anxiety remained high.[10]

That weekend, the team played its worst game of the season, losing 27-0 to Class B Long Branch. On Monday, a packed school board meeting saw students of all backgrounds testify that they were afraid to go to school because of the violence that might erupt. Residents of Cliffwood Beach protested that they were left unprotected from gangs of white teenagers driving through in search of trouble. The school was turning on itself.

Helping to calm the situation was Curtis Edwards, a leader on and off the field. A punishing fullback, Edwards was also a leader of the emerging Black student union. At the height of the tensions, he had helped organize the concerns the group had, much of which centered on feelings that Black students were overlooked at the school.[11]

Tempers simmered, but the team recovered. Edwards ran for 172 yards and four touchdowns in a confidence-boosting win over Asbury Park.[12] The Huskies were rolling just in time for their big showdown with Brick. Matawan's Barry Rizzo and Brick's Warren Wolf were the two longest-tenured coaches in the Shore Conference, and this game marked their first meeting since 1961. The game lived up to the hype.

Vic Kubu's swarming defense took center stage. Edwards managed to rack up 84 yards, but a stout Brick defense, led by end Jeff Lansing and linebacker Don Ayers, held him without any big plays. Matawan's own defense, led by linebacker Mike Herb, matched the Dragons zero for zero. In the end, Brick's special teams made the difference as Mike Slater's long punt return set up Alan Reiser's touchdown run. It was the only score in Brick's 6-0 win.[13]

Meanwhile, down in Lakewood, the offenses were exploding. Don Barnes ran for four touchdowns as the Piners jumped all over Raritan, taking a 33-14 lead into the fourth quarter. Quarterback Brian Brady rallied the Rockets for two fourth-quarter touchdowns, and when Jerry

Restaino blocked a last-minute Lakewood punt at the 10, Raritan's rally was almost complete. Almost, though, remained the key word. On the game's final play, Brady tried to sneak over from the 1-yard line and was denied, leaving the Piners victorious.[14]

The muddy title picture cleared up a week later, when Edwards led Matawan to a 21-7 victory over Lakewood. That eliminated the Piners. Meanwhile, Brick locked in their own title share with wins over Neptune and Toms River North. That left Raritan and Matawan to fight it out for the other half of the crown on Thanksgiving morning.

This rivalry was young (dating only to 1969), but it was also a natural. The two schools were separated by just five miles, and the players on either team knew each other well. The game was a major attraction even before it moved to Thanksgiving. Now that it was on a holiday and a championship was on the line, it drew a standing-room-only crowd.

John Oxley (son of Raritan Head Coach Joe Oxley): *"I grew up on the sidelines of my father at Raritan . . . that [the Thanksgiving game] was humongous. Talking about having a tough game. It didn't matter, the records. I know that's cliché, but honestly—it was right next door, and those kids didn't like each other. It was brutal."*[15]

Early on, the teams traded touchdowns, as Brian Brady's 67-yard strike to Mark Herman was answered by John Connolly's 28-yard touchdown pass to Tom Geran. Matawan led 7-6 at the half and threatened to seize control in the third with a drive to the 10. However, Raritan held on fourth and goal, then took the lead on another long pass from Brady to Herman. Matawan answered by driving 80 yards to an Edwards touchdown and a 15-14 advantage. Both crowds rose to their feet for Raritan's final drive. The key play was a dive to fullback John Iacouzzi.

John Iacouzzi: *"I was quick to hit the hole, absolutely. I had good flat-out speed and a good offensive line. . . . It was my fifteen minutes of fame."*[16]

Iacouzzi was gone, sprinting 40 yards for the touchdown and a 20-15 Raritan lead. Now fighting the clock, Matawan was forced to go to the air, and they couldn't connect. Raritan won, 20-15, and earned a share of the Class A crown. Beaming with pride, Joe Oxley dubbed the victory "the culmination of four years of hard work" by players and coaches alike.[17]

A number of those players went on to fine college careers. Iacouzzi, a three-sport star for the Rockets, won All-County honors in basketball and baseball, then attended South Carolina on a football scholarship. Linebacker Howard Crow went on to All-MAC honors at Albright, while Mark Herman played football at Yankton State College in South Dakota. During Herman's time at Yankton, he played alongside future Oakland Raiders star Lyle Alzado, and himself lasted five years with the CFL's Calgary Stampeders.[18] Matawan's own star, Curtis Edwards, went on to a fine career at Rutgers, leading the team in rushing in 1973 and 1974.

It was the Brick way that although they finished No. 1 in the Shore, they produced no major college prospects. A host of Dragons would play college football at places such as Glassboro State, Montclair State, and Albright, but at Brick it was toughness, discipline, and numbers that won football games. That was the formula that would shape the next four years of Shore football.

THE GLORY OF BRICK

The spring of 1971 confirmed Warren Wolf's status as one of Brick's most beloved citizens. He decided to run for mayor and was promptly endorsed by both the Democratic and Republican parties. Wolf won easily, receiving 52 percent of the vote in a six-way race. He was now simultaneously the assistant superintendent, mayor, and head football coach.[19] In the fall of 1971, it was that last job that gave him the most reason to be excited.

Eight starters returned from the 1970 team, including halfback Larry Sramowicz, middle linebacker Paul Batsel, and nose guard Bob Russo. All three would win All-Shore honors at season's end. Joining them was something rare for Brick, a sophomore starter. But then again, linebacker

Danny McCullough would have been rare anywhere.[20] Both head coach Wolf and defensive coordinator Kubu quickly saw that he was special.

Vic Kubu (Brick defensive coordinator): *"When Dan hits someone . . . they remember it."*

Warren Wolf: *"We think he's emblematic of the true Brick football player. He's an extremely hard worker, very dedicated to football, and he's got his heart and soul in the sport."*[21]

Brick started the season with their usual statewide tour—tying North Bergen and beating both Phillipsburg and East Brunswick. Then they stampeded the whole Shore Conference. The 1970 Raritan defeat was avenged as Sramowicz ran for three scores in a 51-20 romp. He scored twice more in a 30-0 demolition of Matawan's single wing.[22] None of their games were close.

The Thanksgiving game was basically a victory parade. Brick thrashed Toms River North, 65-14, with Sramowicz running for two scores and Don Rutherford catching three more. By the time it was all over, even the usually reserved Wolf was jubilant.

Warren Wolf: *"This was the greatest team that Brick Township has ever had. We got better as the season went on."*[23]

The 1971 Dragons may have been the best team that Brick had ever had, but they were not the best team that Brick would ever have. Even better was right around the corner. The Dragons returned both Mc-Cullough and All-State guard Jim Blackburn. Equally importantly, Wolf had carefully seasoned his underclassmen throughout the 1971 season.

Dan Duddy: *"I became the number-one quarterback junior year. I got to play in the second half of just about every game my sophomore year because our varsity was so good. Then I played in the JV games and sophomore games. I played in twenty-seven games that year. Going into my junior year I was just so fired up because I got a real good taste of being a leader and the number-one guy."*[24]

What Duddy said was also true of halfbacks Greg Riel and Larry Girgenti, linemen Clark Kull and Don Fircullo, defensive back Greg Vocaturo, and end Clark Goldey. This Dragon team expected to win not just games but titles. They started the year on the radar of all the state papers and knew that a second consecutive undefeated season (especially against a schedule as tough as theirs) would give them a chance to do what no Brick team had done before—earn the No. 1 ranking in the state of New Jersey.

It started in the season opener against Matawan. Dan Duddy put on a show in his first start, throwing a touchdown pass to Brian Ayers and then running for another. Brick rolled, 27-6.[25] Next was a visit to Phillipsburg. Those games were always special. Warren Wolf would have the bus park at the edge of town, then lead the team through deserted downtown streets, past closed stores decorated with handmade "Gone to Game" signs. From there, the team walked uphill to the stadium, where a huge crowd awaited. It was not something to be forgotten.

> **Dan Duddy**: *"Recently I've gone out to Pennsylvania for a couple of trips, and you ride past Phillipsburg High School into Pennsylvania. Once I was with my little boy, and I showed him the end zone where I scored in. For myself, I wanted to look at the gate where we came out, and the field, just listen to the crowd echo. The second time I went with my wife, and I showed her too. It stays with you."[26]*

Brick's dominant defense and a well-timed Duddy touchdown run were enough. The Dragons came out with a hard fought 28-0 victory.[27] Back at the Shore, they won their next three games by a combined 77-6. Impressed, the *Star Ledger* rated Brick neck and neck with powerful Westfield. Yet Brick's greatest test still lay directly in their path—Ron Signorino's Toms River South team, ranked sixth in the Shore by the *Asbury Park Press*. After a two-year hiatus, one of the Shore Conference's best rivalries was making its triumphant return.

Asbury Park Press: *"They approach each other for tomorrow's game circling warily, like two old, battle-scarred bulldogs at the same fireplug."*[28]

It turned out that the split hadn't kept Toms River South down for too long. Counting a six-game surge to end the 1971 season, the Indians had won ten out of their last eleven games. They too were dominating teams, including a punishing 36-0 rout of Toms River North in the first-ever game between the two Toms River schools. It was Ron Signorino's love of pageantry that turned what could have been merely a regular-season game into the first edition of what is still known as the Civil War. Fully embracing the North vs. South theme, he had his team take the field "Olympic style," with flags flying and the marching band blaring martial tunes.[29]

Signorino decided to employ that same pageantry for the showdown with Brick. The week of the game, the whole team shaved their heads as a sign of unity. On Saturday, October 28, Toms River South arrived ready to play. Then, it started to drizzle. Warren Wolf, who hated playing in the rain, immediately canceled the game, postponing it to Monday afternoon. The game was so big that Brick schools let out early so that the student body could see it.

A typically large Brick crowd gathered that sunny October afternoon for the game. Concern, however, began to grow when Toms River South didn't show up. Game-time was just a few minutes away, and the Indians were nowhere to be seen. They weren't late. Instead, they were just a few hundred yards away, charging through the backyards of confused Brick residents, who wondered why their Monday afternoon had been disrupted by one hundred screaming football players, led by a middle-aged coach and a high school student carrying a spear.

Bob Fiocco (Toms River South assistant): *"We thought we'd surprise them. . . . We had the buses drop us off on the Parkway, and we came charging through the woods and over the fence."*[30]

Dan Duddy: *"Behind us, to our left, coming over a fence . . . came Coach Sig in a full Indian headdress, followed by their mascot, a sprinting fiery student dressed as an Indian. He took a spear and jammed it violently a few feet in front of Coach Wolf, composed in his gray suit, of course, and then to be followed by war-painted, screaming football players and cheerleaders as they bolted through us to their frenzied sideline. . . . Forget about football, now it was time to fight. . . . Vic Kubu simply twisted his hat backwards, popped a toothpick in his mouth, smirked, and with his high raspy voice turned and said, 'Well, it looks like we got ourselves a game.'"*[31]

And what a game it was . . . for Brick. South's first possession ended in a three-and-out. The Dragons then easily marched to the first touchdown, a short run by Kevin Keeney. South tried to throw on their next possession. Keeney intercepted and returned it 25 yards for a touchdown. South received the kickoff and fumbled. No matter what the Indians did, Brick had the answer. The Dragons built a 49-7 halftime lead and coasted home to a 56-22 final in what the *Asbury Park Press* immediately dubbed "their most awesome display of power."[32] Meanwhile for South, there was one last humiliation to cap their miserable day.

Bob Fiocco: *"To make matters worse, our buses didn't know where to pick us up, and we had to sit around for an hour after the game waiting for them. Their scoreboard stayed lit up with the score for every one of those minutes."*[33]

The Indians rebounded to finish 6-2-1, but the Class A race was basically over. Of Brick's remaining Shore foes, only Neptune challenged them, eventually losing 19-14. The real drama centered on the race for the state championship. Brick's main rival in that chase was Westfield, ranked No. 1 in both 1970 and 1971 and unbeaten since 1968. The two teams didn't play each other, but they did have a common opponent—Montclair.

The Mounties were blessed with one of the oldest, richest traditions in New Jersey. Their reputation was equal to Phillipsburg, and their addition to Brick's schedule showed how high Warren Wolf's ambitions were now reaching. They also were loaded.

Dan Duddy: *"They were like Montclair State University to us, they were unbelievable. They had two Division I running backs, one went to Virginia and the other went to Syracuse. Dale Berra, Yogi Berra's son who wound up playing third base for the Pittsburgh Pirates, a couple of big defensive lineman . . . and we were just little guys."[34]*

Westfield's meeting with Montclair drew 7,000 fans and all the sportswriters from the major state papers. All wanted to see if the Devils could tie a state record by winning their fortieth consecutive game. They saw a classic, maybe the best game played in New Jersey that season. Montclair led 14-12 late, but Westfield's great fullback Glen Kehler saved the Devils with a fourth-quarter touchdown.[35] That opened the door for Brick. If the Dragons could better Westfield's performance, they would have a very strong claim to the state crown.

The crowd at Keller Memorial Field was large (including a CBS-TV camera crew filming a segment on the suburban boom in Ocean County), and the atmosphere was tense. The game stayed scoreless until late in the first half. That's when Dan Duddy struck again. He dropped back to pass, looking over the middle for Bob Walters on a short crossing pattern. Walters hauled it in, slipped a tackle, turned up the field, and didn't stop until he reached the end zone. That not only put Brick up 7-0, but it also broke the ice.

The second half belonged to the Brick offensive line. Jim Blackburn, Bruce Lach, and Paul Batsel carved huge holes in the Montclair defense, and Kevin Keeney charged through them to the tune of two touchdowns. Meanwhile, the Mounties were held under 100 yards rushing. The final score was 19-0, exactly the sort of dominating performance that the Dragons needed to secure their position at the top of the *Star Ledger* poll.[36]

A 27-7 win over Toms River North on Thanksgiving Day completed the dream. McCullough, Larry Girgenti, and Greg Riel all ran for touchdowns, while Duddy added a touchdown pass to Clark Goldey. For first time in the history of Brick Township High School, they stood alone atop the mountain. State champions.[37] Warren Wolf had been at Brick for fifteen years, and in that time his Dragons had claimed eight division titles, seven sectional championships, six undefeated seasons, and now a *Star Ledger* trophy.

Brick had come a long way since 1958. The dirt roads and egg farms were long gone now, replaced with shopping centers, commuters, and traffic jams. People were beginning to ask if more growth was even desirable. The country had changed too. The Vietnam War had taken a heavy toll in lives, money, and the credibility of the federal government. Even the White House was now embroiled in controversy, as a tax evasion scandal closed around Vice President Spiro Agnew, and the word "Watergate" began to cling ever tighter to President Richard Nixon. The economy, too, was starting to cool off. After a seemingly endless boom, inflation (especially felt in rising gas prices) was becoming a part of American life.

Through it all, Brick football had kept winning, and would keep winning. In the fall of 1973, Wolf had every reason to feel that his team had the material to run the table for a third consecutive season. Seven starters returned, most notably fullback/linebacker McCullough. He had earned All-Shore honors in football, wrestling, and baseball as a junior, and going into his senior year had been named to *Parade*'s high school All-American team. Letters from Division I schools across the country were arriving at Brick every day.[38] He wasn't alone. The Dragon offense returned quarterback Dan Duddy and guard Steve Romanowsky, while the defense kept defensive tackle Paul Lawrence, linebacker Mark Heil, and safety Greg Vocaturo. This was an experienced team that expected nothing but victory.

They started with three narrow victories—7-6 over Matawan on a Duddy touchdown pass, 7-0 over Phillipsburg on a Duddy touchdown run, and 14-13 over Raritan when they stopped a late Rocket two-point try.[39] But in the end Brick couldn't be stopped, marching to their fourth-consecutive Class A crown with a 21-0 win over Neptune. That same day, Montclair upset Westfield, ending the Blue Devil winning streak at forty-eight. Brick was now the consensus No. 1 and holder of the state's longest unbeaten string at twenty-eight. That was the good news. The bad news was that the streak-breakers from Montclair were coming for them next.[40] Over 8,000 fans crowded into Woodman Field, eager to see the Mounties avenge their 1972 loss.

Dan Duddy: *"They wanted revenge so badly."*[41]

Montclair struck first, using the punishing runs of Earl Vaughn to build an early 12-0 lead. Touchdown runs by McCullough and Bobby Walters gave Brick a short-lived 13-12 lead, but this was Montclair's night. Vaughn scored once in the second quarter and then added a third touchdown in the third to give the Mounties a 24-13 lead. By the midway point of the fourth quarter, Montclair was ahead 38-20 and Brick's streak was essentially over.

Still, both sets of starters were still on the field, and the revenge-minded Mounties were still throwing the ball. With under a minute to go, linebacker Mark Heil intercepted one of those passes and set off down the sidelines. That's when a Montclair assistant came charging off the bench to tackle him. Pandemonium erupted as players, coaches, and fans poured onto the field.[42]

Dan Duddy: *"It turned into a brawl. . . . The refs gave us seven points, and then ran off the field. Our bus windows got broken, the cops came, there were sirens and we got out of there."*[43]

Mark Heil: *"I do remember as I laid on the ground the mass of people running on the field and Dale Berra, Yogi Berra's son, kneeling over me. I always thought that was first class."*[44]

The final score was recorded as 38-27. Montclair's win snapped the Dragon winning streak and ended their chances of retaining the *Star Ledger* trophy (which eventually went to Clifton), but they still finished their season in winning fashion. A 34-7 win over Toms River North capped an 8-1 season and concluded another year without a Shore Conference loss. McCullough received both All-Shore and All-State honors that winter, then accepted a scholarship to the University of Oklahoma. A two-sport athlete for the Sooners, he wrestled and played football for two seasons, qualifying for the Division I championships as a freshman.

Fellow linebacker Mark Heil would play at Elon, earning All-South Atlantic Conference honors as a senior. It remained the case, though, that the Dragons had done their work mostly with players who ended their football lives on Thanksgiving morning. The holiday morning game had been the traditional finale for football as long as the sport had been played in New Jersey. Just like Brick football, it seemed like that was something that would never change.

CHANGES

From the earliest days of high school football in New Jersey, the season had ended on Thanksgiving Day. That was when teams played their traditional rivals, in front of the season's largest crowds. Alumni came home, family visited from out of town, and everyone bundled up and headed over to the game. Whether a team was 7-2 or 2-7, Thanksgiving was special.

At one time, this was the case everywhere. Little by little, though, other states began adding statewide playoffs, which replaced the Thanksgiving finale and extended the football season into mid-December. That wasn't an option in New Jersey. The state's basketball and wrestling traditions were strong, and those sports were unwilling to have the start of their season squeezed.[45] And so it was that through the 1950s and 1960s, New Jersey had no state playoff system, and only in extreme circumstances were games played after Thanksgiving weekend.

There had been the occasional postseason game. In 1939, Garfield took a train down to Florida to play in the Health Bowl, winning the mythical national championship by beating Miami High School at the Orange Bowl. Asbury Park was invited to the same game in 1940 but had to decline due to budget issues. In 1946, Clifton took a similar trip to Virginia, facing off against Norfolk's Granby High School in the Oyster Bowl. Hudson County's Legion Bowl, played from 1945 until 1956, had pit the county champion against a strong opponent from elsewhere in New Jersey. Warren Wolf, who had been an assistant on seven Legion

Bowl teams at Memorial (West New York), remembered those games well.

As Brick rose to prominence, Wolf became one of the most vocal advocates for the creation of a playoff system. A demand for it was starting to emerge. In 1968, the NJSIAA only narrowly voted down a proposal that would have allowed independent groups to organize "Super Bowls." Support for the playoffs was growing.[46] In 1971, when Brick and Central finished the year undefeated, there were even some halting efforts at the Shore to organize a postseason clash. In 1972, when Brick and Westfield both finished undefeated, the merits of a potential playoff system became even clearer. In 1973, sportswriters were left pondering the possibility of a showdown between undefeated Bloomfield and undefeated Clifton. That December, the NJSIAA finally agreed to try playoffs. They would be limited—very limited.

There was only one round, with two teams from each section meeting in a postseason championship game. The choices would be made by the Colliton Formula, a mathematical ranking system that the state had been using to award sectional titles. This was an invitation to controversy; the formula was not widely understood or highly regarded, and the titles were so arbitrary that local newspapers didn't always report on who was awarded the crown.

The search for a stadium to host the games was equally troubled. It wasn't until October that the NJSIAA settled on the Atlantic City Convention Center. This was not an ideal venue; the field was indoors, oddly shaped, and poorly surfaced. Nonetheless, a system had been created. For the first time, every team in the state was playing for a shot at the playoffs.[47]

Brick was one of the frontrunners, although (as he did every year) Warren Wolf emphasized how much his team had lost to graduation. The Dragons had lost thirty-one lettermen, including a three-year starter at linebacker in McCullough and a two-year starter at quarterback in Duddy. By now, though, the rest of the Shore was tired of hearing it and even the *Asbury Park Press* gently mocked Wolf's worries:

Asbury Park Press: *"According to Warren Wolf, it's the same old story at Brick this season. All the starters are gone, thirty-one lettermen are missing, and he just isn't sure how the 1974 Dragons will measure up. It's an oft-repeated account of the fortunes of the Shore's most successful coach and please forgive the rest of the Shore Conference Class A for not shedding a tear."[48]*

The mockery was well-placed since the Dragons were loaded. Guard Donovan Brown was possibly the best to ever wear the Green and White. He was strong and fast, making him particularly effective blocking for sweeps. He won All-State honors at season's end. Running back Don Gethard and quarterback Paul Durkin looked good, while end Paul Panuska and linebacker Kevin Hughes ably anchored the defense. This was a senior class that had lost just once in their entire high school career; they didn't like it and hoped to avoid doing it again.[49]

As they usually did, the Dragons dominated the Shore. Only Neptune, featuring future Iowa halfback Rod Morton, was able to challenge them. The Fliers led Brick 20-14 in the fourth quarter, which was when Durkin sprang into action. He hit Dale Koch for a 34-yard touchdown pass in the back of the end zone, and kicker Warren Wolf Jr. coolly buried the extra point to give Brick its narrow 21-20 win.[50] No one challenged them again.

One after another, each opponent fell—Rancocas Valley, East Brunswick, Toms River South, and then finally, ten days before Thanksgiving, Montclair. That last one was the highlight of the season. Vic Kubu's relentless defense never allowed the Mounties inside the 20, while Gethard's two touchdowns secured a 20-0 win.[51] On Thanksgiving, the Dragons held off Toms River North, 14-6, to complete their schedule with a 9-0 record. Now they waited.

Then, sometime that evening, word began to spread. Brick was going to Atlantic City to play for the South Jersey Group IV championship. Not everyone was so lucky. The Colliton system's choices made no sense to anyone—four unbeaten teams, including No. 1-ranked Westfield, were left out. So was Red Bank, ranked by most people as one of the best

Group II teams in the state. Their coach, Bobby Strangia, vocally and angrily protested his team's exclusion.

> **Bobby Strangia (RBR head coach)**: *"I don't know how the hell they can do this to our kids. You win seventeen in a row, and they say that's not good enough? How can they cheat us like this? What they're saying is the best teams in the Shore aren't as good as those somewhere else."*[52]

Strangia's anger helped unite the entire Shore Conference behind Warren Wolf and his Green Dragons. On that Friday night in Atlantic City, fans from all over Monmouth and Ocean County, many of whom wanted nothing more than to beat Brick all season long, packed the convention hall in order to support the team that carried the banner of Shore football. Bob Strangia and a busload of his Bucs were among that crowd.

> **Warren Wolf**: *"We'll be playing not only for our own high school but for the conference."*[53]

> **Bob Strangia**: *"I would love nothing more than for Warren Wolf and Brick to do tomorrow night what we have been denied the opportunity to do."*

The SJ IV title game, pitting Brick against Camden, was played on Friday, December 6. It was the first to be played that year and therefore the first in the history of the state. Atlantic City's Convention Hall was jam-packed as the two teams went through their warmups, Brick in their iconic green-and-white jerseys, Camden in their sparkling, bright-gold uniforms. The Purple Avalanche, as South Jersey papers liked to call them, were quite a team. They had a huge defensive end, Calvin Cook, a massive fullback named Frank Green (6-2, 247), and the most dangerous athlete in New Jersey, quarterback/kick returner Anthony Brown.

> **Paul Durkin (Brick quarterback)**: *"They were built up in the newspaper as being so fast and big. . . . Then we go to Atlantic City, and we see them in their flashy gold uniforms. It was kind of scary.*

Anthony Brown was the most electrifying, scariest player I'd ever seen."[54]

Dennis Filippone (Brick graduate, attended the game): *"I was sitting with my brother and a couple of friends, and when you saw Camden come out to warm up, you literally thought they were a small college, like a Rowan."*[55]

Brown struck on the opening kickoff, weaving through the Brick coverage team for an 87-yard touchdown. It didn't count. The referees ruled that the kickoff had occurred before the ready-for-play whistle, nullifying the Panther touchdown. Brick successfully re-kicked and then stopped Camden. The Shore fans settled into their seats and relaxed as the game began to look familiar—the powerful Brick offensive line blowing holes for Don Gethard, the Dragons marching steadily down the field. Gethard scored from the 1 and Tony Aulisi's extra point made it 7-0. Brick forced another three-and-out, but now Calvin Cook and the Camden defense were settling in and forced the Dragons to kick it away.

That was dangerous, because it meant putting the ball in the hands of Anthony Brown and he punished them again with a 60-yard punt return for a touchdown. That sliced the score to 7-6, which was how the game stayed for most of the first half. The Panthers threw another scare into the Shore fans when Anthony Brown raced 65 yards up the sideline with another punt return, but an illegal block nullified the play and kept the Dragons in front.

The next big play went to Brick. Camden had the ball and was approaching midfield when linebackers Ed Smith and Kerry Mattsson gang-tackled a Camden runner. The ball popped out, and Mattsson scooped it up, racing 44 yards to the end zone to give Brick a 14-6 halftime lead. The green-and-white fans roared with delight. Still, there was a lot of football left to be played, and lots of time for Anthony Brown to strike again. He did in the third quarter, returning another punt for a touchdown. A two-point conversion tied the game at 14 apiece.

Now it was Camden with the upper hand. Brick's offense couldn't move (Gethard couldn't find his footing on the thin sod and on a few plays fell when his cleats dug through and hit concrete), and quarterback Paul Durkin was taking an awful beating. Only sheer grit was keeping Brick in it.

Tony Adelizzi (reporter for the Asbury Park Press): *"I've never seen anybody as battered and bruised as Paul Durkin was after that game. He was getting killed but he hung in there."*[56]

The game turned on another big play, midway through the fourth. Mattsson set it up with a leaping interception at his own 49-yard line. After considering the situation, Warren Wolf decided to take a shot at the end zone and called for a long pass to end Dale Koch.

Paul Durkin: *"Coach Wolf called the play, and I liked it. I said, 'OK, Dale. Me and you, we're going to do it.' I had a confident feeling."*[57]

The safety coming over the top to cover Koch tripped and fell down. Durkin's pass was on target, and Koch raced untouched into the end zone. Tony Aulisi buried his third extra point of the evening, and now Brick was out in front 21-14. They were now half a quarter from winning a state championship game. Back came Camden. Suddenly Frank Green was transformed into the unstoppable fullback that South Jersey had come to know so well, and when Brick's linebackers tried to converge on him, Walt Nock swept to the outside.

The Panthers were moving on Brick's defense with an ease that no one from the Shore had seen all year. In all, they covered 68 yards in roughly five minutes, scoring from the 3 when Frank Green pushed over. The Camden side now erupted in cheers. 2:52 remained on the clock, and Brick was clinging to a 21-20 lead. Camden Head Coach Andy Hinson waved for his offense to stay on the field, to go for two and the win. New Jersey's first-ever state championship game was coming down to one play.

Paul Durkin: *"We were all up on the sideline. Once they scored, it got real quiet and then we were screaming for defense."*[58]

Early in the game, Camden had successfully completed a two-point conversion by running a sweep to Walter Nock. Wolf and defensive co-ordinator Vic Kubu guessed that they might try the same play again and warned their defense to be ready for it. They guessed right. The hole was there, but so was Brick linebacker George Gawdun. Nock and Gawdun met just shy of the goal line and toppled to the ground. No good. The Brick sidelines now erupted in joy. The cheers only grew louder when the hands team recovered Camden's onside kick, and when the Dragon offense ground out a few first downs to the run out the clock. When the scoreboard finally hit 0:00, pandemonium erupted in the Convention Center. Brick had won.

Warren Wolf: *"This proves that the Shore Conference can play excellent football. This was my greatest coaching accomplishment. It was even better than being elected freeholder."*[59]

In the locker room, the champions piled on top of each and their coaches. Proud alumni and townspeople stood outside waving flags and hugging. It was the culmination of fifteen years of labor for Warren Wolf and his staff, four years of hard work and dedication for their players, and the fulfillment of the dreams of so many of the town's new residents. Brick was on the map. And what of its exhausted hero, quarterback Paul Durkin? He had given his all, and then joined in the mad celebration after the game. It was only when the buses arrived, and it was time to go home that it all caught up with him. He quietly took his seat and fell into satisfied sleep.[60]

Many of the game's stars went on to play college football, and one of Camden's linebackers would later play in the NFL. Paul Durkin did none of that. Instead, he joined the Marine Corps, eventually rising to the rank of colonel. When the United States invaded Iraq in 2005, Durkin was the operations officer for the 2nd Force Support Group, making him responsible for coordinating and planning the logistics of all Marine forces in Iraq.[61]

EPILOGUE

If 1974 marked the beginning of an era in state football, 1975 marked the end of one in Shore football. It was the last year before the old Class A split into A North and A South. Naturally, the team that took home the final Class A crown was the same team that had taken home the preceding five—Brick. The Dragons assembled their most dominating defense yet, with George Gawdun calling signals from his safety position and junior middle linebacker Doug Conboy wreaking havoc on opposing offenses.

Their toughest test came against Toms River South. Inspired by a halftime speech from assistant coach and Brick legend Sam Riello, the Dragons rallied from a 7-3 halftime deficit to win the game, 17-7. Scott DiMicco's 25-yard touchdown run put Brick ahead and linebacker Hubie Asmar's interception return for a touchdown clinched the win.[62] Three weeks later, the Dragons secured a return to the SJ IV playoffs by shutting down Montclair, 13-0.

The expanded playoffs included four teams from each section, with the semifinal round played the Saturday before Thanksgiving. Brick's first-round opponent was a fearsome Pennsauken team that had allowed just twelve points all season, and the Indians were heavily favored. Brick was giving away somewhere between ten and twenty pounds per man on the lines against Pennsauken's huge front.[63]

> **Warren Wolf**: *"Before the game I was afraid we were going to get blown off the field. That's how big and strong they were and how good they looked. Their quarterback is one of the best quarterbacks I have ever seen."*[64]

On the road in this one, the Dragons faced a hostile crowd, including an overeager member of the chain gang who was ejected from the stadium for attempting to steal signals. Nonetheless, Brick refused to fold. Two goal-line stands kept the Indians from pulling away and provided a late opportunity for Brick to win the game with a kick. The coach's son, Warren Wolf Jr., trotted onto the field with 2:19 to go and his team down 7-6 because of an extra point he had missed earlier in the game. Unfazed, he buried the kick, giving the Dragons a 9-7 lead. On the next series, Mark Anderson stripped Pennsauken's quarterback and Bill Gorcyzka recovered to seal the win.

Ike Willis (Pennsauken AD): *"I think we had more talent. There weren't more than four or five guys there that could start for us, but they were well-coached and executed perfectly and that's why they won."*

On Thanksgiving, the Dragons extended their winning streak to nineteen games by crushing Toms River North, but their dreams of repeating as state champions skidded to a halt against Millville. The Thunderbolts were just too big, especially up front, where they had 6-5, 270-pound nose tackle Bubba Green. Brick hung around for most of the game, but early in the fourth quarter Millville's star halfback Calvin Murray iced the game with his 82-yard touchdown run.[65] The final was 22-12, and it denied Brick a potential claim to the *Star Ledger* trophy. However, it also showed how far the Shore Conference had come.

During the 1950s, Shore teams leaving the area were the underdogs, dismissed by local papers and expected to stay close at best. Now, they were the big dogs. The *Press of Atlantic City*, ecstatic over Millville's stunning upset, described Brick as "the legendary invaders from Ocean County," and Thunderbolt Head Coach Tony Surace called the upset win "a fairy tale."[66]

It was small consolation to the Dragons, who had wanted to win a second SJ IV championship, but Millville's reaction proved that Wolf had achieved his dream. Brick was officially one of the state's leading football powers. At the halfway point of the decade, their 1970s record was an unbelievable 51-4-1 with six division championships, an SJ IV championship, and an overall state ranking of No. 1 in the *Star Ledger*. The Dragons were soaring.

CHAPTER 22
CLASS B FOOTBALL IN THE EARLY 1970s

"One of Monmouth County's most physical football teams, Matawan's ground attack resembles the German Army rolling across Western Europe. They just keep coming."
– Rich Nicoletti, *Asbury Park Press*[1]

During the 1970s, there were few teams in Monmouth County that were tougher to prepare for than Matawan. Their single wing offense was the terror of the Shore Conference. Year after year, Huskie fullbacks slammed like battering rams into opposing defenses, bursting through for long gains. Everybody knew what was coming; no one could stop it.

> **Barry Rizzo**: *"It's football like the young kids play it. You give me the ball, and we'll block for you. It's simple, just wedge blocking and running right at the opponent."*[2]

During the early 1970s, Matawan won game after game. There were plenty of highlights, many of them provided by the next two in the long line of brilliant Huskie backs, tailback Skip Deitz and blockbusting full-back Alan Smutko. Deitz, a two-way star, led Matawan to a 6-3 record in 1972, earned a spot on the All-Shore team, and then went on to play third base and catcher for the West Point baseball team. In 1973, the last year before the creation of the state playoff system, Smutko took the reins and powered the team to a CJ III crown. What Barry Rizzo and his Huskies really wanted, though, was a Shore Conference championship.

In Class A, Brick had always stood in their way, and when they joined Class B in 1974, they had a young team and weren't favorites. A season-opening loss to Long Branch seemingly confirmed that they were destined to finish second again.[3] This team, though, had incredible promise. Junior Kenny Mandeville was a two-way star, an All-Shore safety and a workhorse tailback. Two more juniors, Gary Weber and Ed Steward, split the fullback position. Sometimes, Rizzo would line up all three backs in an "elephant backfield."[4] Since All-Shore linemen Brian Wood and Bob LaDage were leading the charge, this usually worked.

As a result, the team finished the year on an eight-game winning streak and won the Class B title. Along the way, Matawan's defense shut down a variety of offenses, from Southern's all-out aerial assault to Howell's wishbone attack (featuring the explosive running of Bill Hill). The Howell game was Matawan's most impressive showing. A host of maroon-clad defenders contained Hill, while Weber ran for four touchdowns in a convincing 34-12 win.[5] A 28-8 win over Raritan completed a highly successful season.

The only thing missing was a playoff bid. The Huskies were not invited to the inaugural CJ III title game, which was won by Bridgewater-Raritan East. They vowed to change that in 1975. That would be a major challenge. Matawan was now trying to qualify for a Group IV bracket but would be doing so against a schedule of Group III schools. The only realistic way into the playoffs was to go undefeated. Fortunately, they had a loaded lineup, one that Barry Rizzo admitted was "potentially great."

The backfield returned Weber, Steward, and Mandeville, then added Ricky Butler. The line had tackle Bob Kopcho and end Rick Derechallo, a useful deep threat to punish teams that committed too aggressively to stopping the run. All five were named to the All-Shore team at season's end. On defense, Derechallo and junior TR Bethune paired up at end, backed by Steward and Vince Migliore at linebacker. There were seemingly no weaknesses.

Matawan started the year ranked number one in the Shore and never looked back. They won their opener with Long Branch, 14-6, then started mauling people. The team won by wider and wider scores in each game. The *Red Bank Register*'s description of a typical play from their 52-8 win over Jackson could have stood in for the rest of the season.

> **Red Bank Register**: *"Running out of the famous single wing, the Matawan linemen opened up gaping holes, which not only allowed the blocking backs to penetrate and pick up a downfield block, it also allowed the ball carrier to get up a full head of steam and break tackles when the visitors, hampered by slow footing, couldn't pick up a good angle."*[6]

And then there was that defense. Matawan finished the regular season with games against Southern and Howell, their two strongest division opponents. Neither could make a dent in the Huskie line. Southern was bludgeoned, 28-7, and Howell's spectacular Bill Hill was held without a touchdown in a 38-7 loss. Following that game, Rizzo called his team the best he had ever coached.[7] The playoffs went the same way. Watchung Hills, ranked number one in Somerset County, was simply mauled by the Huskies, 38-0. Gary Weber ran for 144 yards and two touchdowns and Kenny Mandeville added a touchdown pass in a 38-0 romp. Watchung Hills coach Bill Baly could do nothing but gape at the talent Matawan had available.

> **Bill Baly (Watchung Hills head coach)**: *"We've seen clubs with bigger people up front, but I've never seen a team with bigger backs than Matawan has."*[8]

Next came a quirk that is unique to New Jersey football—it was back to the regular season. Then as now, New Jersey's playoff system is sandwiched around traditional Thanksgiving rivalry games. Just five days after the semifinals, Matawan would have to play Raritan. In later years, observers would begin to gripe that these so-called "meaningless" games interfered with the supposedly more "meaningful" playoff games. Few felt that way in 1975. Surrendering a year's worth of bragging rights to a Thanksgiving opponent was unthinkable. It was even more unthinkable for Matawan, who needed to stay undefeated in order to preserve their hopes of a No. 1 overall ranking in the state of New Jersey.

That was why not even a heavy downpour the night before could delay this game. There were puddles of water all over the field, leaving it a slippery mess on which no one could find any footing. The muck neutralized Matawan's normally overwhelming size advantage, and the Rockets took advantage by jumping out to a 6-0 lead. It took Kenny Mandeville to turn the tide. His 30-yard jump pass in the third flipped the field position and set up a blocked punt for a safety. After the free kick, Gary Weber ran for a touchdown to put the Huskies in control. Ed Steward's touchdown run soon after wrapped up the 14-6 victory.[9]

It was Matawan's eighteenth consecutive win, and it now left them one game away from their first undefeated season since 1966. The last hurdle, though, would be a high one. Their opponents, Colonia, had run through their own season at 10-0, thanks to the efforts of Maryland-bound quarterback John Baldante. Colonia was ranked No. 2 in the state, behind only No. 1 Matawan. The *Star Ledger* called this, the biggest game of the year, a "dream game that otherwise could only have been dreamt about." On game day, the teams took the field at Colonia to a capacity crowd, with an even larger audience watching at home on the Jerseyvision television network.[10]

Matawan took control from the first snap, forcing a Colonia punt and then running the single wing to perfection. The Patriots were packing the line to stop Weber, so Mandeville went to the air and completed three quick passes to Rick Derechallo, Weber, and Kurt Neal. Then, when Colonia began to backpedal, Mandeville, Weber, and Steward started slashing the line. Weber scored from the 2 to make the score 7-0. Now it was the defense's turn to take over. The towering Matawan line held Colonia's potent offense to 56 yards rushing and sacked Baldante six times. Still, Colonia put up a stout fight. Weber too was limited to just 65 yards rushing, and Matawan's best drives both ended in interceptions at the 18 and 30.

It didn't matter. Matawan controlled the ball for most of the game, and they never let Colonia even start a threatening drive. The Patriots' final threat ended on fourth and 7 deep in their own territory, and Laverne Underwood sealed the title by batting down a Baldante pass. When it was all over, Rizzo's players hoisted him on their shoulders and paraded him around the field. Even when the team returned to school that evening, the fans still wanted more.[11]

> **Bruce MacCutcheon (Matawan athletic director)**: *"It was like V-J Day. We had a huge victory parade involving the band, the cheerleaders, the players, and anyone who wanted to march."*[12]

It had been a glorious run—11-0 in 1975, 26-3 over three seasons— and it had produced some of the greatest players in school history. Ricky Butler and Ed Steward went on to Rutgers, with Steward starting on defense for three years and winning honorable mention All-American honors in 1978. Gary Weber, meanwhile, won first-team All-State honors and went off to Michigan, playing defensive tackle for Wolverine teams that won three Big Ten titles. And Mandeville still had another year of high school football to play.

THE REBEL ALLIANCE

On Thanksgiving Day 1972, running back Steve Pascarella lifted Howell to its second win of the season, a 14-8 victory over Jackson, by rushing for 200 yards and two touchdowns.[13] It was a positive ending to an otherwise frustrating 2-7 season. Whether known as Southern Freehold or Howell, the Rebels hadn't done very much winning—1965 was the last time they'd won more than two games in a season. The whole Freehold Regional district was experiencing the same struggle. Freehold Borough won a total of just eight games between 1964 and 1972, Marlboro was winless in their first season, Freehold Township and Manalapan combined for thirteen wins in their first five seasons—the losses just kept on coming.

Budgets were tight. At one point, the district tried to save money by buying the same blue-and-gold uniforms for all four of their schools—not the best way to promote individual school pride. Fields were not always well-kept, and head coaches were often starved for stipends to hire assistants. Equipment was often purchased out of the head coach's pocket.[14] The schools seemed to split every other year and building a sense of community was hard.

Howell had some unique challenges of its own. The township was sixty-one square miles, and with students traveling such long distances to get to school, it was difficult to promote spirit or encourage athletic participation. There was no town center, and since most of the town's residents were North Jersey transplants, it wasn't easy to develop any sort of identity. Jack Van Etten knew his business and was once described by Warren Wolf as a "coach's coach," but even he stepped down in frustration in 1970 after five consecutive losing seasons.[15]

His replacement, Walt Edick, was a classic Shore character. A three-sport star at Manasquan, he had coached football, wrestling, and even golf at high schools around the Shore. Edick also ran the Manasquan beachfront, served on the Manasquan town council, ran a kennel for Siberian huskies, and wrote a column on dog breeding for the *Asbury Park Press*.[16] His new job at Howell was perhaps the most difficult of all of them, but he had a plan.

Edick switched the Rebels to the wishbone, and after struggling through two losing seasons it all started to click in 1973. Quarterback Ed McCarthy and halfback Byron Stallworth led the team to three wins in the final month and their first winning season in a decade. McCarthy would be back to run the offense again in 1974, but there was even more reason for excitement coming up from the Rebel freshman team.

Howell's youngsters had gone 8-0-1 in 1973, led mostly by a remarkable young back named Bill Hill. The newest member of one of the town's finest athletic families, Hill had first raised eyebrows around Howell in eighth grade, when he led the Howell Lions Pop Warner team with twenty touchdowns. In high school, Hill was even better. All three seasons saw him dominate freshmen competition—twenty touchdowns for the undefeated football team, ten points per game for the basketball team, and a cartoonish .598 batting average for the baseball team.[17] His arrival on the varsity was highly anticipated.

> **Bill Hill**: *"I had an uncle named Herman Hill, and before him there was Doug Hill, who was a running back. Then it was Herman, then Jack, then Larry. I had a bunch of uncles that played ball in the Freehold district. They all went on to play some type of college and even further."*[18]

Hill's relatives had been fine athletes, but he stood out even among that special group. He scored once in his first start, a 12-8 loss to Southern, then scored three times in the second half of a 36-8 win over Monmouth.[19] Howell won four of their last five games and finished with a winning record. The three touchdowns Hill scored in a Thanksgiving rout of Jackson gave him a total of thirteen on the season. McCarthy, meanwhile, completed his own brilliant career by breaking the school's all-time rushing record (soon broken in turn by Hill).[20] The stage was set for a big 1975 season. Nineteen seniors may have graduated, but Bill Hill was back.

At first, he struggled. He had missed the entire spring baseball season with a broken ankle, and he was held to just 31 yards in a season-opening loss to Southern. However, he soon returned to form by running for four touchdowns in a season-saving rout of Monmouth.[21] Over the next month and a half, Hill did "everything but sell popcorn at halftime," leading his team to six straight wins and the Shore Conference scoring title. A loss to Matawan kept them from winning the Class B title, but their 6-1-1 record was still good enough to qualify for the CJ III playoffs. There, they faced North Hunterdon, champions of the Delaware River Conference.

It took a series of bad second-half breaks to beat the Rebels. Early in the third quarter, North Hunterdon went to the air. Danny Hill (Bill's younger brother) managed a leaping interception, but as he lay on the ground a North Hunterdon receiver ripped the ball away from him. Possession was awarded to the Lions, who scored a few plays later to take a 14-6 lead. Howell still had Bill Hill, and his 61-yard touchdown run quickly turned the tide back toward Howell. But a flag was down. Holding. Their biggest play of the day taken away, the Rebels were unable to recover, and the clock ran out on a bitter 14-6 defeat.

> **Walt Edick**: *"I felt we outplayed them. The kids deserved a better fate."*[22]

Howell finished 6-3-1, and Hill finished with a total of 1,072 yards and 14 touchdowns. In 1976, the Rebels moved into Class A South and finished a respectable 4-4-1 against a tough schedule. Despite missing three games with a broken hand, Hill still managed to top 1,000 yards, score twelve touchdowns, and earn All-Shore honors.[23] That winter, he scored his 1,000th point in basketball and that spring he earned All-State honors in baseball.

He briefly played football at Virginia, then came home to play baseball for Brookdale Community College's traditionally strong team. He starred there and spent a season in the New York Mets farm system before walking onto the Rutgers football team. In his last year of college eligibility, he started at cornerback for a 7-4 Scarlet Knights team. From there, he embarked on a wide-ranging career in professional football, playing in the USFL, CFL, and NFL. He would later return to the Shore again, this time as an assistant and head coach.

Hill's alma mater, however, was struggling. Without a superstar talent like Hill, the Rebels were outmatched in Class A South. They didn't win another game for two years.

> **Walt Edick**: *"We were a Group III school, and we played nine Group IV schools. We played a schedule that was not geared to our level of play. . . . We're competing against teams which have as many as ten coaches. As of now, we have myself and Bob Pepe."*[24]

Edick stepped down after the 1978 season. Despite his frustrations, he had laid a foundation at Howell that would be built on in the years to come by his successor, a young head coach named Ty Lewis.

RAMMING SPEED: SOUTHERN REGIONAL

Southern Regional faced many of the same problems as Howell. Their student population was small, and their sending area enormous (250 square miles). Fortunately, the Rams had a coach who knew how to overcome those challenges. Ron Emmert had arrived at Southern in 1963 alongside two of his football teammates from Ursinus College, Dave DiEugenio and Tony Sermarini. The trio stayed at Southern for many years. When Emmert became the head coach in 1972, DiEugenio and Sermarini were among his chief assistants. By then, the Southern formula was established—a powerful running game, a strong offensive line, the occasional deep pass, and Emmert's trademark trick plays.

> **Rob Davis (played for Emmert 1985-86 and future head coach at Barnegat)**: *"He was an icon to me. I looked up to Coach Emmert when I was a little kid. He was God in my family. I was always looking forward to playing for him. I was in Heaven being in his program."*[25]

> **Kevin Williams (Shore sports reporter)**: *"Wins and losses are often forgotten but not life lessons, and if you ask those who played for Emmert, they'll tell you to this day they learned many from him. His ex-players remained a part of his life and he theirs for many years after they took off their pads."*[26]

In 1972, the combination of quarterback Joe DePasquale and end Gary Sheehan helped the Rams tie Asbury Park and Wall for the Class C title. The key game was a 13-12 October win over Wall. The DePasquale-Sheehan connection (and big tackle Russ Asay) shone again in 1973, when the Rams finished 6-2-1. In 1974, the passing combination was between Larry Dunfee and halfback Rich Elkins, both protected by a massive line featuring Steve Smead and Rich Hogan. The Rams started 5-0 and finished 6-3.

All that was a prelude to the 1975 team, Emmert's finest. Quarterback Phil Wayes filled the airways with bullet passes, while the lines were simply dominant. The star of that line was two-way tackle Steve Smead, whom the *Asbury Park Press* dubbed "Southern's Gibraltar." Smead weighed in at an imposing 6-2, 257 pounds, but he was more than just bulk. He was fast and athletic, difficult to block and sure in his tackling (something that would help win two consecutive district championships in wrestling). He was also a reliable kicker, and his extra points were the difference in 7-6 wins over Long Branch and Lakewood.[27]

The Rams stormed through the regular season with a 6-1-1 record, earning their first playoff appearance. Unfortunately, their visit to the SJ III playoffs ended quickly and unceremoniously. Undefeated Sterling took a 32-0 lead just six minutes into the game and coasted to a 54-6 win.[28] The season nonetheless ended on a high note, as Rich Elkins ran for 183 yards and Wayes for two touchdowns in a 19-13 Thanksgiving win over Central. It was Southern's fourth consecutive victory over their biggest rivals, and it closed the best season in school history.[29]

Ron Emmert's program was far from finished. Although the growing school faced new challenges (they went on split sessions and moved into Class A South in the same year), they remained competitive even in their tough new division. Southern's early-1970s run of success gave the program an identity that it would never lose—to this day, Ram football is associated with powerful offensive lines and a strong passing game.

CHAPTER 23
STREAKS AND SHOWDOWNS

A s the biggest of the Shore's powerhouses, Brick Township got most of the attention in the early 1970s. However, this time period also saw tremendous runs by Point Boro, Central, and Manasquan. Those rivals produced some of the most dramatic showdowns and thrilling finishes anywhere in the Shore. The chain started in Point Boro. Al Saner's boys entered 1970 riding a twenty-nine-game winning streak and fresh off four consecutive division championships. They once again had a powerhouse line (led by center Bill Munn) and a workhorse tailback (Mike Swigon). Equally importantly, the town was passionately behind them.

> **Mickey Hart (Point Boro split end):** *"There was virtually no pressure. We expected to win, and we did. . . . We didn't think it was anything special. But you have to remember, at that time, Point Boro had an incredible soccer team . . . and the cross-country teams were the division champs, too. All the male athletic teams were very good."[1]*

The Panthers were joining a new division in 1970, Class D, which had been created for the benefit of the Shore's smallest schools. The schedule, however, was not getting easier. For the first time in school history, the Panthers had booked a game with their local rivals, Manasquan. Jack Hawkins's Big Blue Warriors, now in Class C, had won their last twelve games behind veteran quarterback John Ervin. 'Squan also had some talented youngsters coming up through the ranks, particularly junior nose guard Danny McKelvey and sophomore halfback Ted Raffetto. Like Boro, Manasquan's primary goal was to win their own division, but for many fans the Halloween meeting between Panthers and Warriors was already circled in red.[2]

Before that showdown could happen, however, both Boro and Manasquan would have to get through Joe Boyd's Central team. In 1970, Central had an outstanding junior class—quarterback Robbie Keyes, end John Kilmurray, and halfback Pete Bell. Central and Manasquan, the two main contenders for the Class C title, squared off in the 1970 season opener. The Warrior defense shut down Bell, while Manasquan's Bill Roberts ran for 164 yards in a narrow 6-0 victory.[3]

A week later, Central lost another heartbreaker, this time to Point Boro. Two Mike Swigon touchdown runs staked the Panthers to an early lead, and their defense helped them hold on for a 14-12 victory. Robbie Keyes ran for a touchdown with forty seconds left, but on the two-point try linebacker Dave Ricks smothered Mike Burke short of the goal line. Boro had now won thirty-one games without defeat.[4] From there, Point Boro and Manasquan marched fearlessly toward their inevitable showdown.

By the time it arrived, the Warriors had won seventeen straight, while the Panther streak sat at a Shore Conference-record thirty-four. The whole Shore was excited for the game. The rich rivalry between Manasquan and Point Pleasant dated back many years, but until now only students at Point *Beach* had been a part of it. Now it was the Boro's turn. The game was played in a Thanksgiving atmosphere, with 3,000 fans packing the bleachers. It ended up being fairly one-sided; the Big Blue defense holding Mike Swigon to a mere 28 yards on 16 carries. McKelvey scored the game's first touchdown by falling on a blocked punt in the end zone, while quarterback Ervin tortured the Panthers with perfectly executed bootlegs and screen passes. Manasquan won, 26-0, extending their own winning streak to eighteen games.[5]

Both teams would be upset themselves a week later. Surprising Shore Regional upended the Warriors, 10-0, while the season's biggest stunner saw Wall drop Point Boro, 22-14, to win the Class D title. John Dolan's 77-yard interception return for a touchdown gave Wall its first lead, and Wayne Hirleman's late touchdown run clinched the victory.[6] The Knights clinched the outright crown a week later by beating Marlboro 36-14. Meanwhile, Central was starting a winning streak of their own. They had found an identity—victory through air power.

Robbie Keyes was firing deep pass after deep pass to John Kilmurray, whom no one could cover one on one. Putting two men on him only opened huge running lanes for Pete Bell. Their shell-shocked opponents tried everything, no matter how ridiculous, in a vain attempt to stop them. Toms River South assistant Bob Fiocco even painted a chicken in the red-and-gold colors of Central's jerseys. The idea was that the chicken would run around the locker room in terror, inspiring the Indians to shut down Kilmurray. When Fiocco tried to grab the chicken and bring an end to the demonstration, however, he accidentally tore its head off.

> **Bob Fiocco**: *"It was terrible. Blood was spurting all over and feathers were flying. Some of the kids couldn't stop laughing, others were sick to their stomachs. I stayed behind to clean up the mess. By the time I got to the sidelines, Central was beating us 21-0."*[7]

That game ended 58-0, with Kilmurray catching a touchdown pass and Keyes running for two more. Two weeks later, the pair did even better, crushing Wall 46-14 behind 301 yards and 5 touchdown passes from the unstoppable Keyes.[8] They were even kind enough to do Manasquan a good turn by shutting out Shore 14-0. As a result, the Devils were eliminated, leaving the Eagles and Warriors to share the Class B title. The Eagles closed their season in impressive style, blasting Southern, 50-0, thanks to four touchdowns from Pete Bell.[9]

That strong finish carried over into 1971. Central fans, expecting greatness, dubbed it "the Year of the Eagle." Four starters (Pete Bell, Robbie

Keyes, John Kilmurray, Rich Breitenbach, and Steve Ditchkus) would eventually make the school Hall of Fame. Keyes scored his 1,000th point in basketball, while Bell, Kilmurray, Breitenbach, and Ditchkus led the baseball team to the SJ III semifinals. It was on the football field, though, that they made their mark.

John Kilmurray: *"We had great teams. We had guys sitting on the bench who would have played in a lot of other places."*[10]

Kevin Williams (Central player): *"I don't know, even to this day, how many teams could have beaten us. We were loaded."*[11]

Bell, Breitenbach, and Ditchkus formed a three-headed backfield of which any school would be jealous, with Bell providing the speed and Breitenbach and Ditchkus the power. It was the aerial attack, however, for which no one had any answers.

Joe Boyd: *"If two men go for the ball downfield and one of them is Kilmurray, John is going to get the ball. He has to rate as the best end we've ever had here at Central. He and quarterback Robbie Keyes have been together since their freshman days. They've got their timing down just right and now when John cuts loose, it's mighty tough for anyone to stop him."*[12]

John Kilmurray: *"We worked a lot in the summers, throwing the ball back and forth, and it became a sixth sense. Robbie knew where I'd be, and I knew where he was going to throw it."*[13]

Central opened against Manasquan. It was a clash of field generals— John Ervin (now in his fourth season as a starter) against Keyes. The game was tied 12-12 at the start of the fourth when Keyes started finding Kilmurray. The two connected five times on the final drive, including the 10-yard touchdown that won it.[14] That was the closest anyone came all season to knocking off Central. The Eagles won every remaining regular season game by at least thirty points and ran up huge scores on Point Boro (36-0), Toms River South (64-20), and even Group IV Trenton Central

(54-8). The season ended with a 34-12 Thanksgiving rout of Southern. Their dominance was so complete that there were even opportunities for some midgame fun.

> **Kevin Williams**: *"That 9-0 season, we won a lot of games that were over by halftime. I was a second-string offensive linemen who only got to play when the game was out of hand. . . . My parents had friends who still lived in New York, and they wanted to come down and see a game I might play in. We were winning handily, late in the third quarter, and I figured I might get to play. . . . Well, there were a couple of shenanigans with our opponent that did not make Coach Boyd happy, and the starters were playing the whole game. With about five minutes left, this contingent of eight people, my family, start chanting that 'We want Zelmo,' my high school nickname . . . it's noticeable because we're winning 50-8. My teammates are busting my chops a little bit, and Coach Boyd goes, 'Zelmo, get over here.' And I go to grab my helmet, and I run over, and I think I'm going in. So, he tells me, 'You hear those people over there?' And I say, 'Yes, sir, I do.' 'Can you do me a favor and find out what they want?' and he turns back and looks at the field, and I realize I've been ridiculed. . . . We laughed about it after the season."*[15]

The win was Central's sixteenth straight and capped a remarkable 9-0 season. For the first (and to date only) time in school history, the *Asbury Park Press* named the Eagles number one in the Shore Conference. They also finished fourth in the *Star Ledger* Top Twenty. Kilmurray and Keyes were both All-State and All-Shore, while tackle Mike Curry and defensive back Reggie Brewton also earned All-Shore honors.[16] Both Kilmurray and Keyes headed south to Florida State, while Bell played in-state on the newly reborn varsity football team at Seton Hall.

The season was also a triumph for Joe Boyd, who now had an impressive sixteen-year record of 85-52-3. No one knew then that he had coached his last football game. On March 12, 1972, the only head football coach that Central had ever known died of a heart attack at the age of 51. He created a football program where there was none, and for nearly two decades he built the boys of Central into men. After his death, the football field at the high school was renamed in his honor, an appropriate tribute to a man who dedicated much of his life to Central Regional.

While Central was completing the greatest run in school history, Point Boro was reclaiming the Class D crown. Rich Leibfried was back under center, Mike Swigon and Ken Stahlin were once again carrying the football, and the Panthers were running through the division undefeated. Their final two games, against Marlboro and Wall to decide the league crown, were instant classics. The Mustangs led the Panthers 15-8 late in the fourth, only for the Panthers to win the game with a 12-play, 77-yard drive. Every play was a run, seven of them to Swigon. His touchdown run cut the score to 15-14, and his two-point run capped a 16-15 victory.[17]

The rematch with Wall was even better. Despite losing Leibfried to an early injury, the Panthers took an 8-0 lead on a sneak by backup Ron Stone and a two-point run by Ken Stahlin. Wall scored late, but Swigon batted down a two-point pass to preserve the win and claim the title.[18] The 7-2 season was marred only by another loss to Manasquan. The Big Blue took a 14-0 lead on a touchdown run by Hal Manson and a touchdown pass from Ervin to Steve Merli. Although Boro rallied on touchdowns by Swigon and Stahlin, Manasquan stopped two conversion attempts and won 14-12.[19]

The Warriors also finished 7-2, beating Point Beach on Thanksgiving. John Ervin celebrated his final game by scoring three times, while junior Steve Merli crossed the 1,000-yard barrier during the game[20] It was the end of an era in more ways than one. Ervin was graduating and the Beach-'Squan rivalry was ending. Manasquan was now a Group III school, and Beach was a tiny Group I. They hadn't beaten Manasquan since 1963, and the games were becoming blowouts. Thus, a Thanksgiving rivalry dating back to 1935 was brought to a close.

Although Manasquan had dominated the holiday series, the crowds had always been among the biggest in the Shore and the fans among the most passionate. No one wanted the ancient Manasquan-Point Pleasant rivalry to end. So, Point Boro replaced Point Beach and the Thanksgiving rivalry continued. The regular-season game had drawn huge crowds, and once the series moved to Thanksgiving in 1972 it became a Shore fixture.

> **Jay Price (Current Manasquan head coach)**: *"Two things [made it special]—the teams and the geography. . . . It was the Manasquan River Shootout. And then you had Coach Saner, who was a monument of Ocean County football, and Hawk was a Manasquan legend."*[21]

It also helped that both teams were strong that first year. The Panthers had a stout line (anchored by Dave Corratti and Mike Davinno) and half-back Fred Rogacki. The Warriors had three great two-way linemen (Steve Whitman, Ken Lucas, and Steve Koenig), fullback Hal "Rock" Manson, and the spectacular Merli at halfback. Merli was a speedster, as was the rest of his family (his father was a long-time track coach at Asbury Park and his brother was a record-breaking hurdler at RBC). Steve himself starred on the track in the 220, hurdles, and long jump. It was on the football field, though, that he was truly dangerous.

> **Jack Hawkins**: *"Steve has very good speed and change of pace, plus he utilizes his blockers well and has the ability to slip tacklers. . . . He's not satisfied until he's mastered all the finer details. I feel that when Steve's high school days are over, he's going to make some college coach as happy as he has made our coaching staff."*[22]

Merli ran for 164 yards and three touchdowns in a season-opening romp past Central, then joined with Rock Manson to crush Howell and Jackson.[23] Monmouth's defense, anchored by defensive lineman Pfunandre Redvict (a future starter at the Naval Academy) was tougher, but they couldn't stop Merli and Manson either. The Warriors controlled the clock and the ball on their way to a 22-8 victory. Down the stretch, the Big Blue were unstoppable. Merli scored nine touchdowns in three games, the defense dominated, and the team clinched Class B. The last obstacle between them and an undefeated season was Point Boro Panthers, Class D champions.

Boro had started 4-0, romping over their early opponents and using Rogacki like a battering ram. Then came a Week Five meeting against Shore Regional. The game drew 2,500 fans for what was supposed to be a homecoming romp. Instead, they saw Scott Quillen's Blue Devils claim a surprising 7-0 upset. Shore played a brilliant defensive game and got just enough points to win on Andre Spedaliere's touchdown pass to Jim Delehanty.[24]

The win marked one of the high points of Scott Quillen's tenure as head coach at the West Long Branch school. When he had arrived, the program was in a rut. Lack of numbers had caught up with the Devils, who had struggled through four straight losing seasons. In hopes of changing their fortunes, Quillen switched his offense to the Power-I. The new system got the Devils rolling, with wins over Boro and RBC. Huge crowds were descending on West Long Branch every Friday night, and they were fast closing in on their first division title since 1966.

Then came another upset, this one sprung by Keyport. Nobody gave the 4-2 Red Raiders much of a chance. They had the youngest head coach in the Shore (twenty-five-year-old George Conti) and just one notable offensive threat, halfback Charlie Carter. And yet somehow, the Red Raiders pulled it off, shutting out the Devils in a masterful performance that the *Red Bank Register* compared to the Texans defending the walls of the Alamo.[25]

Conti chose to dare Shore to throw by putting nine defenders at the line of scrimmage. While the weight of numbers contained the Shore rushing game, the Keyport offense was doing just enough to win. Sophomore quarterback Joey Smith started the winning drive by scrambling for 12 yards, and Hal Bell followed that by converting a third and 7 with an 8-yard run. The drive finally ended in Smith's 10-yard touchdown pass to Gil Burlew. As the clock ran out, an exhausted but jubilant Keyport team began to celebrate their stunning 7-0 upset.[26]

That same day, Point Boro was grinding down Freehold Boro, 18-8. It was their third straight win, and it clinched a share of the Class D title. Fred Rogacki crossed the 1,000-yard barrier during the game (he'd eventually finish with 1,200 and 14 touchdowns).[27] It was on that emotional high that they entered their first Thanksgiving game against Manasquan. Memories of how the Warriors had broken their streak two years ago still rankled, and the chance to exact some revenge by ruining Manasquan's undefeated season was a real temptation.

It was not to be. Steve Merli scored three times in the first quarter, including an astonishing 93-yard touchdown run to break open a 39-6 romp. Although Merli left the game after halftime, he still finished with 22 touchdowns, 134 points (enough for the Shore Scoring title), 1,348 yards rushing, and an astonishing average of 10.8 yards per carry. He was honored on the All-Shore first-team, All-Group II first-team, and All-State third-team.[28]

Many of Manasquan's 1972 stars went on to play college football—Merli at Eastern Kentucky, Steve Whitman at Southern Connecticut State, and Ted Raffetto at West Point. Point Boro's Fred Rogacki also went on to play college football, at Sioux Falls College in South Dakota. Despite the graduation of those stars, expectations for both teams remained high in 1973. Manasquan was especially dangerous, with "Rock" Manson back at fullback and Jim Dickson taking over at quarterback. To fill Merli's admittedly large shoes at tailback, the Warriors came up with a talented tandem of John Banta and Tim McCorkrell. Together, that group overwhelmed Central, Howell, and Jackson by a combined 122-20.[29]

Their defensive line was just dominant. Class B was loaded with stars in 1973, great athletes such as Monmouth's Pfunandre Redvict, Rumson's Mike Miles, and Lakewood's Jeff Theibault. None of them could do anything against the Big Blue. By Thanksgiving, the Warriors were 8-0, outright Class B Champions, and winners of eighteen straight. The holiday rivalry was no more competitive. The running of Manson and McCorkell sprung Manasquan for twenty first-quarter points and a 26-0 victory.[30]

It was the finishing touch on a glorious two-year run for the Big Blue, who sent another great crop of athletes off to college. Manson went to Murray State, Dickson to Southern Illinois, John Banta to Gettysburg, and Stew Whitman to Southern Connecticut. The lone downside was that the Big Blue would be very young in 1974.

They weren't quite as happy in Point Boro. The Panthers had compiled a disappointing 5-4 record, finishing third in Class D. The division title belonged to 8-1 Shore Regional, led by end Bill Bell, tackle John Hulta, and halfback Rocky Precopio. Precopio's short touchdown run had been the key to Shore's 6-0 victory over the Panthers.[31] Following that win, Shore waltzed through the rest of the division, then beat Monmouth on Thanksgiving.

Shore had tormented Point Boro for two straight years. In 1974, they would break Manasquan's hearts. The Warriors, newcomers to Class C, scratched and clawed their way to a 12-8 win over Ocean in the season opener. That extended their winning streak to twenty games. However, all that did was give Shore a chance to end it a week later. Quarterback Bruce Bradley led Shore Regional to a thrilling 14-8 victory, throwing two long passes to Steve Capozzi and Jack Kahle before sneaking over for the winning touchdown.[32]

> **Scott Quillen (Shore coach)**: *"Last year I told everybody our team had the best quarterback in the Shore Conference. Now they believe me."[33]*

In the end, neither team was able to lay claim to the Class C title, which was won by a dominant Red Bank team. Shore finished a disappointing 4-5, while Manasquan stumbled through an up-and-down season, entering Thanksgiving at 4-4. This year, the usual rivalry roles were reversed. It was Point Boro's turn to enter as the undefeated favorites, having already clinched their Class D title. That wasn't expected at the start of the season.

The young Panthers entered the 1974 season with a lot of unfamiliar faces in important positions. Junior Scott Kerwin was debuting at quarterback, while New York transfer Charlie Chapel was taking over the key tailback position.[34] In their season-opener, the Panthers battled to an 8-8 tie with Keyport, a result that left nothing settled. The next month did nothing to separate the two teams, as both teams rolled through their schedule. And then, unexpectedly, the Garnet Gulls of Point Pleasant Beach inserted themselves into the title discussion.

Tiny Beach hadn't been involved in a title race of any kind since the opening of Point Boro a decade before. However, the creation of Class D in 1972 gave them hope that they could succeed against a more reasonable schedule. That same year, Jack White arrived to take over the head coaching job. He was the right fit. The school was tiny, but the town's pride in it was large, and the charismatic White embraced the small-town atmosphere.

> **Jack White (Point Beach head coach)**: *"Being small has some advantages. It gives boys who wouldn't have a chance to play if they were at some other schools an opportunity, and a lot really prove themselves. I think something like 75 percent of our student body is active in some athletic activity during the year, and that's very healthy. That doesn't happen elsewhere."*[35]

The 1974 team had only twenty-eight players, but they were good. Quarterback Tom Spiegel and tailbacks Keith Hertling, Chip Sherman, and Pete Cancro led the team to a 4-0 start. That set up a big division showdown with Point Boro. The game was a classic, but it was also a tie. Beach took a 6-0 lead on Spiegel's touchdown pass to Kevin Skinner, but Boro tied it on Kirwan's 35-yard touchdown pass to Tom Mazich. The final was 6-6 and the division was deadlocked.

Those questions remained unanswered a week later, when two late leaping touchdown catches by Gil Burlew allowed Keyport to rally for a 16-16 tie with the Garnet Gulls.[36] As Thanksgiving approached, the division race was still up in the air. Beach and Boro had both clinched shares of the title and had their eyes on holiday clashes against St. Joseph's (Toms River) and Manasquan. Keyport, meanwhile, needed to beat Holmdel in their final Class D game to throw themselves into a three-way tie.

As it turned out, all three teams ended up with broken hearts. Point Boro, so sure that this was the year that they would finally beat Manasquan, was unable to stop Andy Morgan, who ran for 126 yards and a touchdown. The Warriors prevailed, 16-0.[37] Point Beach, too, missed their shot at an unbeaten season, falling to the pounding runs of St. Joseph's star Jim

Freudenberg.[38] Still, at least they had the Class D title to console them. Keyport, which suffered the cruelest fate of all, didn't even get that.

All they needed to do to win the division title was to beat Holmdel. Instead, they lost a heartbreaker to their rivals, 6-0. The winning touchdown was scored early by Hornet back Lou Cella. Keyport mounted a last drive, but on the final play end Larry Vecchio was dragged down inches short of the goal line. Holmdel's players poured onto the field in celebration.[39]

That meant that the two Point Pleasant schools would split the title. For Al Saner's Panthers, it wrapped up a solid run in Class D. Since the end of their streak, Boro had compiled a five-year record of 31-11-3 and won three division crowns. The only team they couldn't seem to beat was mighty Manasquan, on quite a run of its own. The Big Blue had won three division championships, compiling a 36-9-1 record over the same stretch. Most importantly, though, the two teams had created one of the finest rivalries in the Shore, one that would continue as the decade moved into its second half.

CHAPTER 24
THE AUTUMN WIND BLOWS
THROUGH RED BANK

"The Autumn Wind is a pirate.
Blustering in from sea,
With a rollicking song, he sweeps along,
Swaggering boisterously.
. . .
The Autumn Wind is a Raider,
Pillaging just for fun.
He'll knock you 'round and upside down,
And laugh when he's conquered and won."
–Steve Sabol, "The Autumn Wind"

"When I was at Red Bank Catholic, it was like the
British Army. Everything was regimented, everything was

precise. At Red Bank, it was totally different. Those guys
really were buccaneers."
–Lou Vircillo (Red Bank assistant and
later head coach)

After their unexpected 1960 championship, Red Bank became the team of near misses. Seven times, RBR entered November with a chance to win a championship, and seven times they came up painfully short. Even more torturous was their Thanksgiving rivalry with Long Branch. Since World War II, the Bucs had won on Thanksgiving just three times.

Rich Nicoletti (longtime sports editor for the Red Bank Register): *"I remember as a kid going to all of the Red Bank games, and I particularly recall looking forward to the big one against invincible Long Branch every year. It was like death, though. Red Bank never won . . . as an eternal optimist I can remember never leaving my house en route to those Thanksgiving Day games without thinking this year it would be different. It never was."[1]*

In 1970, a new coach arrived to try his hand at the wheel. Bobby Strangia was yet another Hudson County native making his way to the Shore. A standout lineman at Jersey City's Dickinson High School, Strangia was used to big crowds—Dickinson's Thanksgiving rivalry with St. Peter's Prep had always drawn well. After playing left tackle at Kutztown State, he returned to his alma mater. His teams were always competitive, and in 1968 Strangia was named the Hudson County Coach of the Year. However, it was clear that Dickinson was on a downward slide. Not long after Strangia's departure, the Rams slipped into a six-year, forty-three-game losing streak. Besides, Strangia had a young family, and it was the right time to head to the suburbs. So, he became the next man to take the head job at Red Bank.[2]

Bobby Strangia: *"I would tell a kid on my team that I'm on your back for one reason—I want to make you great. If you want to hate me because I want to make you the best football player that I can,*

*go ahead and do that. . . . When you look at thirty or forty kids, you
know there are only about ten out there who will give it everything
they have at all times. They may not be your best athletes . . . but
there will be a certain something in them that will never quit. . . .
They are the kids who make things happen. They make the big plays,
and they make you a winner."[3]*

Strangia, a colorful character and a natural motivator, became an immediate hit at Red Bank. His first team, which had just thirty-three players,
overcame low expectations to find surprising success. The key was a junior
class that featured defensive tackle John Lee, defensive end Greg Norflee,
offensive end Lonnie Allgood, halfbacks Ron Carter and Mike Pitts, and
quarterback Jim Palumbo. Strangia ran a pro-style offense, which allowed
that host of stars to show off their talents.[4] The team started 2-2, but their
fortunes changed with a wild comeback win over Ocean.

Ocean led 14-0 with under four minutes to go, when Pitts took a draw
29 yards, setting up Palumbo's touchdown pass to Allgood. A perfectly executed onside kick handed the ball back to the Bucs, who tied the
game on Palumbo's 13-yard touchdown pass to Bobby Moore. The extra
point was blocked, and Strangia (unwilling to settle for a tie) gambled
with another onside kick. That worked too, allowing Palumbo to win the
game with another touchdown pass to Moore.[5] Ocean hung on to win the
division, but RBR was nonetheless on the move. They won four straight,
setting up a Thanksgiving showdown with Long Branch.

It might have been the best game in the long rivalry. Down 18-8 early, the Bucs rallied behind two Moore touchdown runs to take a 22-18
fourth-quarter lead. Long Branch regained the lead with twenty-five seconds left on Frank Mazza's touchdown pass to Ed Gilmore. Red Bank
frantically drove down the field, and with just five seconds left Moore
scampered out of bounds at the 5-yard line. The magic finally ran out
when Palumbo's last pass fell incomplete, leaving end Greg Norflee and
his teammates sobbing as time expired.[6] However, a high standard had
been set, and with a host of starters returning, Red Bank's potential for
1971 was obvious.

Bob Strangia: *"We had a 6–3 season, but only 13 points separated us from an unbeaten season. I think we all realized then, deep down, that if we worked a little harder, if we pulled together, we could be number one."*[7]

The offense returned halfback Mike Pitts and ends Norflee and All-good. The fearsome defense returned end John Lee (now an All-State player), plus a host of punishing hitters that defensive coordinator George Tardiff molded into a unit known as the "Eleven Sticks of Dynamite."[8] Their road to glory started in September against RBC.

Pitts ran for 156 yards and three touchdowns, and Steve Hill returned an interception for a touchdown in a 35-0 victory. A week later, the Bucs looked even better in a 34-14 rout of Toms River South.[9] This was the start of a dominant 8-0 regular season, one that included five shutouts and a 40-0 rout of previously unbeaten Ocean. That game was over from the first play, when tackle Walt Perry intercepted a screen pass and ran it back for a touchdown.[10]

RBR entered Thanksgiving with a lot on the line. One more win would wrap up their first division title since 1960 and their first perfect season since 1922. Pressure was high, with the *Red Bank Register* warning that the Bucs had "seen many a fine season lost at sea after a confrontation with the Wave." And the Branchers, led by 1,000-yard rusher Steve Schwartz, were playing for the division title themselves. In the first half, it looked like the same old story—the Bucs had 6 yards of total offense and the Branchers had an 8-0 lead.

The second half, though, was different. The Eleven Sticks of Dynamite took over in the second half, while Algood turned the tide of the game by blocking a Long Branch punt at the 8. Pitts tied the game with a touchdown run. On Red Bank's next possession, Bill Jeter and Pitts alternated plunges into the line, with Pitts finally forcing through the middle for his second touchdown and a 16-8 lead. Long Branch never recovered. The celebrations should have started as soon as the game ended. Instead, chaos erupted.[11]

Fighting in the stands started as soon as the final whistle sounded, and a panic erupted after a gunshot rang out. Strangia and the Red Bank players hustled to their buses, while Ken Schroeck rushed his Long Branch team into the high school gym. Fortunately, no one was injured by the shot (fired by an Army private stationed at Fort Monmouth) or in the brawl.

> **Bob Strangia**: *"As the fans poured onto the field, we separated our team from the crowd and started backing off the field. We kept our team together and that's a reason none of our players got hurt. . . . I didn't know anyone had been shot until I heard it on the car radio. I did see one guy carrying a barber's razor."*[12]

The Bucs finished the year ranked third in the Shore and sixth in the state. Lonnie Allgood went on to start at wide receiver for Syracuse, twice leading the team in receptions. A ninth-round choice of the Cincinnati Bengals in the 1976 NFL Draft, he spent five years on the roster. Teammate John Lee enjoyed an even more successful career. He started at nose guard for Nebraska in 1974 and 1975, earning All-Conference honors as a senior and helping the Cornhuskers to a Big Eight title and appearances in the Sugar and Fiesta Bowls. The San Diego Chargers took him in the thirteenth round of the 1976 NFL Draft, and he lasted with them until 1981. Lee later played for the USFL's Arizona Wranglers, leading the league in sacks in 1984.[13]

The loss of twenty-two varsity lettermen doomed Red Bank to a losing year in 1972, but it wasn't a lost season. Linebacker Bill Johnston won All-Shore honors, and two talented sophomores got valuable game experience. Those two, halfback Bobby Tomaino and quarterback Chris Ward, would soon be known throughout the Shore. Most importantly, the Bucs beat Long Branch for the second year in a row. Ward played a key role, throwing a first-half touchdown pass, and the swarming Bucs defense managed to hold off a late Brancher rally to win 12-6.[14] The team entered 1973 with ten returning starters and plenty of confidence.

The Bucs overcame an early loss to RBC to dominate the C division once more. The big game was against Asbury Park; RBR's swarming defense shut down Asbury Park's Lindsey Butler and their offensive line sprang John Summonte for the game-winning 88-yard touchdown run. That was good enough to win the title.[15] An exciting 14-7 win over the Green Wave provided the appropriate cap to an 8-1 season. In that game, Gettis's late fumble recovery set up Tomaino's run for the winning touchdown with forty-six seconds left.

Opposing coaches had a hard time sleeping at night when they thought about what Red Bank returned for 1974. The Bucs' three main offensive threats—quarterback Chris Ward, halfback Bobby Tomaino, and fullback John Summonte—were all back. The addition of receivers Al Ashton and Clarence Algood (Lonnie's younger brother) added another dimension to the attack. The line, featuring veteran John McHeffey, was even better, and the defense, which returned nine starters, was best of all. Defensive back Bill Scott was a first-team All-Shore player, and linebacker Ira Bacon was the Monmouth County defensive player of the year. Bacon, in particular, was a brilliant defender; although one of the smallest players on the field, he often gained the edge over stronger opponents by sheer grit and determination.[16]

Power teams such as RBC, Rumson, and Manasquan combined for just one touchdown against the Bucs. Even Asbury Park, playing at home in front of a packed house, was overwhelmed. John Semliatschenko and Derrick Lewis returned fumbles for touchdowns and Chris Ward threw two touchdown passes to Clarence Allgood in a 26-16 victory that wasn't that close.[17] They trailed just once all year, to scrappy Shore Regional. Even that game eventually turned into a rout, thanks to a little halftime tongue-lashing from Strangia.

> **Bob Strangia**: *"I told them that if they wanted the game they'd have to go out and get it. If they wanted to be recognized as a state power, they'd have to play like a state power."*[18]

The Bucs recovered to win 32-14, then clinched their second consecutive division title a week later by hammering Manalapan 62-6. All that was left was Thanksgiving, where the Buc football seniors had a chance to make history. Not since the early 1920s had Red Bank beaten Long

Branch four years in a row. As usual, the game turned into a low-scoring test of wills, with both defenses rising to the occasion. Red Bank was getting the better threats (driving three times inside the 30) but couldn't punch a hole in the fired-up Green Wave lines.

Ira Bacon finally sparked the breakthrough by recovering a fumble at the 23-yard line. That led to Chris Ward's quick touchdown pass to Al Ashton. A few plays later, Jerry Agee plucked a Branch fumble out of the air and returned it for a touchdown, giving the Bucs a 13-0 lead at the half. From there, they held on to win 16-8. Red Bank had now won seventeen straight and finished 9-0 for the second time in four years. They were ranked second in the Shore, fifth in the state, and were quite confident that an invitation to Atlantic City for the state playoffs was on the way.

That call never came. The state's computer ranking system selected Middlesex and Hillsborough, two undefeated teams that had already played to a scoreless tie, as the two best teams in Central Jersey Group II. The entire town of Red Bank was beside itself with frustration and anger. Bob Strangia's protests gave voice to their emotions.

> **Bob Strangia**: *"I don't know how the hell they can do this to our kids. You win seventeen in a row, and they say that's not good enough? How can they do that? How can they cheat us like this? Those who have seen us play rated us fifth in the state. How can I tell these kids who bust their butts for me that they aren't good enough to go to Atlantic City? The players got nothing, and they deserved a better fate than robbery. What they're saying is the best teams in the Shore aren't as good as those somewhere else."[19]*

The only way Red Bank could get to the state finals that December was by buying a ticket. Many of them did, cheering Brick's victory in the SJ IV finals. Still, it was no substitute for playing the game. The snub left the Bucs hungry heading into the offseason, more driven than ever before to finish unbeaten and reach the state playoffs. The goal wasn't an unreasonable one. They had suffered a key loss in Chris Ward (who went on to start at safety for two years at Maryland), but many of his teammates were back.

Center John McHeffey, tackle Tim Turner, and tight end Steve Scoppetuolo would open holes for one of the most explosive backfields in school history. There, Al Ashton was joined by juniors Tim Johnson and Cookie Lewis. Johnson was a threat to score on every play, the most talented back to that point in school history. Lewis, the new starting quarterback, was no slouch himself. A dual-threat quarterback, he raised everyone's eyebrows in a preseason scrimmage against Brick, slaloming through the Dragon defense for a 58-yard touchdown run.[20] It was the defense, though, that Strangia predicted would be the heart of the team.

Red Bank returned seven of their front-eight defenders in 1975. The line was anchored by two All-Shore players, Nate Stathum and Roger Perry. Stathum was a fast, unblockable defensive end. He was too strong to run at, and he was too fast to run away from. Perry, on the other hand, drew and overpowered double and triple-teams on virtually every play. The linebacking corps, which featured Ashton, Sam Saunders, and Jerry Agee, was just as good.[21] Maurice Hayes was the only junior starter, and he was an All-Shore safety.

> **Chick Bruno (player, 1975)**: *It was absolutely amazing the talent that team had. We had twenty-two seniors, almost two full platoons on offense and defense.*[22]

That year Strangia also added a new assistant, picking up Lou Vircillo from RBC (where he had been the freshmen coach). The Caseys had been enjoying some success with the split back veer, and Strangia wanted to install the new system. His hope was that Vircillo would help implement the system for Red Bank's potentially potent offense.[23]

The town of Red Bank didn't have a lot to be excited about in 1975. Businesses were moving out of the downtown and into the suburbs, leaving behind an increasing number of vacant storefronts. Crime was on the rise, and it seemed like even the physical appearance of the downtown was declining fast. Residents complained of garbage on the streets, potholed roads, and untended storefronts.[24] A weak national economy left local unemployment at 13 percent, and rumors that the army was getting ready to shut down Fort Monmouth threatened to drive that number even higher.

The town itself was divided, with Red Bank's predominantly black and impoverished West Side growing increasingly alienated from the more prosperous East Side and wealthier suburbs such as Little Silver.[25]

The football team was a much-welcomed distraction. Huge crowds attended both home and away games. Strangia and the school administration alike worked hard to make sure that the high school teams became a focus of community pride, sending football players and cheerleaders on tours of local elementary schools, where they offered free tickets to Saturday home games. It helped that the Bucs team was representative of Red Bank's diverse community; they had starters from all over town, and they all shared the single goal of winning a state championship.

> **Bob Strangia**: *"Black kids were in white homes, white kids were in Black homes. And when we got to the stadium all the parents knew each other and were rooting together."*

> **John Semliatschenko (Red Bank player 1975)**: *"We were such a diverse group of players. I was from the West Side of Red Bank. My parents were immigrants from Eastern Europe, but we all mixed well together, and coming out of an era where there was so much racial tension, this team was something Red Bank needed. That's why it was so special."*[26]

RBR opened the season ranked third in the Shore, and their first game against sixth-ranked RBC drew over 6,000 fans. The Bucs used two touchdowns by Timmy Johnson to win handily, 20-0.[27] Happy days were still in town in Red Bank. Then, on the following Monday, the community was jolted by tragedy. During the JV game, sophomore Alton "Bobo" Palmer made a tackle at an awkward angle and went down hard. It was immediately obvious that the injury was serious, and he was rushed to Riverview Hospital. Palmer was paralyzed from the shoulders down. An emotional Red Bank team vowed that they would win the next game against Rumson and bring the game ball to him in the hospital.[28]

The already emotional Battle of Ridge Road was played at a fever pitch. Red Bank led just 7-6 late in the fourth quarter, and their victory wasn't secured until a late Sam Saunders interception set up Al Ashton's clinching touchdown run. After the game, the Bucs dropped to their knees and prayed on the field for Alton Palmer. A delegation of players then traveled to Riverview, where they presented Palmer with a game ball.[29] For the Red Bank team, however, relaxation wasn't even a thought. Manasquan was next.

The Big Blue, featuring quarterback Mark Lockenmeyer's aerial talents, were ranked fourth in the Shore. Fans expected fireworks. Instead, it poured, and both offenses bogged down in the mud. With three minutes to go, Manasquan had a 12-6 lead and the ball, needing just one more first down to run out the clock. Then lightning struck, as backup linebacker Kevin Brown (in the game only because of an injury) dove on a 'Squan fumble. RBR had another chance.

Lewis found Pete Dickerson for 30 yards to the 22, scrambled for 7 more, and converted a fourth and 3 by finding Dickerson for first down to the 7. The next play was a swing pass to Al Ashton. The speedy halfback outraced the Manasquan defense to the pylon, pulling the teams even. Kicker Steve Scoppetuolo's extra point finished the job. RBR won, 13-12.[30] The Bucs won their next five with comparative ease, extending their winning streak to twenty-three games, clinching the Class C title, and qualifying for the CJ III playoffs. Everything was falling into place.

> **Bob Strangia**: *"These guys have been playing together so long they know exactly what they have do in a given situation. That's why I call them my old pros."*

Then came another crisis. A nosebleed that wouldn't heal sent Strangia to the doctor, where he learned that he was suffering from dangerously high blood pressure. The semifinal matchup with Somerville was approaching, and Strangia was laid up in the hospital, receiving advice from doctors that he should not coach in the game. The Palmer injury had left the team in a state of emotional turmoil, and their coach's illness only intensified that.

Lou Vircillo: *"The kids did get emotional. They wanted to win for Bob."*

Al Albrizio (RBR defensive coordinator): *"For the kids, the streak and their pride at stake, but Bob is like their security blanket. It's tough without him."*[31]

Somerville was no easy mark. The Pioneers had gone 6-2 against a tough schedule, riding a powerful wishbone offense to a series of impressive victories over larger foes. Their talent presented a problem that had defensive coordinator Al Albrizio and offensive coordinator Lou Vircillo working overtime to try to solve. On the advice of his doctors, Strangia stayed off the sidelines in the first half, watching the game from the press box and communicating with the sidelines by phone. It was a long twenty-four minutes.

RBR fumbled on the very first play from scrimmage, leading to an early Somerville touchdown. On the next Buc possession, Cookie Lewis was intercepted by Les Johnson, who returned the pass 42 yards for a touchdown. It was 14-0, and the Bucs had run less than five offensive plays. Lewis's 42-yard touchdown pass to Richard Sims made the score 14-8 at the half, but Red Bank was still on the ropes.

Bob Strangia: *"I said 'the hell with that' [about staying in the press box] and went out on the field. The last thing I said to the kids before going out on the field was, 'It all began for us on this field together, and if it ends for us on this field today, it ends together.' And they went wild."*[32]

The inspired Bucs seized control of the game. Jerry Agee started the third with an interception, setting up Lewis's touchdown pass to Pete Dickerson. Steve Scoppetuolo's extra point made it 15-14 and Red Bank was in front. In the fourth, John Waterbury's pick got RBR the ball at the 8, allowing Lewis to scrambled toward the end zone. He fumbled, but Al Ashton dove on top of the ball for the touchdown and a 22-14 lead. Red Bank was going to the finals.[33]

First, though, they had to deal with Long Branch on Thanksgiving. The Green Wave threw a real scare into the Bucs. It took tough defense and a late Lewis touchdown pass to Scoppetuolo to put the game out of reach at 27-14.[34] Now it really was time to turn to the state championship game.

The entire town of Red Bank was on edge as the state championship game approached. If the Bucs could win in their final game, they would finish 11-0 for the first time in school history and avenge their omission from last year's playoffs. Bob Strangia felt that his team was not just carrying the banner of their own school, but also of the Shore Conference as a whole.

Bob Strangia: *"My dream is for Matawan, Brick, and Keyport to win their playoffs, too, and silence a lot of those people who still say that the Shore is second rate. The kids on this year's team haven't forgotten what happened last year."*[35]

Against most teams, Red Bank would be heavy favorites. The undefeated Hightstown Rams, however, were not most teams. Led by the virtually unstoppable Dana Shelton (who set Mercer County records with 1,600 yards rushing and nearly 30 touchdowns), Hightstown was averaging over 40 points per game. In the semifinals, his 326 yards on 28 carries had just about singlehandedly beaten Hillsborough.

Tony Treonze (Manville head coach; lost 58-14 to Hightstown): *"It was more like facing a track team than a football team. Their speed was unbelievable. It was the fastest team I've seen in ten years of coaching."*

Tony Graham (Asbury Park Press sportswriter): *"Shelton was only 5-6, 180, but lightning fast. Hidden behind a huge offensive line, he was difficult to locate and once he sliced through an opening, almost impossible to catch."*[36]

And it wasn't just Shelton. Quarterback Mike Radics had thrown nine touchdown passes to end Brian Ishman, who would later start at Syracuse. And like Red Bank, the Rams had something to prove. Hightstown's Mercer County schedule was often dismissed as weak, and they were eager to prove their critics wrong.

> **Cliff Brautigan (Hightstown defensive coordinator)**: *"We thought we could stop [Red Bank] defensively and score on them, maybe win 28-14. . . . We, at that time, were the highest-scoring team in the state and had beaten a tough Hillsborough team fairly easily."*

Red Bank, meanwhile, was a little wobbly. Not only was Strangia's health still unsteady, but his team was also finally tiring out. Linebackers Rich Ashton and Sam Saunders were both playing on injured legs, and the pressure of the twenty-seven-game winning streak was starting to wear thin. After three years' worth of big games, some feared that Red Bank was running out of gas before the biggest game of all.[37]

> **Lou Vircillo**: *"The atmosphere was very serious, which at Red Bank I had not seen before. It was almost eerie. There were tears before the game in our pregame talks. There was much emotion in the locker room and a spirit that bonded everyone. It was different."*

Lou Vircillo couldn't sleep the night before the game. Up early that morning, the Buc offensive coordinator decided to make a trip he had made several times before. This time, though, he included his head coach.

> **Lou Vircillo**: *"When I was in college and studying football to become a coach, I had this kind of attachment to the Vince Lombardi style. When he died, I was taken aback quite a bit, because I had gotten emotionally attached to him. I found myself in the Red Bank area, and he was buried right next door in Middletown. The way I was brought up, in a religious home . . . to respect and honor the dead . . . going to a gravesite to pay respects was not uncommon. When I was at Red Bank Catholic, I was compelled for some reason to bring players over there. Just one or two a game. In the game of football, it's kind of a funny thing. In all my years of playing and*

coaching . . . it's so physically demanding that it draws you in mentally and emotionally to the point that you're kind of open to a lot of things you're not usually open to as easily in your regular routine. At that time, your senses are so heightened that to be a little bit more spiritual. . . . The kids that went there had that experience. When we went to Red Bank Regional, I would go personally and continue the practice of taking some linemen here and there. Quietly, nobody knew about it except the kids. Then I took Strangia before the Hightstown game."[38]

Bob Strangia: *"He [Lou Vircillo] said to me that he couldn't sleep, and he knew I'd be up. He said, 'Come with me.' He drove us to this little cemetery in Middletown. I didn't even know Vince Lombardi was buried there. He took me over to Lombardi's grave, and we knelt down and prayed for 10-15 minutes without saying anything. Then we got up and walked back to the car. I looked at Louie and the strangest thing came over me. I could see Lombardi's face smiling at me. I could hear his voice saying three times, clear as could be 'Run the ball, run the ball, there's no way they stop you today.' I told Louie. He just looked at me and his eyes glistened. He grabbed me and hugged me and said, 'I hope you're right, coach.'"[39]*

The visit made, the two coaches headed over to the high school, where the undefeated Bucs were waiting. By now, the team's emotions were at a boiling point. It took no speech from Strangia or Vircillo to set them off. Instead, the catalyst was senior starter John Semliatschenko. Before the season, he had seriously considered leaving the team to get a job and support his family. Just before kickoff, he rose to speak about his experience.

Lou Vircillo: *"In the very beginning of the season, he almost did not play. He had a home situation where he had to work, and Bobby did a great job of working with the family and got him an opportunity to continue to play. He was very emotional because of all that, and before that last game he shared his personal feelings about being there. That was a big thing."[40]*

While Red Bank was preparing mentally for the contest ahead, the stadium was filling up with the Shore's biggest crowd of the year (somewhere between 8,000 and 10,000 fans).

Chick Bruno (Red Bank player 1975): *"When we came out into a little bowl at the south end of the field that day, there must have been 10,000 there. The energy was unreal."*[41]

That energy helped power the Bucs to an early strike, as they drove down the field to a Timmy Johnson touchdown run and 6-0 lead. Hightstown went three-and-out, but Red Bank fumbled the punt return into their own end zone for a Ram score. Mike Radics then put the Rams up 8-6 with a two-point pass to John Martini. The Bucs answered by driving 64 yards in 10 plays to a touchdown pass from Cookie Lewis to Steve Scoppetuolo. That lead lasted for less than thirty seconds, as Brian Ishman returned the kickoff 80 yards for a touchdown. The Rams hadn't run an offensive play for nearly ten minutes, but they still led 14-12.

Red Bank answered with a 20-yard touchdown run by Cookie Lewis. Then Shelton scored for Hightstown, then Lewis scored for Red Bank, and then Shelton scored for Hightstown again. Hightstown marched into the locker room with a 30-24 lead. Already it was one of the highest-scoring games of the year and the second half hadn't been played yet.

Bob Strangia: *"I walked in the locker room at halftime and sat my offensive team down. I told them that was the greatest half of offensive football that I'd ever seen a team play, and we were losing. I said, 'Unless you make this the second-greatest half, we're gonna lose.' Then I went over to the defense and, after I gave them a series of expletives, I told them that we'd have to stop them at least twice in a row so we could tie them up and then get the lead. . . . I told Cookie Lewis, a great runner who we hadn't run all year, that there was nothing at this stage to save him for. We knew Hightstown wouldn't be ready for him because they were concerned with Johnson and Al Ashton."*[42]

The first of those two stops came on Hightstown's first possession of the second half. A few plays later, Cookie Lewis found a wide-open Rich

Sims behind the Hightstown secondary for a 34-yard touchdown and a 31-30 lead. The second came on a Maurice Hayes interception, which led directly to a Timmy Johnson touchdown run. Red Bank was in front 38-30. It didn't last. Shelton scored from the 3 to tie the game at 38-38. Cookie Lewis untied it just over a minute later, rolling out of the pocket and scampering 58 yards down the sideline for a touchdown. Red Bank went for two and this time converted, with Lewis again turning the corner to extend the lead to 46-38.

> **Lou Vircillo**: *"It was like watching a tennis match. The game was going back and forth. It ended up that we all felt as the game went on was that the last team with the ball would win."*[43]

The fourth quarter actually slowed down a little bit, and even saw an exchange of punts before Hightstown got going again. Radics found Ishman for a 24-yard touchdown pass, cutting the score to 46-44 with 1:18 to play. Three years of struggle had come down to the biggest play of the biggest game of the best season in the history of Red Bank football.

Dave McIntire called for a rollout pass. Radics took the snap and headed right. He saw no one open and headed for the corner flag. In hot pursuit was defensive end John Semliatschenko, whose pregame speech had so inspired his teammates. The entire game had come down to a footrace.

> **Steve Scoppetuolo (Red Bank tight end)**: *"All I remember seeing was when Radics rolled out. Just seeing the two of them I thought, 'Oh, no!'"*[44]

> **John Semliatschenko**: *"I saw him coming the whole way, and I stepped up and hit Radics hard. I think he came off the ground. It got quiet for a moment, and then it erupted."*[45]

> **Lou Vircillo**: *"He had talked specifically about his gratitude for being part of this football team and no matter what happened he was grateful to be a part of this team. And then he made the hit that*

saved the game. It has a special place in my heart when it comes to one of the finest moments I've ever been a part of." [46]

Incredibly, Hightstown recovered the onside kick, and gave themselves one more chance. Radics hit Ishman for 20 yards up the middle of the field, and suddenly the Rams were almost in range for a game-winning field goal. Yet the Buc defense, shelled for 44 points on the day, still had just enough gas left in the tank for one more big play. Mike Nesci and Ray England broke through the Hightstown line to sack Radics. A screen pass and a draw play to Shelton gained nothing, leaving Hightstown with fourth down and 20 yards to go, with only thirty seconds on the clock. Jerry Agee picked off Radics's desperation pass and fell to the ground, clutching the ball to his chest. Red Bank had won.

It took a moment for it all to sink in. Then the celebration began. There had never been a game like it in the history of the Shore Conference, and when the totals are listed together it remains difficult to believe—ten lead changes, 90 total points, and 706 yards of total offense. The most important number, though, was one. After all those years of frustration and near misses, Red Bank stood alone. They were the champions.

Bob Strangia: *"Rich Ashton never talked. He always looked at me with a sort of an evil eye. After the game, he walked up to me slowly, put out his arms around me and said, 'Thanks to you, I never lost a game in high school.' That's when the magnitude of what we had done set in."* [47]

In 1975, in those immediate moments of joy that followed the greatest victory in the history of Red Bank Regional High School, Strangia put it even more dramatically, shouting joyously, "My god, what a game! I feel like I've been to the mountaintop and seen the other side!" In that moment, the entire area stood on the pinnacle with him. The Shore Conference had reached the promised land, and a new era of glory was about to begin.

PART 5:
THE CATHOLIC GOLDEN AGE

CHAPTER 25
THE MONSIGNOR'S DREAM:
MATER DEI

In the days before the Parkway boom hit the Jersey Shore, there were only enough Catholics living at the Jersey Shore to support two Catholic high schools (Red Bank Catholic and St. Rose in Belmar). Like so much else at the Shore, that changed with the area's exploding population. The wave of new public schools was joined by the opening of four new Catholic high schools—Middletown had both Mater Dei and the all-boys Christian Brothers Academy (which didn't play football), Holmdel had St. John Vianney, and Toms River had St. Joseph's. The wave of parochial education was cresting.

These were golden days for Catholic high school football. The Shore Conference at that time was not open to non-public schools, but there were so many fellow parochials that it was not difficult to build an independent schedule. They attracted enthusiastic crowds, especially for the natural rivalries that emerged between them. And they were good—between 1965 and 1980, every one of the Shore Catholics won at least one sectional championship.

This era ended in 1980, when the Catholic schools joined the Shore Conference for the first time. Leagues such as the Central Jersey Catholic Federation were forgotten, and the championships of the 1960s and 1970s are now only marked by faded banners hanging in gymnasiums and old plaques stacked in closets. Yet they happened, and for those who were there the memories remain vivid.

> **Flora Higgins (New Monmouth resident):** *"When we arrived in New Monmouth in 1950, it consisted of a grocery store, a Baptist church, and a Catholic church. . . . It was a garden or truck farming area and extremely rural."*[1]

In 1940, a young priest named Robert Bulman arrived in Middletown. He was on his very first assignment, a posting as the assistant pastor of St. Mary's Church, located in the rural New Monmouth section of the township. A native of Perth Amboy, he was used to an urban setting, and he struggled to adjust to the sprawling farmland of his new home.

> **Monsignor Robert Bulman:** *"I thought 'How am I ever going to function? How am I ever going to get to know the place as a young priest desires to do?' It was a very rural parish."*[2]

At that time, Middletown was still dotted with dirt roads and the parish was home to just 300 families. By the time Father Bulman became the pastor in 1950, the roads had been paved, but the church was still small. Nonetheless, Bulman had a dream. The church owned an empty lot on Cherry Tree Farm Road, and it was there that he envisioned an elementary school and perhaps, one day a high school. The elementary school came first, opening in 1953 under the leadership of nuns that Bulman personally recruited from upstate New York.[3]

The high school followed ten years later. At the time, it didn't even have its own building, just a wing of the elementary school. Still, there were plenty of students, coming from all over the Bayshore. Bulman's dream was now a reality.

Like the school itself, Mater Dei football had to start from scratch. Fortunately, they had two fine head coaches, veteran Art Schiller and the legendary Army Ippolito. Mater Dei didn't win too many games during those first three years, but they did draw quite a following. Their 1965 game with RBC drew 3,000 fans (RBC won 13-12), and the dedication of the school's own field drew another 2,500. That field was named Monsignor Bulman Stadium in honor of the priest whose vision had produced the tight-knit Seraph community. [4]

The Seraphs would enjoy their first sustained success later that decade, under Dick Hartnett. Hartnett was better known as a baseball coach—he had managed in the minor leagues, and his Mater Dei teams would win three Parochial B South titles—but his football career was nothing to sneeze at. In his first season (1966), Mater Dei beat RBC for the first time, upsetting the Caseys, 13-6, on a trick play. Pat Coyle hit Joe Warrack for a halfback option pass with the winning touchdown, bringing the entire stadium to its feet.

Things got even better a year later. Monsignor Bulman and his athletic director, Father Paul Gluth, wanted to play night football. In 1967, they rented a set of portable lights and played night home games in front of crowds that grew larger as the season wore on. There was magic on those special Friday nights, and they produced some incredible finishes.

Mater Dei went on a five-game winning streak, including one-point wins over Point Beach and Notre Dame High School and a 24-0 shutout of RBC. The skein eventually ended with a loss to Bayley-Ellard. However, the Seraphs finished the year on their highest note yet with a Thanksgiving upset over 6-1-1 Raritan. Brilliant performances from Tom Palagano, Ed Butler, and Ed Vasquez allowed Mater Dei to claim a stunning 13-6 victory. Four thousand fans saw the game, which allowed the team to claim its first winning record at 6-3. [5]

Hartnett stepped down after the 1968 season, but it didn't take the school long to find a capable replacement. George Conti Sr., previously a successful head coach at Newark West Side and Metuchen, commanded respect across New Jersey. In 1969, Conti was living in New Monmouth, and the short commute made the job appealing. [6] The available talent made it even more appealing—Mater Dei had a strong trio of backs (quarterback John Checton and halfbacks Paul Albe and Bob McBride) and a small but spirited offensive line led by center Tim Schnoor.

The Seraphs went 7-2 that year, a record highlighted by an upset of previously unbeaten Immaculata. Albe was the hero of that game, slaying the Spartans with a 61-yard touchdown run.[7] The season ended with a first-ever Thanksgiving meeting against the team that eventually became Mater Dei's archrival—Keansburg. The Seraphs set a school scoring record as McBride ran for two touchdowns and returned a kickoff for a third in a wild 44-32 win.[8] That win secured Mater Dei the Parochial B South crown, the first such title in school history.

The run continued into 1971, when the great passing combination of junior quarterback Mike Corley and end Chris Ryan powered the Seraphs to a 7-2 record. They upset an undefeated Hillsborough team, knocked off RBC, and routed Keansburg, 52-20, on Thanksgiving. At season's end, Mater Dei was crowned champions of the Central Jersey Catholic Federation.

Expectations for 1972 were high since both Corley and Ryan were coming back for their senior year. They looked good in the season opener, shelling St. Joseph's (Toms River), 44-20. However, any state title dreams came to an abrupt end when Corley fractured his ankle, forcing Ryan to move to quarterback and weakening Mater Dei's passing attack.[9] Still, the Seraphs kept their heads above water, and Corley returned in time for the Thanksgiving game against new rivals St. John Vianney. If Mater Dei could beat the Lancers, they would share the CJCF crown with RBC. Most observers expected a close game.

Instead, they saw a rout. Corley ran for a touchdown and threw for two more in Mater Dei's easy 42-0 victory. Ryan earned a well-deserved spot on the All-Shore team, while his team finished a very satisfying 6-3 and won a title for the second consecutive season.

Times on the Bayshore, though, were changing, and the Seraphs were headed for some rough waters. Traditionally, Mater Dei had drawn plenty of students from western Monmouth County. The opening of St. John Vianney in 1969 began to siphon off those students and athletes. Later in the decade, the opening of a second Middletown high school took the public schools off double-sessions and knocked off a reason to choose a Catholic education. The decade's weak economy hit the working class Bayshore particularly hard, and local Catholic families began struggling to afford the tuition bill. As a result, the school's enrollment shrank, and its football team found itself fighting an uphill battle. There were still highlights left in this early golden era, but the weight of numbers was telling its tale.

The team finished 4-5 in 1973 and 3-6 in 1974. Then came the disastrous 1975 season. The Seraphs had great coaches (Conti was assisted by two future state championship coaches in John Amabile and Jerry Schulte) and hard-working, determined players, but they just didn't have enough of them. An outmatched roster of only thirty-three players struggled to a 1-8 finish. Not until 1983 would they enjoy another winning season. Parochial football at the Shore, though, was far from finished. The spotlight was just shifting elsewhere.

CHAPTER 26
SOARING WITH THE GRIFFINS
(ST. JOSEPH'S)

J ust like Mater Dei, St. Joseph's High School in Toms River was the product of a monsignor's dream. From the moment that Father Lawrence Donovan arrived at St. Joseph's Parish in 1949, he wanted a high school. The demand was there; the grade school was already full to overflowing, and by the start of the decade there were two buses full of students leaving the parish parking lot to attend St. Rose.[1] By 1962, the population of Ocean County had grown enough to support a Catholic high school, and St. Joe's became a reality.

Still, it was missing something that Father Donovan loved very much—football. The pastor had always been a big football fan, and despite his high school's small enrollment, he wanted it to have one. Together with athletic director Steve Gepp, he founded the St. Joseph's Angels, a Pop Warner team built entirely from parish families. That helped build interest, and by 1967, there were enough players for the high school to start its own team.

Bob Tormollan (future head coach at St. Joseph's/Monsignor Donovan): *"The school wouldn't have a football program if it wasn't for him. He initiated it when the program started, and he has always been behind it, 100 percent."*[2]

Determined to make that team special, the pastor purchased permanent lights from Philadelphia's Connie Mack Stadium, where the Athletics had once played, for the team's field behind the high school. From their very first season, the Griffins would play all their games on Friday night.[3]

Kevin Williams (longtime Ocean County resident and sports reporter): *"The only two teams in the Shore that played night football were what is now Donovan, St. Joseph's High School, and Point Beach. What was very common on a Friday night was that you would go to a St. Joe's game, and look on the hill, and see clusters of kids with varsity jackets from every school in Ocean County. We went to see them play because nobody else played on Friday."*[4]

The Griffins didn't have an easy time in their first season. St. Joe's was the smallest football-playing high school in New Jersey, and they struggled to a 1-7 record. 1968 was better. Former Brick offensive coordinator George Jeck took over as head coach. Jeck was full of ideas and ambition, and more importantly had a brilliant sophomore quarterback named Kevin Billerman. Billerman had been a force of nature in Brick youth sports, starring in both football and basketball. Even in grade school, it was obvious that he was a special athlete. Getting him away from Brick was quite a coup for the young Griffin athletic program.

Kevin Billerman: *"I wanted to play for Mr. [Steve] Gepp [head basketball coach at St. Joe's]. He had coached my brother Bill, and I had watched how he handled everything. I wanted to be a part of it. I played football because my friends played football and I played with my friends."*[5]

The 1968 Griffins started twenty sophomores, but they managed to win their final three games to finish a respectable 4-5. Jeck left to go back to Brick after the season, but Billerman stayed. The team was just 2-7 that year, but that record was nonetheless good enough to claim the 1969 Parochial C South title, the school's first. Billerman remained the standout player and played his best game yet in the season finale, throwing for five touchdown passes in a 36-18 rout of Keyport.[6] Still, the star entered his senior year without ever having played on a winning football team. That changed in 1970.

This was the year that Al Sica arrived. Sica brought some badly needed stability, a wealth of experience, and local credibility. Any old-time local knew of Sica's brilliant career at Toms River High School and his later exploits for the University of Pennsylvania. During his time at St. Joseph's, he laid the foundation on which all future Griffin football success rested.[7] His first team was his best one. Billerman was back, as was a talented group of linemen featuring Pat Kordan, Marcel Power, John Menter, and Steve Ensor. To that group, the Griffins added Marlboro transfer and big-play running back Nate Kelly.[8]

The key game of the season came in week five. The 2-2 Griffins were embroiled in a crosstown battle with Toms River North (playing just their second year of varsity football). The hero, as expected, was Billerman. His two interceptions kept the Mariners scoreless, while his touchdown pass and two-point run gave the Griffins an 8-0 lead. North managed to drive and score, but their own conversion try was stuffed by Nate Kelly. An All-State buzz started to surround their star quarterback, and the team began to play with a new confidence.[9]

The Griffins won all five of their remaining games, finishing 7-2 and winning a second straight Parochial C South crown. Billerman, the school's first All-Shore football selection, was even better on the basketball court. He racked up nearly 2,000 points during his four years and led the Griffins to a sectional crown in 1969. By his senior year, he had scholarship offers to play football at Notre Dame and basketball at Duke. Billerman chose to stick with roundball and was a two-year captain for the Blue Devils in 1974 and 1975.

The departure of Billerman didn't mean the end of football success at St. Joe's. Sica's team finished 6-2-1 in 1971, winning a third consecutive C South crown. The highlight of the year was an 8-6 win over Red Bank Catholic in which Joe DeTuro returned a Casey fumble 80 yards for the winning touchdown.[10] Sica finished his run at St. Joseph's with two more respectable seasons in 1972-73. A businessman at heart, he then left to take on a new opportunity—buying an ownership share in the WFL's Philadelphia Bell. His departure was followed by the wildest and woolliest football era in the history of the school.

HURRICANE BOB FIOCCO

Kevin Williams *(longtime Ocean County sports reporter)*: *"The most colorful character I ever met covering high school football. . . . There's about a million stories about him, and half of them are true."*[11]

Bob Fiocco was by nature a fiery coach. His stint as the defensive coordinator at Toms River South had been marked by aggressive, hard-hitting defenses and wild motivational tactics (including the accidental decapitation of a live chicken). When the St. Joseph's job opened in 1974, he was recruited by a group of parents to run the program. The Griffin faithful (including Monsignor Donovan himself) dreamed of a football power and hoped that Fiocco was the man to help them take the next step toward football glory.[12]

He inherited a team with potential. They had third-year starter Jim Freudenberg at halfback, strong-armed junior Brian Hanifan at quarterback, talented senior Al Pietrangelo at end. Linemen Dave Froysa and Mike Painter gave the team some punch in the trenches. With a team like that, Fiocco was feeling confident.

They were both good and exciting, roaring to a 3-0 start. Among the wins was a thrilling 14-13 victory against St. Thomas Aquinas (Edison). Al Pietrangelo's perfect pass to Pat Rankin on a fake extra point won the game, 14-13.[13] It was a late-season game with Central, though, that featured the best atmosphere.

Bob Fiocco: *"It was a night game. We shut off the lights and came out with flashlights on our faces. When the lights came back on, we were at an emotional high."*[14]

In reality, the pregame ritual was even more elaborate than that. On top of the flashlights and darkness, the Griffins did a war dance around a wooden effigy of a Central Eagle that defensive tackle Mike Painter proceeded to destroy with a hatchet. The Griffins then destroyed Central, 42-16. After the game, Monsignor Donovan visited the locker room to dub them "the finest Griffin team we have ever had." He proudly announced, "I've been waiting a long time for a team like this."[15] They finished the year 7-2.

Football was fun, and it seemed to be getting better every day. Hanifin was back at quarterback, and more talent was arriving at the high school every day. Linebacker Dan Cook transferred in from Manasquan that winter, while Central stars Dwayne Dillard and Robert Taylor enrolled in September. Taylor, "the Manitou Park Flash," was special indeed, a unique combination of speed and power. Before the season, he set his sights high—"I want to run for 2,000 yards and be the leading scorer in the state."[16] Thanks to those transfers, it looked like the Griffins were going to have a monster team.

Wait . . . transfers? Was it a coincidence that three standout football players had just decided to enroll at St. Joseph's? Charges of illegal recruiting suddenly started to pour in. Central Regional's school board voted to end their rivalry with St. Joseph's after the 1975 season, and other local parochial schools groused that the Griffins had harmed their reputation (and perhaps spoiled their chances of getting into the Shore Conference).[17] The season began under the harsh glare of an unwanted spotlight.

St. Joe's started 2-0 and rose as high as number three in the Shore, but a loss to Southern Regional sent their season into a skid. Hanifin injured his ankle trying to make a tackle, Taylor was held to just 17 yards on 12 carries, and the Rams shredded the Griffins defense with a surprise no-huddle offense. By the end of a nasty game (which featured two benches-clearing brawls), Southern had prevailed, 20-8.[18] The air was out of the balloon, and the season spiraled out of control. The team drifted to a 3-5 finish, with Fiocco resigning after a disheartening 23-0 loss to Central. A scheduled Thanksgiving game against Point Beach was left unplayed.[19]

Fiocco's career was not over. He took the year off in 1976, then used the lessons he learned at St. Joseph's to turn Toms River North into a football power. The Griffins, meanwhile, faced an uncertain future. They still had Robert Taylor at halfback, but they had lost the other transfers to their original schools and their quarterback to graduation. They also needed a coach. That's where Denny Toddings came in.

> **Denny Toddings**: *"I was coaching football and wrestling at the New York Military Academy. It was in the late 1970s, those anti-military years, and I said to my wife that 'We gotta get out of town here.' The only job that was open was St. Joe's . . . at the time I didn't even know where St. Joe's was."*

> **Bill Vanore (St. Joe's player)**: *"We had much respect for him. He was an accomplished football player in his own right, at Brick and at the University of Delaware, and he brought in a great coaching staff. One of his coaches he brought onboard was Kenny Scott, a football standout at Brick. Coach Toddings played at Delaware, and Kenny Scott played at the University of Maryland . . . knowing their background and their knowledge, it was just phenomenal."[20]*

A former Brick center and Long Branch assistant, Toddings knew how to build winning programs, and he immediately saw that this Griffin team had winning potential. Taylor, of course, was something special, but so was John Schroepfer, a junior quarterback with a cannon for an arm. In the middle of the defensive line was a bear of a lineman, Sean Cosgrove.

Denny Toddings: *"The one thing about the Joey kids, the Donovan kids, was that they were tough-ass kids, they were maniacs. Great kids, but they were nasty."[21]*

The Griffins started quietly, and with a 2-2 record were not expected to be a match for Red Bank Catholic in midseason. The Caseys, featuring star running back Lonnie Burgess, were 4-1 and ranked number eight in the Shore. The eventual Parochial A South champions were the unanimous choice of every sports reporter in the area to win and win handily. The only people who believed in St. Joe's were from St. Joe's. A standing-room-only crowd packed the field and watched the Griffin defense play their best game yet.

Charlie Tully thwarted an RBC drive to the 15 by stripping Burgess and recovering a fumble. Dave Del Pizzo, Tim Reil, and Jeff Finley shut down the RBC passing game. Jim Baglio ran for a touchdown, and Vince Canella hit a key field goal. The hero, though, was Sean Cosgrove. He came up with three sacks, including one on RBC's final possession. The Caseys had the ball on the 4, not far from the winning touchdown. Quarterback Mike Mahon dropped back to pass, but before he could find anyone, Cosgrove was on him. The Griffins prevailed.

Denny Toddings: *"Credit has to be given to our twenty-two heroes out there tonight. No one picked us, but we made believers out of most of them tonight. This has to be one of the greatest football wins in St. Joseph history, and it definitely is the greatest thrill I have ever had in athletics."[22]*

Now they had a chance to do something truly special. If the Griffins could beat Orange's Our Lady of the Valley, they would secure the Parochial B South title. It was played on a Sunday morning in Toms River, and it was the most pressure-packed game in school history.

Bill Vanore: *"We had big Saturday night crowds, but this was huge. People were lined up all over the hill, standing room only, and it was packed."[23]*

When OLV took a 12-0 halftime lead, the pressure mounted. But St. Joe's didn't fold. Taylor's long punt return in the third flipped the field position and led to Schroepfer's 37-yard touchdown to Tim Riel. That sparked a rally that tied the game at 12. The Griffins got the ball back late in the fourth quarter, in decent field position, needing to score to win the game and the title. It was Schroepfer's game now. He hit Riel for 13 and Baglio for 11. Donovan was in OLV territory with 50 seconds to play. That was well within the range of kicker Vince Canella.

> **Denny Toddings**: *"Vinny had to come in and hit a 40 yarder. He had a great leg. I think he set the state record at that time. I turned my back and walked away. . . . I said, 'I can't watch this, I can't watch this.' And he made it from about 42, and it was still rising. That thing could've been good from maybe 60."*[24]

The Griffins had won it, 15-12. Monsignor Donovan had wanted a championship, and Denny Toddings and his boys had brought him one. Barely a year after their season had gone down in flames, St. Joseph's was on top of the football world. And they would celebrate.

> **Bill Vanore**: *"Father Donovan every once in a while would come on the PA. All of a sudden you would hear it in the loudspeakers, and then a little fumbling with the microphone, so you kind of knew it was him. That was kind of his trademark. He would start to talk. Everybody would be listening intently, and he wanted to congratulate the football team for winning the state championship, and then there was a little bit of a pause and he'd go 'No school tomorrow!' And everybody cheers. He was famous for doing that for special occasions, giving you the day off for something good that happened. He did that for us."*[25]

CHAPTER 27
THE LUCK OF THE IRISH
(RED BANK CATHOLIC)

In the late 1960s, RBC's football teams had three goals—winning the Parochial A South title, beating Red Bank, and beating Rumson. Under Jim McNamara (the head coach from 1967-71), the Caseys did fairly well by those standards. They enjoyed winning seasons in 1969 and 1970 and grabbed some exciting victories over their traditional foes. Perhaps the most exciting of those was their 1969 Thanksgiving game against Rumson, when Pat D'Aloia returned a blocked punt for the winning touchdown, RBC's first win over the Bulldogs since 1961.[1]

In 1971, McNamara stepped down in favor of assistant Tom Lalli. Lalli was one of the greatest athletes in school history and had seemed destined for football greatness at the University of Maryland until a serious leg injury ended his career. Just twenty-six when he took the reins of the program in 1972, he enjoyed immediate success.

Lou Vircillo (assistant under Tom Lalli): *"One of the reasons I wanted to go to Red Bank Catholic was that it was an exciting place to coach. In our interview, I realized there was a lot of spirit*

there. . . . I liked the new, young coaching staff headed by Tommy
Lalli, who had played there and played at Maryland. He was very
organized, very progressive. It was a great staff."[2]

He led the Caseys to winning records in each of his first three seasons, including a strong 7-2 finish in 1973. The end of the 1974 season, though, marked the beginning of something special. The Caseys were young, featuring junior quarterback John Sutphin, junior halfback Paul D'Aloia, and sophomore tackle Chris Shellenbach. Heavy underdogs on Thanksgiving, they rallied from a 21-6 halftime deficit to upset powerful Rumson. The key play was a punt that John Shellenbach blocked and Chris Morley recovered for a touchdown. RBC then won the game on a fake extra point—Sutphin, the holder, threw for the winning two points to Dave Howell. The Caseys prevailed, 22-21.[3]

The momentum continued into 1975. Seventy-six players came out for the team, highlighted by Shellenbach, D'Aloia, and junior nose guard Bill Barth. Most importantly, though, the Caseys added an incredible junior running back named Lonnie Burgess, one of the finest runners in school history. Behind Burgess (who was scoring at will) and Barth (who almost singlehandedly beat St. John Vianney with five sacks in the regular-season finale), the Caseys finished 6-2 and made their first appearance in the Parochial A South playoffs.[4]

The playoff run ended in a narrow defeat to Camden Catholic. Burgess gave RBC an early 7-0 lead with a 64-yard touchdown run, but he was contained the rest of the game. By halftime, the Irish were back up 9-7, the score by which they eventually prevailed. [5] One week later, the Casey season came to a quiet end with a 6-6 tie against Rumson. Their stars went on to fine careers elsewhere—Sutphin played quarterback at Villanova and D'Aloia played fullback at Bucknell. Lalli, too, was moving on; he became the assistant principal. He turned the program over to his veteran assistant, Lou Montanaro. The cupboard wasn't bare, either. Shellenbach, Barth, and Burgess were all back, and all three would earn All-Shore honors. Burgess, in particular, was outstanding, running for 1,400 yards and 20 touchdowns in an incredible year.

It all started in the season-opener against defending state champions Red Bank. Burgess ran for 134 yards and two touchdowns and led RBC to a crushing 33-6 victory.[6] Eyes across the Shore shot open almost immediately. The Caseys kept that momentum going against a tough schedule; they fell narrowly to Group IV Atlantic City but rebounded with a hard-fought win over St. John Vianney in a battle for supremacy among Monmouth County parochials.

On the first series of the game, Casey QB Mike Mahon hit Jim Lake on a seam pass that ended up going 49 yards for a touchdown. A few minutes later, Chris Fry blocked a punt to set up a Mike Largey field goal and it was 10-0. Vianney trimmed the score to 10-7 at the half, but after the break Bill Barth and the Casey defense dominated, holding the Lancers to just 4 yards rushing. When the clock ran out, the Caseys were still ahead, 10-7.[7]

RBC finished the regular season 6-2, earning another trip to the Parochial A South playoffs. That brought a rematch with St. John Vianney. This one wasn't close; Burgess ran for 134 yards and 2 touchdowns, powering a 27-3 Casey victory. They were going back to the state finals.[8] First, though, they had to deal with Rumson, and the Bulldogs managed to grab one of the season's great upsets. Led by quarterback Bob Scarrone and linebacker Mike Fallon, the Bulldogs took a 12-7 lead into the fourth quarter. On RBC's final drive, Fallon tackled Burgress on fourth down to clinch the Bulldog victory. Papers took note and favored Notre Dame in the state finals. RBC's momentum had been broken. Besides, the Fighting Irish were the miracle team of 1976, rallying from two winless seasons to reach the state finals.[9]

On game day, Lonnie Burgess quickly erased any such thoughts. He ran for 233 yards and 4 touchdowns, powering RBC to a 40-14 romp. When Burgess finally left the field, with the game well in hand, he received a standing ovation from the appreciative Casey faithful.

> **Lou Montanaro**: *"It was just a great effort by all the kids. Our game plan was simply to run, tackle, and block better than they did, and our kids went out and did it."[10]*

"The players who had won RBC's first title in over a decade were off to colleges across the country—Burgess to Springfield College, Barth to John Carroll University (where he started at nose guard), and Shellenbach to Rutgers (where he played on the defensive line). Montanaro's team didn't slow down in 1977, either. Jerry Bruno stepped into Lonnie Burgess's large shoes and ran his way to 1,000 yards and a spot on the All-Shore team. The Caseys finished the regular season 6-2 and earned a return to the Parochial A South playoffs.

There, they grabbed another fantastic upset, shocking undefeated Holy Spirit 13-8. The heroes were Bruno and Mike Madsen, who each had long touchdown runs (Madsen for 80 yards and Bruno for 41).[11] Five days later, RBC ran their record to 8-2 with a 30-15 win over Rumson. They now turned their sights to a potential second consecutive Parochial A South crown.

This time, though, there would be no miracles. Holy Cross was just too much, especially after Bruno limped off with a leg injury in the first half. RBC bowed, 14-6.[12] Still, RBC had finished 8-3 for the second year in a row, and their status as one of Monmouth County's finest football teams, public or private, was firmly established. However, their reign was not undisputed. St. John Vianney was on the rise, and ready to challenge the Caseys.

CHAPTER 28
THE NEW POWER
(ST. JOHN VIANNEY)

R BC beat St. John Vianney twice in 1976, once in the regular season and once in the Parochial A South playoffs. Those losses were bitter disappointments for coach Gary Chapman and his Lancers, all of whom firmly believed that they could have beaten the Caseys. Still, just making the playoffs was quite an accomplishment. Ten years prior, there had been no St. John Vianney football team. There hadn't even been a St. John Vianney.

Unlike Mater Dei or St. Joseph's, Vianney was not the product of one man's vision. Instead, it was the result of careful planning by the Diocese of Trenton, which recognized that the explosive population growth of Western Monmouth County would soon fuel demand for a new Catholic high school. In 1969, St. John Vianney opened its doors to a freshman class of 200 students.[1] Then, 1970 brought JV football, and 1971 brought varsity games for the first time.

The program's foundation was laid well by its very first coach, Ray Geneske. Nearly a third of the school's 300 boys came out for the team that year, and they managed a respectable 5-4 finish, including a 6-0 victory over Red Bank Catholic and a Thanksgiving victory against Keansburg.[2] Still, 1972, SJV's first season with a senior class, was even more exciting. Explosive halfback Barney DiBenedetto led the Lancers to a 7-2 finish and the Raritan Valley Conference title. DiBenedetto shone in the first game of another rivalry—a crosstown clash with Holmdel, the public school less than three miles down the road. The star halfback ran for four touchdowns in a 42-0 rout, the beginning of a rivalry that would last for decades.[3]

After the season, Ray Geneske stepped down as head coach, turning the reins over to his top assistant, Gary Chapman. Chapman maintained SJV's strong sub-varsity programs, which kept the program stocked with talent throughout the 1970s (at one point, the Lancer freshmen won forty-eight straight games).[4] Chapman's other contribution was to move Vianney to the wishbone permanently. That offense would have the same impact on Monmouth County that it was simultaneously having on major college football.

On paper, it just looked like a different formation out of which to run the triple option, but there was more to it than that. With two halfbacks in the backfield, the offense presented the threat of running the option either left or right, and whichever back wasn't the pitch man was able to serve as a lead blocker. It all put tremendous stress on a defense's flanks, and a unit that wasn't disciplined would soon find itself watching helplessly as the halfbacks tore off long touchdown runs down the sidelines. When run right, it could be downright scary.[5]

It took the Lancers a few years to get to that point. Although competitive in each of Chapman's first three years at the helm, they didn't break through until 1976. That was when they tore off a 6-2-1 record and qualified for the playoffs for the first time, losing the aforementioned game to Red Bank Catholic in the semifinals.

In 1977, the Lancers put forth their best team yet. Senior quarterback Terry Deitz was the perfect wishbone quarterback; he was quick with his reads, fast on his feet, and able to throw the deep ball whenever needed. They had two great halfbacks (John O'Brien and Scott Fitzgerald) and a dangerous receiver (Kevin Flanagan). Defensively, they were anchored by roving linebacker Mark Estoch. This was a team that would be tough to beat.

> **Gary Chapman**: *"A kid like Terry Deitz comes along once in a lifetime. He was an emotional leader, fiery. Mark Estoch, a co-captain with Terry, was our practical leader, a little more toned down. The two complemented each other perfectly. . . . The pleasure I had in coaching this season was that when one aspect of our offense was stopped, we could go to another."*[6]

SJV topped forty points four times and came up big in the biggest games. Their most impressive performance came against RBC. The Lancers were on the road and missing nine starters due to a mononucleosis outbreak at the school, but they refused to surrender. The game was tied at 15-15 with 33 seconds left when Scott Fitzgerald ran for the winning touchdown on a perfectly executed draw play.[7] Another big win came against Holmdel, a strong team featuring future NFL tackle John Cannon.

Unfazed, SJV rushed for 284 yards, and with linebacker Estoch everywhere, Holmdel never got anything going. Vianney prevailed, 17-12, and finished the regular season at 8-0.[8] They had earned the top seed in the Parochial A South playoffs and were favored to bring home the school's first-ever state title. Instead, they were rewarded with heartbreak, a narrow 12-7 loss to the eventual state champions from Holy Cross. Vianney had to settle for closing their season at 9-1 with a Thanksgiving win over Mater Dei.

> **Gary Chapman**: *"Everything just fell into place. You couldn't have written it any better for a novel, except maybe the ending."*[9]

Terry Deitz was one of the best multisport athletes that SJV had ever had, and he finished his senior year by winning a district title in wrestling and helping the baseball team to a county title. He continued his baseball career at the Naval Academy, and in 1982 helped the Midshipmen slug their way to within a game of the College World Series.

Deitz was gone in 1978, but the Lancers remained a powerhouse. Chris Mertz was the leader of a strong offensive line that cleared the way for workhorse back John O'Brien (1,243 yards and 20 touchdowns). Both of them, plus disruptive defensive lineman Pat Sheehan, earned All-Shore honors that year. The Lancers dominated almost everyone, scoring sixty points three times and claiming another win over Red Bank Catholic. This one was saved by Mike Sullivan's late touchdown run, which set the final at 14-12 in SJV's favor.[10]

The only blemish was another loss to Holy Cross, which stopped the Lancers 23-9 in the Parochial A South final. Once again, SJV had to settle for the consolation of beating Mater Dei, 32-0, on Thanksgiving. That was the final game in black and gold for Gary Chapman, who was accepting a new job as the head football coach at Manasquan High School. He left with great pride in what his Lancer teams had accomplished, and the future that they had ahead of them.

> **Gary Chapman**: *"Well, beyond the single games, the thing I'll remember most is taking the program up from the start. It's a super program right now. They've got a strong freshman team, and the jayvees have been undefeated for two years."*[11]

His successor, former defensive coordinator Jerry Clarey, found that Chapman was right. The Lancers had a potent wishbone attack featuring quarterback Tommie Deitz, fullback Mike Zupa, and linemen Tony De-Gulis and Jeff Jablonski. Their defense, which pitched two shutouts and held three other teams to a touchdown or less, was just as good.

The year started with another hard-fought win over RBC. Casey back Harry Flaherty ran for two first-quarter touchdowns, but two Mike Zupa touchdown runs and a touchdown pass from Deitz to Bill Cowley rallied the Lancers to a 24-20 victory.[12] RBC ended up finishing the year 6-3, just one game short of the playoffs.

Flaherty, the Caseys' star, was headed for greatness at Holy Cross. He was a four-year starter, a Division I-AA All-American in 1982, and the captain of a playoff-bound Crusader team in 1983. After college, Flaherty played in the USFL and earned tryouts with the Philadelphia Eagles and

Dallas Cowboys before bringing his football career to an end. Vianney, meanwhile, headed back to the playoffs, where they would lose to Holy Cross once again.

This was the most heartbreaking one yet. Deitz's touchdown pass to Bill Cowley helped the Lancers take an 8-8 tie into the half, and Vianney opened the second half with a deep drive into Holy Cross territory before missing a field goal. On the next play, Tim Schoenborn tore off a 73-yard touchdown run to give Holy Cross a 14-8 lead they never relinquished.[13]

The Lancers completed the season with a Thanksgiving win over Mater Dei, lifting their final record to 7-3. A few of their stars went on to college careers, most notably Bill Cowley, who played college ball at Villanova and Holy Cross before earning NFL tryouts with the Cowboys and Patriots. Still, there were frustrations. After three seasons as the best Catholic school team in Monmouth County, the Lancers had only three straight losses to Holy Cross to show for it. They wanted more, and they were hungry to get it in 1980. That was a year that would go down in the history of the Shore Conference, for more reasons than one.

CHAPTER 29
IN COME THE CATHOLICS
(1980)

P laying independent football hadn't been an issue for the parochial schools in 1970. By 1980, it was a major headache. Leagues all over the state began providing their members with full schedules, making it harder to find acceptable games. The Shore's parochials often found themselves traveling the state, playing foes that were poor mixes both in terms of enrollment and talent. As the problem grew more urgent, so did Red Bank Catholic's long-standing ambition to join the Shore Conference.[1]

> **William Himmelman (lawyer for Red Bank Catholic):** *"We were playing golf and [RBC athletic director Jack Rafter] turned to me and asked, 'Can you get us into the Shore Conference?' I said that I thought RBC belonged there and said I would help. Then we got the administration of the school to go along with us, and they were a tremendous help."*[2]

The lawsuit that changed the Shore Conference forever was filed in the winter of 1977 and ruled on that February. Judge Thomas Yaccarino found that the Shore Conference's blanket prohibition on nonpublic schools was discriminatory and ordered them to admit the Caseys.[3] It took time to fully hash out the details, but in the end, RBC was accepted as a full member in time for the 1980 season. Applications from St. John Vianney, Mater Dei, and non-football-playing CBA followed and were quickly accepted. For basketball reasons, St. Joseph's and St. Rose remained independents for a few years more. The Catholic schools had arrived.[4]

Little Mater Dei, which was struggling to beat anyone at this point, went into Class C with little fanfare. The spotlight was on RBC and St. John Vianney, whose reputation preceded them. The Lancers and the Caseys would join the very strong Class B North, where they would be tested immediately against foes such as Red Bank, Rumson, Shore, and Long Branch. They would also be facing each other in what had developed into a very fierce rivalry.

> **Lou Montanaro**: *"We're kind of going to be in the goldfish bowl. I guess a lot of people will be watching to see how we do. It will be like when Arizona and Arizona State entered the Pac-10."*

> **Jerry Clarey**: *"This is the challenge to end all challenges. . . . These kids know they're the lead-off team for this school in the conference. They know the level of competition is high, but it doesn't scare them."*[5]

Both teams were very strong in 1980. SJV featured All-Monmouth linemen Bill Wiegand and Keith Christensen, as well as backs Joe Breen, Joe McQuarrie, and sophomore speedster Scott Navitsky. Defenses that packed the box to stop the run had to fear the downfield threat of All-Shore split end Greg Golden and his partner, Robert Birdsall. On defense, the Lancers had a great linebacking corps led by Robert Quidore and a superb safety in Sean Gioffre. RBC was just as good, returning twenty-one lettermen and fielding the biggest offensive line in the Shore (anchored by 200 pounders Willie Ryan and Wally Case). The heart of the team was fullback and linebacker Jim McHeffey, a pounding runner and a punishing tackler. Both he and Case would earn All-Shore honors.

SJV's entered the Shore Conference with a 14-3 win over Shore Regional in the season opener. A week later, they took on Long Branch, one of the Shore's traditional powers. Greg Golden was everywhere, catching two first-half touchdown passes and returning a punt for a touchdown, but Long Branch still led 24-20 late in the fourth. The day was saved by Bill Wiegand, who scooped up a Green Wave fumble and ran it back to the 20. That set up John Eustace's touchdown pass to Golden, his *fourth* score of the day, and a 26-24 Lancer win.[6]

A 16-0 victory over Red Bank followed, running SJV's record to 3-0 and setting up a showdown with Red Bank Catholic. The Caseys, who had lost only to powerful Middletown North, were unafraid. Their defense shattered the Lancer wishbone, holding SJV to just 64 yards rushing. Jay Colao ran for 117 yards and a touchdown, while Jim McHeffey added 70 yards and another touchdown in an impressive 14-0 victory.[7]

> **Skip Edwards (St. John Vianney assistant)**: *"That was a very big rivalry. Both schools were in contention on the field and for the players that might come to their school. . . . We lost the first game to them. That's when Eustace hurt his knee."*[8]

The Caseys, now flying high, won their next three games and ran their record to 6-1. They entered the regular-season finale needing just one win to clinch the outright B North title. Standing in their path were their old rivals from Red Bank Regional. The annual game had been moved from the season opener, but it was still a highlight of the season, and the Bucs were salivating at the opportunity to derail RBC's title march. The bleachers were packed for one of the greatest games in the history of the long series.

RBR forced seven turnovers, keeping the game tied at 7-7 until late in the fourth quarter. Special teams decided the game, as a bad punt snap led to a safety and allowed RBR to take a 9-7 lead. RBC's final drive was foiled by a sensational one-handed interception from Buc safety Tony

Scoppetuolo, who made the play of the day.[9] The Bucs had prevailed, shocking the Shore.

Lou Vircillo: *"Last year, they were the underdogs and snatched it from us. This year, we were the underdogs and snatched it from them."*[10]

RBR went on to beat Long Branch the next week, finishing 5-4. After a slow start, the Bucs had won their final four games to finish with a winning record, beating their three biggest rivals (Rumson, RBC, and Long Branch) along the way. The win also was good news for St. John Vianney, which clinched a share of the B North crown as a result of RBC's loss. The red-hot Lancers had allowed just one touchdown after their RBC loss, finishing the regular season 7-1 and earning the top seed in the Parochial A South playoffs. RBC, at 6-2, was the second seed. The possibility was there for a state championship rematch between these two fierce rivals.

But the Caseys and Lancers weren't the only Shore parochials in the title mix this year; the Griffins of St. Joe's were back in the mix. Denny Toddings's team had stayed competitive after their 1976 title, finishing 4-4-1 in 1977 and upsetting Red Bank Catholic in 1979. In 1980, the Griffins were as strong as anyone. The combination of quarterback Tony English and end John Metzger gave them a real aerial threat, and their young but talented line featured tough blockers such as Ed Lyons. Still, no one gave the Griffs much of a chance against St. John Vianney. St. Joe's hadn't beaten the Lancers in six years, and just two years earlier their Monmouth County rivals had slaughtered them by an unholy 68-3 final score. Avenging that defeat would require that St. Joseph's play their best game of the season.

They certainly played their hearts out. The Griffin defense refused to buckle against the Lancer wishbone and forced quarterback John Eustace (whose knee injury was still bothering him) to the bench. Meanwhile, English hit Metzger for a touchdown pass, Lou Sepe kicked a field goal, and Sean O'Brien returned a blocked punt for a touchdown to give the Griffins an unlikely 16-7 lead late in the third quarter. Now it was the

Lancers for whom things looked dark. With another playoff loss looming, Eustace could watch no longer, and came off the bench.

Jerry Clarey: *"When John came back, we really started to go. He had a strained knee, and he was forced out in the first half. He was just crying on the bench. They had to ask me to send him in four times before I finally said yes."*[11]

Eustace led a march to the 5, but the Griffins weren't going to fold easily. On fourth and goal, they forced a hurried pass that evaded Robert Birdsall. With their own running game dried up, they then decided to try for a big play, a play-action pass. SJV was ready, however, and Mike Poskonka intercepted the ball at the 6-yard line. One play later, Eustace hit Greg Golden for a touchdown, cutting the score to 16-14. The momentum was now with SJV, and they took the lead for good with four minutes to play when Eustace scrambled away from a St. Joe's rush before finding Bob Quidore for the winning touchdown. The Lancers were finally going to the state finals.[12] RBC would meet them there.

Elsewhere in Monmouth County, the Caseys had just wrapped up a hard-fought 7-0 victory over Holy Spirit. Bob Bauer had scored a short touchdown in the fourth quarter, and the Casey defense made the lead stand up with a fine performance. The game ended with a goal-line stand, with Jim McHeffey and his defensive teammates stuffing the Spartans on fourth down and goal.[13] Both SJV and RBC won on Thanksgiving, setting up the final meeting on December 6.

It was tough to pick a favorite. SJV had the better record and had generally looked like the better team, but RBC had won the first meeting. Most observers ultimately decided that the game was a toss-up. Everyone agreed that it was likely to be a classic.

Much like the first game, RBC dominated the statistics. They ran seventy plays to SJV's forty-four, picked up seventeen first downs to SJV's five, and spent most of the game in Lancer territory. Yet thanks to some well-timed big plays from the SJV offense, they still entered the half down 14-0. First, Eustace converted a fourth and 11 with a 27-yard touchdown pass to Greg Golden. Then, just before the half, the Lancers came out on top of a wild and confusing sequence.

Late in the second quarter, SJV drove to the RBC 4 before the Caseys held. RBC then mounted a drive of their own, reaching a fourth down and 1 from midfield with 15 seconds left in the half. RBC gambled and tried a pass, but it fell incomplete, giving the ball back to the Lancers. Jerry Clarey called for a Hail Mary, and Eustace connected with Golden all the way down to the 7.

Jerry Clarey: *"Typical Golden. Every time we threw the ball today, I just had this feeling the little rascal was going to catch it."*[14]

There was time for one play. Eustace rolled right, looking for Golden again, this time on an out pass. Golden was covered (in fact he was knocked down on the play), so Eustace, sore knee and all, simply raced to the pylon for a touchdown and a 14-0 lead.

The second half was almost all Caseys, but Sean Gioffre's booming punts kept forcing them to try long drives and the disciplined SJV defense refused to allow a big play. RBC managed to cut the score to 14-6 with a Peter McNamara touchdown run, but they could get no closer. RBC's final drive ended with sacks by Tom Clancy and Drew Cowley. The Lancers had done it, winning the Parochial A South title for the first time in school history.[15]

SJV's magical year continued into other seasons. Greg Golden and John Eustace both played key roles on the baseball team, which won both B North and Parochial A South titles that spring. After graduation, those stars continued their fine athletic careers. Golden went to Miami and Bob Quidore to Northwestern. RBC also produced college stars—Jim McHeffey played linebacker at William & Mary, Jay Colao running back at Bucknell. Wally Case went to Springfield College and was a two-time All-American there.

The programs they left behind remained in good shape, too. Their strong performances had proved that they could stand toe-to-toe with anyone in the Shore Conference, and the natural rivalries that emerged made them valued additions to Class B North. In the decade to come, that division would earn a reputation as one of the Shore's toughest.

St. Joseph's, meanwhile, finished their successful 1980 season with a 9-0 Thanksgiving victory over Manchester. Denny Toddings stepped down after the season and was replaced by assistant Bob Tormollan. The Griffins remained strong over the next several seasons. Behind the powerful running of halfback Bob Gould and the dominant line play of defensive tackle Gordon Nelson, St. Joseph's finished with winning records in 1982 and 1983 and earned a trip to the 1983 Parochial A South playoffs.

That last year marked the beginning of a new era. In order to honor its beloved founder, St. Joe's officially changed its name to Monsignor Donovan at the start of the school year. A year later, another new era began, when the Griffins finally gave into scheduling difficulties and entered the Shore Conference. With the exception of Admiral Farragut (which didn't really play an NJSIAA schedule), there were no more independent football programs in Monmouth or Ocean County. An era was over, and a new one was just beginning.

EPILOGUE

NOVEMBER 18, 2005

As I wrote at the start of this book, that was the day we played the game I'll never forget—Monsignor Donovan against Manchester in the season finale. There wasn't a lot of coverage in the newspaper—just two sentences on one of the inside pages of the sports section, as well as a box score listing touchdowns and statistics. However, most of us who were there that evening would have no difficulty recounting what happened.

I remember how Manchester dominated the first half, scoring three touchdowns in the second quarter to build a 23-7 halftime lead. I remember how low I felt as we walked back down the tunnel and into a classroom for our halftime meeting. But then I also remember our coaches quickly going to work, drawing adjustments on the board and urging us to keep playing. They laid out a path for us to get back into the game—which was exactly what we did.

The second half comes to me in flashes. I can see our quarterback, Travis Graga, finding our leading receiver, Tim Finnegan, for a long gain early in the third quarter. Tim leapt to his feet and gave a big, Mark Bavaro-style first down signal. We were moving. Later that drive, he caught a quick touchdown pass to trim Manchester's lead to 23-14.

I can remember Frank Gunteski's field goal bringing us within six. I can remember our leading rusher, Ryan Gabriel, crossing the goal line to tie the game. Frank's extra point broke the tie, and for the first time, we were ahead. And I remember the final drive.

Manchester drove into our territory and with seconds to play was at the very edge of field goal range. They called a timeout to set up their attempt. Players on both teams dropped to their knees and linked arms. A few seniors, knowing that this was their final game, looked away, unable to watch. The crowd quieted, or at least I think they did. This was it.

From the field, Manchester's field goal try looked straight and true almost all of the way, only hooking wide and short at the last second. Our sidelines erupted in joy. Coaches and players leapt, cheered, hugged, and knocked each other flat with chest-bumps. Our offense went out in the victory formation for one play, and then it was over. Our friends and fellow students poured onto the field for another celebration. We had won. MonDon 24, Manchester 23.

There have been countless games like this played in the history of the Shore Conference, mostly unknown outside of those who played in them, coached in them, or watched them. They were not played for championships or for statewide rankings, and as a result they did not receive detailed newspaper accounts. But they *mattered.* They are treasured memories, recounted again and again as the years go by.

It is likely that everyone who has worn pads in the Shore Conference has experienced a game like this at least once, in victory or in defeat. It is one of many common experiences that those who played the game have shared. By strapping on the pads and laying their hearts on the line, they became what Teddy Roosevelt called "the man in the arena":

> *The credit belongs to the man who is actually in the arena, whose face is marred by dust and sweat and blood; who strives valiantly; who errs; who comes short again and again, because there is no effort without error and shortcoming, but who actually does strive to do the deeds; who knows the great enthusiasms, the great devotions; who spends himself in a worthy cause; who at the best knows in the*

end the triumph of high achievement and who at the worst, if he
fails, at least fails while daring greatly, so that his place shall never
again be with those cold and timid souls who neither know victory
nor defeat."[1]

But Shore Conference football players over the years have gained much more than knowing with whom their place is not. They have found others with whom their place *is*. The friends I made through football remain close to me years after we played our final game. The stories we shared and the memories we made have brought joy and laughter many times over, and the lessons we learned together have made my life immeasurably richer. In that, I am certain that I am not alone. One of my favorite parts of writing this book has been the opportunity to talk Shore football with strangers, to hear their stories and to discover with how many people my own stories overlap. That brings me back around to the real point of this book.

When the Shore Conference was first founded in 1936, it was just a scheduling convenience intended to reduce travel time for its members. Nearly a century later, across many seasons and nearly 10,000 football games, it has become something more. Countless players, coaches, families, and fans have transformed it into a community. Every individual who has come through the Shore Conference has contributed something; to remove anyone would make the whole lesser. The Shore Conference has become our home.

This community means so much to so many people. I think that the most appropriate way to finish this book is to allow them to say it in their own words:[2]

> **Bill Bruno**: *"With my family history going back to my dad in high school in the late 1920s and 1930s, and then being part of his legacy as a young kid, on the sidelines as a waterboy, and then just sitting in his office, in his locker room, and taking bus rides . . . then coming full circle, where I'm coaching kids at Asbury, and Manalapan, and Pinelands. . . . I'll look back, and I'm blessed . . . it's a great family legacy. I tell you, I'm getting choked up . . . my family, my siblings,*

we cherish the name Bruno and Asbury Park. We never forgot our roots."

Bob Badders: *"It's fun, and it's meaningful to me because it has such a rich tradition. Such a long history. You've got schools that have been around a long time, and rivalries that have stood the test of time. . . . Football gives a lot of these towns, a lot of these schools an identity. Being around it so long and having an institutional knowledge of a lot of the schools and programs, you see what it means at certain schools, what a Friday night or a Saturday afternoon means. . . . It reminds you that it really is more than just a game. It's a cliché, but it is true. Some will go on to play in college or maybe in the NFL, but some might not ever strap up the helmet again. When you see that end, whether in a regular season game, on Thanksgiving, or in a playoff game . . . you really understand how much it means to them. It really sinks in."*

Brian Kmak: *"It means everything. It's been my entire adult life. Ever since I got out of college, I've been teaching and coaching, and been a part of it ever since. . . . For the last thirty something years of my life, I've been a part of Shore Conference football, and I've loved every minute of it."*

Calvin Thompson: *"The state is so great in football. The public-school programs and the parochial school programs produce some guys. And then you take it to another level, with the amount of champions that the Shore Conference puts out there year in and year out. The fact that we can compete shows how very well prepared we are because of the schedule we played in the Shore Conference."*

LeRoy Hayes: *"I feel as though, personally, that we play the best football. Every year you wind up with four or five champs coming out of the Shore Conference. . . . I don't know if it's coaching,* *athletes, or what. I just feel as though we play better football here. Different brand of football.*"

John Oxley: "*It means a lot. Being a player and a coach, there's not many conferences around like it. So many times, the Shore Conference goes to state games, and they don't realize how good the Shore Conference is. We tended to do very well in the states and things like that. It's a pretty special area.*"

Dan Duddy: "*It's great to talk about the history of football in the Shore Conference. We're just really, really proud of it. You're talking to a guy who played at Brick Township High School for Warren Wolf. We traveled the whole state and Coach Wolf was very bold about the pride he had in Brick football and Shore football.*"

Chip LaBarca Jr.: "*I've been here such a long time and fortunate to coach at so many schools. I think you've got to be proud of it. A lot of fantastic players come from the Shore, a lot of good coaching. Anytime we go up against teams from outside the Shore, we do pretty well. I'm proud to be a part of it.*"

Pete Cahill: "*The Shore Conference as a whole is known through the state as a powerhouse in football. Up and down. We pride ourselves that we want to play the best and be the best, and I think that the Shore Conference is the best football in New Jersey.*"

Brian Lee: "*When you get on Parkway North or South, you have a little respect for your own town, saying, 'We're going to represent Smalltown USA.' There's something about going to Carteret or Roselle and having them say, 'Holy crap, that team from the Shore is pretty good.' I kind of like going out to the state and saying, 'This is what we're bringing to your part of the state. We're not bad.'*"

Cory Davies: *"The Shore Conference is a very unique, but very elite conference. . . . How big it is, not only that there are forty-three teams that play football, but that they've been doing it for ages. There's so much tradition to it. . . . It's an incredible conference."*

Dan Curcione: *"There's been so many great players, so many great coaches. To be able to be a small part of the history of it, just a really small part of it, it means something. . . . Having a legacy means a lot. You can look at the banner and tell your kids that you were a part of it."*

Skip Edwards: *"There's a lot of history in the Shore Conference, a lot of people who have come through the Shore Conference. People that have gone on and done great things. And it is one of the oldest conferences in the state. How can you not appreciate that and not want to be a part of it?"*

Dennis Filippone: *"When I was growing up in the late '60s and early '70s, it was a much smaller community. Football was the binding factor for the entire town. On Saturday afternoons, everybody was at the football game. You couldn't get to a gas station or a delicatessen or anything else. Coach Wolf was an iconic figure, because he was the deputy superintendent, the mayor, and he was the head football coach. It was really fun to be a part of."*

Tom O'Keefe: *"To me, the Shore Conference is phenomenal. It's a tight group. They root for each other, and they hate each other when they're playing each other. It's great to be a part of it, and I go to as many games as I can."*

LJ Clark: *"You play these teams out west and down south, they know about the Shore Conference, I'll tell you that. We play hard. Just a rich tradition of waking up, looking in the paper, and seeing what other schools are doing. It's just a rich tradition. Family-like.*

If no one's playing, and I'm not scouting, I'll go over to Brick and just watch them play. Look at Lakewood-Toms River South on Thanksgiving. You have people who just come watch the game. Manasquan-Wall, Asbury-Neptune. You go to these games, even if you aren't playing in these games. You're just a Shore Conference guy, you go out and support."

Sean Henry: *"My uncle was a principal at Manasquan when I was in high school. Vic Kubu was one of his best friends. I remember talking to him, it was like talking to a legend. That's how much respect I had for him as a king of the Shore Conference. To have been a part of that, it's the greatest tradition . . . give me a great Shore Conference game on a Friday night and there's nothing better than that. I'd take that over a pro game. The atmosphere, wherever it is . . . Toms River, Manasquan, Middletown. It still gives me chills walking up to a game now. To me, that's Shore Conference football."*

Jay Price: *"We should have a Shore Conference tournament. Forget states. Play all forty-two schools down to a Shore Conference champion. If we had a tournament and played it right down to the wire, you'd put 60,000 people in those stands."*

Charlie Diskin: *"When you travel around the state, people are always talking about the Shore Conference, and comparing their conferences to it. I think about the coaches over the years, the guys that kind of are the foundation of it—Coach Wolf, Coach Vircillo, Coach Martucci, Coach Signorino, all those guys. Got it started. To be part of it, and coach in it, it's fun."*

Frank Papalia: *"My first year at Holmdel, I got involved with the Shore Conference coaches association. I'm in a room with Coach Vircillo, and Coach Wolf, and Coach Kubu, and Coach Costantino, and all these legendary guys. Coach Duddy had played for Coach*

Wolf, so it's something I heard a lot about growing up. I felt the pride. I remember Coach Wolf calling people up for state finals and interdivisional games, about how important it was to acquit yourself well.

There's a real unique camaraderie among Shore Conference coaches. You see it every year at the All-Shore game, and every year at the clinics. It's just a real special place to coach."

Fred Sprengel: *"I am very much into the history, the brotherhood of the coaches. . . . I thought it was so cool to go to games and watch and see and learn. When I went to clinics, I wanted to sit down with Coach Vircillo, Coach Signorino, Coach Wolf, Coach Kubu, Coach Amabile. I wanted to be around those people and learn from them."*

Mark Costantino: *"It's awesome. Coach Wolf, Coach Kubu, getting to know those guys . . . my first date with my wife, I had to do a film exchange with Coach Kubu for Bob Rolak. I was nervous. Not about the date, but about going to Coach Kubu's house, because this guy's a legend. He shook my hands talking to me, and I was like a twenty-seven-year-old guy. It's awesome."*

Sal Spampanato: *"I know I'm biased, but I think the Shore Conference is one of the toughest conferences in the state, if not the toughest conference in the state. You look at our records against other counties, we've held up well. And the people in it are awesome. I've been very, very lucky. I've coached with Coach Conti, Hall of Fame; Danny George, future Hall of Fame; Mark Ciccotelli, future Hall of Fame; Al Saner; John Amabile . . . to be around these guys and learn how things are done, is just awesome."*

Greg LaCava: *"When you can say that you coach in the Shore Conference, it's a badge of pride and honor. It's one of the best* *conferences in the state, as far as football is concerned and probably other sports as well. Everywhere you go in the state, everyone knows the Shore Conference. It's good to be part of it."*

Gary Penta: *"It's a great honor to be part of it, with the character of the coaches, and the players, and even the officiating. Just being around high-character, high-quality people who affect lives in a positive way. . . . All the great players and the great coaches. . . . Who could get better people? The best of the best."*

Harry Chebookjian: *"I take great pride in it. I really do. I think the Shore Conference is the premier league in the state of New Jersey. I think we produce great players and great coaches. It's just a pleasure to be involved with it every single week of my life. There really isn't another conference where you get such a great mix of different types of players, different types of offense, different types of defense, different coaching styles, whatever it may be. The Shore Conference has got it, and they are the best conference in the state, bar none."*

John Tierney: *"It's gone on for a hundred years. It's awesome. I've been a part of seven All-Shore football games. Watching them be played is fun, going back and seeing guys I played with. . . . It's a humbling experience, knowing that I had a little, little, little minute part of the Shore Conference. It's pretty awesome."*

Gary Foulks: *"For me, it's as much as anything being part of the history that my grandfather would talk about. Shore Conference football is what I was brought up on. What got me interested in football in the first place. Being a history buff anyway and being brought up on stories from my grandfather, I always wanted to be a part of that growing up."*

Kevin Williams: *"When I first started out, I was a twenty-three-year-old covering football. Here. I really wasn't that much older than the athletes I was covering. Here I sit, thirty-eight years later, as a sixty-one-year-old who could be the grandfather of anyone who plays today. . . . Football's special. For me as an observer, as a player, as someone whose watched football games since I was thirteen years old, it will always be special."*

Scott Stump: *"It's funny. I was an athlete in the Shore Conference, but at the time, when I was in the middle of it, I didn't realize the legacy that's gone on all these years. The timeline that you're part of, that you're joining. As a reporter to be even mentioned or remembered by anyone is humbling. That shows how much the games meant to them. I think it puts an imprint on people's lives that stays there forever. Even athletes who have gone on to great success at the college or even the professional level always look back and remember fondly their time at the Shore. It's a tradition of winning, of great coaching, of immortal athletes.*

It's a place too that people love it here so much they tend to stay. You look at a lot of other places in the country, and guys have success and move away. The area doesn't mean as much to them. People at the Shore, they love this place. The football is such a huge part of the tapestry of this area . . . what else are you doing on a Friday night in the fall? You see so many guys go on to success that it's fun to say 'Hey, I knew him when he was sixteen years old, and he was nervous before a high school game.' It evokes a lot of pride. I grew up here, I'm from here, I never left, and I love it here, like so many other people. That's rare in this country."

Steve Antonucci: *"I grew up here. I played for Mike Ciccoctelli. I was All-Shore, and I played in the All-Shore Classic . . . to always know that I grew up here, to be a part of Shore Conference lore and history of it, it means a lot to me. It really does. It's something* *you can never replace. It's been a tremendous honor to represent Middletown South and Shore Conference football. And to have my children do it. My son played at Manasquan. He was All-Shore, and he played in the All-Shore Classic. I have a younger son right now, who is going to be a junior at Manasquan. I'm excited to watch him play, and I have a son behind him who I think is going to play. And that's been exciting to be a part of it and stay in touch with it. It's always been a part of my life."*

Bill Vanore: *"Moving down here in my junior year was really the turning point of my life. Being part of the football team and playing football has a lot to do with that. It was definitely something I was proud to be a part of. It means a lot to me, and it still does."*

Tyler LaVine: *"The Shore Conference, when I was a student, I didn't recognize the magnitude of it. As I moved into adult life and a career, and I've been coaching baseball, and meeting guys who coach in other conferences, other parts of the state, I say 'We're at Mater Dei, we're in the Shore Conference.' They give you kind of a look. 'Oh, the Shore Conference. OK.' At first you wonder, why is this guy giving me a funny look? Then it started to occur to me that the Shore Conference was a premier ground for athletes.*

Being in the Shore Conference, you can be a Keyport student and be one block away from Keansburg, or Raritan, or something along those lines. At Mater Dei, you could have gone to North, to South, to Red Bank Catholic. That's what was different about the Shore Conference. As competitive as it was, it was a very close-knit group. That's what made it so special."

Chuck Welsh: *"I feel fortunate to have been a part of something so much bigger than what school you're at or what your job is. There is a community of coaches and players. I'm humbled by the opportunity to have been associated with and to have been around really,*

really giants of the game. George Conti, Bob Generelli, Al Saner . . . I could tick off a bunch if I had the time to think about it. Just the tradition—you felt like you were part of something special, that had been going on for quite some time. I don't think I've seen anything like that, anywhere else I've been. It was my privilege to have been part of that, something I'll cherish forever."

Chris Barnes: *"I think back to being a kid on those quiet, hot summer nights, daydreaming of playing football and baseball and sports in the Shore Conference, and competing and wanting to be your very best, and being a part of that as a student-athlete growing up, and then coming back as a teacher, a coach, and an educator. I'd have to say at this point that a lot of dreams were fulfilled, and aspirations of where I wanted to be and what I wanted to do . . . being a part of that, that's just special. It's just a thrill, it's just an absolutely thrill. It's been a great ride, a great experience.*

I've got one daughter with eleven varsity letters, and I've got another who just finished Division I lacrosse at Duquesne University. They're part of the Shore Conference. My wife is an athletic trainer, and together we've explained to them the history of the Shore Conference, and all that's involved. To be a part of that is special. My own family has experience in that now, as much as all the players I was fortunate enough to coach."

Steve Sciarappa: *"I love the Shore Conference, because for all the pageantry that the big names have in the Shore Conference, there's still the fringe. It's so big that you can be who you want to be, or who you are, and still have a place in the Shore Conference. Everywhere you go in the Shore, there's a certain sense of continuity. You know what you're getting any time.*

The crowds will be fun, but they're not going to cross a line of negativity. The games will be really, really well coached and really,

really well played. And it's a bunch of overachievers. It's forty-something schools that are probably overachieving, relative to their talent levels in the rest of the world. As a coach, I came out of that. I didn't know any better. I thought everybody had to work this hard. I thought everybody did the right things on game days and handled themselves professionally. It really means a lot.

Growing up with the Asbury Park Press, the Ocean County Observer, and a couple of local things, every high school had their own beat writer. Every high school had their own box score. It really, really mattered. I couldn't tell you much about the NFL back then. . . . But shoot, man, I had the whole box score from the Ocean–Neptune game. It was awesome, it was a really, really fun thing to grow up and play in. I hope the kids have the same fun today, because it was a lot of fun for us. And I say to a lot of kids today, when you look at what high school sports are supposed to be, take a good look at the Shore Conference."

Although this history of the Shore Conference is coming to a close, the history of the league itself is far from over. Every August, a new crop of rising freshmen snaps on their football helmets for the first time. Like generations of athletes before them, they are discovering a very special world, and in their own way they will leave their mark on the Shore Conference for generations to come. Soon, they'll be telling stories of their own.

ENDNOTES

Newspaper articles from the *Asbury Park Press* are listed by name and date only. Newspaper articles from other papers specify the paper in which they were found.

CHAPTER 1

1   Neptune Seeks Gridiron Dates, p. 16, 2/10/36

2   Group 2 Athletic Authorities Organize Shore Sports Conference, p. 14, 2/11/36

3   "Interview With Phillip May," Monmouth County Library System, Last Modified September 6, 2001, http://www.visitmonmouth.com/oralhistory/bios/MayPhilip.htm.

4   Neptune Protests Two Local Gridiron Players, p. 1, 11/22/28

5   Daniel Wolff, *4th of July Asbury Park,* (New York: Bloomsbury Publishing, 2005), 79.

6   "Interview With Thomas Smith," Monmouth County Library System, last modified May 4, 2001, http://www.visitmonmouth.com/oralhistory/bios/SmithThomas.htm.

7   Classes Resumed at Shore Schools, p. 1, 9/9/1946, and Board Studies Segregation, p. 3, 4/13/1946

8   Wolff 81

9   Towns Joined By the God of the Sea, p. 62, 1/17/2002

10 Neptune Scored by Kraybill For Protest, p. 1, 11/27/28, Asbury Squad Forfeits All Rights to State Honors, p. 16, 11/28/28, and Asbury Bows to Neptune Eleven, p. 1, 11/30/28

11 Flora Higgins, *Remembering the 20th Century: An Oral History of Monmouth County* (Monmouth County, NJ: Monmouth County Library, 2002) 36.

12 "Interview With Daniel Dorn," Monmouth County Library System, last modified August 30, 2001, http://www.visitmonmouth.com/oralhistory/bios/DornDaniel.htm.

13 Federal Writers' Project, *The WPA Guide to New Jersey* (San Antonio: Trinity University Press, 2013), 679 and Randall Gabrielan, *Rumson: Shaping A Superlative Suburb* (Charleston: Arcadia Publishing, 2003) 84

14 Gabrielan 150

15 Muriel J. Smith, "Atlantic's First Library and School," AHHerald.com, https://www.ahherald.com/columns-list/history-and-happenings/23058-atlantic-s-first-library-and-school, Federal Writers' Project 676,

and Jack Jeandron, *Keyport: From Plantation to Center of Commerce and Industry* (Charleston: Arcadia Publishing, 2003). 134

16   Federal Writers' Project 592

17   "History," Middletown Township, accessed May 22, 2021, https://www.middletownnj.org/249/History and 721 Pupils Enrolled From Wide Area, p. 13, 12/19/1938

18   Around Matawan and Aberdeen, p. 7 and Matawan 1686-1936, p. 5 and 8

19   Federal Writers' Project 250-55.

20   Mozeleski Ready to Give Up Hope For Freehold High, p. 18, 9/26/40

21   Federal Writers' Project, 556

22   Federal Writers' Project, 605-607

23   Federal Writers' Project, 672

24   Federal Writers' Project, 585 and 694

CHAPTER 2

1   Tice is Victor in Mound Duel, p. 10, 6/20/1936

2   Asbury Park Opens Scholastic Grid Season, p. 16, 9/25/1936

3   Bishops Are Outplayed in Final Grid Contest, p. 20, 11/27/36

4   Henry is Star In Banker Win, 11/27/36, p. 20

5   Sports Angles, p. 14, 9/21/36, Sports Angles, p. 14, 9/22/36, and Sports Angles, p. 18, 9/18/1936

6   Sports Angles, p. 12, 9/15/36 and Sports Angles, p. 15, 11/16/36

7   Piners Defeat Indian 11, p. 20, 11/27/36

8   Vetrano's Touchdown Dash, p. 11, 9/25/37 and Vetrano Leads Fliers to Second Nocturnal Win, p. 11, 10/2/37

9   Vetrano, Smith Suspended Indefinitely From Neptune Grid Squad, 10/6/37, p. 15

10   Piners Upset Favored Team Under Lights, p. 16, 10/9/37

11   3,500 Witness Bayshore Tilt, p. 18, 11/12/37

12   Piner Fumble Brings Score, p. 12, 11/26/37

13   Meinert Says Team is Thru For Year, p. 14, 12/2/37

14   Vetrano Thrills Crowd With Touchdown Dashes, p. 13, 10/30/37

15   Vetrano Stars As Fliers Top County Rivals, p. 13, 11/7/37

16   Long Branch Stages Rally To Whip Asbury Park, 12-7, p. 1, 12/5/37

17   75 Yard March Brings Victory, p. 10, 11/6/38

18   Neptune Shades Red Bank, 10-7, and Ends Season Undefeated, p. 8, 11/13/38

19   Atlantic Highlands Beats Leonardo, 7-0, For
     First Time Since 1923, p. 11, 11/12/38

20   Indians Topple Truex Machine, p. 10, 11/20/38

21   Toms River Jolts Lakewood, 12-0, To Win Shore, p. 17, 11/25/38

22   6,000 To See All-Star Grid Contest Today, p. 1, 12/3/38
     and All-Stars Tie in Spectacular Game, p. 1, 12/4/38

CHAPTER 3

1   David Kennedy, *Freedom From Fear: The American People in Depression
     and War* (New York: Oxford University Press, 1999), 434, 446, and 476.

2   Jay Price, Oral History Interview Conducted by Author

3   Snappy Game Here Thursday, p. 1, 11/22/1935, Manasquan Coast Star

4   Manasquan Smothers Point Pleasant, p. 18, 11/29/1935

5   Four Gridders Share Scoring, p. 19, 11/26/37
     and Sports Angles, p. 13, 1/29/1950

6   Sports Angles, p. 13, 1/29/1950

7   New Attitude May Swing the Tide in Favor
     of 'Squan This Year, 9/21/39, p. 20

8   Brevoort Star For Manasquan In League Tilt, p. 16, 10/5/39

9   Blue And Gray Aerial Assault Repel Indians, p. 8, 10/15/39

10   Campbell's Dazzling Run Decides Bitter Struggle, p. 8, 10/21/39

11   This year's Manasquan-Point Pleasant game wasn't actually played on
     Thanksgiving. The holiday *should* have fallen on November 30th, but in
     order to promote a longer Christmas shopping season, President Franklin
     Roosevelt had the holiday moved to November 23rd. To keep things
     simple, the Warriors simply moved their game with the Freehold up to
     Thanksgiving, and their game with the Gulls to the following Saturday.

12   Thompson Set Bar High for Warrior Football,
     p. 65, 5/29/2008, Coast Star

13   Dodgers Sign Brevoort, p. 10, 7/23/1940

14   Manasquan's Aerial Attack Routs Neptune, p. 8, 10/19/40
     and Campbell, Moore, Deter Are Stars, p. 9, 10/27/40

15   Big Blue Led By Kurilchyk and Campbell, p. 10, 11/17/40
     and Manasquan Routs Point Pleasant, p. 18, 11/22/40

16   Gil Augustine Resigns Post, p. 8, 4/12/1939, Long
     Branch Daily Record and Middletown Fights Request
     to Switch Highlands Pupils, p. 3, 10/11/1938

17   Atlantic Highlands Loses Truex and Its Bayshore
     Rivals Make a Gain, p. 10, 5/2/1939

18   Jack McCallum, "A Hero for All Time," *Sports Illustrated* January 7, 1980.

19 Hefty Leonardo 11 Ready for RB, p. 16, 9/7/1940, Red Bank Daily Standard and Leon's Powerful, p. 15, 9/23/1940, Red Bank Daily Standard

20 Leonardo Stops Drive From Foot To Goal To Conquer Red Bank, p. 9, 9/30/40

21 Leonardo Eleven Rolls Over Keyport, p. 8, 11/10/40 and Leonardo Turns Back Atlantic Highlands p. 9, 11/17/40

22 "How the RFH Bulldogs Got Their Name," Two River Times, March 8-15, 2018

23 2,000 See Rumson Eleven Overpower Neptune, 15-6, 9/28/40, p. 8

24 Plunge By Mellaci Caps Drive in Fourth Period, p. 9, 11/10/40

25 Bolger Scores Twice, Purple Held in Check, p. 18, 11/22/40

26 500 Wildly Cheering Fans Welcome Leonardo Squad, p. 5, 11/23/1940, Red Bank Daily Standard

27 Manasquan's Streak is Broken, p. 9, 10/12/41

28 Toms River Comes From Behind to End Leonardo's Streak, p. 11, 11/2/41

29 Two Letters About the Sports Situation At Lakewood, p. 8, 11/6/43, Spectators Clash As Lakewood Overwhelms Manasquan, p. 8, 10/26/41, and Red Bank-Lakewood Is A Natural, But They Won't Play, p. 8, 10/25/43

30 Spectators Clash As Lakewood Overwhelms Manasquan, p. 8, 10/26/41

31 Sica Nearly Breaks Away on Final Play of Contest, p. 19, 11/21/41

32 Lakewood Moves to Withdraw From Shore Conference, p. 10, 11/26/41 and Lakewood to Ask Conference Quota of Grid Games, p. 8, 11/29/41

33 Jack Netcher Athletic Director Now at High Point College, p. 17, 10/6/1957

34 All-Monmouth Ocean, p. 10, 12/7/1941

35 Netcher Sparkles Again, p. 8, 9/29/40 and Asbury Park Beats Jefferson On Long Runs, p. 8, 10/5/40

36 Fourth Straight Victory Strengthens Title Hopes, p. 8, 10/13/40

37 Netcher Scores 26 Points As Asbury Park Crushes Red Bank, p. 8, 10/27/40

38 Asbury Park Overpowers Long Branch, 21 to 0, Before 7,000, p. 8, 11/17/40

39 Asbury Park Crushes New Brunswick, 19 to 0, p. 17, 11/22/40

40 Smith Sends Bishops Through Workout, p. 10, 9/3/1941

41 Asbury Park, Camden Gain, p. 18, 3/15/1941, Passaic Herald-News and Asbury Park Defeats West New York, p. 1, 3/23/1941

42 Asbury Park, Phillipsburg Play to Scoreless Tie in Steady Rain, p. 11, 11/2/41

43   Asbury Park Hit By Injuries in 25-0 Win
     Over Long Branch, p. 9, 11/16/41

44   Bishops Bitter Over Tie Game and Asbury Park and New
     Brunswick Play Scoreless Tie, p. 21, 11/21/1941

45   Netcher Captures Batting Title, p. 10, 6/10/1942

46   Word from Camp Wheeler, p. 20, 4/16/1943

47   Netcher is Signed by Senators, p. 8, 8/25/1946

48   Jack Netcher Athletic Director at High Point College, p. 17, 10/6/1957

49   Maroon May Account For Its Lack of Material
     In Sheer Courage, p. 10, 9/16/39\

50   Red Bank Crushes Neptune, p. 9, 11/19/39

51   Red Bank Eleven Conquers Long Branch, p. 8, 11/25/39

CHAPTER 4

1   Kennedy 522 and 617

2   Kennedy 634-35

3   Kennedy 618-619 and 655

4   Kennedy 645-46

5   Kennedy 748

CHAPTER 5

1   Loss is Bishops First On Gridiron Since '39, p. 8, 10/4/42

2   Vetrano Leads Bishops To 20-7 Win Over
    Newark East Side, p. 16, 11/27/42

3   Pete Vetrano Will Know Soon If He Can Play Again,
    p. 8, 2/11/1946 and Petey Vet, H10, 11/13/1988

4   Asbury Park Downs Neptune in Series Renewal, p. 8, 11/21/43

CHAPTER 6

1   The Piners Are Still the Class of the Conference, p.
    10, 9/23/1942 and Truex Expects Another So-So
    Grid Season, So Watch Out, p. 16, 9/25/1942

2   Lions Trounce Rumson Eleven By 53-0 Count, p. 17, 11/27/42

3   Moore, J. Royle Score All Piner Touchdowns, p. 10, 10/11/42,
    Piners Hurl Powerful Attack In First Period, p. 11, 10/25/42, and
    Piners' Scoring Splurge Crushes Freehold, 32-0, p. 9, 11/1/42

4   Football Fans Still Want a Leonardo-Lakewood Tilt, p. 8, 11/28/1942

5   Coach At Lakehurst Tackles Big Job on Gridiron, p. 12, 9/22/1943

6   Lakewood Allowed Conference Rating, p. 10, 9/21/1943

7   The Mail Brings Us News About Russ Wright, p. 10, 9/13/1943

8   Royle Stars As Piners Win, p. 8, 10/3/43 and Royle Scores 22 Points As Line Displays Power, p. 8, 10/10/43

9   Royle Stars As Piners Top Manasquan, 13-7, p. 8, 10/24/43

10   Lakewood Wins, 40 to 7; Royle Scores 26 points, p. 8, 11/26/43

11   Prospects Are Fair For Grid Eleven at Red Bank, p. 9, 9/27/1943

12   Red Bank Holds Big Blue Team to 6-6 Deadlock, p. 8, 10/3/43

13   Buccaneers Score Early To Break 21 Year Jinx, p. 8, 10/24/43 and Bucs Stage Major Upset, p. 7, 10/25/1943, Long Branch Daily Record, and Red Bank Triumphs, p. 8, 10/28/1943, Red Bank Register

14   Long Branch Scores, 13-0, Over Red Bank, p. 8, 11/26/43

15   Royle Set Grid Scoring Mark While At Lakewood, p. 43, 7/26/1964

16   Boxing Upsets Top Firemen's Ring Program, p. 7, 4/29/1944

17   8 Ex-GIs at Red Bank, p. 11, 10/9/1946 and Sports Angles, p. 10, 5/17/1944

18   Toms River Presents Strong Lineup, p. 16, 9/29/1944

19   Truex Lists Lion Starts, p. 7, 9/23/1944

20   Red Bank's Team Has Only Three Veterans, p. 9, 9/18/1944

21   Arnie Truex's Lions Come From Behind, p. 9, 10/24/44

22   Blocked Leonardo Kicks Decide Tilt, p. 12, 11/5/44

23   Red Bank Noses Out Branchers, p. 18, 11/24/44

24   Piners Hold Indians Down, Lose Only 7-0, p. 18, 11/24/44

CHAPTER 7

1   Holiday Crowds Called Biggest in Shore History, p. 1, 9/4/45

2   Gulls Register First Triumph in Three Seasons, p. 11, 10/25/42

3   Jimmy Egidio Goes to War, p. 9, 10/6/1943, Long Branch Daily Record

4   Golden Gulls of 1944-45, D1, 5/26/92

5   Golden Gulls of 1944-45, D1, 5/26/92

6   Garnet Gulls Score by 7-0, Defeat 'Squad, p. 18, 11/24/44

7   Indian Eleven Looks Good, p. 9, 9/22/1945

8   Asbury Park Swamps Lakewood, p. 12, 9/30/45 and Manasquan Scores in Win Over Red Bank, p. 12, 10/7/45

9   Manasquan's Final Period Try Fails As Toms River Ekes Out 7-6 Score, p. 10, 10/14/45

10   Pointers Snap 14-14 Deadlock to Win 20-14, p. 12, 10/21/45

11 Golden Gulls of 1944-45, D1, 5/26/92

12 Pointers Squeeze past Matawan, p. 12, 11/18/45

13 Point Pleasant Ties Manasquan, p. 19, 11/23/45

14 Fifty Years Later, They Honor a Great Team, Coach, H11,9/17/95

15 Golden Gulls of 1944-45, D1, 5/26/92

16 Sica Top Gridder, p. 58, 11/1/1970

CHAPTER 8

1 Matawan Downs Battling Keyport, p. 10, 11/24/1939

2 Fragasso's Touchdown Gives Keyport 6-0 Win, p. 17, 11/27/42

3 Matawan Tops Keyport, 6 to 0, Team Unbeaten, p. 8, 11/26/43

CHAPTER 9

1 Sports Angles, p. 25, 11/11/54

2 St. Rose Takes Final Game Over Queen of Peace, p. 9, 11/17/40

3 Viracola Scores Three As Branchers Whip Asbury Park, p. 12, 11/18/45
and Viracola, Acerra Shine in Brancher Victory, p. 19, 11/23/45

4 Turkey Day Game at Lakewood Park, p. 16, 11/16/45

5 Asbury Park Crushes New Brunswick, 19 to 0, p. 17, 11/22/40

6 New Era in Football Career of Butch Bruno, p. 10, 9/28/46

7 Bishops Come From Behind to Conquer Branchers, p. 15, 11/14/48

8 Elliott Denman, C5, 6/30/81

9 Joseph Bilby and Harry Ziegler, *Asbury Park: A Brief History*
(Charleston: Arcadia Publishing, 2009), 99 and 101

10 Wolff 149

11 Asbury Park Bows To Garfield, p. 10, 9/29/46

12 Asbury Park Scores Convincing Win Over Long Branch, p. 11, 11/17/46

13 Asbury Park Overpowers Long Branch in 42nd Contest, p. 9, 11/16/47

14 Bruno to Resign as Football Coach of Asbury
Park High School, p. 17, 11/27/48

15 Seven Holdovers at Long Branch, p. 15, 9/2/48.

16 Bishops Come From Behind to Conquer Branchers, p. 15, 11/14/48

CHAPTER 10

1 Leonardo Nips Lakewood in Bruising Shore
Conference Tilt, p. 10, 10/13/46

2   "Granville Magee," Manasquan High School, http://www.
    manasquanschools.org/Page/231, accessed May 22, 2021, and "The
    Officers Club at Fort Niagara State Park," http://info-poland.buffalo.
    edu/exhib/murals/themes/POW.html, accessed May 21, 2021.

3   "Alfred Morgan," Manasquan High School, http://www.
    manasquanschools.org/Page/232, accessed May 22, 2021.

4   Morgan's Kick Decides Battle in 4th Quarter, p. 9, 11/3/46

5   Manasquan Rallies to Top Piners, p. 9, 11/2/47

6   Game Reunion Planned, G36, 10/1/97. McIntyre also led the basketball
    team in scoring and was the ace pitcher for the baseball team.

7   Manasquan Edges Point Pleasant, p. 25, 11/28/47

8   Leonardo Belts Tigers, Wins Shore, p. 15, 11/21/48.

9   Sports Angles, p. 13, 10/20/48 and Sports Angles, p. 14, 10/2/49

10 Pagano 'Fires' Six Players on Eve of Asbury Park Game, p. 16, 11/27/46

11 Neptune Loses DeMidowitz, p. 19, 9/18/47, Sports Angles, p. 9, 10/27/47

12 Scarlet Fliers Throw Passes to Beat Lions, p. 9, 11/2/47
    and Neptune Wallops Red Bank, p. 9, 11/16/47

13 Neptune Scores "Upset" Over Asbury Park, p. 25, 11/28/47

14 Neptune Wins Out Over Leonardo in Last-
    Minute Thriller, p. 15,10/30/49

15 Scarlet Fliers Notch 8th, Clinch CJ Title, p. 25, 11/25/49

CHAPTER 11

1   Bishops Run Roughshod Over Long Branch, p. 17, 11/13/49

2   Coach Builds Around Pair of Ace Backs, p. 12, 9/17/51

3   Green Wave Braves Late Aerial Flurry, p. 24, 11/6/51

4   Long Branch Downs Asbury Park, p. 1, 11/11/51

5   Exodus Marks End of Shore Resort Season, p. 1. 9/5/50 and
    The WPA Guide to 1930s New Jersey, p. 250-254

6   Freehold Played Key Role, p. 86, 11/17/54 and "Interview With Barclay
    Carroll," Monmouth County Library, last modified August 9, 2001,
    http://www.visitmonmouth.com/oralhistory/bios/BarclayCarroll.html.

7   Mozeleski Ready to Give Up Hope For Freehold High, p. 18, 9/26/40

8   Russell Nails Down Job, p. 20, 9/13/49 and Scarlet Fliers
    Notch 8th, Clinch CJ Title, p. 25, 11/25/49

9   Van Note Loss Hurts Colonial Chances, p. 27, 9/22/50

10 Freehold Drubs Frenchtown, p. 14, 9/24/50

11 Colonials Rip Unbeaten Foe in Sharp Tilt, p. 13, 10/29/50

12   James T. Patterson, *Grand Expectations: The United States 1945-74* (New York: Oxford University Press, 1996) 221.

13   Patterson 232

14   Patterson 186-205

15   Patterson 236-38

16   Indians Whoop War Call in Celebration, p. 15, 10/28/51, Indians Survive Late Lion Passing Attack, p. 17, 11/7/51, and Four Indians Share Scoring in Finale, p. 32, 11/23/51

17   Piner Eleven is Impressive Under Lights, p. 12, 9/24/49.

18   Worried Wright Makes Changes, p. 20, 9/13/49

19   Lakewood's Football Outlook Darkest in Two Decades, p. 16, 9/17/50

20   Big Blue Squad Romps Against Piners, p. 16, 10/28/51 and Keyport Raps Piners, p. 15, 10/26/52

21   Lakewood Upsets Toms River 11 For First Victory in 22 Games, p. 33, 11/28/52

22   Bayshore Field Is Dedicated, p. 1, 10/2/49

23   Sports Angles, p. 14, 9/19/53

24   Tigers Beat Allentown, p. 13, 10/10/54

25   Then and Now, D1, 11/18/2000

26   Sports Angles, p. 17, 11/2/55

27   Point Pleasant Plays Tie At Ocean City, p. 12, 10/2/49 and Freehold Bows to Powerful Attack, p. 16, 11/6/49

28   Johnson Paces Gulls to Win Over Blue, p. 30, 11/24/50

29   Matawan Victim of Sayreville, p. 7, 11/7/46, Matawan Journal, and Lauer Making Runaway of Scoring Race, 10/25/48. Both were multi-sport stars.

30   Matawan Defeats Sayreville, p. 6, 11/4/48, Matawan Journal, and Matawan Rips Keyport, p. 22, 11/26/48, Star Ledger

31   "Interview With George Jones," Monmouth County Library, last modified on July 17, 2001, http://www.visitmonmouth.com/oralhistory/bios/JonesGeorge.htm

32   RBC Football Players Served 3-Course Meal, p. 9, 10/11/47 and Caseys Defeat Trinity, p. 10, 11/9/46.

33   Red Bank Catholic Building for Future, p. 20, 10/4/46

34   Caseys Topple St. Mary's, 6-0, p. 10, 10/21/46, and Caseys Net Touchdown in First Period, p. 10, 10/26/47

35   Red Bank Catholic, Rumson, Play Scoreless Draw—Both Threaten, p. 10, 11/16/47

36   Sports Angles, p. 13, 11/2/48

37   Sports Angles, p. 13, 11/2/48, Caseys Beaten By Trenton Catholic, p.

14, 10/31/48 and Rumson's Rountree Routs Caseys, p. 16, 11/14/48

CHAPTER 12

1   Joe Valenti, Oral history Interview conducted by author

2   Bill Bruno, Oral History Interview Conducted by Author

3   Letter From Asa Hall, Litchfield Connecticut, published
     on "What Exit? New Jersey and Its Turnpike," Driving
     It: Voices From the Road, http://www.jerseyhistory.org/
     what_exit/d-15.html, accessed on February 18, 2016

4   Bruno Recovers Fumble Scores in Last Minute, p. 10, 10/4/52 and
     Blue Bishops Continue to Win ON the Road, p. 17, 11/2/52

5   Plainfield Edges Bishops, 7-2, p. 15, 10/26/52 and Olympic Star
     Has 14 Points in 33-13 Win, p. 11, 9/28/52. Campbell was one of
     the greatest all-around athletes to ever come through New Jersey.
     In addition to starring in track and football at Plainfield, he was
     an All-American swimmer. He is currently the only man to be
     a member of both the Track and Swimming Hall of Fames.

6   Green Wave Wins 3rd Straight By Lambasting
     Linden's Tigers, p. 17, 10/19/52

7   Army Ippolito Taught Realities of Football, Life, D6, 7/6/80

8   Army Ippolito Taught Realities of Football, Life, D6, 7/6/80

9   Green Wave Players End Bricktown Streak, p. 16, 10/26/52

10   Asbury Park Defeats Long Branch in Rain, Mud, p. 17, 11/16/52

11   Long Branch Downs Red Bank Before 3,500 Fans, p. 33, 11/28/52

12   Same Grid Titans Rule School Roost, p.85,
     9/20/53, Newark Evening News

13   Asbury Park Romps to Easy Victory, p. 13, 10/4/53

14   Asbury Park Comes From Behind, p. 17, 10/11/53,
     and Asbury Park Blasts Cards, p. 13, 10/25/53

15   Bishops Rout Rivals in Grid Tussle, p. 15, 11/15/53

16   Asbury Park Ends Season Undefeated, Tops Barons, p. 29, 11/27/53

17   New Brunswick Upsets Asbury Park in Season Opener, p. 1, 10/2/54

18   Green Wave Tramples Bucs in Finale, p. 21, 11/26/54

19   Hard-Pressed Bishops Defeat Long Branch, p. 15, 11/14/54

20   Green Wave Tramples Bucs in Finale, p. 21, 11/26/54

21   Green Wave Has Same Potential As Championship
     Team of 1951, p. 20, 9/12/55

22   Defense vs. Offense Underlying Argument, p. 22, 11/11/55

23   Long Branch and Asbury Park Tie in Bruising Contest, p. 22, 11/11/55

24 Asbury Park Battles Woodbridge to 6-6 Deadlock, p. 15, 11/20/55 and Steckbeck Sets Pace as Bishops Beat Middletown, p. 31, 11/25/55

25 Red Bank's Linemen Surprise Green Wave, p. 10, 12/1/55, RBR

26 Big Oaks and Little Acorns, p. 12, 1/23/56 and Sports Angles, p. 14, 6/13/60

27 Bobo Reeves A Long Branch Legend, C1, 10/28/88

28 "Sprinter's World Record Legacy Lives on at the Frank Budd Meet," NJ.com, Advance Local Media, http://www.nj.com/ledger-dalessandro/index.ssf/2013/07/sprinters_world-record_legacy_lives_on_at_the_annual_frank_budd_track_meet_at_asbury_park_hs.html and "Asbury Park Track and Field Legend Frank Budd Dies at 54," NJ.com, Advance Local Media, http://www.nj.com/sports/index.ssf/2014/05/asbury_park_track_and_field_legend_frank_budd_dies_at_74.html. Some sources incorrectly state that Budd suffered from polio, but he always insisted this was untrue.

29 A Lasting Legacy, C3, 5/1/2014

30 Bill Bruno, Oral History Interview Conducted by Author

31 Bruno and Budd Lead Bishops to Win, p. 17, 9/23/56 and Bishops Snap Zebra Jinx with Arclight Win, p. 12, 9/29/56

32 David Slays Goliath, p. 1, 11/11/59

33 Bruno, Budd Spark Bishops to Victory, p. 15, 11/11/56

34 Asbury Park's Perfect Play Wins, p. 26, 11/23/56 and Asbury Park Halts Woodbridge, Budd Races 73 yards for One Score, p. 17, 11/18/56

35 Long Branch Blanks Bucs, Reeves Sets Record p. 26, 11/23/56

36 Patterson 257-61

37 You've Got to Give the Guy Credit, p. 8, 11/3/49, Matawan Journal

38 Outlook Not Bright, Lions May Still Roar, p. 22, 9/12/52

39 Crowded Conditions at Freehold Regional, Asbury Park Press School News, 10/4/54

40 Asbury Park and Freehold Renew Rivalry Tomorrow, p. 32, 11/4/55

41 Freehold Regional's Grid Team Can Boast Unusual Locker Room, p. 21, 11/3/55

42 Looking It Over, p. 6, Second Section, *Matawan Journal*

43 Tribute Planned for Schank, H9, 5/19/91

44 Tim Morris, "Mayes, Freeman Enter Borough's Athletic Hall," *News Transcript*, http://nt.gmnews.com/news/2000-06-21/Sports/sp02.html. Accessed September 1, 2015.

45 Well-Deserved Honors, D1, 5/5/99

46 Sports Angles, p. 12, 10/24/53

47 Freehold Tops Middletown, p. 13, 10/25/53

48   "Mayes, Freeman Enter Borough's Athletic Hall," News Transcript,

49   See Overflow Crowd for Game of the Year, p. 24, 11/13/53

50   "Mayes, Freeman Enter Borough's Athletic Hall," News Transcript, Both fast and strong, Freeman was an All-Shore basketball player and a championship hurdler, setting league records in both the high and low events.

51   Title Bound Colonial Eleven Scores, p. 15, 11/15/53

52   Freehold Wins Shore Conference, Lewis Smashes Record, p. 23, 11/27/53

53   "Danny Lewis," NJSports.com, Upper Case Editorial Services, accessed June 28, 2021, http://www.njsportsheroes.com/dannylewisfb.html.

54   Colonials Rebuild for Defense of Class A, Central Jersey Titles, p. 24, 9/24/54 and Freehold Conquers Hard Fighting Point Pleasant, p. 16, 9/26/54

55   Freehold Wins, Unbeaten String at 16, p. 15, 11/21/54. Lakewood had tied for the title in both 1941 and 1942.

56   David Halberstam, *The Fifties* (New York: Villard Books, 1993), 55.

57   Fort Monmouth Integral Part of Shore Economy, p. 90, 11/17/54

58   Probe of Security at Monmouth Set, p. 1, 10/8/53

59   McCarthy Hunting Expedition Still Haunts Fort Monmouth, F1, 11/18/73

60   Bob Glisson Played in All 33 Delaware Grid Victories, p. 36, 10/13/63. Although he played at Delaware, Glisson's offensive system was apparently not related to the later, better-known Delaware Wing-T.

61   Red Bank Studded With Veterans Who Know Glisson's Winged-T, p. 27, 9/9/55

62   NJSIAA Says Nixon Ineligible, Wed Students Face New Curbs, p. 1, 7/12/55

63   Short Denies Ruling Nixon Ineligible, p. 1, 7/15/55

64   Shore Conference Suspends Freehold Regional For 1955-56, Red Bank Register 10/20/55, p. 10

65   Colonials Rebuild for Defense of Class A, Central Jersey Titles, p. 24, 9/24/54.

66   Freehold Trenton Play to Tie, p. 17, 9/25/55

67   Red Bank Beats Lions, p. 15, 10/16/55

68   Spotting Sports, Red Bank Register p. 8, 11/8/55

69   Sports Angles, p. 18, 11/7/55

70   Colonials Clout Fliers, p. 33, 11/25/55,

71   Freehold Regional, Perennial Powerhouse, p. 16, 9/19/56

72   Red Bank Looks to A Banner Season, p. 13, 9/17/56 and

Scotti's Aerials Beat Middletown, p. 15, 10/14/56

73   6,000 Watch Bucs Trip Caseys, p. 17, 9/23/56

74   Stanford at Full Paces Colonial Win, p. 15, 10/28/56

75   Freehold Shells Neptune as Carter Romps, p. 27, 11/23/56

76   Garnet Gulls Trim Rumson, Take Group I Title, p. 18, 11/9/52

77   Nuccio's Marvel-ous Husky 11 Headed for 2nd Group I Crown, p. 28, 9/22/53.

78   Matawan Clinches Title, p. 30, 11/27/53. Marvel was a star in more than just football. He was also the ace pitcher on the Huskie baseball teams, which won the B Division title in both 1953 and 1954.

79   Matawan Insures Group I Title With Victory Over Keyport, p. 23, 11/26/54

80   Keyport Team is Solid; 12 Lettermen Back, p. 20, 9/14/55

81   Fedele Leads Matawan to Win Over Keyport, p. 32, 11/25/55

82   Keyport Outscores Garnet Gulls, p. 6, 10/18/56, Matawan Journal

83   Unbeaten Keyport Nips Tigers, 14-0, p. 26, 11/23/56 and Looking It Over, p. 6, 11/29/56, Matawan Journal

84   Huskies Look for Good Year p. 24, 9/27/56 and Point Pleasant Felled, p. 6, 10/11/56, Matawan Journal

85   Rob Edelman, "Snuffy Stirnweiss," Society of American Baseball Researchers, http://sabr.org/bioproj/person/fdca74a3 and "George H. Stirnweiss," Fordham Preparatory School, http://www.fordhamprep.org/page.cfm?p=4861.

86   The Boys of Winter, C1, 3/22/2015.

87   Rob Edelman, "Snuffy Stirnweiss," Society of American Baseball Researchers.

88   Caseys Build on 19 Lettermen, p. 25, 9/24/53. Saxenmeyer was one of RBC's first great athletes, scoring 1,000 points on the basketball court. He later played basketball at St. Peter's College.

89   Red Bank Catholic Defeats Red Bank, p. 19, 9/27/53

90   Caseys Stage Rally to Tie Trenton Catholic, p. 14, 11/9/53

91   Rob Edelman, "Snuffy Stirnweiss," Society of American Baseball Researchers.

92   Bolger Coaching Caseys, p. 28, 9/23/54

93   Public School Miscues Lead to Trouncing, p. 15, 9/26/54

94   Rob Edelman, "Snuffy Stirnweiss," Society of American Baseball Researchers.

95   Asbury Park's Perfect Play Wins, p. 26, 11/23/56

96   The High School Crisis, p. 8, 10/6/57

97   Asbury Park Scores Win over New Brunswick, p. 13, 10/6/57

98   Bishops in Conference Seen as Aid to Gate, p. 23, 11/10/55

99   Only 5 of 89 Freehold Grid Candidates Lettermen, p. 19, 9/6/57

100   Freehold Falls in Upset, p. 13, 10/27/57

101   Asbury Park Scores Win over New Brunswick, p. 13, 10/6/57
      and Asbury Park Beats Manasquan, p. 13, 9/29/57

102   Asbury Park Grinds out Win over Neptune, p. 13, 10/20/57

103   Asbury Park Buries Red Bank, p. 13, 10/27/57

104   Unbeaten Asbury Park Gridders Outscore Long Branch, p. 1, 11/17/57

105   Middletown Stops Long Branch, p. 12, 11/23/57

106   Middletown Beats Asbury Park to Win A Title, 11/29/57, p. 35

107   Shore Conference Accepts Three More High
      Schools, 12/5/57, Red Bank Register

CHAPTER 13

1   Bilby and Ziegler 106

2   Wolff 174-75

3   Bilby and Ziegler 106

4   Asbury Park Police Arrest Five Students p. 1, 9/21/56 and
      High School Trouble Over, Lembke Feels, p. 1, 9/22/56

5   Freehold Ends Sports Tie With Asbury Park, p. 1, 11/14/61.

6   Long Branch Takes the Big Game, p. 1, 11/12/61 and
      Wave Overcomes Early Deficit, p. 29, 11/12/61

7   Sports Angles, p. 15, 11/16/59

8   Sports Angles, p. 33, 10/18/61. Just a few years earlier, the *Asbury
      Park Press* had lambasted the practice of "overcoaching" players.
      "It would be wise to just let coaching staffs attend huddles to save
      time," the *Press* said. "Or maybe just let the coaches play because
      they obviously don't feel that it is important for the boys to learn
      how to make their own decisions." Sports Angles p. 13, 10/8/56

9   Asbury Park Buries Neptune, p. 17, 10/18/59
      and Bishops Top Bucs, p. 21, 10/27/59

10   Long Branch Wins, p. 17, 11/15/59 and Long Branch
      Whips Red Bank, 40 to 0, p. 37, 11/27/59.

11   Red Bank's Champs Targets For All p. 11, 9/2/61

12   Long Branch Banks on 15 Seniors, p. 26, 9/6/61

13   Asbury Romps, p. 21, 9/24/61, Asbury Nips Trenton, p. 35,
      10/1/61, Asbury Park Stops Union p. 35, 10/8/61

14 Long Branch's Fleet Backs Turn Back Neptune, p. 21, 9/24/61

15 Long Branch Makes Union Victim, p. 35, 10/15/61
and Long Branch Triumphs, p. 35, 10/22/61

16 Asbury Park Wins, p. 32, 11/5/61

17 Long Branch Banks on Phillips, Defense, p. 32, 11/9/61

18 Bishops Confident They'll Beat Wave, p. 31, 11/8/61

19 Joe Valenti, Oral History Interview Conducted by Author

20 Long Branch Takes the Big Game, p. 1, 11/12/61 and
Wave Overcomes Early Deficit, p. 29, 11/12/61

21 Wave's 1st Unblemished Grid Season, p. 47, 11/24/61

22 Bishop Ace Scores 3 in Final Game, p. 47, 11/24/61

23 Beverly's 2 TD Passes Win For Asbury Park, p. 33, 10/24/65

24 Bishops Celebrate Homecoming, p. 37, 11/21/65

25 Bruno Steps Down After 20 Years, p. 13, 11/27/65

26 Army Ippolito Taught Realities of Football, Life, D6, 7/6/80

27 Elliott Denman, C5, 6/30/81

CHAPTER 14

1 Miller, Pauline. *Ocean County Four Centuries in the Making* (Toms River, NJ: Ocean County Cultural and Heritage Commission, 2000), 304-305 and 536-537.

2 Patterson 75-76

3 Patterson 75 and 383

4 Patterson 384 and 399

5 Dover Farmer Not Egged On By Progress, A1, 9/19/87, and "Interview with Josef and Bea Bienstock," Monmouth County Library, last modified July 18, 2001, http://www.visitmonmouth.com/oralhistory/bios/BienstockBea.htm

6 The Farmer and Mirage, p. 21, 9/21/56

7 The Farmer and Mirage, p. 21, 9/21/56

8 Matawan Upset by Bayville Regional School, p. 6, 10/25/56, Matawan Journal

9 Central Nips Neptune, p. 13, 10/13/57 and Eagles Slam Rumson, p. 13, 11/3/57. Warren Wolf is usually given the credit for bringing this innovation to the Shore, but it would seem Boyd beat him by a year.

10 Central Defeats Stubborn Toms River, p. 14, 10/20/57 and Unbeaten Central Wins, p. 14, 10/27/57

11 Central Wins B Title, p. 17, 11/24/57

12 Matawan Runs Over Lambertville, p. 16, 9/28/58 and
    Matawan Tramples Point Pleasant, p. 22, 10/12/58

13 Peeler Scores 3 Times As Matawan Stuns Rumson, p. 20,
    10/19/58, Huskies Roll Over Central, p. 18, 10/28/58,
    and Matawan Rips Lakewood, p. 19, 11/2/58

14 Peeler Gets Lone Score in Win, p. 21, 11/28/58 and
    Matawan Holds Off Keyport, p. 18, Matawan Journal

15 Piners Lose as Len Morgan Stars, p. 16, 10/30/49, Big Blue
    Rips Through Freehold, p. 18, 11/13/49, and Manasquan
    Rolls Up 25 0 Count on Tigers, p. 16, 11/6/49

16 Sun Smiles on Holiday Crowd as Shore Traffic Hits Peak, p. 1, 9/7/54

17 Boy Dies of Polio, p. 1, 9/5/54 and Hines Fears
    Upswing in Shore Polio Rate, p. 1, 10/3/54

18 "Communities," Whatever Happened to Polio? Smithsonian
    National Museum of American History, http://amhistory.si.edu/
    polio/americanepi/communities.htm, accessed on June 28, 2021.

19 "Families," Whatever Happened to Polio? Smithsonian National
    Museum of American History, http://amhistory.si.edu/polio/
    americanepi/families.htm, last accessed on June 28, 2021

20 "Communities," Whatever Happened to Polio? Smithsonian
    National Museum of American History,

21 Polio Hits Manasquan Star, Game Postponed, p. 1, 10/21/54
    and 2nd Polio Case Closes Schools at Manasquan, p. 1,
    10/22/54 and Manasquan Tops Fliers, p. 15, 11/21/54

22 Sports Angles, p. 15, 11/8/54

23 Manasquan Tops Fliers, p. 15, 11/21/54

24 Tears of Heartbreak Shed After Manasquan Beats Gulls, p. 23, 11/26/54

25 The High School Crisis, p. 8, 10/6/57

26 Manasquan Nips Point Pleasant Before Crowd of 7,000, p. 31, 11/25/55.

27 Manasquan Power Wrecks Freehold, p. 18, 11/16/58
    and Sports Angles, p. 21, 11/18/59

28 Squan Football Has Long, Rich Tradition of Success, p.
    29, Coast Star Special Supplement, 9/27/2012

29 Manasquan Rolls to a Win Over Red Bank Catholic, p. 14, 11/3/57

30 Manasquan Stops Asbury Park, p. 15, 9/28/58

31 Manasquan Power Wrecks Freehold, p. 18, 11/16/58

32 Kenney Big Gun in 19-0 Victory, 11/28/58, p. 21

33 Athletic Play is Continued, p. 22, 10/14/59

34 Kubu Paces Manasquan, p. 38, 11/27/59

35 Bob Glisson Played in All 33 Delaware Grid Victories, p. 36, 10/13/63

36   Lincoln Air Attack Tops Bucs, p. 11, 10/1/60, 2
      Long Runs, Tight Defense Defeat Red Bank, p. 21,
      10/9/60, Red Bank Wins, p. 22, 10/16/60

37   Red Bank Defeats Freehold, p. 22, 10/30/60 and
      Red Bank 11 Takes Title, p. 22, 11/13/60

38   Wave-Bishop Game Could Decide Crown, p. 31, 11/9/60

39   Long Branch Continues Hex on Red Bank
      With 19-19 Tie p. 19, 11/25/60

40   Rosati: Forty-Three Years With Bulldogs, C6, 9/23/79, RBR

41   Rumson's Rountree Routs Caseys, p. 16, 11/14/48

42   Rumson Has 11 Holdovers, p. 20, 9/8/49

43   Leonardo Upset By Rumson, p. 27, 11/25/49

44   Rosati Must Build Rumson 11, p. 23, 9/17/53

45   Rosati Builds Team Around Four Veterans, p. 22, 9/25/56

46   Lewis Sets Scoring Record As Bulldogs Trounce Caseys, p. 36, 11/29/57

47   Quick Rumson Scores Down Caseys, p. 21, 11/28/58

48   Lines Stand Out As Red Bank Catholic, Rumson Tie, p. 37, 11/27/59

49   Lines Stand Out As Red Bank Catholic, Rumson Tie, p. 37, 11/27/59

50   Of those players, two would go on to play college football at a high level.
      Abbes would kick for Wagner's 1964 undefeated team, while Doc Corley
      play running back for the University of Virginia, lettering in 1965.

51   Caseys Rebuild Around 18 Vets, p. 28, 9/13/60 and Red Bank
      Catholic Pointing Toward Another Fine Season, p. 25, 9/8/861

52   Caseys Drub Red Bank in Air, p. 21, 9/25/60

53   Red Bank Catholic Triumphs, p. 21, 10/9/60, Caseys Score, p. 21, 11/6/60

54   Caseys Blank Rumson, p. 17, 11/25/60

CHAPTER 15

1   A Call Worked, Brick was Champ, p. 6, Section V, Star Ledger, 12/8/74,

2   Playoff Replay, D1, 11/17/88

3   Oral History Interview With Dan Duddy,
     6/25/2011, conducted by author

4   Playoff Replay, D1, 11/17/88

5   Right as Reign, D1, 9/26/98 and Route 549 Is Northern
     Ocean county's Main Street, D1, 10/21/73

6   Right as Reign, D1, 9/26/98

7   Oral History Interview With Al Saner, Conducted by Author

8   "The Death of A True Legend," Hudson Reporter http://

www.hudsonreporter.com/view/full_story/2379312/article-
The-death-of-a-true-legend-Coviello--long-time-grid-coach-
and-administrator--dies-at-88, accessed on May 7, 2018

9   Right as Reign, D1, 9/26/98 and Warren Wolf, *The History of Brick
    Township Football* (Outskirts Press: Denver, Colorado, 2012), 4.

10 New Faces in Shore Coaching Fraternity, p. 29, 9/11/69,
    Red Bank Register and Right as Reign, D1, 9/26/98

11 Warren Wolf Junior, Oral History Interview Conducted by Author

12 This description is drawn from Wolf's own account, found on Wolf, 5-6.

13 Patterson 28-29

14 Patterson 28-29

15 Wolf 20

16 Oral History Interview With Denny Toddings, Conducted by Author

17 Oral History Interview With Kevin Williams, Conducted by Author

18 Jeff Zillgitt, "The Wing-T Offense: Football's Shell Game," USA
    Today, http://usatoday30.usatoday.com/sports/preps/football/2007-
    08-16-wing-t-football_N.htm, accessed on June 28, 2021.

19 Oral History Interview with Dan Duddy, Conducted by Author.

20 Brick Tosses Scare at Indians, p. 24, 10/12/58

21 Riello Owes Everything to the Game of Football, D4, 9/24/05

22 Wolf, 22

23 Wolf 306

24 Late Central TDs Edge Brick, p. 22, 11/28/58

25 Brick Tops Matawan in Thriller, p. 18, 9/27/59

26 Richard Bonelli, Oral History Interview Conducted by Mike Bonelli

27 Brick Upsets Manasquan, p. 17, 10/4/59 and Toms River
    Recovers 7 Brick Fumbles in Win, p. 17, 10/11/59

28 Sayreville Out Logs Brick in Mud, p. 9, 11/7/59

29 Oral History Interview with Dan Duddy, conducted by author

30 *The Challenge* (Brick Township Yearbook) 1959 and 1960

31 Frosh Football is Long Developmental Process, p. 17, 10/16/73

32 Oral History Interview with Dan Duddy, conducted by author

33 Brick Crushes Matawan, p. 21, 9/25/60, Riello Scores 3,
    p. 21, 10/2/60 and 4 TDs By Riello, p. 21, 10/9/60

34 Dragons Defeat Central, p. 17, 11/25/60

35 *The Challenge 1961* 6

36 19th Straight Posted By Dragons, p. 29, 11/12/61

37   Riello Treasures Acclaim from Kids, p. 48, 12/7/61

38   Brick Ends 2nd Year Unbeaten, p. 47, 11/24/61

CHAPTER 16

1   Skip Edwards, Oral History Interview Conducted by Author

2   Truex Views Football's Changed Face, p. 18, 9/19/72, Red Bank Register

3   Kleva's Scuba Program A Success, F6, 12/15/74 and Emerald 1962 p. 111

4   Gary Foulks, Oral History Interview Conducted by Author

5   200 Welcome Vetrano Back to Neptune, p. 22, 9/22/60
     and Neptune Upsets Long Branch, p. 21, 9/25/60

6   ASD Board Confirms Allen Grid Post for Bednarik, Allentown Morning
     Call http://articles.mcall.com/1989-06-23/sports/2684446_1_vote-
     last-night-board-member-football-circles, Accessed on June 28, 2021

7   Signorino Comes Home Again, Toms River Patch, http://patch.com/new-
     jersey/tomsriver/signorino-comes-home-again, accessed on June 28, 2021

8   "Undefeated Bald Eagle Area Team Celebrates 50th Anniversary,"
     Centre Daily, http://www.centredaily.com/2013/10/11/3832655/
     football-undefeated-bald-eagle.html, accessed on June 28, 2021

9   Ron Signorino, Oral History Interview Conducted by Author

10   Indian Field Goal Edges Freehold, p. 42, 10/25/64

11   Ron Signorino, Oral History Interview Conducted by Author

12   Warren Wolf Junior, Oral History Interview Conducted by Author

13   Unbeaten Red Bank, Brick Gridders Tie, p. 33, 11/7/62

14   Oral History Interview With Joe Valenti, Conducted by Author

15   UVA Football Legend Ready to Join Elite Group,
     Virginia Sports, http://www.virginiasports.com/
     genrel/101510aaa.html, accessed on June 28, 2021

16   Neptune's Davis Starred Despite Problems With Strategy, D12, 9/28/91

17   Neptune's Bednarik is Optimistic, p. 31, 9/6/63

18   Wolf 266

19   Neptune Ends Brick String, p. 37, 10/27/63 and Neptune
     Line Beat Brick to Punch, p. 23, 10/29/63

20   Peter Jennings and Todd Brewster, *The Century*
     (London: Doubleday, 1999), 385.

21   Ex-Brick Athlete Killed in Vietnam, p. 1, 7/12/69

22   38th Clash Can Make, Break Year, p. 25, 11/26/63 and P. 23, 11/27/63

23   LeRoy Hayes, Oral History Interview Conducted By Author

24   Neptune's Last Play Score Downs Asbury Park, p. 41, 11/29/63

25   Hopkins' TDs Pace Neptune to 25-0 Win, p. 39, 9/27/64

26   The Best of the Rest, D13, 9/28/91

27   Middletown Prevails Over Neptune, p. 25, 10/4/64 and
      Middletown Overcomes Brick, p. 47, 10/11/64, Abdella Steers
      Middletown to Win in Last Seconds, p. 57, 11/15/64

28   Hopkins Scores Three Times As Neptune
      Beats Asbury Park, p. 39, 11/27/64

29   Fort Monmouth Integral Part of Shore Economy, p. 90,
      11/17/54 and Monmouth Humbles Brick, p. 35, 10/31/65

30   Tuck's Passing Spree Earns Monmouth 12-12 Tie, 11/7/65, p. 33

31   Warren Stars as Neptune Ruins Bruno's Finale, p. 49, 11/26/65

32   Central Hands Brick Licking in Wolf's Last Game, p. 49, 11/26/65

33   Top Season Claimed for Shore Area, p. 1, 9/7/66
      and Sully's Sports, p. 31, 11/17/66

34   Negro Grievances Heard By Neptune, p. 1, 10/5/66 and
      Lakewood Moves to Improve Slums, p. 1, 9/9/66

35   Students Give Dr. King Good Round of Applause, p. 3,
      10/7/66 and Watkins Injured in Scuffle, p. 1, 10/8/66

36   All Brick Jobs Wide Open, p. 26, 9/11/66 and
      Brick Crushes Central, p. 40, 11/27/64

37   Toms River Counts on Backs, p. 21, 9/5/66

38   Signorino Comes Home Again, Toms River Patch, http://patch.com/new-
      jersey/tomsriver/signorino-comes-home-again, accessed on June 28, 2021.

39   Sendzik's Passing Brings Brick Back, p. 33, 9/25/66

40   Toms River Can Celebrate, p. 52, 11/25/66

41   Oral History Interview with Dan Duddy, Conducted by Author

42   Brick's Speed, Alert Play Upset Phillipsburg, p. 18, 10/1/66

43   Rockefeller and Reagan in Big GOP Successes,
      p. 3, 11/9/66, Red Bank Register

44   Sees Peace Far Off, p. 1, 10/24/66, Red Bank Register

45   Family of Dead GI Wants Second Son Brought Home, p. 1, 11/5/66

46   Monmouth's Constructive Efforts, p. 7, 10/2/67, Red Bank Register

47   One Brick Starter Back, p. 13, 9/9/67 and Neptune
      Coach Starred on Cornell Grid, p. 31, 9/3/67

48   Morris is New Red Bank Coach, p. 16, 9/18/67 and
      Red Bank is Short of Coaches, p. 49, 9/10/67

49   Red Bank Strikes Fast, p. 21, 10/1/67 and Tough Red
      Bank Defense Checks Toms River, p. 34, 10/8/67

50   Middletown Defense Turns Tide, p. 20, 10/1/67, Brick

Defense Forges Victory, p. 33, 10/8/67, Fumble, Pass
Theft Win For Neptune, p. 31, 10/22/67

51 Bucs Chant We're Number One, p. 55, 11/5/67

52 Monmouth Whips Fliers, p. 55, 11/5/67

53 Neptune Keeps Title Hopes Alive, p. 61, 11/12/67

54 Long Branch Senior Power Dashes Bucs Hopes, p. 53, 11/26/67

55 Allies Beat Off Attack, Slay 238, p. 1, 11/2/67, Red Bank
Register, Various Red Bank Register Headlines

56 Urge Party Debate War, p. 1, 11/1/67, Red Bank Register

57 This description of events is drawn from Patterson, 679-701.

58 Unity Humphrey Shore Rally Theme, p. 1, 9/13/68, Red Bank Register
and Nixon Visiting Area Saturday, p. 1, 10/15/68, Red Bank Register

59 Brick Should Have Usual Powerhouse, 7A, 9/27/68

60 Helping Others is Bush's Life, B1, 10/14/76

61 Ron Signorino, Oral History Interview Conducted by Author

62 Hard-Running Toms River Trims Brick, p. 39, 9/29/68

63 Toms River Impossible Dream is Real, p. 31, 11/29/68

CHAPTER 17

1 Brick's Caso Kicks Bishop Egan, p. 33, 11/29/68

2 Big Question At Brick Is How Powerful, 6A, 9/26/69

3 Indians' Big Weakness Will Be On Bench, 44A, 9/26/69

4 Middletown 14, Toms River South 8, D3, 9/22/86

5 Signorino Has a New Problem, p. 24, 11/12/68

6 Split: Big Headache For Coaches, p. 5, 9/22/81

7 Signorino Rates Lions as Toughest at Defense, p.
28, 11/11/69, Ocean County Observer

8 Middletown 14, Toms River South 8, D3, 9/22/86

9 Middletown Grinds Long Branch, 2B, 9/28/69 and
Schools, p. 60, Newark Evening News

10 Toms River South Gridders Romp Over Brick, 1BB, 9/28/69

11 Sports Angles, 10/16/69, p. 36

12 Moratorium Day Off To Early Start, p. 1, 10/15/69, Red Bank Register,
War Protest Biggest in Nation, p. 1, 10/16/69, Red Bank Register, and
State's Moratorium Reaction Mixed, p. 2, 10/16/69, Red Bank Register

13 Even Coviello Happy With North Bergen
win, p. 24, 10/20/69, Jersey Journal

14   Ron Signorino, Oral History Interview Conducted By Author

15   Indians Wallop Bayonne, D1, 10/19/69 and Bayonne
      Meets Its Master, p. 23, 10/20/69, Jersey Journal

16   Middletown Rolls Over Brick, 12-0, Remains Unbeaten, B2, 10/12/69

17   Middletown 14, Toms River South 8, D3, 9/22/86

18   Scherer Has His Own Homecoming, D1, 11/2/69

19   Toms River Shows Title Caliber in Closing Minutes, C1, 11/9/69

20   Toms River Shows Title Caliber in Closing Minutes, C1, 11/9/69

21   Moratorium Attracts Modest Crowd, p. 1, 11/17/69, Red Bank Register

22   Middletown 14, Toms River South 8, D3, 9/22/86

23   Jackie Friedman, "Forty Years Later, Toms River South and
      Middletown Still Remember Greatest Game Ever Played," NJ.Com,
      http://www.nj.com/hssports/blog/football/index.ssf/2009/11/
      forty_years_later_toms_river_south_and_middletown_still_remember_
      greatest_game_ever_played.html, accessed on June 28, 2021

24   Kevin Williams, Oral History Interview Conducted by Author

25   Ron Signorino, Oral History Interview Conducted by Author

26   Middletown 14, Toms River South 8, D3, 9/22/86

27   "Forty Years Later, Toms River South and Middletown Still
      Remember Greatest Game Ever Played," NJ.Com

28   Friedman, "Forty Years Later, Toms River South and
      Middletown Still Remember Greatest Game Ever Played"

29   Middletown 14, Toms River South 8, D3, 9/22/86

30   Friedman, "Forty Years Later, Toms River South and
      Middletown Still Remember Greatest Game Ever Played"

31   Friedman, "Forty Years Later, Toms River South and
      Middletown Still Remember Greatest Game Ever Played"

32   Middletown 14, Toms River South 8, D3, 9/22/86

33   Middletown Strengthens Claim, 1A, 11/16/69, Middletown
      Changes Indians' No. 1 Chant, D1, 11/16/69, Middletown
      Wins, Newark Evening News, S1, 11/16/69, and
      Middletown 14, Toms River South 8, D3, 9/22/86

34   Ole TR's Camelot, p. 19, 11/17/69, OCO

35   Brick Stuns Bishop Egan Again, 37, 11/28/69

36   Friedman, "Forty Years Later, Toms River South and
      Middletown Still Remember Greatest Game Ever Played"

37   Kleva's Scuba Program A Success, F6, 12/15/74

38   "Harry Walters," CFLaPedia, http://www.cflapedia.com/
      Players/w/walters_harry.htm, accessed on June 28, 2021

39   Hermanni Cited for Post Game, p. 38, 10/6/72

40   Middletown 14, Toms River South 8, D3, 9/22/86

41   Middletown 14, Toms River South 8, D3, 9/22/86

42   Friedman, "Forty Years Later, Toms River South and Middletown Still Remember Greatest Game Ever Played"

CHAPTER 18

1   Joe Dunne, Oral History Interview Conducted by Author

2   A Long-Standing Tradition, Coast Star Special Supplement, 9/27/2012

3   Richard Bonelli, Oral History Interview Conducted by Mike Bonelli

4   "Interview with Sarah Ellison," Monmouth County Library, last modified September 6, 2001, http://www.visitmonmouth.com/oralhistory/bios/EllisonSarah.htm.

5   Some Area Municipalities Feel Impact of Levitt Building, C1, 10/1/72

6   "Interview With Sarah Ellison"

7   Aberdeen: Invisible Line Divides, B1, 11/18/79, RBR and Can You Say the Best Ever, High School Football Preview, 9/16/94

8   Manasquan Beats Matawan, p. 21, 11/6/60

9   Manasquan Invades Matawan For B Title Game, p. 11, 11/2/61, Matawan Journal

10   Matawan Has 12 Lettermen Back, p. 32, 9/12/61

11   Matawan Upsets Manasquan, p. 37, 11/5/61 and Matawan Triumphs Over Manasquan, p. 8, 11/9/61, Matawan Journal

12   Matawan Rallies to Tie Keyport, Gains Title, p. 8, 11/30/61, Matawan Journal,

13   "Jake Landfried," Manasquan Athletic Hall of Fame, Manasquan High School, http://www.manasquanschools.org/Page/232, accessed on June 28, 2021

14   Marvin Scores All Three Touchdowns as Central Beats Matawan, p. 24, 9/30/62. Marvin was the Shore Conference low hurdles champion; Norcross a baseball star.

15   "For Manasquan, The Spirits of the Past Inspire Today's Success," Manasquan Patch, http://patch.com/new-jersey/manasquan/for-manasquan-the-1spirits-of-the-past-inspire-today-s-success, accessed on June 20, 2017 and Housing Projects Dot Old Farm Sights, p. 77, 11/17/54

16   Central Clinches Title, p. 21, 11/11/62

17   Mango was one of Monmouth's first great athletes, leading the baseball team to consecutive B South titles in 1963-64 (including a scoreless streak that lasted fifty innings).

18   This Could Be Point's Big Year, p. 13, 9/14/63

19 Joe Dunne, Oral History Interview Conducted By Author

20 Raritan Gives Bulldogs Fight, p. 33, 12/4/63

21 Joe Dunne, Oral History Interview Conducted by Author

22 Garnet Gulls Request Relief on Gridiron, p. 12, 11/19/68, Red Bank Register

23 Joe Dunne, Oral History Interview Conducted by Author

24 Point Beach Rips Jackson, p. 43, 10/25/64

25 Point Holds Manasquan, p. 27, 11/24/67

26 "Jack Van Etten," *Asbury Park Press*, http://archive.app.com/article/20070814/OBITUARIES/708140432/JACK-VAN-ETTEN-87-LAKEWOOD, accessed on May 17, 2015

27 Clifford Blau, "Leg Men: Career Pinch-Runners in Minor League Baseball," Society for American Baseball Research, http://sabr.org/latest/leg-men-career-pinch-runners-major-league-baseball, accessed on March 8, 2017

28 So. Freehold Scores Over Matawan, p. 40, 9/27/64, So. Freehold Defeats Raritan, p. 27, 10/4/64. So. Freehold Led By Hill, p. 48, 10/11/64, Hill Scores All 32 So. Freehold Points, p. 25, 10/20/64 and Hill Scores 5, p. 58, 11/15/64

29 Joseph Wancho, "Ray Fosse," Society for American Baseball Research, http://sabr.org/bioproj/person/b8e6733a, accessed on June 28, 2021, and Blau, "Leg Men".

30 Herman Hill Drowns in Sea, p. 16, 12/15/1970, Red Bank Register

31 An Old Farm Town Looks Back, Ahead, D1, 12/4/88 RBR

32 Manasquan Rally Tops Point, p. 40, 11/27/64

33 Manasquan's Second-Half Rally Overcomes Raritan, 26-25, p. 37, 10/10/65

34 Footballs Take Funny Bounces, p. 19, 10/12/65

35 Southern Freehold Offense Clicks, p. 31, 10/17/65

36 Raritan Rallies, p. 34, 10/17/65

37 Raritan Edges Out Mater Dei, p. 54, 11/26/65 and Roper, Ferreira Pace Manasquan, p. 53, 11/26/65

38 Matawan Wins In Last Minute, p. 50, 11/26/65

39 Matawan, p. 15, 10/15/66

40 All-Around Davis is Husky Ace, p. 11, 10/10/66, Red Bank Register

41 Matawan Wallops Southern, p. 35, 9/25/66

42 Roper's 5 TD Passes Pace Manasquan, p. 36, 10/30/66

43 The B Game, p. 12, 11/11/66, Red Bank Register

44 Matawan Rides Lambertville Special to Victory, p. 61, 11/13/66

45   4 For Davis as Matawan Ends Unbeaten, p. 49, 11/25/66.

46   Matawan Aims at 2nd Title in a row, p. 17, 9/12/67

47   Davis Serves TD Dish for Matawan, p. 26, 10/26/67, Red Bank Register

48   Raritan Confident Before Edging Matawan, p. 31, 10/29/67

49   Rocket-Ocean Tie Clouds B Race, p. 21, 11/6/67, Red Bank Register

50   Ocean Crushes Raritan Hopes For B Title, p. 56, 11/5/67

51   Manasquan Edges Matawan, p. 61, 11/12/67

52   Ex-Matawan Star to See Son Rise, D1, 4/19/97

53   Post-War Building Pace Impressive, p. 95, 11/17/54 and City School Plan Reaction Varies, p. 1, 10/3/59

54   Drugs in Suburbia USA: The Ocean Township Story, p. 1, 10/25/71

55   Ocean Appears Headed for First Title, 36A, 9/27/68

56   Ocean Defeats Squan p. 72, 11/3/68

57   Two Distinct Towns, One Common Goal, D1, 12/3/05

58   Big Blue Holds Off Wall For 8-6 Win, B2, 9/28/69, Warwick, McKelvey Carry Manasquan Over Bucs, C3, 10/5/69 and Unbeaten Manasquan Checks Matawan, D1, 10/26/69

59   Squan Spirit Overcomes Ocean Statistics, p. 84, 11/3/69, Red Bank Register

60   Manasquan Finishes Perfect Year, 35, 11/28/69

61   Skip Whitman Is Army's Gain and Manasquan's Loss, D1, 5/10/70

62   "Skip Whitman," Manasquan Athletic Hall of Fame, Manasquan High School, http://www.manasquanschools.org/Page/230, accessed on June 28, 2021

63   Iraci Leads Lakewood to Victory over Toms River, p. 36, 11/25/62

64   This Could Be Lakewood's Year, p. 23, 9/15/64

65   Lakewood Shades Point Beach, p. 41, 9/27/64

66   Wall, Lakewood Play 13-13 Tie, p. 47, 11/1/64. That trio enjoyed significant college success. Przyblwoski became an offensive end, while both Fortier and McGowan became ends at Gettysburg.

67   Sharpe's 76 Yard Run Gave Lakewood Win, p. 41, 11/8/64

68   Lakewood Wins Southern B Title, p. 58, 11/15/64

69   Lakewood Grinds Out 41-13 Win, p. 39

70   Ron Signorino, Oral History Interview Conducted by Author

71   Lakewood Shy Depth as Title Threat, 17, p/13/65,

72   Bad Pass Helps Rebels Post Upset, p. 33, 10/24/65

73   DeCausey Hero as Lakewood Holds Off Point Boro, p. 33, 11/14/65

74   Toms River and Lakewood Defenses Star in Tie, p. 51, 11/26/65

CHAPTER 19

1   Sports Angles p. 13, 11/2/68

2   Shore Beats Monmouth, p. 41, 11/29/62

3   Oral History Interview With Joe Dunne, Conducted by Author

4   Oral History Interview with Al Saner, Conducted by Author

5   Oral History Interview With Denny Toddings, Conducted by Author

6   Al Saner, Oral History Interview Conducted by Author

7   Point Panthers Open Hostilities, p. 27, 9/10/64

8   "Eugene Monahan," University of Vermont Athletic
      hall of Fame, http://www.uvmathletics.com/hof.
      aspx?hof=117&path=&kiosk=, accessed on June 28, 2021

9   Point Boro in Building Year, p. 29, 9/22/66

10   Rola Retaining Enthusiasm for His Medical Endeavors, B2, 11/24/75

11   Al Saner, Oral History Interview Conducted By Author

12   Franks Has His Day for Shore, p. 38, 10/9/66. The multi-talented Franks
      was also a basketball star, leading the Devils to a CJ II championship
      and a trip to the Group II finals, which they lost to Gloucester City.

13   Kampf in MCIT History, B2, 5/20/88, RBR

14   Wall Upsets Shore to Create Class C Deadlock, p. 37, 11/6/66

15   Blocked PAT Wins For Point Boro, p. 52, 11/25/66

16   Panthers Should Be Tough, p. 15, 9/23/67 and
      Point Panthers Halt Wall, p. 30, 10/1/67

17   Point Boro Finishes 9-0, p. 53, 11/26/67

18   Wall Gives Point Boro Stiff Battle, p. 38, 10/6/68

19   Wagner Destroys Kings Point, *The Wagnerian*, 10/31/1972

20   Al Saner, Oral History interview Conducted by Author

21   Point Panthers Rely on Youth, Hustle, p. 35A, 9/26/69

22   Hart, Windle, Team Up To Spark Point Boro Win, B4, 9/28/69

CHAPTER 20

1   Red Bank Catholic Eleven Rolls over Rumson-
      Fair Haven, p. 51, 11/24/61

2   Fumbles Help Caseys Rip Red Bank, p. 49, 9/29/63 and
      Seton Hall Gains Tie With RBC, p. 17, 10/14/63

3   Casey's Win over St. Peter's, p. 19, 11/18/63

4   Patterson 523

5   In Red Bank—Shock and Grief, p. 3, 11/23/1963, Red Bank Register

6   Rumson, Red Bank Catholic Fight To Scoreless Tie, p. 46, 11/29/63

7   Rumson Protests SC Grouping, p. 10, 3/23/65, and GSC
    President Sounds Off, p. 22, 9/12/68, Red Bank Register

8   Rumson Crushes Caseys, p. 54, 11/25/66

9   Rumson Reenters Shore Door, p. 10, 6/29/70, RBR

10 Allen Hall of Fame, C3, 12/22/1985, Allentown Morning Call

11 3 Schools Rise, 3 Fall on NJSIAA List, p. 24, 11/1/66

12 Sully's Sports, p. 31, 11/17/66

13 Monmouth's Constructive Efforts, p. 7, 10/2/67, Red Bank Register

CHAPTER 21

1   Oral History Interview with Dan Duddy, Conducted by Author

2   Master vs. Protégé as North Bergen Hosts
    Brick, p. 18, 9/25/70, Jersey Journal

3   Dennis Filippone, Oral History Interview Conducted By Author

4   Brick Falls in Last Minute, p. 13, 9/26/70 and Bruins
    in Comeback, p. 12, 9/26/70, Jersey Journal

5   Raritan is Victor on Rally, D1, 10/25/70

6   Raritan Edges Brick, D1, 11/1/70

7   Angry Black Students March in Matawan, p. 1, 9/12/68, Red Bank
    Register, Sit-In At Matawan High Slows Movements, p. 1, 9/18/68,
    Red Bank Register, and Matawan's Integrated History Project
    Enthuses Student Activists, p. 1, 10/16/68, Red Bank Register

8   The text of the relevant articles from the Matawan Independent
    (October 1, 1970) are reproduced in "History: Racial Conflict
    at Matawan Regional HS-Late Sept 1970," Aberdeen NJ Life,
    http://aberdeennjlife.blogspot.com/2011/03/history-racial-
    conflict-at-matawan.html, accessed on June 29, 2021.

9   Huskies Board A Train For Ride By Middletown,
    p. 10, 9/29/70, Red Bank Register

10 Matawan Student Aims Set, p. 17, 10/1/70, Red Bank Register and
    Trouble Area Has Uneasy Calm, p. 1, 9/30/70, Red Bank Register

11 Matawan Student Aims Set, p. 17, 10/1/70, Red Bank Register

12 Matawan Rips Asbury Park, D1, 11/1/70

13 Brick Defense Forges Triumph, C5, 11/8/70

14 Lakewood Takes A Lead, D1, 11/8/70

15 John Oxley, Oral History Interview Conducted by Author

16 39 Enshrined in Raritan Hall of Fame, p. 21, Community Reporter, 10/23/02

17 Raritan Earns Title Share, p. 38, 11/27/70

18 Jennifer Kotila, "From the Streets of New York to DC," Herald-Journal, http://www.herald-journal.com/archives/2014/stories/herman-yankton.html, November 17, 2014.

19 New Freeholder Wears Many Hats, E14, 11/10/74

20 Brick's Wolf Building Around 8 Seniors, 8A, 9/24/71

21 Dan McCullough is Typical Brick Footballer, E6, 10/8/72

22 Brick Coasts over Raritan, D5, 10/31/71 and Brick Easily Beats Matawan, D4, 11/7/71

23 Brick Sets Mark in Final Victory, E4, 11/28/71

24 Oral History Interview with Dan Duddy, Conducted by Author

25 Brick Cracks Opening Day Jinx, E1, 9/24/72

26 Oral History Interview with Dan Duddy, Conducted by Author

27 Brick Romps to 99th Win, p. 13, 9/30/72

28 Brick Seeks Revenge in Game of the Week, p. 47, 10/27/72

29 Toms River South Wins This Battle, p. 30, 10/10/72

30 Bob Fiocco: You Love Him Or Hate Him, B5, 9/15/79

31 Wolf 273-274.

32 Brick Machine Drubs Toms River South, p. 21, 10/31/72

33 Bob Fiocco: You Love Him Or Hate Him, B5, 9/15/79

34 Oral History Interview with Dan Duddy, Conducted by Author

35 Westfield Equals Unbeaten Mark at 40, p. 1, Section V Star Ledger, 11/5/72

36 Brick Clinches No. 1 Ranking, p. 17, 11/13/72

37 Brick Works for 27-7 Win, p. 81, 11/24/72

38 Sully's Sports, p. 23, 3/18/73

39 Brick Wins as Matawan Misses PAT, E3, 9/23/73, Late Drive Wins For Green Dragons, F3, 9/30/73, and Brick's 2 Second Half TDs Defeat Raritan, E1, 10/7/73

40 Westfield String Ends at 48, p. 1, 11/14/73, Star Ledger

41 Oral History Interview with Dan Duddy, Conducted by Author

42 Montclair Puts End to Brick Streak, E1, 11/11/73

43 Oral History Interview with Dan Duddy, Conducted by Author

44 Wolf 276

45 Round n Bout Sports Beat, p. 32, 11/21/68, Red Bank Register, Grid

Playoffs on Horizon, p. 28, 9/23/69, Red Bank Register, and Group Grid Playoff Gets Chilly Nod From Shore, p. 29, 11/26/71, Red Bank Register

46   Round n Bout Sports Beat, p. 32, 11/21/68, Red Bank Register

47   NJSIAA Sets Grid Playoffs in Aycee's Convention Hall, p. 26, 10/10/74, Red Bank Register and School Grid Playoff Clearer Dec. 1, p. 28, 11/20/74, Red Bank Register

48   Brick's Wolf Sees Challenges Ahead, p. 10 APP Preview 9/23/74

49   Alvarez, Brown, Young on All-State, Section 5 p. 6, Star Ledger 12/22/74

50   Brick Gets Super Scare, E1, 10/13/74

51   Brick Avenges '73 Loss, F1, 11/17/74

52   Red Bank: Unbeaten, Untied, and Uninvited, F1, 12/1/74

53   Bucs Want Brick To Show Shore Play High Caliber, D1, 12/5/74

54   Playoff Replay, D1, 11/17/88

55   Dennis Filippone, Oral History Interview Conducted by Author

56   Playoff Replay, D1, 11/17/88

57   Playoff Replay, D1, 11/17/88

58   Playoff Replay, D1, 11/17/88

59   A Call Worked, Brick was Champ, p. 6, Section V, Star Ledger, 12/8/74,

60   Playoff Replay, D1, 11/17/88 and Brick Dream Comes True By Slimmest of Margins, B1, 12/7/74

61   Sports Prepared Durkin for Life, D7, 11/5/05

62   Late Surge By Dragons Nips Indians, B1, 10/27/75

63   Brick Facing Formidable Foe, C1, 11/21/75

64   Brick's Wolf Jr. Nervous But Wins Game on Kick, D1, 11/23/75

65   Millville Outcoached Brick in 22-12 Triumph, D1, 12/7/75

66   T-Bolts Defeat Brick, D1, 12/7/75, Press of Atlantic City

CHAPTER 22

1   Huskies, Rams Clash For Title, C1, 11/8/74

2   Huskies Simple Little Offense Tough to Defend, p. 15, 10/6/75, Red Bank Register

3   Branchers Rally to Win, E5, 9/29/74

4   Rams Fall to Huskies, F1, 11/10/74

5   Matawan's Elephant Backfield Stashes Away B Crown, p. 22, 11/18/74, Red Bank Register

6   Matawan-Jackson Showdown: No Contest, p. 19, 10/27/75, Red Bank Register

7   Rizzo on Huskies: Best Team I've Coached, p. 19, 11/17/75, Red Bank Register

8   Matawan Overpowers Watchung Hills, B4, 11/15/76, Home News

9   Matawan Wins But Has to Struggle, C1, 11/28/75

10   School Football: Decision Day, p. 13, 12/6/75, Star Ledger and Matawan, Brick to Hit Road in Quest of Football Titles, B5, 11/24/75

11   Defense Boosts Matawan To Crown, D1, 12/7/75

12   Matawan, Red Bank Hail Grid Champions, p. 1, 12/8/75, RBR

13   Pascarella Shines in Howell Win, p. 84, 11/24/72

14   Poor Sis . . . Schoolboys Reluctant to Kiss, p. 10, 11/3/70, Red Bank Register

15   Van Etten Remembered as a Great Coach and Friend, http://tri.gmnews.com/news/2007-08-30/sports/043.html

16   Manasquan's Edick Has Many Interests, D3, 2/8/70

17   Bill Hill's Talents Make Howell History, E13, 10/12/75, APP

18   Bill Hill, Oral History Interview Conducted by Author

19   Rams Conquer Rebels, E7, 9/29/74 and Howell's Late TD Spree Defeats Monmouth, E9, 10/6/74

20   Howell Parlays Jackson's Mistakes Into Rout, C5, 11/29/74

21   Field Conditions Fail to Halt Explosive Howell, B4, 10/20/75 and Edick Hopes Rebels Gain Respect, E5, 11/2/75

22   North Hunterdon Spoils Strong Effort By Rebels, D7, 11/23/75

23   Middletown South makes Debut But Hill Brothers Steal Show, B4, 9/25/76, Hill Outduels Rams Elkins, F2, 10/17/76, and Signorino Calls Howell Powder Keg, C1, 10/8/76

24   Howell is Thrown into A North, p. 15, 9/11/78

25   "Former Southern Coach Ron Emmert Dies," USA Today High School Sports, http://usatodayhss.com/2014/former-southern-coach-ron-emmert-dies, accessed on June 28, 2021

26   Kevin Williams, "Remembering a Father To A Thousand Sons," 92.7 WOBM, March 24, 2014, http://wobm.com/remembering-a-father-to-a-thousand-sons/.

27   Smead is the Rock in Southern's Defense, F5, 10/19/75,

28   Early Spree By Sterling Routs Southern Regional, D5, 11/23/75

29   Strong Play By Elkins, Wayes, Ignites Southern Regional Over Central, C3, 11/28/75

CHAPTER 23

1   Point Pleasant Boro Has Winning Tradition, 24, 9/18/90

2   Squan Brings Question marks to C, p. 47, 9/22/70, Red Bank Register

3   Manasquan Stuns Central, D2, 10/27/70

4   Boro Extends Streak to 31, D1, 10/4/70

5   Manasquan Ends Boro Reign, D1, 11/1/70

6   Wall Checks Boro, D1, 11/8/70

7   Bob Flocco: You Love Him or Hate Him, B5, 9/15/79

8   Central Humbles Indians, D2, 10/18/70, Central Crushes
     Wall, Keyes Throws For Five, D3, 11/1/70

9   Central Tops Shore, D1, 11/15/70, and Bell's 4
     Pace Central Romp, p. 37, 11/27/70

10 Kilmurray's Exploits Legendary at Central, C1, 7/7/85

11 Kevin Williams, Oral History interview conducted by Author

12 Kilmurray A Reason Eagles Rated With Best in Football, D7, 10/10/71

13 1971: Year of the Eagle, Year of Robbie Keyes, D12, 9/28/91

14 Central Defeats Manasquan, D1, 9/26/71

15 Kevin Williams, Oral History Interview Conducted by Author

16 Central Gets By Stubborn Rams, p. 43, 11/26/71

17 Stangs Emerge Mighty Even After First Defeat,
     p. 20, 10/25/71, Red Bank Register

18 Reserve QB Carries Boro Over Wall, D5, 11/7/71

19 Manasquan Edges Point Boro, D2, 10/31/71

20 Merli Paces Manasquan Romp, p. 13, 11/27/71

21 Jay Price, Oral History Interview Conducted By Author

22 Manasquan's Tailback Merli One Big Reason
     Big Blue 11 Wins, E1, 11/5/72, APP

23 Manasquan Snaps Central Streak, E5, 9/24/72

24 Shore Defeats Point Boro, p. 16, 10/21/72

25 Red Raider Handful Holds Down Fort, p.
     23, 11/13/72, Red Bank Register

26 Keyport Upsets Shore, E3, 11/12/72

27 Point Boro Clips Freehold, E4, 11/12/72

28 Manasquan Ends Up Unbeaten, p. 83, 11/24/72

29 Banta Scores in Manasquan Romp, E6, 9/23/73 and
     Manasquan Crushes Howell, F4, 9/30/73

30 Manasquan Streak Hits 19 Games, p. 79, 11/23/79

31 Blue Devils Fight Off Rally, p. 14, 10/22/73

32 Shore Ends Squan's Streak, E7, 10/6/74

33   Bradley A Real Devil to Squan, p. 16, 10/7/74, Red Bank Register

34   Raider Holdover 13, p. 59, 9/27/74, Red Bank Register

35   Beach's Philosophy: Keep Em Healthy, p. 35, 9/23/74, APP Preview

36   Keyport's Frantic Charge Deadlocks Class D Race, F1, 11/10/74

37   Big Blue Jinx Alive, C5, 11/29/74

38   St. Joseph's Ends Gulls Hopes, 11/29/74, C4

39   Hornets Top Raiders, C2, 11/29/74

CHAPTER 24

1   Palumbos Remember Red Bank, p. 55, 2/22/89, Red Bank Register

2   Dickinson's Strangia Will Coach Red Bank
    Grid Team, p. 28, 6/18/70, RBR

3   Bucs' Strangia Tells Secrets of His Success As a
    Football Coach, p. 48, 7/25/85, RBR

4   Buc Coach Sees Busy Schedule, p. 11, 7/28/70, RBR and
    Red Bank Sports New Look, p. 19, 9/22/70, RBR

5   Red Bank Scores 3 in 80 Seconds, D5, 10/25/70

6   Branchers Win In Last 25 Seconds, p. 39, 11/27/70

7   Red Bank Earns First Rutgers Cup, 12/3/71, 41

8   Dynamite in Grid Uniforms, p. 25, 10/28/71, Red Bank Register

9   Pitts Powers Red Bank Win, D5, 9/26/71 and
    Pitts Paces Red Bank, p. 22, 10/5/71

10 Bucs Crush Ocean, D1, 10/24/71

11 Buccaneer 11 Register First Unbeaten Season in 42
    Years, p. 19, 11/29/71, Red Bank Register

12 Students Absolved of Blame in Melee, p. 1, 11/29/71, Red Bank Register

13 Other Bucs from the 1971 team who played college football included
    Teddy Taylor (at Livingstone College, a historically black school
    in North Carolina) and Bill Jeter (at Bates College in Maine).

14 Bucs Celebrate Golden Win, p. 45, 11/24/72, Red Bank Register

15 Summonte's 88 Yard Run Carries Bishops, E13, 10/21/73

16 Bacon, a three-sport star, reached district finals in wrestling,
    then in the spring hurdled and threw the javelin.

17 Buc Defense is Sharp in 6th Victory, E1, 11/3/74

18 Bucs Elated With Comeback Blitz, p. 18, 11/11/74, Red Bank Register

19 Red Bank: Unbeaten, Untied, and Uninvited, F1, 12/1/74

20 Bucs Coach Planning to Copy Brick, D1, 9/11/75

21   Agee went on to play at Montclair State, while Saunders earned All-NJAC honors twice at Trenton State.

22   "Red Bank's Impossible Dream Season Remembered," 10/1/2015, Asbury Park Press, http://www.app.com/story/ sports/high-school/football/redzone/2015/09/30/red-bank-impossible-dream-season-remembered/73116692/.

23   Oral History Interview With Lou Vircillo, Conducted By Author

24   Borough Beautification Urged, p. 1, 10/8/68, Red Bank Register

25   Welfare Rolls Rise, p. 1, 10/30/75, Red Bank Register and Fort Question Hanging, p. 1, 10/31/75, RBR

26   Red Bank's Impossible Dream Season Remembered, 10/1/2015

27   Those People Up Front Pace Bucs 18th, B1, 9/29/75

28   Buc Soph Paralyzed in Grid Game, p. 20, 9/30/75, Long Branch Record

29   Bucs Knew Pass Was Coming, p. 20, 10/6/75, Long Branch Record

30   Buc Warrior Game Rates As Classic, p. 15, 10/13/75, Red Bank Register

31   Red Bank Old Pros Get By Asbury, E1, 11/2/75

32   Red Bank's Impossible Dream Season Remembered, 10/1/2015

33   Strangia's House Call Cures Bucs, p. 23, 11/24/75, Red Bank Register

34   Bucs Whip Branchers For No. 27, C1, 11/28/75

35   Bucaneer Strangia: Once More in Style, p. 36, 12/4/75, Red Bank Register

36   The Shootout At Ridge Road, D12, 11/24/90

37   The Shootout At Ridge Road, D12, 11/24/90

38   Lou Vircillo, Oral History Interview Conducted By Author

39   The Shootout At Ridge Road, D12, 11/24/90

40   Lou Vircillo, Oral History Interview Conducted By Author

41   Red Bank's Impossible Dream Season Remembered, 10/1/2015, http://www.app.com/story/sports/high-school/football/redzone/2015/09/30/red-bank-impossible-dream-season-remembered/73116692/

42   The Shootout At Ridge Road, D12, 11/24/90

43   Lou Vircillo, Oral History Interview Conducted By Author

44   The Shootout At Ridge Road, D12, 11/24/90

45   Red Bank's Impossible Dream Season Remembered, 10/1/2015

46   The Shootout At Ridge Road, D12, 11/24/90

47   The Shootout At Ridge Road, D12, 11/24/90

CHAPTER 25

1   "Interview With Helene Moore," Monmouth County

Library System, Last Modified August 15, 2001, http://www.
visitmonmouth.com/oralhistory/bios/MooreHelene.htm.

2   Building a 52 Year Career, D4, 3/26/92

3   Construction at Mater Dei to Begin Soon, p. 17, 7/25/64

4   Caseys Score First Victory, 13-12, p. 28, 11/1/65 and
    Notre Dame Beats Mater Dei, p. 10, 9/26/66

5   Mater Dei Defense Paves Way for Upset Win, p. 54, 11/26/67

6   New Faces in Shore Coaching Fraternity, p.
    29, 9/11/69, Red Bank Register

7   Mater Dei, Toms River North Triumph, 13, 10/25/69

8   Mater Dei Ground Attack Overcomes Keansburg, 57, 11/28/69

9   Corley Throws 5 TD Passes, p. 18, 9/25/72

CHAPTER 26

1   St. Joseph's High School Opens in Fall, p. 1, 2/24/62 and
    New School, Church are Priest's Goals, p. 12, 5/2/62

2   St. Joe's Becomes Donovan, C2, 8/16/83

3   New School, Church are Priest's Goals, p. 12,
    5/2/62 and Sports Angles, p. 27, 10/2/68

4   Kevin Williams, Oral History Interview Conducted by Author

5   Billerman's Memories Staying Fresh, D1, 5/17/94

6   Billerman Tosses 5 TDs for St. Joseph's, 36, 11/28/69

7   St. Joseph's High to Try Al Sica as Football Coach, p. 25, 12/19/69

8   Kelly Runs Wild For Griffins, p. 13, 9/26/70

9   Billerman Keys St. Joseph's Win, D4, 10/25/70

10 Griffins Surprise Caseys, 8-6, 18, 10/4/71

11 Kevin Williams, Oral History Interview conducted by Author

12 Fiocco Wanted Rest; St. Joseph's Called, p. 44,
    9/23/74, Asbury Park Press Preview

13 St. Thomas Aquinas Suffers 14-13 Setback, p. 10, Home News, 10/14/74

14 Bob FIocco: You Love Him Or Hate Him, H5, 9/15/79

15 Griffs Prove Their Worth, p. 13, 11/18/74, OCO

16 Taylor Eyes Grid Goals, p. 10, 9/23/75, OCO

17 Transfers Prompting Outcries, F1, 8/31/75 and TRN
    Transfer Raises New Issues, p. 23, 1/27/77, RBR

18 Southern Stuns Griffins in Fight-Marred Contest, 10/4/75

19 Coachless Teams Call Final Football Contest, D1, 11/19/75

20   Bill Vanore, Oral History Interview Conducted by Author

21   Denny Toddings, Oral History Interview Conducted by Author

22   Griffs Prove Themselves in Red Bank Cath. Win, B4, 10/31/76, OCO

23   Bill Vanore, Oral History Interview Conducted By Author

24   Denny Toddings, Oral History Interview Conducted by Author

25   Bill Vanore, Oral History Interview Conducted By Author

CHAPTER 27

1   Rosati Ends Career With 99 Victories, p. 39, 11/27/70

2   Oral History Interview With Lou Vircillo, Conducted by Author

3   Caseys Rally Late to Shock Rumson, C5, 11/29/74

4   Berth Improves Defensive Play, B15, 10/15/75

5   Two Casey Fumbles Aid Camden Catholic Victory, D7, 11/23/75

6   Casey Game Plan Ends Red Bank's Streak At 28, F1, 9/26/76

7   Caseys Go to the Air Against St. John Vianney, C5, 10/12/76

8   RBC Rips Vianney, ND Next, F1, 11/21/76

9   Rumson Trips RBC, C4, 11/26/76

10   Burgess Calls RBC Rout the Best Game I Have Ever Had, G1, 12/5/76

11   Tears of Joy Fall as RBC Prevails, D1, 11/20/77

12   Fumble Proves Costly in RBC Loss, C1, 12/4/77

CHAPTER 28

1   Saint John Vianney Has Priest as Principal,
     p. 13, 9/15/69, Red Bank Register

2   St. John's Air Game Works, E4, 11/28/71

3   Lancers Feast on Holmdel, E2, 10/22/72

4   Vianney Frosh: Losing, what's that? C7, 12/3/78, RBR

5   John Underwood, "Oklahoma Stampede," *Sports Illustrated* 10/2/72

6   Chapman Directs Lancer Success, p. 20, 12/2/77, RBR

7   Last-Minute Score Hurls St. John Past RBC, C9, 10/9/77

8   Vianney Offense Too Much For Holmdel to Contain, D7, 10/23/77

9   Chapman Directs Lancer Success, p. 20, 12/2/77, RBR

10   St. John Vianney Topples Red Bank Catholic, C5, 10/8/78

11   Chapman Takes Over Manasquan Post, p. 19, 5/18/79, Red Bank Register

12   Lancers Outlast Caseys, C15, 10/7/79

13   Lancers Fall to Holy Cross, C13, 11/18/79

CHAPTER 29

1   Red Bank Catholic Sues to Join Shore League, p. 27, 1/5/77

2   Caseys Reach Goal, Enter SC in '79, p. 14, 12/5/78, RBR

3   Court Rules Conference Must Accept RBC, F1, 2/10/77

4   Shore Conference Relents, Will Admit RBC, C1, 12/1/78

5   Barriers Ready to Crumble, D2, 8/5/80

6   Lancers Celebrate Golden Moment, C6, 10/5/80, RBR

7   RBC Blanks Third Ranked St. John's, C5, 10/19/80, RBR

8   Skip Edwards, Oral History Interview Conducted by Author

9   Red Bank Upsets RBC, B9, 11/16/80

10   Bucs Shock RBC to Turn Season Around, C4, 11/16/80, RBR

11   St. John Vianney Rally Beats Griffins in 4th, C5, 11/23/80, RBR

12   Lancers Shed Monkey, B8, 11/23/80

13   RBC Holds Off Holy Spirit, B8, 11/23/80

14   Defense Paves Way for St. John Vianney, B1, 12/7/80

15   Defense Paves Way for St. John Vianney, B1, 12/7/80

EPILOGUE

1   Theodore Roosevelt, "The Man in the Arena," 4/23/1910

2   The quotations that follow are all from oral history
     interviews conducted by the author.

ABOUT THE AUTHOR

NICK SCERBO learned to love football as a child and grew to love Shore Conference football while playing in high school for the Monsignor Donovan Griffins. He was a history major at Gettysburg College, after which he became a high school history teacher and football coach in New Jersey. This is his first book.

 @ShoreConferenceFootballHistory